Constitutional Law and Regionalism

ELGAR MONOGRAPHS IN CONSTITUTIONAL AND ADMINISTRATIVE LAW

Series Editors: Rosalind Dixon, *University of New South Wales, Australia,* Susan Rose-Ackerman, *Yale University* and Mark Tushnet, *Harvard University, USA*

Constitutions are a country's most important legal document, laying the foundation not just for politics, but for all other areas of law. They allocate power among different levels and branches of government, record and promote a society's shared values, and protect the rights of citizens. Countries around the world are adopting written constitutions, though what defines a constitution is evolving to include a variety of sources beyond canonical texts, such as political conventions, statutes, judicial decisions and administrative law norms.

This cosmopolitan monograph series provides a forum for the best and most original scholarship in constitutional and administrative law, with each book offering an international, comparative or multi-jurisdictional approach to this complex and fascinating field of research.

Titles in the series include:

Constitutionalism and Religion
Francois Venter

The Arab Spring
An Essay on Revolution and Constitutionalism
Antoni Abat i Ninet and Mark Tushnet

American Judicial Power
The State Court Perspective
Michael L. Buenger and Paul J. De Muniz

Citizen Journalists
Newer Media, Republican Moments and the Constitution
Ian Cram

Against the New Constitutionalism
Tamas Gyorfi

Autonomous Public Bodies and the Law
A European Perspective
Stéphanie De Somer

Constitutional Preambles
A Comparative Analysis
Wim Voermans, Maarten Stremler and Paul Cliteur

Comparative Constitutional Studies
Between Magic and Deceit
Günter Frankenberg

Constitutional Law and Regionalism
A Comparative Analysis of Regionalist Negotiations
Vito Breda

Constitutional Law and Regionalism

A Comparative Analysis of Regionalist Negotiations

Vito Breda

Senior Lecturer in Law, School of Law and Justice, University of Southern Queensland, Australia

ELGAR MONOGRAPHS IN CONSTITUTIONAL AND ADMINISTRATIVE LAW

Edward Elgar
PUBLISHING

Cheltenham, UK • Northampton, MA, USA

Published by
Edward Elgar Publishing Limited
The Lypiatts
15 Lansdown Road
Cheltenham
Glos GL50 2JA
UK

Edward Elgar Publishing, Inc.
William Pratt House
9 Dewey Court
Northampton
Massachusetts 01060
USA

A catalogue record for this book
is available from the British Library

Library of Congress Control Number: 2018943996

This book is available electronically in the **Elgar**online
Law subject collection
DOI 10.4337/9781783470136

FSC www.fsc.org MIX Paper from responsible sources FSC® C013056

ISBN 978 1 78347 012 9 (cased)
ISBN 978 1 78347 013 6 (eBook)

Typeset by Columns Design XML Ltd, Reading
Printed and bound in Great Britain by TJ International Ltd, Padstow

In memory of the extraordinary Jeremy Thompson

Contents

Acknowledgements

This book would not have been possible without the generous sponsorship of the University of Edinburgh's MacCormick Fellowship programme. I must thank Professor Stephen Tierney for his unparalleled support during the MacCormick Fellowship. I also owe thanks to the Australian National University Centre for European Studies and to its director, Professor Jacqueline Lo, for her continuous support. I am particularly grateful to the Washington and Lee University School of Law, the University of Deusto, the Pontifical University in Madrid and the University of Brescia. Much of the material in this book was presented in those institutions. I owe a debt of gratitude to Professor Iñigo Navarro, Professor Luis Gordillo and Professor Luca Passanante for their support and friendship. Finally, I must express my gratitude to the University of Southern Queensland for allocating me the time to travel. This has been a long project, and I am deeply grateful to my publisher, Edward Elgar, and their wonderful staff for their help, kindness and, above all, patience.

Parts of Chapter 1 appeared in different forms in a chapter entitled 'An Odd Partnership: Identity-Based Constitutional Claims', in F. Jenkins, M. Nolan and K. Rubenstein (eds), *Allegiance and Identity in a Globalised World* (Cambridge University Press 2014). I am indebted to Professors Jenkins, Nolan and Rubenstein and Cambridge University Press's anonymous referees for their invaluable feedback. The author and the publisher would like to thank Cambridge University Press for the permission to reprint extracts from the chapter. As per usual, all errors are my own.

Finally, I would like to thank Stefania Morandini for patiently and diligently reading my work. Without her, this book would never have been completed.

Vito Breda
January 2017

Introduction

During the past three decades, regionalist political parties and minority groups in Australia, the UK, Canada, Italy, New Zealand, Spain and the US have revived claims of ethnic ownership of local, regional and state institutions. Depending on the type of relationship between regional and central states, the constitutional effects of such ethnic revival have been antagonism or participation. For instance, Spanish nationalists and regionalist parties had an uneasy relationship. There is, at the time of writing this introduction, still great tension between Spanish and Catalonian institutions. Whether such tension is part of a cycle of simulated identity politics or a real constitutional crisis will be discussed at length in the Spanish chapter.

However, in the great majority of instances, regionalists seek to negotiate with the central governments. This process is often a manifestation of the distinctive perception of what is acceptable in a constitutional system. For instance, the overarching principles of formal equality, as they have been constructed by the US Supreme Court, limit negotiations over the recognition of identity claims within US states and territories. The narrow construction of the principle of equality is shared, albeit with different implications, in Australia and Canada. In these legal systems that have a rigid amendment process, courts have taken the role of updating their constitutional systems in a way that reflects their multinational nature.

A review of the literature on Australian, Canadian and American constitutional law, reproduced in the respective chapters, reveals a genuine concern. Identity-based constitutional demands might endanger the commonwealth and individual rights. This concern has almost ironic effects in Australia, where negative racial discrimination is protected by federal heads of power, and yet equality and protection of rights narratives are used to prevent the constitutional recognition of minority rights.

This book compares the stability of the legal systems that adopt rigid constitutions with those that foster a dynamic interaction between regional minorities and central institutions. New Zealand, the UK and Italy went through a progressive reform of their decentralization policies that led to an increase in regional legislative competences. New Zealand's Tokelau, several of the Italian regions and Scotland have obtained, in a relatively short period of time, both fiscal autonomy (known as fiscal federalism) and quasi-federal legislative competences. In reviewing the Scottish devolution, Robert Hazell noted that, in Europe, only the Swiss Confederation allocated more political power to its regions.

Although some of these processes have been analysed, the book intends to cover a gap within political and constitutional literature that I believe has prevented a comparative understanding of the constitutional effects of regionalist movements in Australia, the UK, Canada, Italy, New Zealand, Spain and the US. Sub-nationalism is perceived as a niche area. Analyses tend to focus on empirical factors (e.g. What are the voting behaviours of Welsh speakers? Where does the support for party X come from? Are you more French Quebecois or Canadian?). However, these analyses acknowledge the constitutional implications of regionalism rather than explaining the role of regionalist parties in amending the constitution or changing the interpretation via constitutional review.

There is a strong body of evidence indicating that constitutional analyses might produce a richer understanding by integrating legal and political methods of investigation. For example, the University College London Constitution Unit, directed with acuity by Robert Hazell, adopted a political studies methodology to deliver a series of ground-breaking publications: 'Constitutional Futures: A History of the Next Ten Years' (1999) and 'Constitutional Futures Revisited: Britain's Constitution to 2020' (2008). Constitutions and their systems of territorial governance are changing under the pressure of identity groups. Sub-nationalism and minority groups are what Hazell calls 'drivers of change'. The political activities of regionalist parties and minority groups seldom look for rupture (e.g. secession) and even when they do, it is part of simulated politics in which bombastic claims are used to obtain better terms in the negotiation that unavoidably follows. Yet these negotiations do not occur in a vacuum. They happen within a distinctive constitutional structure that, in different forms, ensures the democratic coherence of the agreements that emerge from the negotiation processes. A selection of the elements (e.g. constitutional jurisprudence) that helped develop or that trammelled those negotiation processes is discussed in this book. *Constitutional Law and Regionalism* is therefore not a comprehensive comparative constitutional analysis.

The book is divided into eight chapters. The first chapter explains why and when an identity-based constitutional claim should be inserted into a democratic constitutional system. The chapter explains that sub-state national identities, from the Maori to the Basque and from Native

Hawaiians to the Scottish, should be considered as an element of modern constitutional democracy. I argue that a constitution is the manifestation of a distinctive identity and that any attempt to explain it as a culturally neutral endeavour is contrafactual. The idea of 'neutered' public bureaucracy, that Hegel saw as the 'universal class' in the Philosophy of Right, is a projection of a self-directed and imagined national community. The characterization of the state as neutral is potentially undemocratic because it allows the majority group that has already selected the cultural features of a democracy, such as its language and its established church, to exclude political claims because they are not culturally neutral.

Chapters 2–4 evaluate the past two decades of British, Spanish and Italian decentralization policies. European nation states are under pressure externally from the expanding role of international organizations, such as the European Union, and internally by regionalism. Central institutions in Italy, Spain and the UK have different constitutional traditions and have chosen different strategies to grapple with the new regionalism. Italy's federal reform has been driven by its amoral political system, called 'neo-patrimonial' by Fukuyama. Spain continues to experience an extensive constitutional litigation and political tensions. Hundreds of central and regional statutes have to go through the review of the Constitutional Court. However, there are strong indications that such high levels of constitutional litigation, and the political tension related to it, are partly due to the political commodification of nationalist narratives by both regional and unionist political parties.

Chapters 5–8 review Canada, the US, New Zealand and Australia's constitutional systems, respectively. New Zealand has adopted its own variation of the Westminster Model so it has a relatively flexible constitution. Maoris and Pacific Islanders have well-supported constitutional claims (e.g. the Treaty of Waitangi) that have progressively re-shaped the economic and territorial structure of New Zealand. Canada, the US and Australia all have rigid constitutions. These, like New Zealand, are large, multicultural and mostly unbidden immigration nations that endorse civic nationalism and their distinctive, substantive constitutional patriotism. A democratic constitution should be, amongst other things, a historical manifestation of a covenant between individuals who might otherwise have nothing in common. This assumption is unproblematic insofar as it is not engaged by identity groups that pre-existed that model of political association. The chapters on Canada, New Zealand, the US and Australia discuss the effects that identity-based constitutional claims by national minorities, such as Native Hawaiians, Puerto Ricans, Quebecois and Aboriginals, have on these constitutional systems.

1. Identity-based constitutional claims: negotiating with regionalists

INTRODUCTION

This chapter discusses constitutional claims proposed by national identities. Constitutional debates over the roles of national identities are traditionally associated with the protection of minority rights. However, there is perhaps a larger group of constitutional demands that is fostered by identity groups. These identity-based constitutional claims are organized into a constitutional programme by an institution with a democratic mandate (for example, by a political party in a state or by a government in an international organization). The programme normally includes 'a path for constitutional recognition' of the distinctiveness of a national-identity group within the state. So the aim of this section of the book is to clarify the distinctive status of identity-based constitutional demands in modern and pluralist constitutional theory by explaining that some of the objections against their recognition are unfounded.[1] In particular, I argue that constitutional programmes proposed by national identities should not be rejected in advance by advocating the irrational foundations of nationalism[2] or by associating identity-based constitutional claims with the history of the ideology.[3] Both objections are unfounded. They confuse, albeit at different levels of their respective critiques, an assessment of the reasons for the existence of a national community (whether it be religious, historical or political) with a deliberative evaluation of group constitutional claims. I will contend that a modern constitutional

---

[1] David Haljan, *Constitutionalising Secession* (Hart 2014).

[2] See, eg, Claus Offe, 'Homogeneity and Constitutional Democracy: Coping with Identity Conflicts through Group Rights' (1998) 6 Journal of Political Philosophy 113.

[3] See, eg, Jürgen Habermas, 'Citizenship and National Identity: Some Reflections on the Future of Europe,' (1992) 12 (1) Praxis International 1. Vito Breda, 'The Incoherence of the Patriotic State: A Critique of Constitutional Patriotism' (2004) 10 Res Publica 247.

system that aspires to create a set of communal alliances between strangers should seek to retrieve rational discourses, not to impose them.

The chapter is divided into two parts. The first part addresses the normative case against assessing identity-based constitutional claims and argues that a great level of enrichment might be achieved from inserting normative arguments into the debate over the procedural requirements of modern constitutions. The second part looks at the interplay between the development of the modern republican tradition and national identity.

A METHODOLOGICAL OVERVIEW

In the past three decades, identity-based constitutional claims have become more common, but their implications have not been fully researched. The Māori Party in New Zealand, the Catalonian Socialists in Spain, Parti Québécois in Canada and the Lega Nord in Italy rally their supporters around a programme of proposed constitutional reforms.[4] Whilst the great majority of these reforms aim to readjust the balance of constitutional recognition for a particular community, a minority of these political parties such as the Scottish National Party (SNP) and a coalition of Catalonian political parties seek independence for their respective nations.[5] However, even the radical process of transformation suggested by the SNP requires a constitutional programme and, in its implementation stage, a series of international treaties. The recent separation of the former Czechoslovakian Republic is a reminder of the complexity of

[4] Kerensa Johnston, 'Maori Legal Developments' (2017) New Zealand Law Review 131; Daniele Albertazzi and Duncan McDonnell, 'The Lega Nord Back in Government' (2010) 33 West European Politics 1318; Legislative proposal, pursuant to Section 2 [2] of the Regional Law of the 19th June 2014, n 15: 'Modalities and Contents for the Recognition for the Increase of Specific Forms of Autonomy for the Veneto Region, Pursuant to the Third Paragraph of Article 116 of the Constitution' 2017; Jean-François Caron, 'The Exclusive Nature of Quebec's Contemporary Nationalism: The Pitfalls of Civic Nationalism' (2014) 47 International Journal of Canadian Studies 221; Robert Hazell, *Devolution and the Future of the Union* (The Constitution Unit 2015); Elisenda Casanas Adam, 'The Referendum on Catalonian Independence: The Position of the Catalan Authorities' https://ukconstitutionallaw.org/2017/10/03/elisenda-casanas-adam-the-referendum-on-catalonian-independence-the-position-of-the-catalan-authorities/ (accessed 4 January 2018); Kathryn Nalani Setsuko Hong, 'Understanding Native Hawaiian Rights: Mistakes and Consequences of Rice v. Cayetano' (2008) 15 Asian Am. LJ 9.

[5] SNP, 'Manifesto (2017)'; Casanas Adam (n 4).

the internal and international procedures required to disentangle (without violence) two ethnic communities. At the international level, it is the increasing power of international organizations that worries national identities. For instance, an analysis of the documents considered by the European Constitutional Convention shows a plurality of perceptions regarding what a constitution should protect in terms of national cultural diversity, and what should be ignored for the benefit of the common good.[6]

The deliberative process during the making of the un-ratified Treaty for a Constitution for Europe was also an occasion for discussing the principle of constitutional sovereignty. However, this debate needs to be distinguished from the debate regarding the protection of national identities as a hindrance to the European Union's (EU's) integrating project. Concerns based on the protection of a national identity were dismissed by two distinctive narratives. The first advocated separation between (European) constitutional law and national identity;[7] the second argument suggested, instead, endorsing the concept of the 'nation' as the most attractive channel of institutional self-identification for a European Federation.[8] This process had limited success in the United Kingdom of Great Britain and Northern Ireland (hereafter the UK or Britain).[9]

In this chapter and the ones that follow, I will explain how identity-based constitutional claims (within the limits of democratic reasonableness) could be considered a helpful expression of democratic dissent, and therefore silencing them might hinder the perceived democratic coherence of a constitutional system. Before turning to the development of my argument, I must set a series of terminological and methodological qualifications. The term 'national identity' is descriptive of a sociological phenomenon. The paper will refer to national identity as inclusive of both

---

[6] Vito Breda, 'A European Constitution in a Multinational Europe or a Multinational Constitution for Europe?' (2006) 12(3) European Law Journal 330; Ailsa Henderson and others, 'England, Englishness and Brexit' (2016) 87 The Political Quarterly 187.

[7] Jürgen Habermas, 'The European Nation-State. Its Achievements and its Limitations. On the Past and Future of Sovereignty and Citizenship' (1996) 9(2) Ratio Juris 125; Jürgen Habermas, 'Citizenship and National Identity: Some Reflections on the Future of Europe' (n 3).

[8] Prodi's suggestion of a European 'melting pot' cannot be considered an alternative since it displaces the national identity with a European national identity. Specifically, he does not explain why we should prefer European common cultural national identity to the nation-state identity. Romano Prodi, *Europe as I See It* (Polity Press 2000) 4.

[9] Henderson and others (n 6).

civic nationalism – the form of nationalism easily tolerated in most modern democracies – and ethnocentric nationalism – which might be democratically problematic.[10]

I will use the term 'constitutional principles' to refer to those principles that discover, engage and deal with political claims in a way that a constituency considers reasonably acceptable. The concept is inspired by Habermas's early idea of communicative democracy. Some constitutional principles are equality for those who intervene in a public debate, the openness of the debate and the acceptance of reason.[11]

The role of national identity and identity-based constitutional demands in modern constitutional systems is charged with political tension.[12]

---

[10] There is also the pragmatic difficulty of distinguishing the two because most national identities have blended (civic and ethnic) aspirations. For a general analysis of how sociologists distinguish the different stages (tribal, ethnocentric, multicentric) of development of nationalism, see Anthony D Smith, *Theories of Nationalism* (Duckworth 1971); Anthony D Smith, *Nationalism: Theory, Ideology, History* (Polity Press 2001).

Anthropological accounts tend to focus more on languages and how official languages shaped a national identity by creating out of thin air a communal civic conscience: Benedict Anderson, *Imagined Communities: Reflections on the Origin and Spread of Nationalism* (Verso 1983). Political studies tend to suggest instead a putative definition of the separation between civic and ethnic: Margaret Canovan, 'Patriotism is not Enough' (2000) 30 British Journal of Political Science 413; Yael Tamir, *Liberal Nationalism* (Princeton University Press 1993). Constitutional theorists tend to adopt a less prescriptive view of the social phenomenon. See, eg, how different narratives are developed in the UK: Robert Hazell, *The English Question*, Devolution Series (Manchester University Press 2006); Neil MacCormick, *Can Nationalism Be Intellectually Respectable?* (Oxford University Press 1991); Neil MacCormick 'The English Constitution, the British State and the Scottish Anomaly' (1998) 25 Scottish Affairs 129.

[11] Habermas developed his modern deliberative democracy from his critical analysis over several years. Jürgen Habermas, *Between Facts and Norms: Contributions to a Discourse Theory of Law and Democracy* (Polity Press 1996); Jürgen Habermas, *Toward a Rational Society: Student Protest, Science and Politics* (Heinemann Educational 1971); Jürgen Habermas, *The Theory of Communicative Action* (Heinemann Educational 1984).

[12] Javier García Oliva, 'Javier Garcia Oliva: The Referendum on Catalonian Independence: The Position of the Spanish Authorities' https://ukconstitutionallaw.org/2017/10/03/javier-garcia-oliva-the-referendum-on-catalonian-independence-the-position-of-the-spanish-authorities/ (accessed 4 January 2018); 'Javier García Oliva: Catalonia in Spain? The Future Ahead' https://ukconstitutionallaw.org/2014/11/10/javier-garcia-oliva-catalonia-in-spain-the-future-ahead/ (accessed 4 January 2018); Vito Breda, 'La Devolution de Escocia y El Referéndum de 2014: Cuáles Son Las Repercusiones Potenciales En España?' [2013] Teoria y Realidad

Arguing that national-identity constitutional claims should be individually assessed by a process of deliberation (and therefore not constrained by a superimposed system of norms/criteria) might be misread as a plea for considering national-identity claims as normatively 'worthy' of substantive recognition. They are not. At the theoretical level, a polity should generate a sense of solidarity and alliance among its members by discussing their aspirations without any reference to identity, gender, sexual preference and so on. Haljan, for instance, calls this sense of participation associative constitutionalism.[13] However, claims are often drawn from a sense of belonging to a group (for example, a perception of a necessary relationship between faith and constitutional law) or where the national identity is the political conveyer of economic concerns (for example, the preoccupations generated by excessive immigration). The aspirations of creating an ideal, culturally neutral constitutional polity cannot prevent these debates from generating constitutional norms.[14]

The desire for a separation between constitutional principles and the political underpinnings of constitutional principles (for example, the liberal free market adopted in Europe and many modern Western-style democracies) has important epistemic implications for constitutional theory. For instance, direct discriminatory political claims (for example,

---

Constitucional 69; Scottish Goverment, *Your Scotland, Your Referendum. Time Table to 2014* (2012); Kimberly A Costello, 'Rice v. Cayetano: Trouble in Paradise for Native Hawaiians Claiming Special Relationship Status Notes' (2000) 79 North Carolina Law Review 812; Haljan (n 1).

[13] Haljan (n 1) 50–63.

[14] Hazell (n 4); Henderson and others (n 6); Johnston (n 4); Albertazzi and McDonnell (n 4); Paul Williams and others, 'The Legitimacy of Catalonia's Exercise of its Right to Decide: A Report by a Commission of International Experts' (Global Studies Institute University of Geneva – Departament d'Afers i Relacions Institucionals i Exteriors i Transparència 2017) http://exteriors.gencat.cat/web/.content/00_ACTUALITAT/notes_context/FULL-REPORT-Catalonias-legitimate-right-to-decide.pdf (accessed 21 April 2018); Richard Wyn Jones and Roger Scully, *Wales Says Yes: Devolution and the 2011 Welsh Referendum* (University of Wales Press 2012); Gregory Ablavsky, '"With the Indian Tribes": Race, Citizenship, and Original Constitutional Meanings' (Social Science Research Network 2017) SSRN Scholarly Paper ID 3082038, https://papers.ssrn.com/abstract=3082038 (accessed 2 January 2018); Antony Hooper, 'Tokelau: A Sort of "Self-Governing" Sort of "Colony"' (2008) 43 The Journal of Pacific History 331; Scottish Goverment (n 12).

British jobs for British workers)[15] might logically have little legal traction in the EU. However, the assumption that European institutions or any modern state's institutions, by way of comparison with some nationalist political parties, are culturally neutral is equally misleading.[16]

The last theoretical stance is imprecise because it fails to acknowledge the dynamic nature of the constitutional qualification of principles such as equality, freedom and democracy, against which identity claims are made. It is the process of parliamentary deliberation (coupled in common law countries with jurisprudential qualification) that relentlessly fills constitutional principles with actual significance. Cultural neutrality is either proposed at the expense of the prerogative given to each individual to challenge the democratic coherence of constitutional norms[17] or by setting an intersubjective (often unquestioned) set of values. The assumption in this book is that if normative prescriptions can be constructed as immutable ideals, constitutional principles ought to be discovered by a process of dialectical refinement within a distinctive constituency (in civil law systems) and/or discovery (in common law countries). It is this 'dynamic variability' of constitutional principles that prevents a selective reading of identity-based constitutional claims and that promotes the idea of a constitutional polity that works in partnership with national identities.

I will refer to the term 'cosmopolitanism' as the intellectual movement that forecasts and/or argues for establishing a global society without nation-states. The term is inclusive of the theoretical submission of Habermas that speculates about a boundless, open deliberative democracy and a forthcoming global order.[18] It also includes the deductive analyses of, for instance, Held, who predicts the collapse of the nation-state as a side effect of an ever-expanding global economy and its international organizations.[19]

---

[15] Gordon Brown, 'First Speech to the Labour Party Conference as Party Leader' (speech delivered at the 2007 New Labour Conference, Bournemouth UK, 24 September 2007).

[16] Anthony D Smith, *Nationalism: Theory, Ideology, History* (Polity Press/ Blackwell 2001); Henderson and others (n 6); Jocelyn Maclure, *Quebec Identity: The Challenge of Pluralism* (McGill-Queen's University Press 2014).

[17] Haljan (n 1) 51.

[18] Jürgen Habermas, *The Postnational Constellation: Political Essays* (Polity Press 2001).

[19] David Held, *Democracy and the Global Order: From the Modern State to Cosmopolitan Governance* (Polity Press 1995).

The chapter is divided into two sections. The first section discusses whether the irrationality of nationalism as a political doctrine might provide an argument against all identity-based constitutional demands. This argument is developed as a response, firstly, to Offe's idea of egalitarian society, in which he appears to argue that there should be little space for identity-based constitutional demands. It is also a response to Habermas's theory of constitutional patriotism, in which the concept of national identities is considered an irrational doctrine that has no right to intervene in a constitutional debate. It will be argued that the internal incoherence of a political stance might not prevent a national identity from making reasonable constitutional demands. The second part of the chapter focuses, conversely, on the argument that considers identity-based constitutional demands to be historically incompatible with modern republican tradition. I will refer to this stance as the republican/historical critique, and I will argue that it confuses the historical process that formed the present conception of the nation-state (for example, the process of imperial decolonization) with its republican constitutional achievements.

THE NORMATIVE CASE AGAINST NATIONALISM: TWO CRITIQUES

Normative critiques of identity-based constitutional claims hold that these claims must not find their way into an ideal constitutional system. The argument against identity-based constitutional claims is, in general, well articulated and goes a long way towards finding a reason for excluding national-identity claims from a democratic arena,[20] but its conclusions are unsound. The aim of a constitutional system, I argue, is to retrieve the rational validity of a claim (by way of democratically discussing it), not to exclude political parties and/or to police constitutional debates.

The normative case against nationalism is drawn from the assumption that identity-based claims are based on an ideology that is philosophically rooted in the misinterpretation of a Kantian philosophy.[21] If the

---

[20] A methodologically similar critical analysis is drawn from a liberal conception of modern state in Stephen Tierney, *Constitutional Law and National Pluralism* (Oxford University Press 2004) 52.

[21] Jürgen Habermas, 'The European Nation-State: Its Achievements and its Limitations. On the Past and Future of Sovereignty and Citizenship' in Pablo De Grieff (ed), *The Inclusion of the Other: Studies in Political Theory* (MIT Press 1998); Michael Rosenfeld, 'Rethinking Constitutional Ordering in an Era of

complexity and nuances of nationalist narratives are reduced to a set of crude deductions then an individual is free if she/he acts in accordance with communally accepted moral prescriptions. Because of that assumption, it is the imperative duty of every individual to strive and/or to protect a communal freedom, namely the self-determination of the nation. An early historical example of a nationalist narrative that combines the right of individual freedom with communal destiny might be found in the Declaration of Arbroath (1320 AD): '[a]s long as a hundred of us remain alive, never will we on any conditions be subjected to the lordship of the English. It is in truth not for glory, nor riches, nor honours that we are fighting, but for freedom alone, which no honest man gives up but with life itself'.[22] The Declaration of Arbroath was an early attempt to establish a link between individual freedom and national self-determination. Nonetheless, from a normative perspective, the boundaries between the individual and the communal rights of self-determination are not easy to retrieve.

However, in constitutional theory, two specific perspectives engage the normative unsteadiness of identity-based constitutional claims. Firstly, constitutional norms must refer to universal and absolute moral principles;[23] secondly, the right to individual self-determination has a mainly procedural function in the process aimed at finding those principles (that is, individuals must be free to engage in a debate over what freedom means). The philosophical persuasiveness of these two critiques is conceded; however, I argue that they do not have the same valence in modern constitutional theory.

From a constitutional perspective, the process of normative discovery, that is perhaps part of the enlightened project, is procedurally different from the practices that qualify the valence of constitutional claims in an indirect democracy. I draw this distinction from Tully's analysis of the relations between ancient and modern democracies.[24] Deliberative practices in ancient democracy, with some important qualifications such as

---

Legal and Ideological Pluralism' (2008) 6(2) International Journal of Constitutional Law 415.

[22] Translation of the *Declaration of Arbroath* based on Sir James Fergusson, The Declaration of Arbroath 1320 (1970) 5–11, with reference to A A M Duncan, 'The Nation of Scots and the Declaration of Arbroath' (Historical Association pamphlet, 1970) 34–37 and D E R Watt (ed), *Scotichronicon* Vol. 7 (Edinburgh University Press 1996) 4–9.

[23] Offe (n 2).

[24] James Tully, 'The Unfreedom of the Moderns in Comparison to Their Ideals of Constitutional Democracy' (2002) 65(2) Modern Law Review 204.

gender and class discrimination, might be considered proxies for a potential common *enlightenment* and the discovery of normatively poignant principles.

Modern constitutional democracy, in contrast with ancient democracy, is dependent on procedural rules that channel political claims into parliaments and constitutional conventions. One key role of these procedures is to reduce the risk of restricting the admissibility of political claims beyond a level of reasonableness and to transform a constitutional democracy into a self-referential system that reproduces previous decisions rather than to democratically assess constitutional claims.[25] It is from such an awareness of the implications of restricting the role of identity groups that this book calls for an open assessment of identity-based constitutional claims.

The argument is not only that constitutional rules have to be conventionally posited (for example, constructed in clear, general terms), and that necessity should trump political and moral discourses (identity-based constitutional claims are part of all of the legal systems considered in this book), but also that constitutional theories should not downplay the important role of democratic procedures in modern democratic systems. However, the universal/particular critique and the relentless reference to the irrationality of national identity appear to insert a procedural limitation on modern democracy. That is, identity-based constitutional demands are not worth discussing by default, so to speak, because national identities are the political manifestation of an incongruent doctrine. This position is democratically incoherent.

---

[25] Four authors have developed the epistemic implication of Tully's work in their own narratives: Zoran Oklopcic, 'Constitutional (Re)Vision: Sovereign Peoples, New Constituent Powers, and the Formation of Constitutional Orders in the Balkans' (2012) 19 Constellations 81; Martin Loughlin, 'Reflection on the Idea of Public Law' in Emilios Christodoulidis and Stephen Tierney (eds), *Public Law and Politics: The Scope and Limits of Constitutionalism* (Ashgate 2008) 47–68; Frank Michelman, 'Constitutionalism as Proceduralism: A Glance at the Terrain' in Emilios A Christodoulidis and Stephen Tierney (eds), *Public Law and Politics: The Scope and Limits of Constitutionalism* (Ashgate 2008) 69. A general overview of the issue of the self-referential aspect of law is provided in Hans Lindahl, 'Democracy, Political Reflexivity and Bounded Dialogues: Reconsidering the Monism–Pluralism Debate' in Emilios A Christodoulidis and Stephen Tierney (eds), *Public Law and Politics: The Scope and Limits of Constitutionalism* (Ashgate 2008) 103–117. Hans Lindahl, 'Democracy , Political Reflexivity and Bounded Dialogues: Reconsidering the Monism-Pluralism Debate' in Emilios A Christodoulidis and Stephen Tierney (eds), *Public Law and Politics: The Scope and Limits of Constitutionalism* (Ashgate 2008) vi.

The Universal/Particular Critique

The first normative critique against identity-based constitutional claims argues that there is a paradoxical relationship between identity demands and the universal aspiration of constitutional norms. For instance, the refusal to consider (even the refusal to recognize) regional-identity groups as proxies for constitutional demands should be the default stance in an egalitarian society.[26] A similar narrative is also in Haljan.[27]

It is so, Offe argues, for good reasons. Identity-based constitutional claims are very difficult to substantiate because they are derived from dogmatic assumptions such as a right to be treated differently. However, the prima facie incongruity of some identity-based claims (for example, we have a right over this land because a deity told us that we are different) does not prevent democratic debates that encourage mediation between normative principles (for example, equality) and a political stance.[28] For instance, the SNP has led an open consultation, called the National Conversation, aimed at testing the possible financial and institutional aspirations of Scotland's future.[29]

The plan led to a consultative referendum on independence.[30] The Scottish aspirations of autonomy could be considered antithetical to Offe's idea of an egalitarian society. Nevertheless, if analysed in detail, the National Conversation and the consultation for a referendum concerning Scotland's independence promote a political dialogue via a series of initiatives that have, for instance, raised awareness of a distinctive Scottish constitutional history, produced a number of documents concerning policies and that have received substantial backing by the independent Commission on Scottish Devolution. Although debate over the referendum on independence led to a great deal of tension between the

---

[26] James Tully, *Strange Multiplicity: Constitutionalism in an Age of Diversity*, The John Robert Seeley Lectures 1994 (Cambridge University Press 1995) Ch 2.

[27] Haljan (n 1) 204.

[28] This point is analysed by Rosenfeld. See in particular Chapters 2 and 3 of Michel Rosenfeld, *The Identity of the Constitutional Subject* (Routledge 2010).

[29] The Scottish Executive, 'List of Contributions: Scotland's Future: A National Conversation' (2012) http://www.scotland.gov.uk/Topics/a-national-conversation/NC-contributions-inds-org.

[30] 'Agreement between the Scottish Government and the United Kingdom Government on the Referendum on Independence for Scotland' (2012) http://www.scotland.gov.uk/About/Government/concordats/Referendum-on-independence.

Scottish and the UK parliaments, the result of the consultative referendum would not alter the UK's constitutional system (that prerogative remains with the UK parliament).

The consultative referendum is, instead, an opportunity given to Scottish residents to say whether the Scottish parliament should be given the 'powers' to enable negotiation over independence.

Offe's idea of egalitarian society appears to argue that these initiatives should be assessed against the principle of equality, yet this submission overlooks the antidemocratic implications of considering equality to be a procedural limit. A more pertinent observation would consider the Scottish bid for a referendum over national self-determination to be part of a democratic process that maintains the democratic coherence of a multinational polity such as the UK. Such a process cannot be restricted a priori by focusing on its normative implausibility or its outputs without questioning the democratic structure of the constitutional system.

Again, there is a tension generated around national-identity demands, and so I must be precise. The principle of equality that allows national-identity groups to intervene in constitutional debates should not be confused with an attempt to redeem nationalism or, even worse, to speculate on a substantive link between folk and constitutional norms. Regionalist political groups, such as the Lega Nord in Italy, are the institutional proxy for constitutional demands that might be in logical opposition to an egalitarian society.

For instance, the implementation of the Italian 2001 constitutional reform (ex art 119 of the Italian constitution) promoted by the Lega Nord entrenches economic disparity between the North and South of Italy.[31] In this case, Offe's critique inspires a helpful narrative, given that it reminds all those involved in a constitutional debate of the logical limits of political demands in a constitutional polity that endorses the principle of equality (ex art 3 of the Italian constitution). However, the principle of equality cannot prohibit arguments that demand adjustments to the allocation of public resources (for example, infrastructure) if such an allocation better matches the needs of heavily industrialized areas in the north.[32]

---

[31] Luca Antonini, *Federalismo all'italiana* (Marsilio 2013); Francesco Palermo, 'Italy: A Federal Country without Federalism?' in Michael Burgess and G Alan Tarr (eds), *Constitutional Dynamics in Federal Systems: Sub-National Perspectives* (McGill-Queen's University Press 2012).

[32] Emma Lantschner, 'History of the South Tyrol Conflict and its Settlement' in Jens Woelk, Francesco Palermo and Joseph Marko (eds), *Tolerance Through Law: Self Governance and Group Rights in South Tyrol* (Brill 2007).

The argument is that the principle of equality demands reasonable limits on all political claims by projecting a limit, we might say a floodgate, on the effects of those claims (for example, avoidance of groundless discriminatory demands) on a polity. However, those procedural limitations do not sustain Offe's demand for a preventive assessment of the 'normative worthiness' of identity-based constitutional claims.

The Irrationality of Identity-Based Constitutional Claims

In the previous section, we dwelt on the normative critique, and I suggested that there is a procedural incompatibility within identity-based constitutional claims that starts or continues a political project by implying the superiority of one identity group over another. However, I argued that such procedural limits do not prevent the admissibility of all identity-based constitutional claims. Even without considering constitutional systems that are designed to be decentralized, Offe's critique supports a substantive understanding of the principle of equality that is at odds with the normative requirement for a modern constitutional polity to have democratic openness.

In this section, I will dwell, instead, on a second critique of the role of identity-based claims, one that denounces the internal incoherence of nationalism as a political doctrine. The internal critique holds that nationalists confuse the Kantian idea of individual freedom with a national right of self-determination. The focus of this internal critique is on the lack of normative links between the two rights.

I will argue that a debate concerning the existence of a link between individual and national rights of self-determination might clarify the relationship (or lack thereof) between the two but should not support the exclusion of identity-based groups from a constitutional system. Specifically, I suggest that internal incoherencies of identity-based constitutional claims might logically limit their persuasiveness, but not substantively reduce their admissibility, in constitutional dialogues. Before going further, it might be useful to note how the right of self-determination of groups is a principle recognized by international institutions and state constitutions. The 1945 Charter of the United Nations, for instance, asserts that the purpose of the United Nations is 'To develop friendly relations among nations based on respect for the principle of equal rights and self-determination of peoples, and to take other appropriate measures to strengthen universal peace'.[33] A similar assertion can be found in the

[33] United Nations, Charter of the United Nations and Statute of the International Court of Justice, UNTS XVI (24 October 1945). Art 1 [2].

1957 Treaty of Rome, which set the foundations for today's EU: 'DETERMINED to lay the foundations of an ever-closer union among *the peoples* of Europe'.[34] The assertion of a right to be a self-determinate national population is also part of many post-Second World War constitutions. For instance, *La Constitution du 4 October 1958* ('French constitution') states that 'The French people solemnly proclaim their attachment to the Rights of Man and the principles of national sovereignty as defined by the Declaration of 1789'.[35] However, enthusiasm for the legal and/or constitutional right of self-determination was not echoed in political theory. In particular, a very strong critique against identity-based communal rights was developed at the end of the Second World War by authors who saw and/or directly experienced the pathological effects of the right of self-determination of the nation. Back then, Kedourie argued that nationalists misinterpreted the underpinning premises of Kant's philosophy and associated the concept of the nation with the idea of a common moral community.[36]

In contrast with the model of governance provided by the Empire, which nationalists perceive as amoral, the self-determination of the nation is a vessel for the development of a national democratic culture. Nationalists argue that the web of cultural relations between people that underpins the political and administrative structure of the state has a twofold effect on the legal system. Firstly, it is a source of democratic and moral legitimacy for the state. Secondly, it provides a criterion (for example, the ability to speak the national idiom) for distinguishing members of the national community from aliens.[37]

There are few doubts about the internal incongruence of this assumption and its tragic historical consequences. Certainly, the post-war case against the right to national self-determination is rhetorically powerful (there is strong evidence associating nationalism with discrimination) and, to a great extent, convincing. There is a plethora of nationalist

---

[34] *Treaty Establishing the European Economic Community*, opened for signature 25 March 1957, 298 UNTS 11 (entered into force 1 January 1958) 2 ('*Treaty of Rome*').

[35] La Constitution du 4 Octobre 1958 [French Constitution of 4 October 1948] Preamble.

[36] Elie Kedourie, *Nationalism* (Hutchinson 1960) 18.

[37] Ibid 5: 'Nationalism is a doctrine invented in Europe at the beginning of the nineteenth century. [...] Briefly, the doctrine holds that humanity is naturally divided into nations, that nations are known by certain characteristics, which can be ascertained, and that the only legitimate type of government is national self-determination'.

groups (for example, the Lega Nord) that make undemocratic claims.[38] However, the dilemma is whether a modern template for a constitutional democracy requires an a priori rational test of the internal structure of any political doctrine. In addition, if the test fails, could claims made by supporters of that doctrine be prevented from entering the democratic arena? Theoretically, yes.

The assumption might be made, for instance, that in an ideal constitutional polity, only communal claims that bear some normative values (for example, economic benefits for the entire polity) deserve democratic recognition. However, there is still a great deal of disagreement over what an ideal legal system might look like and what substantive and procedural steps and practices will drive us in the direction of such an ideal constitutional polity.

By way of comparison, there is more consent among constitutional theorists regarding the role of democracy as an imperfect procedural system for retrieving rational decisions. We have seen, for instance, that Tully gleans from the distinction between indirect democracy (that is, modern democracy) and ancient democracy the idea that procedures allow norms to be questioned by all those affected.[39] It is from this perspective that the internal critique of the nation-state may appear less convincing.

For instance, let us assume that the 2005 French referendum that rejected the Treaty to Establish a Constitution for Europe is an exclusive expression of the right of self-determination of the French people entrenched in the preamble of the 1958 French constitution and that the UK's Brexit referendum is an expression of a narrow-minded perception of the common good.[40] These rejections might be considered incoherent as an exclusive expression of national self-determination and, thus, normatively irrational. The dilemma is whether the irrationality that motivated such a democratic expression could also be considered a reason for flaunting the result of the referendum. The answer is in the

---

[38] James Tully, 'The Challenge of Reimagining Citizenship and Belonging in Multicultural and Multinational Societies' in Catriona McKinnon and Iain Hampsher-Monk (eds), *The Demands of Citizenship* (Continuum 2000); Tully (n 24). For a well-known analysis of the theoretical feasibility of an ideal constitutional polity (that follows his Theory of Justice) see, eg, John Rawls, *Political Liberalism* (Columbia University Press 1993).

[39] Tully (n 24).

[40] Henderson and others (n 6).

negative.[41] Again, the argument here is not that the 'nationalist will of the French people or the British' has to be respected because it is legally recognized by the French constitution and international organizations such as the EU, or because they are in compliance with UK statutes. Rather, we should assume that, in a modern indirect democracy, we cannot impose stringent limitations on the reasons that support a claim.

However, recent proposals appear to have rediscovered the stance that, first, denounces the internal incoherence of nationalism as a political doctrine and then 'muddles' the distinction between constitutional and normative assessments of identity-based constitutional claims. Habermas, for instance, argues that a substantive and direct relationship between the idea of a homogeneous national population and the state's right to self-determination is normatively unsupported. Habermas echoes Kedourie, saying that a claim for the right to self-determination of the nation can promote a policy of ethnic and racial persecution against minorities: 'The positive self-understanding of one's own nation now becomes an efficient mechanism for repudiating everything regarded as foreign, for devaluing other nations, and for excluding national, ethnic, and religious minorities, especially Jews'.[42] The link between nationalism and ethnocentrism is conceived. The national community must define the others to set its boundaries. However, in the quotation, Habermas appears to pursue Kedourie's idea a step further and suggests an explicit constitutional exclusion of nationalism from modern constitutional democracy: 'The nation-state must renounce the ambivalent potential [the linkage between it and nationalism] that once propelled it'.[43] The idea of 'an in-advance exclusion' of nationalism from modern democracy and the endorsement of his idea of constitutional patriotism might be appealing to European elites[44] for whom the association between the two might be seen as one of the major obstacles to a fully integrated EU. Nonetheless, the argument suggests a great limitation on the reasons that drive a constitutional polity.

For instance, if we were to regard the EU as the most likely laboratory for a patriotic state, a series of dilemmas would need careful consideration. Firstly, is the mere risk of an exclusive stance by a nation that is heavily invested with a particular view of itself as ethnically homogenous

---

41 James Tully, 'A New Kind of Europe?: Democratic Integration in the European Union' (2007) 10 Critical Review of International Social and Political Philosophy 71.

42 Jürgen Habermas, *Between Facts and Norms* (n 11), 111.

43 Ibid 117.

44 Breda (n 3).

a danger that requires nationalism to be excluded entirely? Secondly, even if the nation-states relinquished their egoist perspective of creating a patriotic state, what would be the guarantee that EU institutions would not develop their own European ethnocentric national identity? Are not those references to European humanism in the preamble of the failed Constitution for Europe a manifestation of a nationalism (very similar to Smith's polycentric nationalism)[45] that might limit the democratic openness of constitutional debates?

We might speculate that Habermas's purpose is less radical than it appears and that we are constructing rhetorical 'straw men'. This is, for instance, the interpretation suggested by Müller.[46] Müller holds a less radical interpretation of Habermas's historical account, one that disfranchises some of the normative implications of his critique of the nation-state. Müller starts by questioning the consistency of the English translation of Habermas's works and suggests, for instance, an interpretation of constitutional patriotism in tune with a dynamic cosmopolitan democracy. However, the use of terms such as 'must' (in the English translation) might need further clarification in order for these words to escape their prima facie normative charge.[47]

Still, a second reading suggests that, in his idea of constitutional patriotism, Habermas's critique of nationalism stretches the logical internal requirements of a constitutional narrative into an assessment of a political stance.[48] For Habermas, a constitutional system is not a mere executor of normative prescriptions but works as a conveyor of moral demands that have transcended historical political discussion and found their way into constitutional prescriptions. For instance, many aspects of the doctrine of human rights are perceived by Europeans as evidence of a common apolitical inheritance. It is from this common tradition that Habermas appears to extract an in-advance exclusion (what we might call an a priori exclusion) of identity-based constitutional claims from the political arena. Put simply, we have to exclude identity-based constitutional claims because that is a lesson that our forebears taught us.

---

45 Anthony D Smith (ed), *Ethnicity and Nationalism* (Brill 1992).

46 Jan-Werner Müller, 'On the Origins of Constitutional Patriotism' (2006) 5 Contemporary Political Theory 278. See also Pablo De Greiff, 'Habermas on Nationalism and Cosmopolitanism' (2002) 15(4) Ratio Juris 418.

47 Vito Breda, 'Constitutional Patriotism' in Mortimer Sellers and Stephan Kirste (eds), *Encyclopedia of the Philosophy of Law and Social Philosophy* (Springer 2017).

48 Ibid.

This conclusion cannot be accepted – again, not because we live in a world dominated by nationalist, self-determined democracies and thus a 'contingent state of affairs trumps normative reasoning', but because the irrational internal structure of nationalism-based communities is unrelated to the functioning of a deliberative arena in an ideal constitutional polity.

Specifically, Habermas should consider that civic cohesion in a patriotic sense, that is, the attachment of a system of constitutional values perceived to be worthwhile, should spring from an inherited system of values and a dynamic process of democratic deliberation that relentlessly adjusts those values. There are positive and negative implications of recognizing the dynamic nature of republican values. One positive consequence is the development of a process that relentlessly seeks to adjust the perception of normative validity to a specific situation. Habermas's early critique of liberal democracy has been, perhaps, one of the most lucid reminders of the importance of democratic dissent as a procedural building block of modern open society.[49] The negative implication is that antidemocratic political claims (and we know that identity-based constitutional claims such as the one by the Lega Nord in Italy are at odds with the idea of an egalitarian society) might collect enough political capital to seriously restrict the process of democratic deliberation.[50]

However, restricting a priori the admissibility of identity-based claims because they do not fit the pre-existing set of republican values is derived from the conclusion that in debates about national identity, we have to find the optimal balance between openness and the protection of civic virtues. This is not very convincing. I share Habermas's unease about the potentially dangerous implications of a revival of regionalism and nationalism, and indeed, we can retrieve from a republican tradition a series of persuasive arguments, but we cannot prevent identity-based claims from entering constitutional debates at the state level and/or in international organizations such as the EU.

The motivations that support the attempt are admirable, that is the prevention of discriminatory policies, but the reasoning attracts critiques

[49] The critical contributions of Habermas are developed in Jürgen Habermas, *Toward a Rational Society* (n 11); Jürgen Habermas, *The Structural Transformation of the Public Sphere: An Inquiry into a Category of Bourgeois Society* (Polity Press 1989).

[50] Patrik Macklem, 'Militant Democracy, Legal Pluralism, and the Paradox of Self-Determination' (2006) 4(3) International Journal of Constitutional Law 488.

both from those who support, in principle, the idea of a global democracy and from nationalists. Those enthused by the idea of global democracy or, at this stage, a stateless European democracy, note the confusion between the aspiration for an open and culturally diversified cosmopolitan society and the imposition of a 'historically learned' republic version.[51] The debate that such a critique generates is concerned with what a cosmopolitan constitution ought to be (for example, should it defend humanism?)[52] and what it is that civil states should learn from their historical mistakes.[53]

The republicans consider, instead, a selective reading of the history of constitutional law, one that omits key historical developments of modern constitution making, that spans from the Declaration of Arbroath to the 1958 Charter of the United Nations via the US Declaration of Independence, in which the right of a people's self-determination is considered a key element of any political association.

The Historically Learned Republican Critique

The previous section discussed both the normative critique and the role of identity-based political claims in modern constitutional democracy. It has been argued that we cannot find a normative reason for the a priori exclusion of identity-based constitutional claims from a modern constitutional polity. The following section engages squarely with the epistemic error of the republican critique. Specifically, it discusses the republican historical rendering of modern constitutional democracy.

This section will argue that, whilst historical analyses might help us comprehend the present functioning of constitutional systems, a historical argument cannot support or negate a connection between state and identity. My argument here is that the republican achievements of modern constitutional democracy can be separated from the development of nationalism and, thus, that historical arguments in favour of (as supported

---

[51] Breda (n 47); Robert Nichols and Jakeet Singh, *Freedom and Democracy in an Imperial Context: Dialogues with James Tully* (Routledge 2014); James Tully, 'The Unfreedom of the Moderns in Comparison to Their Ideals of Constitutional Democracy' (2002) 65 Modern Law Review 204.

[52] P C J Lobeira, 'Is Europe Still Worth Fighting for? Allegiance, Identity and Integration paradigms revisited' in F. Jenkins, M. Nolan and K. Rubenstein (eds), *Allegiance and Identity in a Globalised World* (Cambridge University Press 2014).

[53] Jan-Werner Müller, *Constitutional Patriotism* (Princeton University Press 2007) 38.

by nationalists) or against (proposed by republicans) a connection between state and nation are constructed with equal precariousness.

Modern constitutional democracy often favours a common language (for example, a set of idioms/symbols/codes that can be easily understood across cultures). The sharing of a common language, however, helps the expansion of nationalism as a political doctrine.[54] However, the historical paths that favoured the establishment of modern democracy, on the one hand, and modern nationalism, on the other, can be logically separated.

There is no evidence, for instance, that multinational states (for example, the Swiss Confederation and the UK) are less democratic than ethnically homogenous polities (for example, Japan).[55] As contended in the previous sections, nationalism is, and has been, a manifestation of a culturally diversified society that has, as with other sociological groups, historically influenced the understanding of constitutional values. An analysis of the distinctive historical developments of set constitutional principles, for instance, might supply further details about the comparative account of a constitutional system. However, the history of societal interaction with principles (the fact that, in the past, lawyers and politicians might interpret the same rules in different ways) does not support and/or preclude future constitutional recognition of claims made by identity groups.

The formation of the nation-state has followed three different paths. Some nation-states began when an already-established kingdom transformed its subjects into a quasi-uniform national population (for example, France). Others have been the result of intellectual campaigns conducted by romantic writers and poets against imperial powers (for example, Italy and Germany). Finally, some have been the result of a process of decolonization (for example, the USA, Australia, Canada and New Zealand). These three historical processes have led to some confusion over the historical development of nationalism and its role in modern constitutional democracy.[56]

Despite the nationalist rhetoric of some political parties and the historical fact that both constitutional democracy and nationalism expanded from Europe to the rest of the world during the same era, nationalism and the protection of republican values (for example, equality) should be considered distinct processes. There is strong evidence that, since the late eighteenth century, large-scale nation-states have

---

[54] Maclure (n 16); Casanas Adam (n 4); Lantschner (n 32).

[55] Ernest Gellner, *Nations and Nationalism* (Blackwell 1983).

[56] Eric J Hobsbawm, *Nations and Nationalism since 1780: Programme, Myth, Reality* (Cambridge University Press 1990).

developed in tandem with an increased concern for the protection of a set of republican principles. Ernest Gellner argues, for instance, that the identity-formation processes that shaped today's modern nation-states developed during the industrialization of Europe.[57] Although the term 'nation' was used during the Middle Ages by universities and knight orders, the concept of a nation, Gellner explains, did not exist until the eighteenth century. In fact, it was during industrialization that modern states needed a reliable language. The adoption of a national language, in turn, stimulated the spread of nationalism.

The key features of the industrial era were constant development, social mobility and the need for a continuous increase in communication between different individuals (for example, high-society capital holders, middle-class professionals and labourers) who worked at different stages of the industrial process. Before industrialization, different classes could speak different languages without any detrimental effect on the economic or institutional efficiency of a state. For instance, most of the European nobility spoke French, intellectuals and the clergy spoke ancient Greek and Latin, and the lower classes spoke the local vernacular.

However, Gellner notes that the manipulation of goods in an industrialized society required the development of a common language. The distinctive side effect of communication across classes was the formation of a national standard idiom that was intelligible to all. The idiom that would become the nation-state's language was often selected based on its popularity among the middle classes. For instance, Italian, made popular by Dante's 'Divina Commedia',[58] was the vernacular spoken in the regions around Florence.

Having a common language had two consequences. The first was an increase in social mobility: gifted entrepreneurs who might have been from very poor backgrounds but who could speak the national language aspired to join the middle classes. Such an opportunity was historically unprecedented. The second consequence was that the move towards a more egalitarian society (vis-à-vis mediaeval society) favoured the perception that belonging to a community (which provided a common language) and to a modern state were synonymous. This misconception had a multifaceted impact on the relations between individuals who did not share anything apart from being arbitrarily included inside the same state's borders.

---

[57] Ernest Gellner, *Nations and Nationalism* (n 55) 33. Similar narratives are in Anthony D Smith, *Theories of Nationalism* (n 10).

[58] Dante Alighieri, *La Divina Commedia* (Italian edition) (Scrivere 2010).

Firstly, the subjects of a given royal family became 'citizens'. Citizens would use a common language to express their equal status. Secondly, the national group chosen as the proxy for the nation language often perceived the values expressed in the constitution to be a manifestation of national (not republican) moral values. Such a perception is, Gellner argues, based on an imprecise historical narrative. There is a historical overlap between the modern state benefitting from having a common language and the development of an egalitarian society, yet the two are unrelated.

The dilemma for constitutional theorists is whether the nationalist claim of ownership of republican values, which is precariously constructed, should be prevented from entering into constitutional debates at a state level. The short answer is no. The perception that an identity is the historical repository of an idea (for example, equality) taken, perhaps, from a historical document (for example, the Magna Carta) should be separated from the process that accommodates these claims in a constitution.

For instance, MacCormick holds that the plurality of the national community provides the backdrop for developing different patterns of interpretations of commonly endorsed liberal principles in the UK constitutional system. MacCormick argues that the individual and group senses of freedom, which democracy provides, require a sense of loyalty regarding collective decisions – specifically, the acceptance of communal choices. MacCormick suggests that this is possible only if democracy takes into account the individual self-realization that depends on a substantial degree of economic and social support. 'It is clearly not possible to understand humans as extrinsically extra-social atoms who come together voluntarily or otherwise to form human societies or communities, in the manner envisaged by contractarian thought'.[59] Developing this reasoning, MacCormick argues that the collective sense of belonging that supports democracy might be a proxy for a range of constitutional claims (for example, regional autonomy).

MacCormick's concept of identity-based constitutional claims is drawn from the historical accommodation of republican principles, but what is not clear is whether it is compatible with the basic values of a modern democratic society (for example, openness, the respect of pluralism and so on). To pre-empt this critique, he argues that democracy requires a sense of loyalty to collective decisions. Nationalism is one of these

[59] Neil MacCormick, *Questioning Sovereignty Law, State and Nation in the European Commonwealth* (Oxford University Press 1999) 176.

sociological phenomena that contribute to the process of assessing the valence of constitutional principles.[60]

MacCormick's suggestion is that some nationalist perceptions that link together institutions (regional, national and European) and cultural aspects (religion, language and cultural heritage) might be irrational as well as undemocratic. However, it is the process by which these perceptions are accommodated or rejected by a constitutional system that sustains a communal acceptance of constitutional principles.

The argument here is not that, in a context in which all democracies are nationalistic, identity-based constitutional claims are superior. MacCormick's argument instead seeks to explain the importance of a historical partnership between a national identity (for example, the one shared by Scottish public lawyers) and a system of values endorsed by a constitutional system. By starting from a historical analysis of the origin of the UK, he explains that there is a dialectical partnership between the development of the constitutional principle (for example, sovereignty and the rule of law) and UK national identities (British, English, Northern Irish, Scottish and Welsh). The dialectical partnership is, however, only one of the processes that helps maintain a communal acceptance of the values held in the UK constitutional system.

MacCormick's analysis focuses on the rule of law, but it also has general relevance. He explains that historical processes that have given a distinctive cultural qualification to a set of universal values in a society (for example, the Supreme Court's historical qualification of freedom of speech in the First Amendment to the US Constitution) and the entrenchment of nationalist symbols (for example, the colours of the 'Ensigns Armorial of the said United Kingdom be such as Her Majesty shall appoint and the Crosses of St Andrew and St George be conjoined in such manner as Her Majesty shall think fit' set in section 1 of the 1707 Act of Union) are not mutually exclusive. Instead, both processes (that is, the process of legal qualification of right and the assertion of partnership between the constitution and an identity) are asserting the people's ownership of a legal text that they perceive as fundamental for their political community.

---

60 Ibid 167.

CONCLUSION: ARGUMENTS FOR AND AGAINST IDENTITY-BASED CONSTITUTIONAL CLAIMS

This chapter analysed the arguments that refuse to consider national identity as a proxy for constitutional claims. It was argued that a number of normative criticisms of identity-based constitutional claims are misconceived. Calls for a substantive implementation of the principle of equality confuse the logical limitations imposed on all political claims (for example, avoidance of groundless discriminatory demands) with the less stringent procedural limits of deliberative democracy. Habermas's normative critique is, instead, mis-shaped. It has been shown to rest on a misunderstanding of the partnership between civic cohesion in a patriotic sense (that is, the attachment to a system of virtues) and the deliberative process that adjusts those universal values to a specific society.

The second part of the chapter focused on the historical/republican critique of identity-based constitutional claims. The republican/historical case against identity-based constitutional claims and the idea of the nation-state is powerful, yet the role of these claims cannot be completely dismissed, as some critics suggest. Certainly, nationalist beliefs can be democratically dangerous and national-identity groups can be proxies for potentially undemocratic constitutional demands. However, a distinction must be made between the internal incongruence of nationalism as an overarching doctrine and the constitutional demands (for example, regional autonomy) proposed by those whom it inspires.

This chapter argues that the internal or historical oddities of nationalism might be difficult to accept but that there is no reason for a constitutional system to assess whether identity groups have or do not have an inherent moral right to promote constitutional claims. It has been argued that modern constitutional policies depend on deliberative activities aimed at retrieving or restoring rationality within a pluralist and dynamic constitutional polity rather than at imposing it.

The last section of this chapter has focused on seeking out a historical account that separates the development of the constitutional state and nationalism. Whilst the two can be historically and sociologically separated, the dilemma for constitutional theorists is whether the state has developed a republican tradition that independently protects the rule of law – for instance, from contributions made by national-identity groups. The short answer is no.

National identities have been considered one of a number of political proxies for the qualification of republican principles (for example, the protection of minorities) and cannot be distinguished from other groups' contributions. The idea that identity-based constitutional claims ought to be separated from a culturally neutral republican tradition is both implausible and democratically precarious. In the following chapter I will explain how identity-based constitutional claims are recognized and negotiated in a variety of legal systems.[61]

[61] Parts of this chapter first appeared in: Vito Breda, 'An Odd Partnership: Identity-Based Constitutional Claims', in F. Jenkins, M. Nolan and K. Rubenstein (eds), *Allegiance and Identity in a Globalised World* (Cambridge University Press 2014) 52–76.

2. The UK: identity-based constitutional claims in a parliamentarian system

INTRODUCTION

First-year British law students are told that the British constitution can be summed up in eight words: 'What the Queen in Parliament enacts is law'.[1] However, a comparative analysis of the system of governance requires a further qualification. The UK has an uncodified,[2] highly flexible,[3] multinational constitution.[4] The stipulation of what text constituted the British constitution might vary, but a few texts such as the Magna Carta,[5] the Bill of Rights 1688,[6] the Act of Union 1707[7] and a series of conventions are normally essentially considered part of the UK constitutional assets.[8] The British system of territorial governance recognizes four national minorities that are the Northern Irish Catholic, the

---

[1] Vernon Bogdanor, *The New British Constitution* (Hart 2009) 13; Andrew Le Sueur, Maurice Sunkin and Jo Eric Murkens, *Public Law: Text, Cases, and Materials* (third edition, Oxford University Press 2016) 24.

[2] Le Sueur, Sunkin and Murkens (n 1) 17; Bogdanor (n 1) 10; Albert Venn Dicey, *Introduction to the Study of the Law of the Constitution* (Macmillan 1889).

[3] Le Sueur, Sunkin and Murkens (n 1) 52; Bogdanor (n 1) 12, 14.

[4] Le Sueur, Sunkin and Murkens (n 1) 161.

[5] Katherine Fischer Drew, *Magna Carta* (Greenwood 2004).

[6] Bill of Rights [1688] Chapter 2 1 Will and Mar Sess 3 1689.

[7] Union with Scotland (Amendment) Act 1707 Chapter 40 6 Ann.

[8] Bogdanor (n 1) 4–10, Ch 4; Le Sueur, Sunkin and Murkens (n 1) 9, 20, 34; Colm O'Cinneide, 'The New Human Rights Culture' in Robert Hazell (ed), *Constitutional Futures Revisited: Britain's Constitution to 2020* (Palgrave Macmillan 2008).

Northern Irish Protestant, the Scots and the Welsh.[9] The English represent the national majority.[10] Each of these nations bears a distinctive set of cultural features and political perceptions of the common good.[11] British minorities, in the recent past, were subjected to policies that should be considered equivalent to an attempt at cultural genocide.[12]

All constitutional systems considered in this book are based on the doctrine of constitutional sovereignty, the division of powers, and they might also consist of a jurisdictional watchdog to guarantee the interpretation of the constitutional text.[13] The UK constitutional system instead adopts parliamentarism.[14] There is no distinction between Her Majesty's government and Her Majesty's parliament. Parliament, often referred to in the UK with the trope 'the Queen in Parliament', holds the entirety of the state's political powers.[15]

In 1998, with a series of ordinary acts, the UK changed its system of governance from unitary and regional to decentralized and asymmetric.[16] The three acts (Government of Wales Act 1998; Scotland Act 1998; The Northern Ireland Act 1998) created three different systems of regional

---

[9] Le Sueur, Sunkin and Murkens (n 1) 168–190.

[10] Robert Hazell, *Devolution and the Future of the Union* (The Constitution Unit 2015) 39; Le Sueur, Sunkin and Murkens (n 1) 190; Robert Hazell, *The English Question* (Manchester University Press 2006).

[11] Tom Nairn, *The Break-Up of Britain: Crisis and Neonationalism* (second expanded, NLB and Verso editions 1981); Ailsa Henderson and others, 'England, Englishness and Brexit' (2016) 87 The Political Quarterly 187; N MacCormick, 'Is There a Constitutional Path to Scottish Independence?' (2000) 53 Parliamentary Affairs 721; Richard Wyn Jones and Roger Scully, *Wales Says Yes: Devolution and the 2011 Welsh Referendum* (University of Wales Press 2012); K Boyle and T Hadden, 'The Peace Process in Northern Ireland' (1995) 71 International Affairs 269; Hazell, *The English Question* (n 10).

[12] Geoffrey Plank, *Rebellion and Savagery: The Jacobite Rising of 1745 and the British Empire* (University of Pennsylvania Press 2015); R R Davies, 'Colonial Wales' (1974) Past & Present 3; Garth Stevenson, *Parallel Paths: The Development of Nationalism in Ireland and Quebec* (McGill-Queen's University Press 2006).

[13] Janet L Hiebert, 'Parliamentary Bills of Rights: An Alternative Model?' (2006) 69 The Modern Law Review 7.

[14] Bogdanor (n 1) 10.

[15] Le Sueur, Sunkin and Murkens (n 1) 52; Bogdanor (n 1) 10; Dicey (n 2).

[16] Government of Wales Act 1998 Ch 38 (Ch 38); Scotland Act 1998 c 46; The Northern Ireland Act 1998 Ch 47 (Ch 47); Le Sueur, Sunkin and Murkens (n 1) 161; Robert Hazell, *Constitutional Futures Revisited: Britain's Constitution to 2020* (Palgrave Macmillan 2008) pt 1; Le Sueur, Sunkin and Murkens (n 1) 173–190.

governance for devolved regions and kept the unitary regional structure for the English regions.[17] Wales initially received limited administrative competencies which were later extended to a list of direct legislative prerogatives.[18] The Northern Ireland Act 1998 was part of an international agreement that had the effect, among others, of ceasing the civil war.[19] Anyhow, Northern Ireland will not be discussed in this chapter because it is substantially different from the other processes considered in this book.

The Northern Ireland Act 1998 is an act of the UK parliament but it is better understood as part of an international agreement that has been inserted into the process of the decolonization of Ireland.[20] This decolonization process commenced with the allocation of Home Rule to the counties of Northern Ireland by the Northern Ireland Act 1920.[21] The parliament in Northern Ireland, established as one of the effects of the Home Rule system, functioned as a devolved institution until 1971.[22] The relatively short and troubled life of the Home Rule system in Northern Ireland was due, among other social and economic reasons, to a lack of consideration in the Northern Ireland Act 1920 of the internal dynamics of consociative politics in a community divided along sectarian lines.[23] By the time Home Rule in Northern Ireland was suspended in 1971 and the region moved towards a civil war, the Welsh and, subsequently, Scottish Labour considered the possibility of creating

---

17 Le Sueur, Sunkin and Murkens (n 1) 164, 190; Hazell, *The English Question* (n 10); Hazell, *Devolution and the Future of the Union* (n 10).

18 Government of Wales Act 2006 Ch 32; Wales Act 2014 Ch 29; Wales Act 2017 Ch 4.

19 Stefan Wolff, 'The Institutional Structure of Regional Consociations in Brussels, Northern Ireland, and South Tyrol' (2004) 10 Nationalism and Ethnic Politics 387; Stevenson (n 12); Boyle and Hadden (n 11); T Hadden and K Boyle, 'Northern Ireland: Conflict and Conflict Resolution' in K Rupesinghe (ed), *Ethic Conflict and Human Right* (United Nations University Press); The UK Government and The Government of Ireland, 'The Belfast Agreement: An Agreement Reached at the Multi-Party Talks on Northern Ireland 1998. CM 3883 (the Belfast Agreement)'.

20 Boyle and Hadden (n 11); The Northern Ireland Act 1998 Ch 47 (n 26).

21 'Articles of Agreement for a Treaty Between Great Britain and Ireland, London, 6/12/1921'. http://www.nationalarchives.ie/topics/anglo_irish/dfaexhib2.html (accessed 19 August 2015).

22 Bogdanor (n 1) 90.

23 Hadden and Boyle (n 19); Wolff (n 19).

democratic decentralized regional assemblies in Wales and Scotland.[24] The Belfast Agreement established a consociative system of governance in which representatives of religious communities shared a government.[25] Given the level of sectarian tension that still afflicts the area and the specificity of Northern Ireland's history, the region will not be discussed in this book.[26]

As one of the measures to win back nationalist votes in Wales, in 1974, George Thomas, a Welsh Labour Member of Parliament (MP) and Secretary of State for Wales (which is a UK central government office) explained his party's intention to have a deliberative assembly in Wales. The proposal would be the harbinger of the current Welsh devolution: 'What we are considering [...] is a body with powerful executive authority, but which is not a legislative assembly'.[27] The plan was opposed, with some insight perhaps, by the Scottish section of the Labour Party.[28] The Labour Party's historical commitment to launching regional deliberative assemblies coincided with the publication of the Royal Commission on the Constitution 1969–1973, which considered, among other aspects, the potential implications of the Welsh and Scottish nationalist movements in the UK's system of governance.[29]

The report included an evaluation of the Northern Irish, Scottish and Welsh identity-based constitutional claims and considered them of limited relevance.[30] However, the Labour Party read the Royal Commission report as a proposal to have an asymmetric allocation of powers in

---

[24] Wyn Jones and Scully (n 11) 32.

[25] Wolff (n 19); Stevenson (n 12) Ch 9; Robin Wilson and Rick Wilford, 'Northern Ireland: Polarisation or Normalisation?' in Robert Hazell (ed), *Constitutional Futures Revisited: Britain's Constitution to 2020* (Palgrave Macmillan 2008).

[26] Stevenson (n 12); Le Sueur, Sunkin and Murkens (n 1) 176; Gerry Moriarty, 'Arlene Foster Seeks Return to Direct Rule if Deadlock is Not Broken' (1 January 2018) https://www.irishtimes.com/news/ireland/irish-news/arlene-foster-seeks-return-to-direct-rule-if-deadlock-is-not-broken-1.3342249 (accessed 7 January 2018); Stevenson (n 12).

[27] As reported in Wyn Jones and Scully (n 11) 32. Original Source: Labour Party, Policies for a Brighter Future for Wales (1974) 2.

[28] *The Scottish Political System* (Cambridge University Press 1989) 145–147.

[29] 'Royal Commission on the Constitution 1969–1973, Volume I, Report (Cmnd 5460)' http://web-archives.univ-pau.fr/english/kilbrandonchap10.pdf (accessed 20 August 2015).

[30] Ibid 325–366.

Wales and in Scotland.[31] The Welsh, the Labour Party leadership decided, should only have administrative powers, whereas the Scottish parliament would have legislative powers. The reason for differentiating the two institutions is a matter of speculation, but the distinction was maintained in the Labour-sponsored Scotland Act 1998 and in the Government of Wales Act 1998.[32]

In 1979, however, the idea of an asymmetric devolution in Scotland and in Wales was rejected by regional referenda. The results were definitive in Wales and marginal in Scotland, where the referendum did not reach the quorum of 40 per cent of the electoral franchise.[33] The end of the cycle of Labour as a party of government was followed by a series of Conservative governments which put the issues related to UK recognition of identity-based constitutional claims at rest. The same Conservative policies which fostered a liberal economy in a homogenous system of governance had the effect of alienating most voters in the Labour Party's strongholds in Wales and Scotland.[34]

In 1998, and after 18 years of Conservative government, the Labour Party (which at the time had decided to call itself the New Labour Party) took control of the House of Commons, and revived the idea of decentralized deliberative assemblies for Northern Ireland, Scotland and Wales. This was the beginning of the end, so to speak, of the British unitary state. The 1997 pre-election manifesto included a clear commitment to devolution.

> Subsidiarity is as sound a principle in Britain as it is in Europe. Our proposal is for devolution not federation. A sovereign Westminster Parliament will devolve power to Scotland and Wales. The Union will be strengthened, and the threat of separatism removed. As soon as possible after the election, we will enact legislation to allow the people of Scotland and Wales to vote in separate referendums.[35]

The explicit commitment to the policy in the manifesto allowed Labour to pass legislation without the review of the House of Lords, which was still controlled by hereditary peers.[36]

---

31 Wyn Jones and Scully (n 11) 33.

32 Ibid; Scotland Act 1998 c 46; Government of Wales Act 1998 Ch 38.

33 Bogdanor (n 1) 90.

34 Ibid 91.

35 Extract taken from Le Sueur, Sunkin and Murkens (n 1) 175. Full text: '1997 Labour Party Manifesto' http://www.labour-party.org.uk/manifestos/1997/1997-labour-manifesto.shtml (accessed 12 March 2014).

36 House of Lords Act 1999 Ch 34.

After obtaining the control of the House of Commons, the Labour Party prompted a series of debates, which in the case of Northern Ireland took the form of internationally supported peace negotiations aimed at changing the UK system of governance. The debates were followed by a series of regional referenda, which in Northern Ireland included a nationwide Republic of Ireland referendum and concluded with a series of UK parliamentary statutory measures.[37] The Republic of Ireland's constitution was also amended in a way that explicitly made the Republic of Ireland renounce its territorial claims over the Northern Irish counties.[38]

The Scotland Act 1998 established a quasi-federal relationship between the Scots and the UK central institutions.[39] Scotland already had its own legal and educational systems, but the Scotland Act 1998, among other aspects, put the Scottish parliament back into session and established the conditions for some level of fiscal autonomy.[40] The final report of the 2009 Commission on Scottish Devolution reviewed the past decade of Scottish devolution and made a series of recommendations.[41] Some of these recommendations such as the ability of Scotland to collect fiscal resources (and to borrow money) inspired the 2012 Scotland Act.[42] The activity of the Commission on Scottish Devolution was not supported by the Scottish government. At that time, the SNP was preparing for a consultative referendum on independence.[43]

---

[37] Northern Ireland Act 1998 (UK) (c 47); Government of Wales Act 1998 (UK) (c 38); Scotland Act 1998 (UK) (c 46).

[38] The Nineteenth Amendment of The Constitution Act, 1998; Boyle and Hadden (n 11); Wolff (n 19); Stevenson (n 12).

[39] Le Sueur, Sunkin and Murkens (n 1) 164; Robert Hazell, 'Constitutional Reform in the United Kingdom: Past, Present and Future', in Caroline Morris, Jonathan Boston and Petra Butler (eds), *Reconstituting the Constitution* (Springer 2011) 6.

[40] Scotland Act 1998 c 46; Chris Harrop, 'The Sewel Convention. An Assessment of the Process of Westminster Legislating on Devolved Matters Report Prepared for the Scottish Executive Constitution Unit' http://archive.scottish.parliament.uk/business/committees/procedures/papers-05/prp05-02.pdf (accessed 29 October 2015); Alan Trench, 'Tying the UK Together?' in Robert Hazell (ed), *Constitutional Futures Revisited: Britain's Constitution to 2020* (Palgrave Macmillan 2008).

[41] Commission on Devolution, 'Serving Scotland Better: Scotland and the United Kingdom in the 21st Century' (2009) 10–11.

[42] Scotland Act 2012 pt 3.

[43] Scottish Government, *List of Contributions, Scotland's Future: A National Conversation*, vol 2012 (2012); The Scottish Government, 'A National Conversation – Your Scotland Your Voice' (The Scottish Government 2009).

In 2011, the Welsh Assembly obtained, following a referendum, direct legislative powers.[44] In 2012, the First Minister of Scotland and the Prime Minister of the UK signed an agreement over the procedures of a 2014 consultative referendum over Scotland's independence (hereafter, the 2014 referendum). In 2014, the majority of Scottish residents voted against independence; however, in the weeks before the vote, a sudden spike of support for the secession motivated the UK government to promise some significant concessions to Scotland.[45] This set of promises was articulated in Lord Smith of Kelvin's report and inspired the Scotland Act 2016.[46]

The Scotland Act 2016 gives power to set rates and to create new taxes. It also set the process that both parliaments had to follow in case they wished to legislate in an area not covered by their respective competences.[47] The 2012 Agreement and the recent Scotland Act 2016 are, it is reasonable to suggest, manifestations of what is currently perceived as essential to the Scottish sub-state constitutional polity (for example, democratic and fiscal accountability) and of the dynamic approach that the UK parliament has taken in relation to identity-based constitutional claims.[48]

The new quasi-federal Scotland reinforced the perception of Scottish distinctiveness within the Union,[49] and it might have prepared the UK constitutional system for the new emerging level of asymmetric recognition from the English regions and English municipalities.[50] Welsh legislative powers were further extended by the Wales Act 2017,

---

[44] Wyn Jones and Scully (n 11).

[45] Lord Smith of Kelvin, 'The Smith Commission' 1.

[46] Scotland Act 2016 2016 (Ch 11); Lord Smith of Kelvin (n 45).

[47] Scotland Act 2016 (n 46).

[48] St Andrew's House Scottish Executive, 'Agreement between the Scottish Government and the United Kingdom Government on the Referendum on Independence for Scotland' (12 October 2012) http://www.scotland.gov.uk/About/Government/concordats/Referendum-on-independence (accessed 27 October 2012); Scotland Act 2016 (n 46); Hazell, *Devolution and the Future of the Union* (n 10).

[49] Stephen Tierney, 'Towards a Federal United Kingdom? Lessons from America' (2015) 6 Political Insight 16.

[50] Hazell, *The English Question* (n 10); Iain Mclean, 'Report of the Commission on the Consequences of Devolution for the House of Commons (the McKay Commission)' (2013) 84 The Political Quarterly 395; Tom Gash, Joe Randall and Sam Sims, 'Achieving Political Decentralisation' (2014) Institute for Government; Sarah Ayres, 'Examining the Role of "Informal Governance"' (Political Studies Association 2016) https://www.bristol.ac.uk/sps/research/projects/completed/2016/examining-the-role-of-informal-governance/ (accessed 8 January 2018); Cities and Local Government Devolution Act 2016 Ch 1.

and the same statute included the requirement of a Welsh referendum for a UK statute that intended to abolish the Welsh Assembly and its government.[51]

In relation to Brexit, the Supreme Court explained that such a procedure should be separated from debates over the implications that Brexit might have on political agreements between central and devolved institutions.[52] 'Judges therefore are neither the parents nor the guardians of political conventions; they are merely observers [...] they cannot give legal rulings on its operation or scope, because those matters are determined within the political world'.[53] In short, the UK Brexit process should be considered, in relation to sub-state entities, as a manifestation of the parliament's sovereignty and will not be discussed in this book.[54] Furthermore, a comprehensive analysis of the sociological and political drivers of the British constitutional system are in the 'Constitutional Futures' series and its subsequent updates by the Constitution Unit at University College London.[55] This chapter will only focus on a selection of the aspects (the role of nationalist political parties and the effect of a flexible constitution) that influenced the negotiations between central and regional institutions and that could be compared with other legal systems considered in this book.

DRIVER OF CHANGE: THE DIVERGING NATIONALISM OF THE SCOTTISH NATIONAL PARTY AND PLAID CYMRU

The devolution acts were part of a Labour strategy that intended to stop the erosion of its support by regional nationalist parties such as the SNP

---

[51] Wales Act 2017 Ch 4 (n 18); Alan Trench, 'Making "Reserved Powers" Work for Wales' https://constitution-unit.com/2015/09/24/making-reserved-powers-work-for-wales/ (accessed 8 January 2018).

[52] *Miller & Anor, R (on the application of) v Secretary of State for Exiting the European Union (Rev 3)* [2017] UKSC 5 [6, 9–10, 117–118, 126–152].

[53] Ibid 146.

[54] Tom Mullen, 'The Brexit Case and Constitutional Conventions' (2017) 21 Edinburgh Law Review 442.

[55] Hazell (n 16); Robert Hazell, *Constitutional Futures: A History of the Next Ten Years* (Oxford University Press 1999); Hazell, *The English Question* (n 10); Hazell (n 39); The Constitution Unit, 'Publications' http://www.ucl.ac.uk/constitution-unit/publications (accessed 11 January 2018).

in Scotland and Plaid Cymru in Wales.[56] The strategy was partly successful. Plaid Cymru's electoral results, since devolution, have been decreasing.[57] The SNP has, after a post-devolution poor performance, managed to recover its electoral base.[58] However, the role that the two parties play in regional and national politics is a manifestation of two types of nationalism. I will discuss the two parties' roles as drivers of change distinctively, yet, and on a general level, Plaid Cymru focused its political strategy on the protection of ethnic Welsh identity and Welsh-speaking minorities.[59] The SNP embraced a polycentric version of nationalism that cared for the Scottish Gaelic-speaking minorities, but also tried to represent all those individuals who resided in Scotland and who perceived Scandinavian social democracies as an alternative to the liberal model adopted in England.[60]

Successive leaders of the post-devolution SNP steered the party towards a polycentric conception of national identity that ensures freedom and the protection of rights.[61] This was a modern and inclusive idea of a Scottish national community which had the distinct advantage of elevating the SNP above a persistent sectarian antagonism between Catholic and Protestant communities which still lingers in some areas of Scotland.[62] The SNP denounced sectarianism and focused its political campaigns on promoting social policies that responded to national needs such as free care for the elderly and accessible university education.[63] Scotland tends to have, by way of comparison with the rest of the UK, a higher percentage of old people.[64] In particular, the combination of

---

[56] As reported in Wyn Jones and Scully (n 11) 32. Original Source: Labour Party, 'Policies for a Brighter Future for Wales' (1974) 2.

[57] Hazell, *Devolution and the Future of the Union* (n 10) 25.

[58] Ibid.

[59] Wyn Jones and Scully (n 11).

[60] Lindsay Paterson, 'Sources of Support for the SNP' in Catherine Bromley and others (eds), *Has Devolution Delivered?* (Edinburgh University Press 2006).

[61] Anthony D Smith, *Theories of Nationalism* (Duckworth 1971) 158.

[62] Kay Goodall and others, 'Community Experiences of Sectarianism' http://storre.stir.ac.uk/handle/1893/21622 (accessed 13 July 2015); Paterson (n 60) 52.

[63] St Andrew's House Scottish Government, 'Free Personal and Nursing Care' (30 July 2012) http://www.gov.scot/Topics/Health/Support-Social-Care/Support/Adult-Social-Care/Free-Personal-Nursing-Care (accessed 8 January 2018).

[64] Alan Trench, 'Scotland and Wales: The Evolution of Devolution' in Robert Hazell (ed), *Constitutional Futures Revisited: Britain's Constitution to 2020* (Palgrave Macmillan 2008) 34.

policies such as free personal care and free college education attracted the support of the middle classes that might have had to choose between supporting their elderly parents or their children.[65]

From the 1990s, the SNP channelled the steady increase of support from the middle classes into a series of post-devolution electoral victories.[66] The leadership of the Scottish government, when it finally arrived in 2007, provided a platform for increasing the awareness of the SNP's macro aspirations such as an independent or highly decentralized Scotland.[67] The government sponsored a series of open public meetings chaired by MPs or Members of the Scottish Parliament.[68] These public engagements provided the impression of a party that was not afraid to leave the 'corridors of power' of Edinburgh or London to attend local meetings. The experience of government also increased awareness of the internal administrative structure of devolution. It is perhaps this increased awareness of the inner workings of devolution that prepared the way for the support for increased fiscal autonomy.[69]

The plan was for devolution-max, which would, if successful, provide a framework for increased fiscal and financial autonomy that might be compared with the one allocated to regions such as the Basque Country and South Tyrol.[70] Again, the idea of having more control over fiscal revenues appeared in the political arena with a distinctive serendipity. During the 2008 economic crisis in which the UK central government was cutting services, the Scottish parliament tried, given that the crisis was affecting the poorest sectors of society, to maintain the level of

---

[65] Paterson (n 60) 50.

[66] Ibid 52; Alice Brown, David McCrone and Lindsay Paterson, *Politics and Society in Scotland* (Macmillan 1996).

[67] Paterson (n 60) 53; David McCrone, *Understanding Scotland: The Sociology of a Nation* (second edition, Routledge 2001).

[68] The Scottish Government, 'A National Conversation – Your Scotland Your Voice' (The Scottish Government 2009).

[69] 'The Barnett Formula and the Financing of Devolution' https://devolutionmatters.wordpress.com/the-barnett-formula-and-the-financing-of-devolution/ (accessed 25 October 2015).

[70] Hazell, *Devolution and the Future of the Union* (n 10) 30; Stephen Tierney (n 49); Michael Keating, 'Rethinking Sovereignty: Independence-Lite, Devolution-Max and National Accommodation' [2012] Revista d'Estudis Autonomics i Federals 21; Commission on Scottish Devolution and Kenneth Charles Calman, *Serving Scotland Better: Scotland and the United Kingdom in the 21st Century* (The Commission 2009).

support across the Scottish population.[71] The SNP took the role of representing a social democratic Scotland 'against' liberal and utilitarian England.[72]

The message that the SNP was broadcasting was that Scotland was different (from England). The differences might have been more about perceptions than reality.[73] The 2011 manifesto, which prepared for the forthcoming regional election, included a commitment to call for a consultative referendum over independence.[74] There was also a less obvious suggestion that devolution-max would be an acceptable arrangement for Scotland.[75] The election gave the SNP a clear majority and the government commenced the negotiation process with the UK government. Negotiations followed the procedure set in the Legislative Consent Motion.[76] The process was given, by the Scotland Act 2016 (2), statutory status.[77] I will discuss the structure of the Legislative Consent Motion process later, but, as an institution, it was originally designed to reduce the number of bordering administrative and legislative disputes between central and Scottish institutions.[78]

The discussion over the Scottish referendum was carried out behind closed doors and it included, it is reasonable to expect, the two government representatives, civil servants and MPs' staff. The result of the negotiation was the Edinburgh Agreement.[79] In an eight-page document, the UK Prime Minister committed his government to giving the power to the Scottish parliament via a procedure defined by sec 30 (2) of the Scotland Act 1998, to decide on the terms of a referendum over

---

[71] Keating (n 70) 24.

[72] Ibid.

[73] Trench (n 64).

[74] SNP, 'Scottish National Party Manifesto 2011' (2011) 2, 3, 9, 28. http://votesnp.com/campaigns/SNP_Manifesto_2011_lowRes.pdf (accessed 1 November 2015).

[75] Ibid 3, 10.

[76] Hazell, *Devolution and the Future of the Union* (n 10) 4. Scotland Act 2016 (n 46); Scotland Act 1998 c 46. In section 28 of the Scotland Act 1998 (Acts of the Scottish Parliament) at the end add '(8) But it is recognised that the Parliament of the United Kingdom will not normally legislate with regard to devolved matters without the consent of the Scottish Parliament'. Harrop (n 40); St Andrew's House Scottish Government, 'Key Facts on the Sewel Convention' (1 July 1997).

[77] Scotland Act 2016 (n 46).

[78] Harrop (n 40); Hazell (n 39) 84.

[79] St Andrew's House Scottish Executive (n 48) 1.

secession from the UK.[80] The First Minister for Scotland, instead, agreed that such a referendum should have a single question (the initial proposal included two queries) and that it had to take place before the end of 2014.[81] The original plan was to insert a second question that asked whether Scotland should have more fiscal and legislative autonomy (for example, devolution-max).[82]

The Edinburgh Agreement is, in terms of identity-based constitutional negotiation, unique. It was preceded, it is reasonable to assume, by a series of protracted and open negotiations between two governments led by parties that were perceived as representatives of their respective national identities.[83] The Conservative and Unionist Party was perceived as a defender of the liberal, independent, Eurosceptic British identity that, until relatively recently, was confused with a distinctively English identity.[84] The SNP's raison d'être was the idea of promoting an independent social democracy tilted towards Scandinavian and European values.[85] It is reasonable to suggest, given that an agreement was reached, that the representatives had discussions in good faith over the effects that the secession might have in Scotland and the rest of the UK.[86]

---

[80] Ibid.

[81] This agreement is part of the Memorandum of Understanding and Supplementary Agreements Between the United Kingdom Government, Scottish Ministers, the Cabinet of the National Assembly for Wales and the Northern Ireland Executive Committee (Section 4 CM 5240, December 2001) allowing the formation of agreements that might alter the legislative competences and the power to regulate devolved and UK parliaments. Other important aspects of the agreement include the acceptance by both parties of the legal framework within which the referendum will take place (eg Political Parties, Elections and Referendums Act 2000, 7) and supervision of the referendum procedures by the Electoral Commission. Ibid 12.

[82] 'One Question or Two? Let's Have a Referendum | Straight Statistics' http://straightstatistics.fullfact.org/article/one-question-or-two-lets-have-referendum (accessed 8 January 2018); 'Scottish Independence Referendum Deal Signed by Cameron and Salmond' https://www.theguardian.com/politics/2012/oct/15/scottish-independence-referendum-cameron-salmond (accessed 8 January 2018).

[83] Harrop (n 40).

[84] Hazell, *The English Question* (n 10); Henderson and others (n 11).

[85] Paterson (n 60).

[86] Stephen Tierney, 'The Referendum on Scottish Independence: A Process as Well as an Event' (2014) 18 Edinburgh Law Review 245; 'Trident Missiles "could Be Relocated to Plymouth from Independent Scotland" | UK News | The Guardian' https://www.theguardian.com/uk-news/2014/aug/14/trident-missiles-relocate-plymouth-independent-scotland-rusi-report (accessed 10 January 2018);

In the aftermath of the signature of the Edinburgh Agreement, a series of analyses and eminent debates engaged the potential repercussions for the UK, the EU and other decentralized countries.[87] The referendum results favoured those who supported the Union but, a few weeks before the vote, and perhaps to stop the progression that secessionist supporters were making, the UK government announced that, if the Scots were to vote against secession, they would receive a level of fiscal autonomy that was comparable with the so-called devolution-max option.[88] As predicted, in October, the Scots rejected independence and, with the Scotland Act 2016, obtained a level of fiscal autonomy that was comparable with a federal state.[89]

The 2017 SNP manifesto for the UK general election provides some minor tuning on the policies and on the aspirations of Scottish nationalists. The first pages state the support for social policies that, in many ways, distinguish the SNP in the UK political arena.[90] The manifesto also

---

Damian Carrington, 'UK Cancels Pioneering £1bn Carbon Capture and Storage Competition' *The Guardian* (25 November 2015) http://www.theguardian.com/environment/2015/nov/25/uk-cancels-pioneering-1bn-carbon-capture-and-storage-competition (accessed 10 January 2018).

[87] 'Debate: Sionaidh Douglas-Scott: Why the EU Should Welcome an Independent Scotland' http://ukconstitutionallaw.org/2014/09/10/debate-sionaidh-douglas-scott-why-the-eu-should-welcome-an-independent-scotland/ (accessed 13 August 2015); 'Debate: J. H.H. Weiler: Scotland and the EU: A Comment' http://ukconstitutionallaw.org/2014/09/10/debate-j-h-h-weiler-scotland-and-the-eu-a-comment/ (accessed 13 August 2015); Gavin W Anderson and others, 'Gavin Anderson and others, 'The Independence Referendum, Legality and the Contested Constitution: Widening the Debate' http://ukconstitutionallaw.org/2012/01/31/gavin-anderson-et-al-the-independence-referendum-legality-and-the-contested-constitution-widening-the-debate/ (accessed 24 November 2012); Vito Breda, 'La Devolution de Escocia y El Referéndum de 2014: Cuáles Son Las Repercusiones Potenciales En España?' [2013] Teoria y Realidad Constitucional 69; Great Britain: Parliament: House of Commons: Scottish Affairs Committee, *The Referendum on Separation for Scotland: Making the Process Legal, Second Report of Session 2012–13, Report, Together with Formal Minutes* (The Stationery Office 2012).

[88] Severin Carrell and Scotland correspondent, 'Scotland Promised Extra Tax and Legal Powers for Referendum No Vote' *The Guardian* (4 August 2014) http://www.theguardian.com/politics/2014/aug/05/scotland-promised-new-powers-no-vote-referendum (accessed 8 January 2018).

[89] Stephen Tierney (n 49); Stephen Tierney, 'Reclaiming Politics: Popular Democracy in Britain after the Scottish Referendum' (2015) 86 The Political Quarterly 226.

[90] SNP, 'Manifesto (2017)' 5–7.

includes the intention to seek another referendum over independence.[91] The request to consider the possibility of another referendum was refused by the UK government and so was the claim that regional institutions should have a voice in the Brexit process.[92] The refusal to engage, this time with the Scottish government, is one of the elements of the historical relationship between central and regional institutions.[93]

Plaid Cymru

Plaid Cymru has taken the role of representing Welsh national identity into the UK political arena and it does, like the SNP, support social democratic policies.[94] It had, like the SNP, the possibility of attracting voters from the traditional left who were disappointed by the new liberal attitudes of the Labour Party.[95] This has not occurred in a way that has concerned the dominance of the Welsh Labour Party in Wales. One of the reasons for this is that Plaid Cymru has associated its policies with the protection of Welsh-speaking minorities.[96] The pledges to support low-income families and to protect both the level of public services and free education, which could have the potential to change voting partners in Wales, were not coupled with a campaign that dislodged the perception of Plaid Cymru as a party for and of Welsh speakers.[97]

A commitment to bilingualism is also one of the SNP's policies,[98] and there are indications from the analysis of voting patterns in areas that have the most Gaelic speakers that bilingual Scots perceive the SNP as

---

[91] Ibid 8, 29.

[92] Heather Stewart, Peter Walker and Severin Carrell, 'Theresa May Rejects Nicola Sturgeon's Referendum Demand' *The Guardian* (16 March 2017) http://www.theguardian.com/politics/2017/mar/16/theresa-may-rejects-nicola-sturgeons-scottish-referendum-demand (accessed 9 January 2018); *Miller & Anor* (n 52); Mullen (n 54).

[93] SNP (n 90) 44.

[94] Trench (n 64) 32.

[95] Justin Fisher, 'Whither the Parties' in Robert Hazell (ed), *Constitutional Futures Revisited: Britain's Constitution to 2020* (Palgrave Macmillan 2008).

[96] Plaid Cymru, 'Manifesto 2017' 27.

[97] Ibid 3–12, 26–28; Hazell, *Devolution and the Future of the Union* (n 10) 23.

[98] Johann Wolfgang Unger, *Discursive Construction of the Scots Language: Education, Politics and Everyday Life* (John Benjamins 2013) 17.

the party that better represents them in Scotland and in the UK.[99] However, bilingualism is not central to the policy of the SNP in Scotland nor in the UK. Plaid Cymru has consistently chosen, from the decision not to change its name, to give the perception that it is the Welsh-speakers' political party. So, whilst the SNP has used the magnifying effect provided by the Scottish parliament to show the distinctiveness of the Scottish identity (real or perceived), Plaid Cymru has decided not to change its image of a party that associates national distinctiveness with a linguistic minority. In the long term, this might be a successful strategy. The number of young Welsh speakers who are being educated in the Welsh medium is increasing.[100] However, the reliance of a political party on its ability to provide representation for a narrowly constructed national group tends to require a narrow conception of the common good and, on a more general level, it is more difficult to accommodate in a multi-national country such as the UK.[101]

DRIVER OF CHANGE: A FLEXIBLE CONSTITUTION AND THE UNION ON THE BRINK

Most regionalist political parties when they are at the helm of devolved institutions tend to demand more decentralization.[102] This assumption is based on past experiences and has the effect of increasing the level of accountability of regional administrations and of fostering competition between territorial authorities.[103] Constitutional conventions such as the Sewel Convention[104] limit the prerogative of local and central parliaments, but not in a way that is comparable with a codified constitution. The 2012 Edinburgh Agreement, however, might have had the effect of bringing an end to the 1707 parliamentary union between Scotland and

---

[99] Ibid 67, 75; National Records of Scotland, 'Scotland's Census 2011 – Interactive Maps | Census Data Explorer', http://www.Scotlandscensus.Gov.Uk/Ods-Web/Datavis.Jsp?Theme=Language_September_2013 (accessed 9 January 2018).

[100] Welsh Government, 'Wales in Figures 2010' 7, http://gov.wales/statistics-and-research/wales-figures/?lang=en (accessed 9 January 2018).

[101] Wolff (n 19); Stevenson (n 12).

[102] Hazell, *Devolution and the Future of the Union* (n 10) 30.

[103] Robert Hazell and Mark Glover, 'Introduction: Forecasting Constitutional Futures' in Robert Hazell (ed), *Constitutional Futures Revisited: Britain's Constitution to 2020* (Palgrave Macmillan 2008) 5–10; Hazell (n 39) 84; Tierney (n 49).

[104] Scotland Act 2016 (n 46).

England.[105] The prerogative to bring the UK to the 'brink of the dissolution', as Hazell describes it, is one of the effects of the adoption of the Westminster Model.[106] In this section, I will elaborate some of the implications of the principle of absolute legislative sovereignty as a driver of change in the UK system of territorial governance. Again, a much wider analysis of the drivers of change of UK devolution can be found elsewhere, but this book seeks to provide an indication of distinctive drivers of change that might help to qualify the UK in a comparative context.[107]

As the most relevant of all the UK constitutional values, the principle of absolute legislative sovereignty has 'positive' and 'negative' logical implications. The positive implications have been virtually unchanged since its first theorization by Dicey.

> The principle of Parliamentary sovereignty means neither more nor less than this, namely that Parliament thus defined has, under the English constitution, the right to make or unmake any law whatever: and, further, that no person or body is recognised by the law of England as having a right to override or set aside the legislation of Parliament.[108]

The positive logical implication demands that the UK parliament is the only institution to have the power to make statutory instruments in the UK and its colonies. The negative logical interpretation demands that no other institution can repeal or amend a statute approved by the UK parliament.[109]

The 'negative logical interpretation' of the principle of parliamentary sovereignty has a twofold effect on devolution. Firstly, the judiciary, including the UK Supreme Court, cannot alter UK legislation that changes the system of governance in the UK.[110] This is the case even if

---

[105] Hazell, *Devolution and the Future of the Union* (n 10) 6; St Andrew's House Scottish Executive (n 48).

[106] Hazell, *Devolution and the Future of the Union* (n 10) 6.

[107] Hazell, *Devolution and the Future of the Union* (n 10); Hazell (n 16); Robert Hazell and University College London Constitution Unit, *An Unstable Union: Devolution and the English Question: State of the Union Annual Lecture* (Constitution Unit, School of Public Policy, University College London 2000); Hazell, *Constitutional Futures* (n 55); Bogdanor (n 1) pt 2; Bogdanor, *Devolution in the United Kingdom* (n 4); Trench (n 64); Trench (n 50); Le Sueur, Sunkin and Murkens (n 1) Ch 5.

[108] Dicey (n 2) 37.

[109] Vito Breda, 'Lingering with Intent: The UK Constitutional Review' in Miodrag A Jovanovic (ed), *Constitutional Review and Democracy* (Eleven 2015).

[110] Schedule 6, Scotland Act 1998.

such an act might have the effect of dissolving the Union. For instance, the Scotland Act 1998 (Modification of Schedule 5) Order 2013, which allowed the Scottish parliament to prepare a consultative 2014 referendum over independence, could not have been subjected to judicial review.[111]

Once the act of the Scottish parliament setting the procedure for the referendum was within the terms set by the aforementioned Order, the UK Supreme Court could not discuss the substantive aspects of the referendum.[112] In other words, once the Order (ex sec 30 (2)) has been approved by the UK parliament, the UK Supreme Court cannot assess whether a referendum over Scottish independence is compatible with the implicit or explicit principles (*à la* Canadian, so to speak) of the UK constitutional system.[113] This is the case even if the Scottish Act and the Order might have been, following the result of the 2014 referendum, the proxy for the dissolution of the UK.

It is the unwritten principle of the absolute legislative sovereignty of parliament that prevents the UK Supreme Court from delivering a decision analogous to the one provided by the Canadian Supreme Court over the Quebec referendum.[114] The Canadian Supreme Court in *Reference re Secession of Quebec* explains that the will expressed by the majority of Quebecois has respected the basic principles of a modern constitutional democracy: 'federalism, democracy, constitutionalism and the rule of law, and respect for minorities'.[115] These principles (some of them were implicit) helped the Canadian Supreme Court to decide in favour of the illegitimacy of a Quebec referendum over the secession. In contrast with Canada, the UK parliament has the power to decide over radical changes to the institutional structure of the UK, and that includes the prerogative to set whatever procedures it decides upon for dissolving it.[116]

It is also important to note that the parliament and all devolved institutions tend to exercise restraint and to avoid real or simulated

---

[111] That complied with Sec 30 (2) of the Scotland Act 1998.

[112] Schedule 6, Scotland Act 1998.

[113] Scottish Independence Referendum Act 2013; Scottish Independence Referendum (Franchise) Act 2013; Scottish Government and UK Government, 'Agreement between the United Kingdom Government and the Scottish Government on a Referendum on Independence for Scotland'.

[114] *Reference Re Secession of Quebec [1998] 2 SCR 217* [1998] 217.

[115] Ibid para 90.

[116] Hazell, *Devolution and the Future of the Union* (n 10) 6; Bogdanor (n 1) Ch 2.

institutional frictions.[117] This is the so-called principle of political morality implicit in the UK constitutional system.[118] 'The term might be defined as an unwritten ethical commitment for all UK constitutional institutions to serve the common good and, as a corollary, to avoid needless constitutional crises.'[119] In the case of Scotland, there is also a specific assumption that parliamentary sovereignty is not part of the Scottish constitutional tradition.[120] The assumption is taken from an obiter in the case of *MacCormick v Lord Advocate* in which Lord President Copper makes an explicit judicial reference to the existence of a Scottish public law tradition that does not include the principles of parliamentary sovereignty.[121]

However, even within the potential limitations of Lord President Copper's obiter, the UK and devolved institutions can, and did, change the system of governance in a way that is distinctive of the British system. One of the innovative elements of the 1998 devolution was the Sewel Convention. The mechanism of the Sewel Convention allows parliaments and executive administrations to coordinate legislative activities and policies. The first of these memoranda was called 'Memorandum of Understanding Between the United Kingdom Government, Scottish Ministers, the Cabinet of the National Assembly for Wales and

---

[117] See the chapter discussing Spain; Paul Williams and others, 'The Legitimacy of Catalonia's Exercise of Its Right to Decide: A Report by a Commission of International Experts' (Global Studies Institute University of Geneva – Departament d'Afers i Relacions Institucionals i Exteriors i Transparència 2017) 20 http://exteriors.gencat.cat/web/.content/00_ACTUALITAT/notes_context/FULL-REPORT-Catalonias-legitimate-right-to-decide.pdf (accessed 21 April 2018).

[118] John Stuart Mill, *Considerations on Representative Government* (Prometheus 1991) Ch 5. A similar analysis is in John Austin, *The Province of Jurisprudence Determined* (John Murray 1832) 282. The historical origin of the principle is discussed in H Patrick Glenn, *Legal Traditions of the World: Sustainable Diversity in Law* (Oxford University Press 2010) 102.

[119] Breda (n 109) 268. Mill (n 118) Ch 5. A similar analysis is given in Austin (n 118) 282. The historical origin of the principle is discussed in Glenn (n 118) 102.

[120] S Tierney, *Constitutional Law and National Pluralism* (Oxford University Press 2004) 110.

[121] 'The principle of the unlimited sovereignty of Parliament is a distinctively English principle which has no counterpart in Scottish Constitutional Law [...] I have not found in the Union legislation any provision that the parliament of Great Britain should be free to alter the treaty at will [...]' *MacCormick v Lord Advocate* 1953 SC 396 411. Breda (n 109); Vito Breda, 'La Devolution de Escocia y El Referéndum de 2014: Cuáles Son Las Repercusiones Potenciales En España?' [2013] Teoria y Realidad Constitucional 69.

the Northern Ireland Executive (CM 4444)', but it is colloquially known as the Sewel Convention.[122] The document has been revised several times,[123] but its colloquial name has not been changed. The memorandum is not an Act of Parliament and it cannot be enforced on the devolved administrations or indeed bind the parliament (as discussed), yet the procedure was consistently complied with by both central and regional institutions.[124]

As with other regional–central interface institutions such as the Standing Committee on South Tyrol inside the Italian parliament,[125] the Sewel Convention is a deliberative arena that seeks to coordinate and enhance the efficiency of executive policies and reduce 'adjoining' issues in which one of the parliaments perceives that its competence has been trumped by legislations or by the administrative document.[126] The Standard Note SN/PC/2084 warns the staff of the UK departments that their views on

---

[122] UK Parliament, 'Memorandum of Understanding and Supplementary Agreements between the United Kingdom Government, Scottish Ministers and the Cabinet of the National Assembly for Wales (CM 4444)'.

[123] UK Government, 'Memorandum of Understanding and Supplementary Agreements Between the United Kingdom Government Scottish Ministers, the Cabinet of the National Assembly for Wales and the Northern Ireland Executive Committee (CM 4806)'; UK Government, 'Memorandum of Understanding and Supplementary Agreements Between the United Kingdom Government Scottish Ministers, the Cabinet of the National Assembly for Wales and the Northern Ireland Executive Committee (CM 5240)'; UK Government, 'Memorandum of Understanding and Supplementary Agreements Between the United Kingdom Government Scottish Ministers, the Cabinet of the National Assembly for Wales and the Northern Ireland Executive Committee (CM 7864)'; UK Government, 'Memorandum of Understanding and Supplementary Agreements Between the United Kingdom Government Scottish Ministers, the Cabinet of the National Assembly for Wales and the Northern Ireland Executive Committee (2011)'; UK Government, 'Memorandum of Understanding and Supplementary Agreements Between the United Kingdom Government Scottish Ministers, the Cabinet of the National Assembly for Wales and the Northern Ireland Executive Committee (2013) UK Government, Devolution: memorandum of understanding and supplementary agreements (2016)'.

[124] Royal Commission on Auckland Governance, 'Report of the Commission on the Consequences of Devolution for the House of Commons (McKay Report)' 1 http://webarchive.nationalarchives.gov.uk/20130403030652/http://tmc.independent.gov.uk/wp-content/uploads/2013/03/The-McKay-Commission_Main-Report_25-March-20131.pdf (accessed 21 October 2015); Hazell, *Devolution and the Future of the Union* (n 10) 50.

[125] Decree no. 670 31.08.1972 Article 107.

[126] Royal Commission on Auckland Governance (n 124) 4.

the boundaries of devolved matters must be checked with their respective counterparts working for the Scottish government:

> Always consult your Legal Adviser and the Scotland Office if you are in any doubt about whether a proposal may trespass on devolved matters. Do not assume that the Scottish Executive will necessarily share your view about where the boundaries lie as between reserved and devolved matters [and] departments should approach the Scottish Executive on the same basis for Bills being published in draft, even though there is no formal requirement to do so.[127]

The Standard Note also requires public servants to add a note to any policy documents affecting Scotland saying that a Scottish assent was sought and retrieved.

The discursive process between regional and central governments ingrained in the Sewel Convention has several beneficial effects. Firstly, the unavoidable issues related to the overlapping of territorially divided administrative activities are engaged and discussed by civil servants who are directly invested with the task of carrying out those tasks. The public sector in both central and devolved institutions is statutorily independent and normally perceived as a-political.[128] The combination of the expertise of those involved, the relative clarity of the policy aims and the independence of the institutions that must carry out the tasks necessary to achieve an agreed aim contribute to an efficient accommodation of most of the administrative issues.[129] This commitment appears to be lacking in the activity of the Joint Ministerial Committee.[130]

The second positive implication of the Sewel Convention is that it stimulated open and frank political debates between central and regional politicians. Central government cabinet members who oversee specific bills will, before the bill is submitted to parliament, start confidential negotiations with their regional parliamentary counterparts. Regional and central ministers, if their presence is required, will focus only on aspects of a bill that demand a political agreement between the central and Scottish governments. The scope of these political debates is, after the

---

127 Ibid.

128 Francis Fukuyama, *Political Order and Political Decay: From the Industrial Revolution to the Globalisation of Democracy* (Profile 2014) 169; Oxford University Act 1854 (c 81); Cambridge University Act 1856 (c 88); Scott L Greer and Holly Jarman, 'What Whitehall?: Definitions, Demographics and the Changing Home Civil Service' (2010) 25 Public Policy and Administration 251.

129 Royal Commission on Auckland Governance (n 124) 5.

130 Hazell, *Devolution and the Future of the Union* (n 10) 51.

technical issues have been dealt with by experts, narrow, and this, in turn, expedites negotiations and reduces the risk of drafting mistakes.

The third beneficial effect is the establishment of working relations between central and devolved politicians. The UK political system benefits, by way of comparison with other constitutional systems considered in this book (for example, the Australian and the Italian systems), from long-term political cycles.[131] Again, a similar beneficial effect was reported in the work of the South Tyrol Joint Committees.[132] New Labour, for instance, had control of the parliament from 1997 to 2010.[133] The stability of the guarantee is that those involved in the closed-door meetings, who are part of the Sewel Convention, tend to have past long-term working relationships and seek to achieve long-term solutions. Disagreements are instead, it is reasonable to assume, hidden from public scrutiny by the secrecy of the deliberative process. There are questions over the transparency of the Sewel Convention system but, for a negotiator that wants to appear successful, it is an ideal political setting.

CONCLUSION

This chapter has discussed two of the drivers of change that helped (and reduced) the process of the recognition and negotiation of identity-based constitutional claims in the UK. The first section focused on the role of sub-state nationalist parties such as the SNP and Plaid Cymru. The second driver of change considered was the high level of flexibility of the UK constitution. These are just a sample of the complex political and institutional factors that are inserted in the Constitution Unit's 'Constitutional Futures' series.[134] To suggest that multinational constitutional systems should adopt the Westminster Model would be a panglossianism.

The aim of the chapter was instead to show the effects of having an open process for the negotiation and accommodation of regionalist

---

[131] Philip Norton, *Parliament in British Politics* (Palgrave Macmillan 2013) 62. Emma Lantschner, 'History of the South Tyrol Conflict and Its Settlement' in Jens Woelk, Francesco Palermo and Joseph Marko (eds), *Tolerance Through Law: Self Governance and Group Rights in South Tyrol* (Brill 2007). Georg Grote, *The South Tyrol Question, 1866–2010: From National Rage to Regional State* (Peter Lang 2012) 128.

[132] Jens Woelk, Francesco Palermo and Joseph Marko, *Tolerance through Law* (Martinus Nijhoff 2008).

[133] Fisher (n 95); Hazell, *Devolution and the Future of the Union* (n 10) 50.

[134] Hazell, *Constitutional Futures Revisited* (n 55); Hazell (n 16); Hazell (n 39).

demands. The analysis of the SNP's and Plaid Cymru's political strategies shows, for instance, the advantages and disadvantages of associating a national identity with a minority language.[135] The SNP has continued to gain the support of Scottish Gaelic speakers, but has strategically decided to be a polycentric political party that represents all of Scotland.[136] In particular, the SNP has chosen to champion a form of inclusive social democracy that is ideologically distinct from the liberal stance adopted in English politics.[137] The difference in terms of voting trends between the two parties has been substantial.[138] Plaid Cymru has improved, but not enough to claim the control of the Welsh Assembly.[139]

The SNP's demand for the re-negotiation of the Scotland Act 1998 has shifted the system of governance in Scotland from the status of a region within a unitary state (albeit with a distinctive legal system) to a quasi-federal state.[140] It is outside the scope of this book to assess whether such a transformation was good for Scotland. The outcomes of constitutional negotiations, and indeed the political success of a party, are related to multifarious elements and so there is no substantive link between the political strategies and the changes in a system of governance. However, the SNP's careful crafting of inclusive and deliberative policies managed to persuade the electorate in multiple elections of its ability to negotiate with the UK government.[141]

The second of the selected drivers of change in the UK constitutional system is the flexibility of the British uncodified constitution and the related principle of absolute legislative sovereignty. The idea that 'what the Queen in Parliament enacts is law'[142] allocates substantial discretion to the law-making powers of the UK parliament and to Her Majesty's government.[143] The Edinburgh Agreement, in which the UK government

---

135 Paterson (n 60); Welsh Government (n 100).

136 Paterson (n 60).

137 Conservative and Unionist Party, 'Conservative Manifesto 2015' https://s3-eu-west-1.amazonaws.com/manifesto2015/ConservativeManifesto2015.pdf (accessed 10 May 2015); Scottish National Party, 'Scottish Election: SNP Manifesto' http://votesnp.com/campaigns/SNP_Manifesto_2011_lowRes.pdf (accessed 8 January 2018).

138 Hazell, *Devolution and the Future of the Union* (n 10) 25.

139 Conservative and Unionist Party (n 137); Scottish National Party (n 137).

140 Tierney (n 49); Hazell, *Devolution and the Future of the Union* (n 10) Ch 2.

141 Hazell, *Devolution and the Future of the Union* (n 10) Ch 2.

142 Bogdanor (n 1) 13; Le Sueur, Sunkin and Murkens (n 1) 24.

143 Martin Loughlin, 'Constituent Power Subverted: From English Constitutional Argument to British Constitutional Practice' in Martin Loughlin and Neil

and Scottish government decided over a process that might have had the effect of dissolving the UK is perhaps one of the most explicative examples of the potential effect of the untrammelled power of the British parliament and the benefits of the Sewel Convention.[144]

The Joint Ministerial Committee, composed of central and regional cabinet members, had a role in negotiating identity-based constitutional claims,[145] but it appears that the Sewel Convention has been the preferred channel of communication between the UK and Scottish governments.[146] The Sewel Convention was inserted into the 1998 devolution as an informal channel of institutional communication between central and regional institutions.[147] The mechanism of confidential meetings facilitated the activity of both central and regional institutions by reducing bordering disputes and by coordinating overlapping policies.[148]

Again, the narratives proposed in this chapter are not meant to suggest that the UK system of governance could be transplanted into a political system where relations between regionalism and central institutions are acrimonious.[149] The narrative is rather this: the UK experience of decentralization over the past two decades suggests that open negotiations and constant engagement between central and regional institutions tend to facilitate both the recognition and accommodation of real or perceived cultural diversity.

Walker (eds), *The Paradox of Constitutionalism: Constituent Power and Constitutional Form* (Oxford University Press 2007).

144 St Andrew's House Scottish Executive (n 48).

145 Hazell, *Devolution and the Future of the Union* (n 10) 50.

146 Harrop (n 40).

147 Hazell, *Devolution and the Future of the Union* (n 10) 34.

148 *Axa General Insurance Ltd, Petitioners*, vol 2 (2010); *Recovery of Medical Costs for Asbestos Diseases (Wales) Bill (Reference By The Counsel General For Wales) [2015] UKSC 3*; *R. (on the Application of Jackson) v Attorney General*, vol 1 (UKHL 2005).

149 Williams and others (n 117); Michele Graziadei, 'Legal Transplants and the Frontiers of Legal Knowledge' (2009) 10 Theoretical Inquiries in Law 723.

3. Spain: constitutional negotiations and ethnocentric nationalisms

INTRODUCTION: THE DISPOSITIVE PRINCIPLE IN A RIGID CONSTITUTION

Spain has one of the most advanced constitutional systems considered in this book. The 1978 constitution is lengthy and rigid,[1] and it explicitly recognizes the pluralist sociological fabric of Spain,[2] yet allocates all of the sovereignty to the Spanish nation.[3] At the time of writing this book, Spain had 17 autonomous regions and two overseas cities. The autonomous regions, which were intended as a form of recognition for the distinctive social aspects of the Spanish territory, cover the entire landmass of Spain and overseas territories.[4] The prerogative to set up multiple regional institutions is considered one of the effects of the dispositive principle.[5] Regional institutions hold the power to change

[1] *Spanish Constitution 1978* Part X [Constitution Española [C.E.], B.O.E. no. 168, 29 December 1978]. Richard Albert, 'The Structure of Constitutional Amendment Rules' (2014) 49 Wake Forest Law Review 913, 913, 926, 929, 931; Carles Viver, 'Spain's Constitution and Statutes of Autonomy: Explaining the Evolution of Political Decentralization' in Michael Burgess and G Alan Tarr (eds), *Constitutional Dynamics in Federal Systems: Sub-National Perspectives* (McGill-Queen's University Press 2012) 218, 221.

[2] *Spanish Constitution 1978* Preamble [3], section 3 [2–3], 4 [2], pt VIII. Albert (n 1), 926, 929, 931; Viver (n 1), 219–225.

[3] Vito Breda, 'La devolution de Escocia y el referéndum de 2014: ¿cuáles son las repercusiones potenciales en España? = The Scottish devolution and the 2014 referendum: what are the potential reverberations in Spain?' [2013] Teoría y Realidad Constitucional 69.

[4] Antoni i Ninet and Adrià Mateu, 'Spain's Multinational Constitution: A Lost Opportunity?' (2008) 17 Constitutional Forum 19.

[5] Carles Viver, 'Por Favor, No Disparen Contra El Pianista. Mito y Realidad Del (Mal Llamado) Principio Dispositivo' [2008] 84 Revista Española de Derecho Constitucional 339.

their institutional settings within the constitution in a way that dynamically meets their cultural or geo-political needs.[6] However, the decision of the central parliament to extend the prerogative to set up autonomous institutions in all of the geographical communities that might ask for them is colloquially known as the 'café para todos' policy.[7] That is, translated literally, coffee for everyone, yet in this context it means 'a benefit which is intended for the historical nationalities (the Basque Country, Catalonia, Galicia) was granted to all regions of Spain'.[8] During Franco's regime, the Basques and Catalonians were subjected to policies that should be considered equivalent to cultural genocide and that might justify their special status.[9]

---

6 Ibid.

7 Francesc Morata and Lucia Popartan, 'Spain' in Michael J Baun and Dan Marek (eds), *EU Cohesion Policy after Enlargement* (Palgrave Macmillan 2008) 73, 75.

8 *Ley Orgánica 3/1979, de 18 de Diciembre, de Estatuto de Autonomía Para El País Vasco. 1979*; *Ley Orgánica 1/1981, de 6 de Abril, de Estatuto de Autonomía Para Galicia. 1981*; *Ley Orgánica 1/2007, de 28 de Febrero, de Reforma Del Estatuto de Autonomía de Las Illes Balears. 2007*; *Ley Orgánica 1/2011, de 28 de Enero, de Reforma Del Estatuto de Autonomía de La Comunidad Autónoma de Extremadura. 2011*; *Ley Orgánica 2/1995, de 13 de Marzo, de Estatuto de Autonomía de Melilla. 1995*; *Ley Orgánica 2/2007, de 19 de Marzo, de Reforma Del Estatuto de Autonomía Para Andalucía. 2007*; *Ley Orgánica 3/1979, de 18 de Diciembre, de Estatuto de Autonomía Para El País Vasco. 1979*; *Ley Orgánica 3/1983, de 25 de Febrero, de Estatuto de Autonomía de La Comunidad de Madrid. 1983*; *Ley Orgánica 4/1982, de 9 de Junio, de Estatuto de Autonomía Para La Región de Murcia. 1982*; *Ley Orgánica 5/1982, de 1 de Julio, de Estatuto de Autonomía de La Comunidad Valenciana. 1982*; *Ley Orgánica 5/2007, de 20 de Abril, de Reforma Del Estatuto de Autonomía de Aragón. 2007*; *Ley Orgánica 6/2006, de 19 de Julio, de Reforma Del Estatuto de Autonomía de Cataluña. 2006*; *Ley Orgánica 7/1981, de 30 de Diciembre, de Estatuto de Autonomía Para Asturias. 1982*; *Ley Orgánica 8/1981, de 30 de Diciembre, de Estatuto de Autonomía Para Cantabria. 1982*; *Ley Orgánica 9/1982, de 10 de Agosto, de Estatuto de Autonomía de Castilla-La Mancha. 1982*; *Ley Orgánica 10/1982, de 10 de Agosto, de Estatuto de Autonomía de Canarias. 1982*; *Ley Orgánica 13/1982, de 10 de Agosto, de Reintegración y Amejoramiento Del Régimen Foral de Navarra. 1982*; *Ley Orgánica 14/2007, de 30 de Noviembre, de Reforma Del Estatuto de Autonomía de Castilla y León. 2007.*

9 Joseba Zulaika, 'Specificities: Tropics of Terror: From Guernica's "Natives" to Global "Terrorists"' (1998) 4(1) Social Identities 93, 94; Helen Graham, *War and Its Shadow: Spain's Civil War in Europe's Long Twentieth Century* (Sussex Academic Press 2012) 17, 120, 223.

The constitutional amendment process is highly articulated and the text is perceived as virtually unmodifiable.[10] The long constitution entrenched an extensive list of rights that were systematically ignored by the previous regime.[11] Since 1978, the constitution has been amended only twice, and in both situations the changes were motivated by external factors (for example, the pressure of external investors and the European Union [EU]).[12] A rigid (almost paralysed) constitution is, as in other legal systems considered in this book, a severe limitation in a multinational society where minorities are seeking the recognition and accommodation of their identity-based constitutional claims.[13] In section 1 [2], the constitution affirms the centrality of the Spanish nation and the regional rather than federal structure of the state: 'National sovereignty belongs to the Spanish people, from whom all State powers emanate'.[14] However, in section 3, there is a reference to the unity of Spain that is a normative requirement of the newly established constitutional monarchy and a (sociological) recognition of the different nationalities that inhabit the Iberian Peninsula.[15]

This recognition of the 'nationalities', coupled with the provisions of Part VIII, allowed for the development of a system of territorial governance.[16] Spain is, as are most European countries, a highly culturally and historically diversified political community.[17] The historical national communities, albeit not identified in the constitution, are made up of the Basques, the Catalans and the Galicians.[18] All territorial communities

---

[10] Viver (n 1), 220.

[11] *Spanish Constitution 1978* Part I; Luis Lopez Guerra, 'Luis Lopez Guerra Former Judge, Tribunal Constitutional (Constitutional Court) Spain' (2005) 3(4) International Journal of Constitutional Law 567; Graham (n 9); Zulaika (n 9).

[12] Mireia Estrada-Cañamares and Leticia Díez Sánchez, 'National Law Changes in Spain – Constitutional Change through Euro Crisis Law' (19 September 2014) http://eurocrisislaw.eui.eu/country/spain/topic/national-law-changes/.

[13] Albert (n 1); i Ninet and Mateu (n 4); Breda (n 3); Germa Bel, *Disdain, Distrust and Dissolution: The Surge of Support for Independence in Catalonia* (Sussex Academic Press 2015).

[14] *Spanish Constitution 1978.*

[15] Michel Rosenfeld, 'Constitutional Identity' in Michel Rosenfeld and András Sajó (eds), *The Oxford Handbook of Comparative Constitutional Law* (Oxford University Press 2012) 756, 765.

[16] *Spanish Constitution 1978.*

[17] Francis Fukuyama, *The Origins of Political Order: From Prehuman Times to the French Revolution* (Profile Books 2012) 315.

[18] Viver (n 1) 222.

might become autonomous regions after their status has been recognized by a special act of parliament called *Ley Orgánica* (literally translated as 'organic law'). The regional institutions have relatively wide discretion on the content of such a document, but the constitution requires that it must establish an elected assembly using a proportional system, a president, an executive council and a regional jurisdictional system.[19] Both the council and the president are accountable to the regional assembly.

Spain is not considered a federal system, but section 149 lists the central state's exclusive legislative competences.[20] The article has been interpreted as a federal clause that limits the central state's legislative prerogatives.[21] The list of competences that an autonomous region can claim is set in section 148, and it includes, for instance, tourism, transport facilities, planning and economic development.[22] The double list of head of powers was a proxy for confusion since regions could claim (and did claim), in addition to the competences listed in section 148, also all the competences not explicitly allocated to the central state in section 149.[23]

Among the many effects, there are two crucial implications of this ambiguity. First, most of the autonomous communities sought the most extensive level of administrative and legislative powers admissible within the constitution.[24] Second, there is a tendency among regions to expand administrative and legislative prerogatives, whereas the central state's head of power remains static.[25] This is one of the effects of the so-called dispositive principle, in which listed regional powers are interpreted as open-ended and as the basis for a permanent dialogue with the central state.[26]

---

[19] *Spanish Constitution 1978* 151 (1).

[20] *Spanish Constitution 1978.*

[21] Viver (n 1) 220.

[22] *Spanish Constitution 1978.*

[23] Viver (n 5).

[24] Viver (n 1) 222–224; Enric Espadaler Fossas, 'El Control de Constitucionalitat Dels Estatuts d'autonomia' [2011] 43 Revista catalana de dret públic 21, 160.

[25] Viver (n 1) 223–225; Espadaler Fossas, 'El Control de Constitucionalitat Dels Estatuts d'autonomia' (n 24) 156.

[26] Viver (n 1) 222; Enric Espadaler Fossas, 'El principio dispositivo en el Estado autonómico' [2008] 71–72 Revista de Derecho Político; Espadaler Fossas, 'El Control de Constitucionalitat Dels Estatuts d'autonomia' (n 24). '*Su* incorporación *al* texto constitucional fue *una* "opción consciente" adoptada *en el* proceso constituyente, fruto *del* consenso, e inspirada *en la.* Constitución *de* 1931. *Su*

The process of open negotiation increased the complexity of the Spanish system of territorial governance and it has been largely unproblematic.[27] The notable exceptions in terms of frictions have been the partnership between central government and the autonomous regions of Catalonia and the Basque Country, which will be discussed later in this paper.[28] The statute of autonomy normally establishes the internal rules and regulations of the autonomous community and cannot be amended or repealed by an act of the Spanish parliament. However, the statute of autonomy is not an annex of the constitution that is immune from constitutional review.[29]

The statute of autonomy of an aspiring autonomous region can be approved via a normal or a special process. The normal process, which was assumed should have applied to all regions except the Basque Country, Catalonia and Galicia, requires multistage regional and central approval.[30] One of the last steps in this process is the approval by the

---

esencia consiste *en* atribuir *a las* entidades *territoria- les a las que* se reconoce *el derecho a la autonomía (art. 2 CE) una capacidad decisiva en la configuración de la organización territorial, que la misma Constituciónno habría llevado a cabo, pues habría remitido esta operación a unospoderes constituidos mediante su "desconstitucionalización" parcial, introduciendoasí una apertura en aquella organización, que de este modo se ve sometidaa permanente discusión y definición desde la aprobación del texto constitucional*'. Espadaler Fossas, 'El principio dispositivo en el Estado autonómico' (n 26) 152.

[27] Espadaler Fossas, 'El principio dispositivo en el Estado autonómico' (n 26) 154.

[28] Espadaler Fossas, 'El Control de Constitucionalitat Dels Estatuts d'autonomia' (n 24) 153–157; Viver (n 1) 233; Paul Williams and others, 'The Legitimacy of Catalonia's Exercise of Its Right to Decide' (2017); Michael Keating and Zoe Bray, 'Renegotiating Sovereignty: Basque Nationalism and the Rise and Fall of the Ibarretxe Plan' (2006) 5(4) Ethnopolitics 347; Javier García Oliva, 'Javier Garcia Oliva: The Referendum on Catalonian Independence: The Position of the Spanish Authorities' https://ukconstitutionallaw.org/2017/10/03/javier-garcia-oliva-the-referendum-on-catalonian-independence-the-position-of-the-spanish-authorities/; Elisenda Casanas Adam, *Too Little, Too Late? The Spanish Government's Proposals to Resolve the Current Conflict with Catalonia | ConstitutionNet* http://www.constitutionnet.org/news/too-little-too-late-spanish-governments-proposals-resolve-current-conflict-catalonia.

[29] Francesco Palermo, 'Italy: A Federal Country without Federalism?' in Michael Burgess and G Alan Tarr (eds), *Constitutional Dynamics in Federal Systems: Sub-National Perspectives* (McGill-Queen's University Press 2012) 238–254; Luca Antonini, *Federalismo all'italiana* (Marsilio 2013).

[30] *Spanish Constitution 1978* 146.

Spanish Senate of the organic law.[31] After approval, the newly established regional institutions have to go through a transitional period of five years during which they gradually prepare for carrying out their new functions.[32] The historically recognized communities (the Basque Country, Catalonia and Galicia) could obtain the full use of their competences without waiting for the five-year transitional period and the process required for state approval is less taxing.[33] Andalucía also managed to benefit from the use of the special process.[34]

The distinctive feature of the Spanish system of governance, by way of comparison with the other legal systems considered in this book, is that each of the regional governments has the prerogative to start the legislative process that might alter its own statute of autonomy.[35] The bill, and often the new set of claimed new prerogatives, becomes part of the regional constitution after it has been approved by a simple majority in central parliament.[36] In theory, the approval of parliament should guarantee a level of scrutiny, but a parliament controlled by a party that has a vested regional interest tends to rubber stamp pre-existing political agreements.[37]

Constitutional lawyers considered the recent proliferation of amendments to regional statutes as hindering the stability and economic prowess of the Spanish constitutional system,[38] yet the system of governance set out in the 1978 constitution has the distinct advantage of dynamically altering systems of governance to meet social changes.[39] However, the system of governance set in the constitution was not intended to cover the entire landmass of Spain. The 'café para todos' policy had the effect of a proportional reduction of the institutional distinctiveness of the Basque, Catalan and Galician peoples. In addition, the bargaining process between the central government and the historical regions was constructed as a confrontational engagement rather than as a

---

31 Ibid 81.

32 *Spanish Constitution 1978* 148 (2). Please note that Andalucía managed to take advantage of a lack of specific restrictions on the special process set in section 151 (1).

33 *Spanish Constitution 1978* 145 (1).

34 Viver (n 1) 228.

35 Ibid 226. *Spanish Constitution 1978* 143.1.

36 *Spanish Constitution 1978* 147 (3).

37 Viver (n 1) 227, 230; Viver (n 5).

38 Viver (n 5).

39 Viver (n 1); Espadaler Fossas, 'El Control de Constitucionalitat Dels Estatuts d'autonomia' (n 24); Espadaler Fossas, 'El principio dispositivo en el Estado autonómico' (n 26).

collaborative activity, which had unexpected effects.[40] For instance, the Basque Country and Navarra managed to obtain extensive control over their fiscal revenues, which might be very difficult to justify.[41]

The extensive level of autonomy granted to the region by the so-called dipositive principle in the Spanish constitution is balanced by a series of powers granted to central institutions to protect national interests and individual rights.[42] The idea of balancing central and decentralized institutional power, as it was envisaged in the constitutional text, presumed a level of institutional collaboration which never materialized.[43]

The interaction between central and autonomous institutions was, from the outset, quite tense.[44] Even after approval of the statutes of autonomy, constitutional litigation over state–region border disputes was extensive.[45] A few of the Constitutional Court's decisions reminded the parties of the hierarchical structure of the constitution;[46] others tried to protect the regions. Agranoff and Gallarin report that, during the 1990s, the Constitutional Court decided over 100 cases brought by autonomous regions against central government legislation. Similar numbers of cases were brought by the central government against regional legislation.[47] In 2004,

---

[40] Francesc Morata and Lucia Popartan, 'Spain' in Michael J Baun and Dan Marek (eds), *EU Cohesion Policy after Enlargement* (Palgrave Macmillan 2008) 73. Morata and Popartan (n 7) 73; Williams and others (n 28) 20.

[41] *Ley Orgánica 13/1982, de 10 de Agosto, de Reintegración y Amejoramiento Del Régimen Foral de Navarra. 1982*; *Ley Orgánica 3/1979, de 18 de Diciembre, de Estatuto de Autonomía Para El País Vasco. 1979*; *Ley 12/1981, de 13 de Mayo Por La Que Se Aprueba El Concierto Economico Con La Comunidad Autónoma Del Pais Vasco 1981* 12. Please note that, even during the dictatorship, Navarra regional institutions had a special status which allowed the survival of the foral system. José María Ruiz Soroa, *Números y Razones* eldiario.es http://www.eldiario.es/norte/vientodelnorte/Numeros-razones_6_724837516.html.

[42] Hurst Hannum, *Autonomy, Sovereignty, and Self-Determination: The Accommodation of Conflicting Rights* (University of Pennsylvania Press 2011); i Ninet and Mateu (n 4); César Colino and Eloísa del Pino, '15. Spain: The Consolidation of Strong Regional Governments and the Limits of Local Decentralization', in Frank Hendriks, Anders Lidström, and John Loughlin (eds), *The Oxford Handbook of Local and Regional Democracy in Europe* (first edition, Oxford University Press 2010) vol 1, 356.

[43] Morata and Popartan (n 7) 75.

[44] Viver (n 1) 232.

[45] Robert Agranoff and Juan Antonio Ramos Gallarín, 'Toward Federal Democracy in Spain: An Examination of Intergovernmental Relations' (1997) 27(4) Publius: The Journal of Federalism 1.

[46] Constitutional Court Decision n40 18/12/1981 193 12 B.O.E. 14/1/1982.

[47] Agranoff and Gallarín (n 45) 16–17.

the year in which the Constitutional Court decided over the admissibility of a plan to alter the statute of autonomy of the Basque Country,[48] another 80 cases involving bordering disputes between central and regional institutions were decided.[49] This is, for a final appellate jurisdiction, an enormous jurisprudential activity.[50]

After the 1980s and following a period of intense litigation, the Court showed its ability to maintain a balanced, autonomous and well-reasoned judicial position.[51] Tierney describes the effect of such a large case load on the reputation of the Court. 'The Tribunal Constitucional seems to have trodden a careful path but one in which it has emerged with considerable credibility'.[52] The Constitutional Court has shown itself as prepared to uphold actions by the central government to validate policies.[53] The role of the Spanish Constitutional Court in these bordering disputes is typical of what Alec Stone Sweet defined as a 'Constitutional Court triatic entity response in which an institution seeks to maintain stability and the cooperation of the dyadic interaction between Central and Regional governments'.[54] There is, for obvious reasons, a limit to the role of a tribunal as a political mediator.

In the past two decades, seven of the 19 communities amended their statutes of autonomy.[55] The new statutes of autonomy further increased the differences among the regions, and between the regions and the state.[56] For instance, the 1979 statute of autonomy of Catalonia contained

---

[48] *Order 135/2004* [2004] (Unreported, Constitutional Court (Spain), 20 April 2004).

[49] Constitutional Court (Spain), *List of 2004 Orders* Constitutional Court Database http://www.tribunalconstitucional.es/en/jurisprudencia/Pages/Autos.aspx?sel=2004.

[50] Neil Walker, Scotland and Scottish Government, *Final Appellate Jurisdiction in the Scottish Legal System* (Scottish Government 2010).

[51] Stephen Tierney, *Constitutional Law and National Pluralism* (Oxford University Press 2004) 276.

[52] Ibid.

[53] Ibid.

[54] Alec Stone Sweet, 'Judicialization and the Construction of Governance' (1999) 32(2) Comparative Political Studies 147, 150.

[55] Cesar Renedo Aguado, 'Nuevos Estatutos de Autonomía Comparados (Ministero de La Presidencia)' http://www.cepc.gob.es/docs/boletin-de-documentacion-n%C2%BA35/presentacionrev1.pdf?sfvrsn=0.

[56] *Ley Orgánica 1/2007, de 28 de Febrero, de Reforma Del Estatuto de Autonomía de Las Illes Balears. 2007*; *Ley Orgánica 1/2011, de 28 de Enero, de Reforma Del Estatuto de Autonomía de La Comunidad Autónoma de Extremadura. 2011*; *Ley Orgánica 2/2007, de 19 de Marzo, de Reforma Del Estatuto de Autonomía Para Andalucía. 2007*; *Ley Orgánica 6/2006, de 19 de Julio, de*

only 53 sections,[57] whereas the version approved by the Spanish parliament in 2006 includes over 200 sections.[58] The 2006 Catalan statute was, as was expected, subjected to an in-depth constitutional review and several of its new sections were curtailed, or their interpretation limited by the Constitutional Court.[59] Decision no. 31 is considered one of the triggers of the 2017 Spanish constitutional crisis.[60]

DRIVER OF CHANGE: NEGOTIATING NATIONALISMS AND THE FAILED IBARRETXE PLAN

In the previous section, I explained the key features of the dispositive principle. The constitution explicitly acknowledges the sociological multiplicity of Spain, and implicitly establishes, with the dispositive principle, an open-ended process of negotiation that allows for the legal recognition of Spanish 'nationalities' within the Spanish nation.[61] The application of the dispositive principle has been one of the most important drivers of change in the process of the constitutional recognition of Spanish minorities,[62] but in this section, I discuss the tendency of Spanish political institutions and the political parties that lead them to adopt an ethnocentric idea of national identity which hinders the process of the recognition and negotiation of identity claims. Negotiations tend to

---

Reforma Del Estatuto de Autonomía de Cataluña. 2006; *Ley Orgánica 14/2007, de 30 de Noviembre, de Reforma Del Estatuto de Autonomía de Castilla y León. 2007*; *Ley Orgánica 2/1995, de 13 de Marzo, de Estatuto de Autonomía de Melilla. 1995*; *Ley Orgánica 1/1995, de 13 de Marzo, de Estatuto de Autonomía de Ceuta. 1995.*

[57] *Ley Orgánica 4/1979, de 18 de Diciembre, Estatuto de Autonomía de Cataluña. 1979.*

[58] *Ley Orgánica 6/2006, de 19 de Julio, de Reforma Del Estatuto de Autonomía de Cataluña. 2006.*

[59] Constitutional Court Decision n31 28/06/2010 172 (Suplemento 11409) B.O.E. 1. Montserrat Guibernau, 'Calls for Independence in Catalonia are Part of an Evolution of Spain's Democracy That the Country's Constitution May Have to Come to Accommodate. | EUROPP' http://blogs.lse.ac.uk/europpblog/2012/10/08/catalonia-independence-spain-constitution/; Bel (n 13); Renedo Aguado (n 55).

[60] Elisenda Casanas Adam, 'The Referendum on Catalonian Independence: The Position of the Catalan Authorities' https://ukconstitutionallaw.org/2017/10/03/elisenda-casanas-adam-the-referendum-on-catalonian-independence-the-position-of-the-catalan-authorities/; Williams and others (n 28); García Oliva (n 28).

[61] *Spanish Constitution 1978* 2.

[62] Viver (n 5).

become empty sabre-rattling exercises. In this section, I will consider the failed Ibarretxe plan to reform the Basque statute of autonomy and, in the next section, I will analyse the 2017 Catalonian referendum.

In 2003, the Basque government reached an agreement – albeit with a minute majority – within the Basque parliament to start the process of amending the 1979 statute of autonomy.[63] As mentioned earlier, from the 1990s, most of the autonomous regions sought to increase their legislative and administrative competences.[64] Juan Jose Ibarretxe was, at the time, leader of the Basque coalition government, and he had its proposal approved later in 2004 and sent to the Spanish parliament. On a general level, the amendment of the statute of autonomy intended to establish, among other administrative and legislative changes, a new framework for the accommodation of identity-based constitutional demands. The new proposed statute of autonomy envisaged, for instance, the establishment of a freewill partnership between the Basque Country and the Spanish state. It was an attempt to undermine the narrative that assumed a Spanish dominium over the Basque Country and that supported the rhetoric of political violence of the recently disarmed paramilitary organizations such as the Euskadi Ta Askatasuna (hereafter ETA).[65]

The struggle between ETA and Franco's dictatorship is a distinctive element of Spanish constitutional history and is still influencing the political perceptions of many Basque residents.[66] During General Franco's dictatorship, ETA could count on popular support in the Spanish part of the Basque territories and toleration from the French government in French Basque regions.[67] However, after the collapse of General Franco's regime, violence increased and the majority of the Basque political parties rejected the use of politically motivated violence.[68] The Ibarretxe plan aimed to engage some of the thorny issues which are perceived as part of ETA's historical struggle for constitutional recognition of the

---

[63] *Ley Orgánica 3/1979, de 18 de Diciembre, de Estatuto de Autonomía Para El País Vasco. 1979*; *Ley 12/1981, de 13 de Mayo Por La Que Se Aprueba El Concierto Economico Con La Comunidad Autónoma Del Pais Vasco 1981.*

[64] Viver (n 5).

[65] Joseba Zulaika, *Terrorism: The Self-Fulfilling Prophecy* (University of Chicago Press 2010).

[66] Jose Santiago, 'Religion, Secularisation and Nationalism in Quebec and the Basque Country: A Comparative Approach' (2015) 21(1) Nations and Nationalism 120, 124–125. For a more general analysis: Joseba Zulaika, *Basque Violence: Metaphor and Sacrament* (University of Nevada Press 2000).

[67] Santiago (n 66) 124–125. For a more general analysis see Zulaika (n 67).

[68] Keating and Bray (n 28) 351.

Basque peoples. These political issues included the historical accommodation of Basque national sovereignty in the Spanish constitutional system, the protection of linguistic minorities and the enlargement of the welfare state, which is perceived as a distinctive feature of the Basque conception of social democracy and as antithetical to the idea of Spanish identity (as it is perceived, it is advocated by the People's Party).[69]

After 2001, the popular, political and international support for ETA decreased.[70] ETA's actions had a progressively negative effect on the international reputation of the Basque government and it also generated some economic costs for the region.[71] The Ibarretxe plan intended to engage directly with the underpinning reasons for the lingering popular support for political violence among Basque nationalists.[72] In the first section, for instance, the proposed amendment of the statute of autonomy included the assertion of free association of the Basque region with the central Spanish state.[73] Such an assertion has symbolic rather than constitutional implications. There is no indication, for instance, that the plan intended to give the Basque Country a regime analogous to Tokelau.[74] However, the legal irrelevance of these symbolic statements was lost in the debate that followed the approval of the plan by the Basque parliament. The People's Party interpreted section 1 of the bill as anti-Spanish and as part of the Basque government's explicit 'secessionist programme'.[75]

Whilst there is, in the second paragraph of the preamble, a reference to the right to self-determination of the Basque people, it is a right which is explicitly inserted in the pluri-national constitutional setting of the Spanish constitution (in the fourth paragraph of the preamble). Again, as was the case in the 2006 statute of autonomy of Catalonia, the preamble has no legal implications and it could be interpreted as a mild articulation of section 2 of the 1978 constitution. However, the People's Party's critique focused on the symbolic nature of the bill. There was even an

---

69 Ibid.

70 Leslie Turano, 'Spain: Banning Political Parties as a Response to Basque Terrorism' (2003) 1(4) International Journal of Constitutional Law 730.

71 Alberto Abadie and Javier Gardeazabal, 'The Economic Costs of Conflict: A Case Study of the Basque Country' (2003) 93(1) The American Economic Review 113.

72 Basque Goverment, Propuesta Estatuto Político de La Comunidad de Euskadi 2003 1 ('Propuesta Estatuto Político de La Comunidad de Euskadi').

73 Ibid.

74 Antony Hooper, 'Tokelau: A Sort of "Self-Governing" Sort of "Colony"' (2008) 43(3) The Journal of Pacific History 331.

75 Keating and Bray (n 28) 356.

attempt to prevent the debate within the Spanish parliament.[76] The Spanish Court was asked, in an ancillary process, by the Spanish government led by the People's Party, to discuss the possibility of preventing a parliamentary debate over the Basque Country's proposal to amend its statute of autonomy.[77] The request to prevent a parliamentary debate, before the submission of a bill, was squarely dismissed by the Constitutional Court. In point 6(a) of the Order that followed the ancillary procedures, the Court explained that an agreement between the Basque parliament and its government to send a bill to the Spanish parliament could not be considered a violation of the legislative competences granted by the constitution.[78] The Court explained that a political agreement between Basque MPs and their government was a manifestation of democratic activity and outside the remit of a jurisdictional review.[79]

The request to a Constitutional Court to prevent a parliamentary debate might be perceived as quite an extravagant use of public resources. It is reasonably clear that neither the People's Party nor the Spanish Socialist Party had the intention of politically reviewing any substantive aspects of the plan. The request to the Constitutional Court to prevent a debate over the statute was a symbolic act in which the People's Party took the role as the defender of Spanish national identity, and with such an action, it gained the political capital of nationalist voters. The Basque government also benefitted from the process. By presenting a reform to a hostile Spanish parliament, the Basque government reinforced the perception of an antagonistic relationship between the Basque Country and Spain. It was, in other words, a case of a simulated institutional engagement.

---

[76] *Order 135/2004* [2004] (Unreported, Constitutional Court (Spain), 20 April 2004) 135.

[77] Ibid.

[78] Ibid.

[79] Original Text: 'El Acuerdo del Gobierno Vasco no es expresivo de ninguna asunción de competencia con la que se lesione el ámbito competencial propio del Gobierno del Estado o de otra Comunidad Autónoma. La única competencia de la que ese Acuerdo puede ser expresión es la que asiste al Gobierno Vasco para proponer una reforma del Estatuto de Autonomía de su Comunidad Autónoma o, en general, para remitir al Parlamento autonómico cualesquiera propuestas de debate y discusión, con independencia de que se formalicen o no finalmente en textos normativos, para lo que es necesaria la voluntad de la Cámara que aquella inicial propuesta ha podido contribuir a conformar. Tal atribución no puede ser, por principio, cuestionada o discutida'. Ibid 6 (a); *Ley Orgánica 3/1979, de 18 de Diciembre, de Estatuto de Autonomía Para El País Vasco. 1979*; *Spanish Constitution 1978* 161.2.

The debate on the Ibarretxe plan never reached the stage at which it could have been considered a constitutional negotiation, and the public was misinformed.[80] The Ibarretxe plan was an attempt to promote a level of social integration, which is perceived as distinctive to Basque society, and to disenfranchise ETA. It intended, among other aspects, to establish the conditions of what Keating calls meso-level governance.[81] For instance, the bill considered the legal implications of the European integration in regional governance, which could not be envisaged in the original statute of autonomy.[82] The Ibarretxe plan and the new statute of autonomy of the Basque Country might have been another innovative aspect of the Spanish constitutional system, yet the ideological undertone of the political debate hindered the possibility of accommodating identity-based constitutional demands.[83]

It could be argued that a communication channel between the Basque government and Spanish government, analogous to the one set up in the Sewel Convention, might have helped both parties.[84] For instance, a series of preliminary meetings between regional and central civil servants, as expected in the UK concordats, could have ironed out some of the Ibarretxe plan's technical issues.[85] The activity of a joint legislative committee (analogous to the one adopted within the Italian parliament for South Tyrol), with an equal number of representatives for the Basque

---

80 Keating and Bray (n 28) 358.

81 Michael Keating, *Rescaling the European State: The Making of Territory and the Rise of the Meso* (also available as an eBook 2013).

82 Basque Goverment, Propuesta Estatuto Político de La Comunidad de Euskadi 2003 13 (1).

83 Keating and Bray (n 28); Colino and Pino (n 42); Silvia Acierno and Julio Baquero Cruz, 'The Order of the Spanish Constitutional Court on the Proposal to Convert the Basque Country into a Freely Associated Community: Keeping Hands off Constitutional Politics' (2005) 3(4) International Journal of Constitutional Law 687.

84 Andrew Scott, 'The Role of Concordats in the New Governance of Britain: Taking Subsidiarity Seriously?' (2001) 5(1) Edinburgh Law Review 21; Francesco Palermo, 'South Tyrol's Special Status within the Italian Constitution' in Jens Woelk, Francesco Palermo and Joseph Marko (eds), *South Tyrol's Special Status within the Italian Constitution* (Brill 2007) 33; New Zealand and Waitangi Tribunal, *Report of the Waitangi Tribunal on the Te Reo Maori Claim (WAI 11)* (Waitangi Tribunal, Department of Justice 1989); Karyn Paringatai, 'Maori Identity Development Outside of Tribal Environments' (2014) 26(1) Aotearoa New Zealand Social Work 47.

85 Scott (n 84).

Country and central government, might have instead ensured the protection of both regional and national interests.[86] Again, these are speculations and institutions that are transplanted across jurisdictions seldom have similar effects.[87]

The issue that emerged from the analysis of the failed Ibarretxe plan is that the current system of governance in Spain is ill suited to accommodating the level of complexity that was, and still is, generated by the statute of autonomy system.[88] In particular, it allows political parties that have taken on the role of promoting a national identity to use ethnocentric narratives charged with symbolism but with limited technical implications.[89] Again, there are strong indications that both regional and central institutions broadcast ethnocentric narratives to gain support from their respective constituencies, yet they are aware of the implausibility of their claims. The sabre-rattling phase (or the 'chicken-out' phase as it is called by the Commission of International Experts)[90] is used by the representatives of central and regional governments as a device that prepares the stage for the real negotiations in which substantial concessions are made by both parties.[91]

For instance, in 2014, the Basque parliament and the Spanish parliament updated the economic agreements which distributed taxes between central and Basque regional institutions.[92] The economic agreements are quite intricate statutory measures that establish a matrix for the

---

[86] Jens Woelk, Francesco Palermo and Joseph Marko, *Tolerance through Law* (Martinus Nijhoff 2008).

[87] David Cabrelli and Mathias Siems, 'Convergence, Legal Origins, and Transplants in Comparative Corporate Law: A Case-Based and Quantitative Analysis' (2015) 63 American Journal of Comparative Law 109; Alan Watson, *Legal Transplants: An Approach to Comparative Law* (new edition, University of Virginia Press 1988); Vlad Perju, 'Constitutional Transplants, Borrowing, and Migrations' https://papers.ssrn.com/sol3/papers.cfm?abstract_id=1982230.

[88] Viver (n 1).

[89] Andras L Pap, 'Ethno-Racial Identity (Politics) by Law: "Fraud" and "Choice"' (2017) 45(5) Nationalities Papers 968.

[90] Williams and others (n 28) 22.

[91] Soroa (n 41).

[92] *Ley 12/1981, de 13 de Mayo Por La Que Se Aprueba El Concierto Economico Con La Comunidad Autónoma Del Pais Vasco 1981*; *Ley 7/2014, de 21 de Abril, Por La Que Se Modifica La Ley 12/2002, de 23 de Mayo, Por La Que Se Aprueba El Concierto Económico Con La Comunidad Autónoma Del País Vasco 2014* 97 ('*El Nuevo Impuesto Sobre Los Gases Fluorados de Efecto Invernadero*'); Ignacio Zubiri Oria, *The Economic Agreement between the Basque Country and Spain* (Ad Concordiam 2010) 38–48 http://www.nber.org/papers/w2588.

redistribution of fiscal revenues among state and regional institutions which have significant repercussions for Basque and Spanish residents. It would be logical to expect a proportional level of interest; however, the approval of the economic agreements attracted little political attention,[93] whereas the preamble of the Ibarretxe plan, which by way of comparison with the 2014 economic agreements had no legal or financial implications, was depicted by the People's Party as an attack on the ethnocentric conception of the Spanish national identity.[94]

DRIVER OF CHANGE: THE CHICKEN-OUT STRATEGY AND THE CATALONIAN CONSTITUTIONAL NEGOTIATION

In the previous section, I explained the implications of having a negotiation process influenced by the ideological conception of the nation-state in a de facto multinational political system.[95] In this section, I discuss the process of reform of Catalonia's statute of autonomy, its qualification by the Spanish Constitutional Court and the unfortunate effect of the 2017 unconstitutional referendum on independence. It will be argued that the series of events that led to police repression with many Catalonians being injured and an arrest warrant for the Catalonian First Minister is, among other elements, a manifestation of the strategic use of an ethnocentric narrative which seeks to exclude rather than engage with constitutional demands.[96] This is a temporary segment in the process of the recognition and negotiation of constitutional demands that the Commission of International Experts called the 'chicken-out' phase.[97] Representatives of both central and regional governments use ethnocentric narratives to gain political capital whilst making demands that will not be accepted by the other party.

---

[93] Soroa (n 41); Zubiri Oria (n 92) 71–102.

[94] Soroa (n 41).

[95] Vito Breda, 'Constitutional Patriotism' in Mortimer Sellers and Stephan Kirste (eds), *Encyclopedia of the Philosophy of Law and Social Philosophy* (Springer Netherlands 2017) 1; Vito Breda, 'An Odd Partnership: Identity-Based Constitutional Claims' in Fiona Jenkins, Mark Nolan and Kim Rubenstein (eds), *Allegiance and Identity in a Globalised World* (Cambridge University Press 2014) 52; Anthony Appiah, *Cosmopolitanism: Ethics in a World of Strangers* (Allen Lane 2006).

[96] Williams and others (n 28).

[97] Ibid 20.

Ethnocentric narratives can be found in most processes of the recognition and negotiation of identity-based constitutional negotiations.[98] The Spanish constitution is, as mentioned earlier, one of the latest examples of a European multinational constitution. The constitution recognizes, in section 2, the 'nationalities', but considers Spanish national identity as the only Nation with a capital N, so to speak.[99] Given that modern national identities are normally considered based on ideological assumptions, the distinction is, from a sociological perspective, precarious.[100]

The animosity between the Catalonian and Spanish central states has a long history, but it is, by way of comparison with other processes of recognition considered in this book, not distinctive.[101] The recent spat commenced, within a margin of approximation that is related to any political assessment, with the approval of the *Ley Orgánica 6/2006, de 19 de julio, de reforma del Estatuto de Autonomía de Cataluña.*[102] As discussed earlier, it was the case that the socialist central government (the People's Party was opposed to the reform throughout the negotiation process) passed the statute in collaboration with the Catalonian government.[103] The approval by parliament and by a regional referendum[104] was

---

[98] Jean-François Caron, 'The Exclusive Nature of Quebec's Contemporary Nationalism: The Pitfalls of Civic Nationalism' (2014) 47(1) International Journal of Canadian Studies 221; Florence Di Bonaventura, 'Italy and Lega Nord: Stories of Communities, National (Dis)Integration and Spaces of (Restricted) Citizenship' (2016) 7(13) Società Mutamento Politica: Rivista Italiana di Sociologia 289; Conrad Gershevitch, Amy Lamoin and Cassandra Dawes, 'Racism in Australia: Is Denial Still Plausible?' (2010) 3(2) Race/ethnicity: Multidisciplinary Global Contexts 229; Frank Pommersheim, *Broken Landscape* (Oxford University Press 2009); Tom Nairn, *The Break-Up of Britain: Crisis and Neonationalism* (second expanded NLB and Verso editions 1981).

[99] 'La Constitución se fundamenta en la indisoluble unidad de la Nación española, patria común e indivisible de todos los españoles, y reconoce y garantiza el derecho a la autonomía de las nacionalidades y regiones que la integran y la solidaridad entre todas ellas.' [The Constitution is based on the indissoluble unity of the Spanish Nation, the common and indivisible homeland of all Spaniards; it recognizes and guarantees the right to self government of the nationalities and regions of which it is composed and the solidarity among them all.] (My emphasis.) *Spanish Constitution 1978.*

[100] Benedict Anderson, *Imagined Communities: Reflections on the Origin and Spread of Nationalism* (Verso 1983).

[101] Graham (n 9); Williams and others (n 28) 12.

[102] *Ley Orgánica 6/2006, de 19 de Julio, de Reforma Del Estatuto de Autonomía de Cataluña. 2006*; Williams and others (n 28) 18–20.

[103] Williams and others (n 28) 19.

[104] Ibid.

followed by a request for a constitutional review by 99 MPs of the Spanish People's Party.[105]

The decision that followed (Decision no. 31) is a remarkable example of jurisdictional activity.[106] The complexity of the decision and its length, which is over 300 pages, confirms the role of a normative third party in a triatic relation.[107] It is worth mentioning again that the Spanish constitution[108] explicitly recognized the nationalities.[109] Given the lack of legal relevance and the existing constitutional recognition, it might be logical to suggest that asserting the existence of the Catalan nation is no more controversial than asserting the existence of the four nations that, after 1707, made up the UK.[110] However, the Constitutional Court decided to

---

[105] *Ley Orgánica 6/2006, de 19 de Julio, de Reforma Del Estatuto de Autonomía de Cataluña. 2006*; Constitutional Court Decision n31 28/06/2010 172 (Suplemento 11409) B.O.E. 1, 172; Josep Andreu Castellà, *La Sentencia Del Tribunal Constitucional 31/2010, Sobre El Estatuto de Autonomía de Cataluña y Su Significado Para El Futuro Del Estado Autonómico* (Fundación Ciudadanía y Valores 2010); Enric Espadaler Fossas, 'Competencia En Materia de Cultura. Comentario a La Sentencia 31/2010' [2010] 1 Revista catalana de dret públic 328; Enric Espadaler Fossas, 'El Estatuto Como Norma y Su Función Constitucional. Comentario a La Sentencia 31/2010' [2010] 1 Revista catalana de dret públic 91; Espadaler Fossas, 'El Control de Constitucionalitat Dels Estatuts d'autonomia' (n 24); Lucía Payero López, 'El Derecho de Autodeterminación En España: Breve Explicación Para Extranjeros Estupefactos y Nacionales Incautos' [2016] 23 Revista d'estudis autonòmics i federals 46; Casanas Adam (n 60); Casanas Adam (n 28).

[106] From the perspective of media and doctrinal attention, Decision 31 of 2010 can, perhaps, be compared with *Reference Re Secession of Quebec [1998] 2 SCR 217* [1998] (Unreported, 20 August 1998) 217.

[107] From the perspective of media and doctrinal attention, Decision 31 of 2010 can, perhaps, be compared with ibid.

[108] *Spanish Constitution 1978* 2.

[109] Constitutional Court Decision n31 28/06/2010 172 (Suplemento 11409) B.O.E. 1, 272.

[110] AB Desjardins, 'Minority Nationalism and the Changing International Order' (2002) 8 Nationalism and Ethnic Politics 120; Michael Keating, 'So Many Nations, so Few States: Territory and Nationalism in the Global Era' in James Tully and Alain Gagnon (eds), *Multinational Democracies* (Cambridge University Press 2001) 39; Michael Keating and Alex Wilson, 'Regions with Regionalism? The Rescaling of Interest Groups in Six European States (2014) 53(4) European Journal of Political Research 840; Nairn (n 98); Vernon Bogdanor and British Academy, *The British Constitution in the Twentieth Century* (published for the British Academy by Oxford University Press 2003).

consider the reference to the national symbol of Catalonia as incompatible with the idea of the unity of the Spanish nation.[111]

Article 8 of the statute of autonomy has been challenged for classifying as 'national' the symbols of Catalonia listed in the various subsections of the provision.

> Under no circumstances can any nationality be claimed other than the one specified in the constitution proclaimed by the will of that nation, nor through an ambiguity that is completely irrelevant in the judicial/constitutional context, the only guide that this Court can follow, by referring the term 'nation' to any other subject that is not the people holding that sovereignty.[112]

In short, the reference to 'a nation', which the Court distinguished from a reference to 'a nationality', is perceived as antithetical to the unity of the Spanish nation protected by section 2 of the constitution.[113] However, the differences between the terms 'nation' and 'nationality' are not supported by normative reasoning.

As I mentioned in several sections of this book, sociological and political literatures tend to focus on the implications that such nationalism has in modern societies and not on what it might be in ethnic terms.[114] The terms 'nation' and 'nationalities' are, in a sociological

---

[111] Original Text 'La referencia del art. 8 EAC a los símbolos nacionales de Cataluña podría inducir a esa indebida confusión si pretendieran extraerse de la mención del preámbulo a determinada declaración del Parlamento de Cataluña sobre la nación catalana unas consecuencias jurídico constitucionales contradictorias con el sentido preciso del art. 2 CE en punto a la sola y exclusiva relevancia constitucional de la Nación española. Sin embargo, cabe interpretar, de acuerdo con la Constitución, que con la calificación como "nacionales" de los símbolos de Cataluña se predica únicamente su condición de símbolos de una nacionalidad constituida como Comunidad Autónoma en ejercicio del derecho que reconoce [...] En tanto, sin embargo, ello no ocurra, las normas del Ordenamiento no pueden desconocer ni inducir al equívoco en punto a la "indisoluble unidad de la Nación española" proclamada en el art. 2 CE, pues en ningún caso pueden reclamar para sí otra legitimidad que la que resulta de la Constitución proclamada por la voluntad de esa Nación, nipueden tampoco, al amparo de una polisemia por completo irrelevante en el contexto jurídico-constitucional que para este Tribunal es el único que debe atender, referir el término "nación" a otro sujeto que no sea el pueblo titular de la soberanía.' Constitutional Court Decision n31 28/06/2010 172 (Suplemento 11409) B.O.E. 1, 272.

[112] Ibid.

[113] *Spanish Constitution 1978* 2.

[114] It is beyond the limits of this chapter to provide an overview of the literature on nationalism. In other parts of this book, I explain the interplay between nationalism and the development of modern state. For a general

analysis, descriptive of a set of cultural assumptions that are normally associated with the ideology of nationalism. For instance, a community might be associated with the speaking of the same language, as is the case with the Catalans, a shared religion, as is the case with most Jews around the world, and a sense of belonging to a specific territory, as is the case with the rest of the Spanish peoples, as one of the factors that constitute a nation.[115] However, it is not a common language, a shared religion, a place of residence, or indeed any combination of those elements that makes a nation or a nationality. In other words, nation and nationality cannot be scientifically differentiated.[116] Distinctive of most modern national communities is, by way of comparison with blood and belonging to national identities,[117] the acceptance of the role of democracy, equality and the existence of groups that make their own claim of being an identity.[118]

The current literature on nationalism suggests that modern nations are often one of the side products of industrialization and of the adoption of a vernacular language as the official language.[119] The adoption of an official language, as was the case with Catalonia, might predate the development of industrial society and of the modern state.[120] However, an efficient taxation system, a well-organized operating civil sector and

---

overview of the relationship between democracy and nationalism see Anthony D Smith, *Ethnicity and Nationalism* (Brill 1992); Anthony D Smith, *Nationalism: Theory, Ideology, History* (Polity Press; Blackwell 2001); Anthony D Smith, *The Ethnic Origins of Nations* (Basil Blackwell 1986). For an analysis of the development of modern nation-states see Fukuyama (n 17); Francis Fukuyama, *Political Order and Political Decay: From the Industrial Revolution to the Globalisation of Democracy* (Profile Books 2014). For an analysis of the negative implications of nationalism in modern democracy see Nairn (n 98); Michael Ignatieff, *The Warrior's Honor: Ethnic War and the Modern Conscience* (Vintage 1999); Elie Kedourie, *Nationalism* (Hutchinson 1960); Michael Billig, *Banal Nationalism* (Sage 1995).

115 Anderson (n 100).

116 Smith, *Nationalism* (n 114); Vito Breda, 'Constitutional Identities in a Liquid Society' in Jiri Priban (ed), *Liquid Society and its Law* (Routledge 2007); Breda, 'An Odd Partnership' (n 95).

117 Ignatieff (n 114).

118 Smith, *The Ethnic Origins of Nations* (n 114) 171.

119 Eric Hobsbawm, *Nations and Nationalism since 1780: Programme, Myth, Reality* (Cambridge University Press 1992); Ernest Gellner, *Nationalism* (Phoenix 1998); Anderson (n 100).

120 Smith, *Nationalism* (n 114).

democracy create the conditions for the establishment of a state's sponsored official language.[121]

All of these elements are shared, at different levels, in both Catalonia and the rest of Spain. It is thus difficult to find a normative explanation for the decision of the Constitutional Court that considers the reference to a nation and to national symbols in the preamble of the 2006 statute of autonomy of Catalonia as incompatible with the concept of the 'Spanish nation' (whatever that means) of section 2 of the constitution. The reasoning for inserting a distinction between nation and nationalities in Decision no. 31 is to be found in the contextual setting in which the Court carried out its third-party mediating role.[122] In particular, there is a strong indication that ideological aspects of the dyadic interplay between the central state and regional national identities, which we have to assume are of limited rational persuasiveness, were so deeply embedded into the claims made by both parties that the Court decided to intervene.[123] Stone Sweet describes the outcome of the activity of the third-party adjudicator in a compelling narrative: 'The dispute resolver may have done so in a relatively conservative manner, fashioning a partial victory for each disputant and appealing to rules whose prior existence is relatively unquestioned. In so doing, [it] has reinforced existing structure while clarifying its domain of relevance and application'.[124] So the relative implausibility of the claim of an exclusive role of the Spanish nation or the demand for recognition of the Catalan nationality of Catalan nationalists might not have substantive legal relevance.[125] It is, perhaps, an attempt to legalize the dyadic interaction.[126] However, it also shows an indication that the Court has taken its role as arbitrator into precarious grounds.

Modern national identities are polycentric and the decision to arbitrate over what an exclusive national identity ought to be might, in the long term, hinder the Court's ability to deal with regions and central institutions. Again, the central state retains the prerogative to enact statutes to protect the national common interest by enacting a legislation that harmonizes regionally delegated policies.[127] The Spanish parliament

---

[121] Fukuyama, *Political Order and Political Decay* (n 114) 76.
[122] Stone Sweet (n 54).
[123] Ibid 156, 158.
[124] Ibid 158.
[125] Constitutional Court Decision n31 28/06/2010 172 (Suplemento 11409) B.O.E. 1, 272.
[126] Stone Sweet (n 54) 164.
[127] Spanish Constitution 1978 150 (3).

retains, for instance, the power to protect the equality of treatment of all Spanish citizens,[128] the power to delegate centrally reserved competences to regional institutions and, in the case of a conflict between central and regional laws in areas of non-exclusive regional competence, the central state's statutory provision prevails.[129]

In the aftermath of the publication of Decision no. 31, several hundred thousand Catalonians descended on the streets of Barcelona to protest against the ruling,[130] yet the furore generated by Decision no. 31 could have been considered a storm in a tea cup.[131] Some aspects of the *Ley Orgánica 6/2006, de 19 de julio, de reforma del Estatuto de Autonomía de Cataluña* were altered in a way that might be considered substantial,[132] and that is expected by a final appellate jurisdiction that is dealing with an acrimonious dyadic relationship.[133] However, the level of popular support that the Catalonian government received in the aftermath of Decision no. 31 increased the level of cross-party support for independence.[134] The report of the Commission of International Experts used the term the 'radicalization' of opinions among representatives of civic society and political parties.[135] Independence, it is important to note, was not on the agenda of the majority of Catalan MPs before the publication of Decision no. 31 and there are no indications that the Constitutional Court tried to antagonize a national minority.[136]

Decision no. 31 was, according to the report of the Commission of International Experts, the harbinger of a new phase in the acrimonious relationship between Spain and Catalonia. The report uses the term 'chicken out' to describe a political strategy in which both parties willingly took positions that they were certain the other party would not

---

[128] Ibid 149 (1).

[129] Ibid 149 (3).

[130] 'Huge Catalan Protest in Barcelona', BBC News, 10 July 2010 http://www.bbc.com/news/10588494; Williams and others (n 28) 20.

[131] Casanas Adam (n 60).

[132] Ibid; Andreu Castellà (n 105).

[133] Andreu Castellà (n 105); Constitutional Court Decision n31 28/06/2010 172 (Suplemento 11409) B.O.E. 1.

[134] Casanas Adam (n 60); Williams and others (n 28) 14, 21; Catalonian Parliament, 'Resolution 5/X of the Parliament of Catalonia, Adopting the Declaration of Sovereignty and Right to Decide of the People of Catalonia' 1 https://www.parlament.cat/document/intrade/7176.

[135] Williams and others (n 28) 20.

[136] 'Javier García Oliva: Catalonia in Spain? The Future Ahead' https://ukconstitutionallaw.org/2014/11/10/javier-garcia-oliva-catalonia-in-spain-the-future-ahead/.

accept. The other party is forced, often based on bombastic political promises, to continue its policy without engagement which makes its stance illegitimate, or to 'chicken out' from the confrontation.[137]

Based on the history of the Basque Country and central state interaction, it is reasonably clear that Spanish and regional institutions consider the 'chicken-out phase' as temporary. Both parties (for example, the representative of the central government and the representative of the regional government) are cognisant that eventually the confrontation will be followed by a normalization period and concessions will be made.[138] For instance, the failed Ibarretxe plan could be considered, from the perspective of the central government, as a successful use of the chicken-out strategy.[139] The Basques stood down in their plan to amend the statute of autonomy, but in the negotiations that followed, the regional government managed to obtain substantial economic benefits.[140]

So, the sabre-rattling is, it is reasonable to suggest, a political strategy that aims to gain political capital and to delay negotiations until more fruitful conditions have matured.[141] There were, in addition to the ideological disputes, several attempts to negotiate a rebalancing of the fiscal transfer from Catalonia to the Spanish central state.[142] However, the central government refused to engage with the Catalan government.[143] Again, there are good reasons for the Spanish government to be very conservative in its financial planning. The country had recently been 'bailed out',[144] and the request for several billion euros' worth of

---

137 Williams and others (n 28) 23.

138 K Boyle and T Hadden, 'The Peace Process in Northern Ireland' (1995) 71(2) International Affairs 269; Georg Grote, *The South Tyrol Question, 1866–2010: From National Rage to Regional State* (Peter Lang 2012); Caron (n 98).

139 Keating and Bray (n 28).

140 Soroa (n 41); *Ley 12/1981, de 13 de Mayo Por La Que Se Aprueba El Concierto Economico Con La Comunidad Autónoma Del Pais Vasco 1981*; *El Nuevo Impuesto Sobre Los Gases Fluorados de Efecto Invernadero 2014* 97; Zubiri Oria (n 92) 38–48.

141 Williams and others (n 28) 24–42.

142 Maiol Roger, *Las 23 Demandas de Mas a Rajoy: Financiación, Competencias y Lengua* (1 August 2014) EL PAÍS https://elpais.com/ccaa/2014/08/01/catalunya/1406913058_166638.html; Xabi Barrena, *Estas Son Las 46 Peticiones de Carles Puigdemont a Mariano Rajoy* (20 April 2016) elperiodico, http://www.elperiodico.com/es/politica/20160420/las-cuarenta-seis-peticiones-puigdemont-rajoy-moncloa-5070904.

143 Casanas Adam (n 60).

144 Raphael Minder, Nicholas Kulish and Paul Geitner, 'Spain Accepts Bailout Deal From Europeans for Its Banks', *The New York Times*, 9 June 2012

legislative competences from a region might be perceived as extravagant.[145] These are 'big numbers', but in relative terms, the 2017 referendum in Veneto, if all the requests were to be accepted by the central government, would be the proxy for higher fiscal transfers.[146] Independently from the impact that the transfer measures might have, the central government refused to start a dialogue, and in 2015, the Catalans voted again.

The political parties that favoured secession won a substantial majority.[147] The new Catalan government initiated the process to prepare for a referendum in which several decentralization measures, some of which were relatively mild, were considered, but again the central government refused to engage with the Catalonian government.[148] One of the key aspects of the programme was to carry out a referendum which, if the majority of the voters supported independence, would legitimate the Catalan government in declaring unilateral secession. The statute [*Ley de Cataluña 4/2017*] that prepared for the referendum was reviewed by the Constitutional Court and declared unconstitutional.[149] The Catalonian parliament ignored the Court's decision, and a referendum, which was *de jure* illegal, took place on 1 October. The voting was characterized by a series of violent clashes between voters and security forces.[150] The result favoured independence and on 27 October 2017, the Catalan parliament approved the unilateral declaration of independence. The central government, pursuant of section 155 of the 1978 constitution, established direct rule, suspended, among other activities, the Catalonian parliament and called for a new election.[151] The new election that took place on

---

https://www.nytimes.com/2012/06/10/business/global/spain-moves-closer-to-bail out-of-banks.html.

[145] 'Catalonia Asks Spain for 9bn Euros', BBC News, 29 January 2013, http://www.bbc.com/news/world-europe-21254010.

[146] *Legislative Proposal, Pursuant to Section 2 [2] of the Regional Law of the 19th June 2014, no. 15: 'Modalities and Contents for the Recognition for the Increase of Specific Forms of Autonomy for the Veneto Region, Pursuant to the Third Paragraph of Article 116 of the Constitution'. 2017.*

[147] Williams and others (n 28) 39; Casanas Adam (n 60).

[148] Joan Vintró, 'Legalidad y Consulta Soberanista En Cataluña, Por Joan Vintró' 2, http://idpbarcelona.net/legalidad-y-consulta-soberanista-en-cataluna/.

[149] *Recurso: 1638–2017* (unreported, Constitutional Court (Spain), 7 May 2017); García Oliva (n 28).

[150] *Recurso: 1638–2017* (unreported, Constitutional Court (Spain), 7 May 2017).

[151] *Spanish Constitution 1978.*

21 December 2017 gave the majority of the Catalan parliament to pro-independence parties.[152]

The repeated electoral successes of the pro-secession political parties are expected. The Catalonian government and the central government, controlled by a right-wing party, have a vested interest in continuing the chicken-out strategy.[153] It is less clear whether the Spanish Constitutional Court might be benefitting from maintaining an irrational division between nation and nationalities.[154]

CONCLUSION

The Spanish constitutional system is designed to promote a dynamic interaction between regional and central institutions. The dispositive principle, which is the first driver of change considered in this chapter, allows regional identities to initiate the process of an amendment of their statutes of autonomy in a way that meets their social and economic needs. New reforms, over the past two decades, increased the complexity and the articulation of the Spanish system of governance. By way of comparison with the other constitutional systems considered in this book which seek to crystallize the interaction between 'centre and periphery', the Spanish constitutional system fosters negotiations and temporary agreements which are a manifestation of the multinational nature of Spain. The flip side of the dispositive principle is an almost unmanageable level of institutional–territorial complexity. The complexity is manifested in the fiscal regimes and in the gamut of variations of legislative competences allocated to each region. The complexity of the system of governance has also been a proxy for a high level of constitutional litigations.

A second distinctive element of the Spanish process of the recognition and negotiation of identity claims is the reference to ethnocentric fictitious assumptions as a supporting narrative in both legal and political arenas. For instance, in Decision no. 31, the constitution intervened in a debate over the constitutional legitimacy of having a reference to

---

152 Alice Cuddy, *Live: Pro-Independence Parties Claim Victory in Catalan Election* (21 December 2017) euronews, http://www.euronews.com/2017/12/21/follow-live-catalonia-votes-in-regional-election.

153 Williams and others (n 28) 23.

154 Constitutional Court Decision n31 28/06/2010 172 (Suplemento 11409) B.O.E. 1, 31.

Catalonia as a nation in the 2006 Catalonian statute of autonomy. The Constitutional Court answered in the negative.

Decision no. 31 was the harbinger of a period of increased tension between Catalan institutions and the central government controlled by the People's Party. The acrimonious relation fostered ethnocentric narratives from both sides and politically increased the chasm between a popular perception of a Spanish and Catalan common good. The report of the Commission of International Experts on 'The Legitimacy of Catalonia's Exercise of its Right to Decide' called this phase the 'chicken-out' period. Political parties that claim the right to represent the will of Spanish or Catalan communities 'farm' electoral support in their respective franchises by promising ethnocentric measures. The hope, from both parties, is that the other will stand down. The recent unconstitutional 2017 referendum, the suspension of the Catalan parliament, the arrest warrants made against Catalan cabinet members and the new elections are part of a process in which both parties refuse to negotiate. Based on the historical experience of the relation between central government and the Basque Country, these confrontation phases are temporary and tend to prepare for a new transfer of fiscal and legislative prerogatives from the central state to the region.

4. Italy: constitutional negotiations and tolerance in a patrimonial political system

INTRODUCTION

The Italian constitutional system is rigid[1] and adopts a system of governance that is legislatively and fiscally federal.[2] The central state has a limited number of legislative competences and the remaining competences are automatically allocated to the regions. Fifteen of the 20 regions have an ordinary system of governance and five have special constitutional autonomy.[3] Twelve linguistic national minorities have their officially recognized languages. These officially recognized languages are Friulian (526 000 speakers), German (295 000 speakers), Ladin (a Rhaeto-Romanic language that includes 28 000 speakers), Sardinian (175 000 speakers), French (120 000 speakers), Occitan (50 000 speakers), Franco-Provençal (70 000 speakers), Arberesh (a variant of contemporary Albanian that includes 100 000 speakers), Slovene (85 000 speakers), Croatian (1700 speakers), Catalan (18 000 speakers) and Greek (3900 speakers).[4] A few of these national communities reside in the five autonomous regions: the Aosta Valley, Friuli, South Tyrol and Trento, Sardinia and Sicily. The remaining 15 regions can, pursuant to article 116 of the constitution, negotiate a limited expansion of their legislative (and financial) competences.

---

1 Constitution of the Italian Republic 1948 section 116.

2 Constitution of the Italian Republic (n 1) Title: 5. Luca Antonini, *Federalismo all'italiana: Dietro le quinte della grande incompiuta. Quello che ogni cittadino dovrebbe sapere* (Marsilio Editori 2013); Francesco Palermo, 'Italy: A Federal Country without Federalism?' in Michael Burgess and G Alan Tarr (eds), *Constitutional Dynamics in Federal Systems: Sub-National Perspectives* (McGill-Queen's University Press 2012).

3 Constitution of the Italian Republic (n 1) sections 116–117.

4 Law no. 482 15 December 1999 Article 2; Aline Sierp, 'Minority Language Protection in Italy: Linguistic Minorities and the Media' (2008) 4 Journal of Contemporary European Research 303.

Italy also includes two sovereign micro states in its territory: the Republic of San Marino with a population of 37 000[5] and the Holy See with a population of circa 1000.[6] These two independent states will not be discussed in this book, but the oddity of San Marino as an internationally recognized independent state is a constant reminder of the aleatory nature of nation-building in Europe, and albeit incidentally, refocuses the debate on the 'suitable size' for an independent nation-state or a sub-state administrative division.[7]

Italy might have rich history, yet as an internationally recognized political entity, it is one of the youngest considered in this book. The official date of birth of the current polity is set at 1861. Rome was not included in the 1861 Kingdom of Italy and three of five autonomous regions (a large part of Veneto, South Tyrol and Friuli) were not included in the Kingdom until the end of the First World War.[8] Several regions have a series of linguistic minorities such as the South Tyrol region,[9] the Aosta Valley[10] and Friuli.[11] Large sections of the population use Italian, a Tuscan dialect selected as the state's official language,[12] as a second language.[13] The levels of education, economic development and criminality vary across regions.[14] The industrialized areas around Milan are

---

5 Central Intelligence Agency, 'The World Factbook: San Marino' https://www.cia.gov/library/publications/the-world-factbook/geos/sm.html (accessed 19 December 2017).

6 Central Intelligence Agency, 'The World Factbook: Holy See' https://www.cia.gov/library/publications/the-world-factbook/geos/vt.html (accessed 19 December 2017).

7 Ernest Gellner, *Nations and Nationalism* (Basil Blackwell 1983).

8 Mario Cervi and Indro Montanelli, *L'Italia Del Novecento* (Rizzoli 1998) http://rizzoli.rcslibri.corriere.it/libro/6014_l_italia_del_novecento_montanelli_cervi.html (accessed 25 January 2013).

9 Constitutional Law no. 5 26.02.1948.

10 Constitutional Law no. 4 26.02.1948.

11 Constitutional Law no. 1 31.1963.

12 Paolo Nencioni, 'L'Accademia Della Crusca e La Lingua Italiana' in Paolo Ramat, Hans-Josef Niederehe and E F K Koerner (eds), *History of Linguistics in Italy* (John Benjamins Publishing Company 1986) 110; Domenico Santamaria, 'Orientamenti Della Linguistica Italiana Del Primo Ottocento' in Paolo Ramat, Hans-Josef Niederehe and E F K Koerner (eds), *History of Linguistics in Italy* (John Benjamins 1986) 229.

13 ISTAT, 'L'uso Della Lingua Italiana, Dei Dialetti e Di Altre Lingue in Italia, Statistiche, Rapporto 2012' (2014) 3.

14 Paolo Di Martino, Emanuele Felice and Michelangelo Vasta, 'The Curious Case of the Coexistence of Two "Access-Orders": Explaining the Italian Regional Divide' (Department of Economics, University of Siena 2017).

among the richest in the world, whereas the South of Italy is currently one the largest economically depressed geographical areas in the European Union.[15] These variations have been instrumental in the development of some unsavoury ideological narratives of the Lega Nord which will be discussed later in this chapter.[16]

The central state legislative competences are set in a closed list of heads of power, listed in article 117, and the remaining legislative competences are granted to regional councils.[17] In comma 3 of section 117, there is a list of concurrent heads of power.[18] A region, as mentioned earlier, can negotiate (pursuant to article 116) the allocation of concurrent legislative prerogatives.[19] All five autonomous regions can retain most of their territorial fiscal income. The Aosta Valley, Friuli and South Tyrol are among the wealthiest regions of Europe,[20] whereas Sardinia and Sicily are among the poorest and are subsidized by the central state.[21] The islands of Sicily[22] and Sardinia[23] have special constitutional status.[24] Two regions were and still are, by way of comparison with the rest of Italy, economically depressed in a way that is similar to Southern Italy.[25]

In 1963, Friuli Venezia Giulia was the fifth area of Italy to be added to the list of regions with special autonomy.[26] The motivation for the latest addition was to compensate for the disruption created by NATO's strong

---

15 Eurostat, 'Gross Domestic Product (GDP) per Inhabitant in Purchasing Power Standards (PPS) in Relation to the EU-28 Average, by NUTS 2 Regions, 2015 (% of the EU-28 Average, EU-28 = 100)'.

16 Anna Cento Bull, 'Lega Nord: A Case of Simulative Politics?' (2009) 14 South European Society and Politics 129.

17 Antonin considers the wording of Article 117 'scellerato' which literally translated means 'wicked'. Antonini (n 2) 165. The Italian definition from a dictionary add a criminal qualification: 'Act, thought, behavior, which comes from evil heart or of which have a criminal end'. 'Scellerato' http://www.treccani.it/vocabolario/scellerato/ (accessed 9 May 2015).

18 *Decision no. 39 2014* (Constitutional Court [Italy]).

19 Palermo (n 2) 239–240.

20 Antonini (n 2) 2560; Banca d 'Italia, 'Economie Regionali L'economia Delle Regioni Italiane Dinamiche Recenti e Aspetti Strutturali' 5; Eurostat (n 15).

21 Banca d 'Italia (n 20) 52; Di Martino, Felice and Vasta (n 14) 8–13.

22 Constitutional Law no. 2 26.02.1948.

23 Constitutional Law no. 3 26.02.1948.

24 Paul Ginsborg, *A History of Contemporary Italy: Society and Politics, 1943–1988* (Palgrave Macmillan 2003).

25 Banca d 'Italia (n 20) 5; Eurostat (n 15); Di Martino, Felice and Vasta (n 14) 8–13.

26 Constitutional Law no. 1 31.1963 (n 11).

military presence. Following the 1955 Austrian Declaration of Neutrality, the American army and a large section of the Italian army relocated to Friuli.[27] That included the bulk of the US–Italy's nuclear tactical assets, which, in turn, provided grounds for high levels of land expropriation and military restrictions on private rights.[28] The Friulian population includes three officially recognized linguistic groups: Friulian, Slovenian and German.[29] However, the language groups in Friuli did not form political consociations comparable with the one in South Tyrol and, after the collapse of the communist regimes, the strategic role of Friuli has declined. Since the 1990s, the numbers in the Italian Army have been cut.[30] Furthermore, there are strong indications that the size of the nuclear arsenal has also been reduced.[31] Following the Presidential Nuclear Initiatives and the subsequent NATO Ministerial Communiqué by the Nuclear Planning Group, which announced a reduction of 80 per cent of the nuclear weapons in Europe, it is reasonable to assume that Friuli has lost strategical significance.[32] In short, it is reasonable to say that the historical reasons that made Friuli a suitable candidate for autonomous-region status have lapsed.

A constitutional amendment of the Italian constitution is a rigid multitrack and multistage process analogous to the processes of constitutional reform adopted by the Australian, Canadian and Spanish constitutional systems.[33] A proposal for a constitutional amendment must be approved by both houses of parliament twice and the process must include a three-month pause between votes. If a constitutional law is not approved by two-thirds of the parliament on the second vote, then a fifth

---

27 Georg Grote, *The South Tyrol Question, 1866–2010: From National Rage to Regional State* (Peter Lang 2012) 74.

28 Laura Spagnuolo, 'Italy's Tactical Nuclear Weapons | BASIC – British American Security Information Council' http://www.basicint.org/publications/laura-spagnuolo-research-and-policy-officer/2011/italys-tactical-nuclear-weapons (accessed 8 July 2015).

29 'Regione Autonoma Friuli Venezia Giulia – Comunità Linguistiche Regionali' http://www.regione.fvg.it/rafvg/cms/RAFVG/cultura-sport/patrimonio-culturale/comunita-linguistiche/ (accessed 18 December 2017).

30 'NATO Mini. Comm. Taormina, Italy, 17–18 Nov 1991'; Susan Koch, *The Presidential Nuclear Initiatives of 1991–1992* (National Defense University Press 2012).

31 'NATO Mini. Comm. Taormina, Italy, 17–18 Nov 1991' (n 30).

32 Koch (n 30).

33 Constitution of the Italian Republic (n 1) section: 138; Richard Albert, 'The Structure of Constitutional Amendment Rules' (2014) 49 Wake Forest Law Review 913, 937.

of the Members of Parliament (MPs) can still trigger a national referendum.[34] For historical reasons, some aspects of the Italian constitution cannot be amended.[35]

However, in article 116, the constitution allows a region to negotiate for an increase (or decrease) in legislative competences in a way that facilitates the accommodation of identity-based constitutional claims. At the time of writing this chapter, three regions (Emilia Romagna, Lombardy and Veneto) had initiated the process of negotiation aimed at amending the current allocation of their respective legislative competences. A change in legislative competences is automatically coupled with a change in financial allocations.[36]

The Italian political system is, by way of comparison with the other legal systems considered in this book, distinctive. Fukoyama uses the term 'neo-patrimonial' to qualify the Italian political system.[37] Patrimonial systems, like the ones adopted in most of medieval Europe, are based on networks of relationships where a close network of personal alliances trumps institutional efficiency.[38] A neo-patrimonial system might have a formal setting that makes reference to institutional efficiency and openness, but de facto still functions as a patrimonial system.[39]

The 1948 Italian constitution, for instance, makes direct reference to a type of political association which might be associated with a Weberian state. For instance, in article 1, there is a direct reference to democracy and meritocracy as the founding elements of the new republic: 'Italy is a democratic Republic founded on labour'.[40] Article 97 instead ensures that there is a system of competent and impartial public institutions: 'Public offices are organised according to the provisions of law, so as to ensure the efficiency and impartiality of administration [...] Employment in public administration is accessed through competitive examinations,

---

34 Constitution of the Italian Republic (n 1).

35 Basic Law for the Federal Republic of Germany in the revised version published in the Federal Law Gazette Part III as last amended by the Act of 11 July 2012 (Federal Law Gazette I p. 1478) 100–101.

36 Constitution of the Italian Republic (n 1) Article 118.

37 Francis Fukuyama, *Political Order and Political Decay: From the Industrial Revolution to the Globalisation of Democracy* (Profile 2014) 7.

38 Francis Fukuyama, *The Origins of Political Order: From Prehuman Times to the French Revolution* (Profile 2012) Ch 7.

39 Di Martino, Felice and Vasta (n 14).

40 Constitution of the Italian Republic (n 1).

except in the cases established by law'.[41] There are, in short, strong indications that, in 1948, the drafters aspired to set up the meritocratic institutions of a modern state, but the modern democratic Weberian state mentioned in the Italian constitutional text has never been fully implemented.[42] The resistance to modernization is particularly strong in the depressed South of the peninsula where the network of patronages has a vested interest in reducing openness and meritocracy in all public-sector areas.[43]

So, neo-patrimonialism is a distinctive element of the Italian political system, and this chapter relies on the studies of primary sources such as constitutional laws and secondary sources drafted by academics working inside and outside of Italy.[44] However, Italian academia, as with all aspects of the civil sector, is historically colonized by the patrimonial activity of political parties, and both tenured and temporary positions are often linked to a clientele.[45] The network of favours goes beyond the group mentioned in Morano-Foadi's description. It includes, for instance, individuals who are promoted in the network rankings owing to their political associations but who have no family ties with an academic patron.[46]

The negative implications of a patrimonial system in academia are beyond the unbalanced distribution of human capital.[47] For instance, the

---

41 Ibid.

42 Fukuyama (n 37) 7; Di Martino, Felice and Vasta (n 14); Emanuele Felice, *Perché Il Sud è Rimasto Indietro* (Il Mulino 2013).

43 Di Martino, Felice and Vasta (n 14); Ginsborg (n 24) 418; Vito Breda, 'How to Reverse the Italian Brain Drain: A Master Class from Australia' (2014) 52 International Migration 64.

44 Di Martino, Felice and Vasta (n 14); Antonini (n 2); Francesco Palermo and Alex Wilson, 'The Dynamics of Decentralization in Italy: Towards a Federal Solution?' [2013] European Diversity & Autonomy Papers http://webfolder.eurac.edu/eurac/publications/edap/2013_edap04.pdf (accessed 19 June 2015).

45 Sonia Morano-Foadi, 'Key Issues and Causes of the Italian Brain Drain' (2006) 19 Innovation: The European Journal of Social Science Research 209, 216.

46 Redazione Scuola, 'Augusto Fantozzi e i 7 Arrestati: Ecco Chi Sono i Docenti Dello Scandalo Concorsi Truccati' (*Corriere della Sera*, 25 September 2017) http://www.corriere.it/scuola/universita/cards/corruzione-universita-ecco-chi-sono-docenti-arrestati-dove-insegnano/ex-ministro-fantozzi_principale.shtml (accessed 20 December 2017); 'Firenze, Concorsi Truccati: "E" Il Vile Commercio Dei Posti' (*Repubblica.it*, 25 September 2017) http://firenze.repubblica.it/cronaca/2017/09/25/news/firenze_concorsi_truccati_arrestati_sette_docenti_universitari-176440964/ (accessed 20 December 2017).

47 Breda (n 43).

connection between political parties and the allocation of academic jobs might be the springboard for questioning the academic plausibility of some of the narratives used in this analysis. It could be argued, for instance, that the pervasive effect of clientelism within Italian academia and the related practice of associating individuals with a political activity might question, by extrapolation, the scientific value of academic research.[48] It is beyond the scope to this book to discuss and evaluate the persuasiveness of such a deduction.

DRIVER OF CHANGE: THE CASES OF THE SOUTH TYROLEAN PEOPLE'S PARTY AND THE LEGA NORD PARTY

Italy is a highly culturally diversified multinational society and this chapter focuses on a sample of aspects that are indicative of the benefits and shortcomings of having a flexible system of territorial governance.[49] This section will focus, in particular, on the case of the German-speaking national community in the Autonome Region of Trentino–Südtirol and on the political movement associated with the Lega Nord that has taken on the role of representing the Northern Italian identity. In the past 70 years, the Autonome Region of Trentino–Südtirol has been politically controlled by the Südtiroler Volkspartei (SVP), which negotiated a series of identity-based constitutional claims with the Italian government.[50] The result of this process is an efficient system of institutional cooperation, like the one linked to the Joint Commission on the implementation of South Tyrol autonomy, which, over the years, has ensured a relatively pacific interaction between the central state, the region and the autonomous provinces.[51] The Lega Nord has been considered the conveyor of grievances by the industrialized North against the perceived corrupt

---

48 Morano-Foadi (n 45).

49 Beverly Allen and Mary Russo, *Revisioning Italy: National Identity and Global Culture* (University of Minnesota Press 1997) 4 http://ebookcentral.proquest.com/lib/usq/detail.action?docID=310410 (accessed 18 December 2017); Gianni Toniolo (ed), *The Oxford Handbook of the Italian Economy Since Unification* (Oxford University Press 2013); Sierp (n 4).

50 Emma Lantschner, 'History of the South Tyrol Conflict and Its Settlement' in Jens Woelk, Francesco Palermo and Joseph Marko (eds), *Tolerance Through Law: Self Governance and Group Rights in South Tyrol* (Brill 2007).

51 Jens Woelk, Francesco Palermo and Joseph Marko, *Tolerance through Law* (Martinus Nijhoff 2008).

politics of the South of Italy.[52] It will be argued that, even without considering the precarious ideological assumptions, the Lega Nord represents a manifestation of economic nationalism in a patrimonial political system.[53]

As mentioned in the introduction, Italy is constitutionally divided into 20 regions.[54] Several officially recognized linguistic minorities reside in one of the five autonomous regions set out in the 1948 constitution.[55] Trentino Alto Adige is one of the five regions that includes multiple national identities. It covers 13 000 km^2 of alpine area in the northernmost part of Italy and encompasses two autonomous provinces. One is the Italian-speaking province of Trento and the other is the German-speaking province of Bozen.[56] Both provinces are recognized as having special statutory autonomy.[57] Overall, two-thirds of the regional residents (that is, the combined number of residents in the autonomous provinces) are German speakers.[58] The Ladin population represents less than 5 per cent of the regional population and the remaining regional residents are Italian speakers and immigrants.[59]

The Autonome Region of Trentino–Südtirol is, as it appears from this skeleton description, demographically complex and its system of governance mirrors that complexity.[60] The region and the two provinces that constitute it have a series of exclusive legislative and fiscal competences that ensure the protection of linguistic minorities and the cultural preservation of national identities and provide for the specific geographical needs of alpine communities which provide services in a sub-arctic environment.[61] The SVP has been the political entity that, in the past

---

[52] Thomas W Gold, *The Lega Nord and Contemporary Politics in Italy* (Palgrave Macmillan 2003); Cento Bull (n 16).

[53] Gold (n 52); Cento Bull (n 16); Z Bauman, 'Identity in the Globalising World' (2001) 9 Social Anthropology 121.

[54] Constitution of the Italian Republic (n 1) Title V.

[55] Law no. 482 15 December 1999 (n 4) Article 2; Sierp (n 4).

[56] Constitutional Law no. 5 26.02.1948 (n 9).

[57] Constitutional Law no. 5 26.02.1948 (n 9); Constitution of the Italian Republic (n 1) Article 116 [1].

[58] 'Trentino-Alto Adige' http://www.regione.taa.it/biblioteca/minoranze/tn_bz.aspx (accessed 20 December 2017).

[59] Ibid (n 58).

[60] Constitutional Law no. 5 26.02.1948 (n 9); Constitutional Law n.1 10.11.1971 1; Law n.482 15 December 1999 (n 4); Constitutional Law no. 3 18.10.2001.

[61] ISTAT, 'Trentino Alto Adige (Environment and Energy Data Set)' (13 December 2010) http://www.istat.it (accessed 20 December 2017).

seven decades, has taken on the role of pursuing German constitutional identity claims within Italian politics.[62]

In its activity, the SVP sought to foster tolerance and collaboration between three South Tyrolean linguistic communities.[63] Palermo and Verena Wisthaler, among others, use the term 'tolerance through law' to describe the effect of a complex system of rules managed to establish a political system that allows for a fair allocation of public resources and, at the same time, protects national identities.[64] Distinctive of this process of the accommodation of identity-based constitutional demands was, quite early on, the acceptance of the dynamic interaction between the linguistic groups and the avoidance of 'definitive solutions' which in the past escalated the tension between 'ethnic communities'.[65]

The Autonome Region of Trentino–Südtirol is a historical oddity and the German-speaking community has been the target of policies that could have had the effect of cultural genocide.[66] In 1915, article 4 of a secret agreement between France, Russia and Great Britain established that, in case of an Allied victory, the new Italian border with the Austro-Hungarian Empire would be the alpine pass of Brennero.[67] That included a large territory which was the home of German- and Ladin-speaking communities. Given the confidential nature of the agreement, the reasons for pushing the border of the Italian state deep into the German-speaking ethnic group are a matter of speculation; commentators appear to agree that military reasons prompted the request.[68] Given that a

---

62 Rolf Steininger, *South Tyrol: A Minority Conflict of the Twentieth Century* (Transaction 2003); Woelk, Palermo and Marko (n 51); Francesco Palermo, Walter Obwexer and Esther Happacher (eds), *I 40 Anni Del Secondo Statuto Di Autonomia: L'autonomia Speciale Della Provincia Autonoma Di Bolzano Nel Contesto Dell'integrazione Europea* (Wolters Kluwer Italia; CEDAM 2014); Palermo and Wilson (n 44).

63 Verena Wisthaler, 'Identity Politics in the Educational System in South Tyrol: Balancing between Minority Protection and the Need to Manage Diversity' (2013) 13 Studies in Ethnicity and Nationalism 358, 359.

64 Wisthaler (n 63) 359; Woelk, Palermo and Marko (n 51).

65 Lantschner (n 50).

66 Federico Scarano, *Tra Mussolini e Hitler. Le opzioni dei sudtirolesi nella politica estera fascista: Le opzioni dei sudtirolesi nella politica estera fascista* (FrancoAngeli 2012) 213; Grote (n 27) 29–38, 42–45, 51.

67 'Agreement between France, Russia, Great Britain and Italy, London 26/04/1915'; Grote (n 27) 18–22.

68 Steininger (n 62) ii. Antony Alcock, 'The South Tyrol Autonomy' [2001] A short introduction. University of Ulster 5 http://www.geography.ryerson.ca/wayne/Geo773-F2013/South-Tyrol-Autonomy.pdf (accessed 5 July 2015).

large section of the Italian alpine border is with neutral Switzerland, there are relatively few major North–South military routes across the Dolomites. One of those routes connects München, Innsbruck and Verona, and it has a natural obstacle in the Brenner Pass. The second, which is less direct and easier to defend militarily, connects Vienna to Venice via Klagenfurt and Vittorio Veneto. However, the control of the Puster Valley, which runs East–West from the foothills of Brennero to the Italian valley of Cadore, allows for the control of both transalpine routes.[69] It was therefore reasonable for the 1915 Italian government, which was about to embark on Italy's fourth war in 67 years against the Austro-Hungarian Empire, to demand a strategic strong point on its northern border.[70]

Article 4 of the Paris Agreement does exactly that. It explicitly allocates South Tyrol to Italy and specifies the new border: 'Italy shall obtain the Trentino, Cisalpine Tyrol with its geographical and natural frontier (the Brenner Pass frontier)'.[71] The new natural border between the Empire and Italy was duly ratified by the Saint Germain Treaty.[72] In the period between the World Wars, German speakers of South Tyrol were subjected to a policy of ethnic cleansing and progressive cultural genocide by the Italian authorities.[73] One of the most tragic events of this period was the mass deportation of German-speaking South Tyroleans to Germany.[74] The so-called 'Blut oder Boden' diaspora.[75] By 1943, over 20 per cent of the German-speaking population had been relocated to temporary residences in the German Reich.[76]

---

69 Steininger (n 62) VIII.

70 Grote (n 27) 2–9; Lantschner (n 50) 7.

71 'Agreement between France, Russia, Great Britain' https://archive.org/stream/agreementbetween00franrich#page/n5/mode/2up (accessed 4 July 2015); Grote (n 27) 30.

72 The new border was set in Article 3: 'from Piz Umbrail to north of Stelvio it will follow crest of Rhetian Alps to sources of the Adige and Eisach, passing thence by the Reschen and Brenner and the heights of Oetz and Ziller'. 'Treaty of Peace between the Allied and Associated Powers and Austria; Protocol, Declaration and Special Declaration [1920] ATS 3'.

73 Steininger (n 62) 1–13.

74 Scarano (n 66) 213.

75 Grote (n 27) 69; Georg Grote, 'Gehen Oder Bleiben? – Die Identitätskrise Der Deutschsprachigen Südtiroler in Optanten- Und Dableibergedichten Der Optionszeit' (2004) 37 Modern Austrian Literature 47.

76 Grote (n 27) 69; Lantschner (n 50) 7.

In 1947, the unfortunate consequences of three decades of a fascist regime in South Tyrol were recognized by the Peace Treaty with Italy.[77] In article 10, there is an explicit obligation to guarantee the free movement of persons on the border.[78] In addition, the Treaty recognized the 1946 Austrian and Italian agreement, also known as the Gruber–De Gasperi Agreement, which provided a series of rights to the German-speaking minority in South Tyrol.[79] Annex IV also set a list of private rights such as the right to use their language (article 1), prerogatives to remedy some of the effects of xenophobic policies that preceded the agreement such as the Italianization of family names (article 1) and an obligation for the Italian government to grant special legislative and executive powers to the region (in article 2). Critically, in article 3, the Italian government is committed to consulting with the Austrian government before legislating on citizenship, trade and the free movement of individuals between the borders of the two German communities.[80]

The Peace Treaty and the Italian–Austrian agreement set the international relevance of the debate over the recognition of German-speaking identity-based political claims. However, this process was not automatic. In 1948, the SVP was founded as a party for the South Tyrolean German speakers.[81] From the outset, it denounced the historical connection between South Tyrol and Germany. The decision to relinquish the claim of a connection with Germany was not easy and hurt many of the South Tyroleans who fought during the Second World War in the German Wehrmacht. However, in the aftermath of the Second World War, many German sympathizers continued to provide asylum to escaping Nazi war criminals.[82] From Eichmann and Hesse to Mengele, whose family still lives in South Tyrol, a long list of Nazi criminals relied on South

---

77 Steininger (n 62) 78; 'Declaration on the Italian Peace. Concluded between: United Kingdom, France, and the United States [1951] 3 UST 2873', refers to the Peace treaty with Italy, 10 February 1947; Grote (n 27) 78.

78 'Declaration on the Italian Peace' (n 77).

79 Ibid Article 10 (2).

80 Ibid Annex IV.

81 Grote (n 27) 78–80.

82 'Mengele Family Keeps Uneasy Silence' (*Tribune Digital – Chicago Tribune*) http://articles.chicagotribune.com/1985-06-09/news/8502060229_1_guenzburg-martha-mengele-dr-josef-mengele (accessed 21 December 2017); 'Nazisti, in Sud Tirolo Il Rifugio Delle SS in Fuga – La Repubblica.It' (*Archivio – la Repubblica.it*) http://ricerca.repubblica.it/repubblica/archivio/repubblica/2008/10/28/nazisti-in-sud-tirolo-il-rifugio-delle.html (accessed 20 December 2017).

Tyrolean support to escape to South America.[83] The explicit and unconditional denouncement of a connection between the SVP and Germany was perceived as essential.

The year 1948 was also that in which the Italian constitution included South Tyrol in the list of autonomous regions.[84] There were, however, indications than the Italian government might tilt its policies towards a literal, rather than purposive, interpretation of the Gruber–De Gasperi Agreement.[85] The Italian government perceived that the legislative autonomy for the German speakers might be interpreted as one of the stepping stones for South Tyrol's reunification with Austria and again implemented a series of policies aimed at the Italianization of the province of Bozen.[86] German-speaking civil servants, many of whom had fought in the Italian Army, were forbidden from using their German family names when dealing with the public.[87] Italian speakers were also favoured in the allocation of basic services and, given that the quality of those services in South Tyrol was much higher than in the South of Italy, the region became a destination for mass Italian immigration.[88] These policies, as expected, increased the tension between ethnic groups and allowed the SVP to gain the disgruntled votes of the German speakers who might have had little interest in the ethnic policies.[89]

In particular, the SVP associated itself with Catholic values shared by both Italian and German communities, rejected secessionism and focused on protecting the linguistic minority.[90] The combined effects of being a moderately conservative political party and of being successful in regional elections made the leadership of the SVP an ideal interlocutor for both the Italian and the Austrian governments, which were often populated by representatives of the Christian Democrat Party.[91] Consequently, after a relatively short phase of organized ethnic violence,[92]

---

83 'Mengele Family Keeps Uneasy Silence' (n 82); 'Nazisti, in Sud Tirolo Il Rifugio Delle SS in Fuga – La Repubblica.It' (n 82).

84 Constitution of the Italian Republic (n 1); Constitutional Law no. 5 26.02.1948 (n 9).

85 Grote (n 27) 85; Lantschner (n 50) 11.

86 Grote (n 27) 85.

87 Ibid 89.

88 Ibid 89.

89 Ibid 90.

90 Ibid 93.

91 Ibid 95.

92 Hans K Peterlini, *Südtiroler Bombenjahre: Von Blut und Tränen zum Happy End?* (Raetia 2005).

two UN resolutions,[93] a change in public opinion in Italy[94] and a shift to the left of the Italian central government's policies, the conditions were created for a more effective negotiation process aimed at engaging the international commitments set up in the 1947 Peace Treaty and the Gruber–De Gasperi Agreement.[95] In 1961, the Italian government organized a committee composed of representatives of all of the South Tyrol linguistic communities with the aim of designing a series of policies and legislative competences. Almost at the same time, government representatives and the leadership of the SVP started a process of negotiation which resulted in the South Tyrol Package. The Package, as it is commonly known, combined the recommendations of the commission with the government–SVP agreement.[96]

The Italian parliament, with votes from the Christian Democrats, the SVP and the Socialist Party, entrenched some part of the agreement into a new constitutional law.[97] The Package included 137 policies and competences, of which 97 were introduced by the Italian parliament through constitutional law.[98] The remaining points were implemented with ordinary law and with extremely well-articulated administrative regulations.[99] It was the beginning of the 'tolerance through law' system.[100]

The agreement over the Package provided a watershed moment in the history of South Tyrol. The SVP representatives became the permanent referent with government. The establishment of the Joint Commission composed by an equal number (six each) of South Tyrolean and Italian government representatives, for instance, ensured that legislative and administrative policies in South Tyrol would be agreed by both central and regional representatives before reaching the parliament or the cabinet.[101] If the legislative or administrative measures were to engage only

---

93 United Nations, 'Article 14, Analytical Summary of Practice – Resolutions 1497 (XV) and 1661 (XVI) 31/10/1960 346–357' http://legal.un.org/repertory/art14/english/rep_supp3_vol1-art14_e.pdf (accessed 5 July 2015).

94 Grote (n 27) 109.

95 Ibid 97.

96 Giuseppe Avolio, 'Institutions of Self-Government' in Jens Woelk, Francesco Palermo and Joseph Marko (eds), *Tolerance Through Law: Self Governance and Group Rights in South Tyrol* (Brill 2007).

97 Constitutional Law no. 1 10.11.1971 (n 60); Decree no. 670 31.08.1972.

98 Ibid.

99 Woelk, Palermo and Marko (n 51).

100 Lantschner (n 50).

101 Decree no. 670 31.08.1972 (n 98) Article 107.

the Italian-speaking autonomous province of Trento, then the Joint Committee would be reduced to six and the three representatives of the province would be Italian speakers.[102] Given that European, central, regional and provincial policies often require multiple forms of institutional cooperation (for example, manging the environmental impact on public transport in Garda Lake region requires the coordination of institutions from Veneto, Lombardy, the Italian government and the province of Trento),[103] and that cooperation has to be agreed separately by the regional and provincial Joint Committees, it is no surprise that the system of governance in South Tyrol is based on micromanaging the rules and statutes.[104]

The 'tolerance through law' system via the extensive work of the Joint Committee ensures that all parties must agree on changes to their respective status.[105] More importantly, given the stable regional governance of the SVP and the volatility of Italian politics, the Joint Committee ensures that subsequent central governments are precluded from forcing policies that might push the accommodation process of identity-based constitutional claims backwards in either province. The activity of the Joint Committee is parallel to the one of the Standing Conference of the State and Regions chaired by a government representative and that aims at coordinating regional policies across the territory.[106]

The recent reform of the Package might be constructed as a consociational agreement since it confirmed the ethnical division of South Tyrol rather than solving the problematic interaction between the two communities.[107] That is only partially correct. The real achievement of the Package was in the acceptance that a highly articulated multinational negotiation would become part of life for the South Tyrolean nation. The

---

[102] Ibid.

[103] Grote (n 27) 128.

[104] Francesco Palermo, 'South Tyrol's Special Status within the Italian Constitution' in Jens Woelk, Francesco Palermo and Joseph Marko (eds), *South Tyrol's Special Status within the Italian Constitution* (Brill 2007) 44; Avolio (n 96) 56.

[105] Woelk, Palermo and Marko (n 51).

[106] Jens Woelk, 'What It Means to Be Special in Relations with the Central State: Institutions and Procedures' in Jens Woelk, Francesco Palermo and Joseph Marko (eds), *Tolerance Through Law: Self Governance and Group Rights in South Tyrol* (Brill 2007) 126.

[107] Brendan O'Leary, 'Debating Consociational Politics: Normative and Explanatory Arguments' in Sidney John Roderick Noel (ed), *From Power Sharing to Democracy: Post-Conflict Institutions in Ethnically Divided Societies* (McGill-Queen's University Press) 18; Palermo (n 104) 35.

process took almost a decade and its implementation required the engagement of central, regional and local institutions.[108] The length of the negotiation, however, helped with internalizing choices before they were entrenched in constitutional law[109] and into national legislation.[110]

In 1999, constitutional law no. 1 established the direct election of the regional president and set a new amendment procedure for regional statutes which are considered quasi-regional constitutions. An amendment to the regional statute requires two successive approvals by the regional assembly and, if requested by voters or regional MPs, a referendum.[111] The 2001 reform, as mentioned earlier, established a federal system in which the central state only has the competences allocated to it by the constitution.[112] Regions such as Veneto and Lombardy are painfully aware of the performance of the civil sector of the South Tyrol institutions and wish to have a similar level of autonomy.[113] The SVP has also lost some of its political support.[114] The newer generations are more concerned with developing a regional identity within Europe and are less worried about the parochial debates of the recent past.[115]

It is reasonable to suggest that the SVP, by carefully managing the German-speaking community's political aspirations, steered the debate with central institutions away from ethnic and jurisprudential conflicts.[116] Indeed, there are strong indications that three alpine linguist groups (the Venetians, Germans and Ladins) had a long history of pacific connivance and that an elite class of merchants that controlled the three communities had a vested interest in solving and minimizing conflicts.[117] However, the

---

108 Stefan Wolff, 'The Institutional Structure of Regional Consociations in Brussels, Northern Ireland, and South Tyrol' (2004) 10 Nationalism and Ethnic Politics 387; Grote (n 27) 113.

109 Constitutional Law no. 1 10.11.1971 (n 60); Law no. 482 15 December 1999 (n 4); Decree no. 670 31/08/1972 TULSPTA 2015 67.

110 Steininger (n 62); Wolff (n 108).

111 Constitution of the Italian Republic (n 1) Articles 121–123, 126. Constitutional Law no. 1 22.11.1999.

112 Lantschner (n 50) 36; Constitutional Law no. 3 18.10.2001 (n 60).

113 Legislative proposal, pursuant to Section 2 [2] of the Regional Law of the 19th June 2014, no. 15: 'Modalities and Contents for the Recognition for the Increase of Specific Forms of Autonomy for the Veneto Region, pursuant to the third paragraph of Article 116 of the Constitution' (2017).

114 Grote (n 27) 132.

115 Ibid 12.

116 Avolio (n 96) 61.

117 O'Leary (n 107) 28.

SVP's leadership, over the years, has managed to convince the Italian government that institutions can only provide a vessel for an open dialogue and not a solution to ethnic tension.

DRIVER OF CHANGE: THE LEGA NORD PARTY AND THE 2017 REFERENDA

In the previous section I explained that the SVP has been a driver of change in the Italian constitutional system, and in this section, I will discuss instead the Lega Nord. The Lega Nord is perceived as one of the drivers of change of the 2001 federal reforms of the Italian system of governance. However, it will be explained that, whilst the Lega Nord is one of the new elements of Italian identity politics, it tends to act as a patrimonial political party which seeks to distribute resources among its network of affiliates and not to promote identity-based constitutional claims.

The success of the Lega Nord as a national political party is due to multiple factors. However, two factors helped its rise to the level of a coalition partner in several Italian governments. Firstly, in the early 1990s, a series of political scandals reduced the number of Italian political parties, and a string of mafia attacks on the state's institutions (in which two Sicilian judges and their bodyguards were killed) increased the perception of an ever-enlarging gap between an industrialized civil North and a mafia-controlled violent South.[118] Secondly, and at the same time as the mafia terrorist attacks, a small group of judges in Milan uncovered a clientele network that over the years had funnelled large amounts of public money into private businesses that were willing to pay hefty bribes to corrupt public servants and politicians.[119] Neither the role of the mafia nor the effect of patrimonialism was new, yet a regional party called Lega Nord in Lombardy, with a charismatic leader and unorthodox political views, managed to ride the wave of dissent generated by the then-recent events.[120]

---

[118] Paul Ginsborg, *Italy and Its Discontents 1980–2001: Family, Civil Society, State* (new edition, Penguin 2003); Di Martino, Felice and Vasta (n 14).

[119] Massimo Sargiacomo and others, 'Accounting and the Fight against Corruption in Italian Government Procurement: A Longitudinal Critical Analysis (1992–2014)' (2015) 28 Critical Perspectives on Accounting 89, 90.

[120] B Giordano, 'The Contrasting Geographies of "Padania": The Case of the Lega Nord in Northern Italy' (2001) 33 Area 27, 27.

The support for the Lega Nord came from the middle classes residing in the North of the peninsula who aspired to reducing the hindering effects of patrimonialism in Italian politics and the level of criminality in the South.[121] However, the support for the modernization of Italian politics was cut short by the leadership of the Lega Nord, which steered its political programme towards xenophobic policies and, in many ways, mimicked the system of patronage adopted by political parties in the Southern regions of Italy.[122] In particular, the Lega Nord's political programme focused on protecting a middle class of small and medium-sized entrepreneurs.[123] Initially, immigration from Northern Africa and Eastern Europe brought a new source of cheap labour, but subsequently, these new Italian residents became entrepreneurs themselves and competed against the middle class that favoured the Lega Nord.[124] From this perspective, the Lega Nord does not represent an ethnic group, like the SVP does, but rather it funnels the political aspirations of an interest group that is localized in a small group of regions.[125]

It is reasonable to say that the Lega Nord has been distinctively effective in channelling the discontent in the industrialized North into political support, yet the proposed xenophobic policies were almost certainly constitutionally unworkable and in violation of international law that is automatically applicable in Italian law. The 1948 constitution includes a series of extensive systems of rights granted to all residents and, in article 10, it explicitly adopts the so-called monist system which automatically imposes the compliance of all jurisdictions to the general principle of international law.[126] Even during the period of the coalition government in which the Lega Nord controlled the Ministry of the Interior, it had little influence on Italian immigration policies. One of the reasons is, again, the general inefficiency of the Italian public sector, yet there are clear indications that at the legislative level, the Lega Nord had little intention of hindering the flux of immigration that provided the cheap labour for the industrial North.[127] For instance, in 2008, the Lega Nord Ministry of Interior-sponsored government legislative decree no. 92

[121] Fukuyama (n 38) 96; Di Martino, Felice and Vasta (n 14) 8.

[122] Cento Bull (n 16) 136.

[123] Ernesto Calvanese, *Media e immigrazione tra stereotipi e pregiudizi: la rappresentazione dello straniero nel racconto giornalistico* (FrancoAngeli 2011).

[124] Calvanese (n 123).

[125] Giordano (n 120) 29; Bauman (n 53); Zygmunt Bauman, *In Search of Politics* (Polity 1999).

[126] Constitution of the Italian Republic (n 1).

[127] Breda (n 43).

(hereafter LD 92) included a series of measures aimed at regulating illegal immigration in Italy. Article 5 (para 3) of the decree introduced the possibility of the police being able to seize properties leased to illegal immigrants, yet the sanction applies only if the rent is deemed excessive and the manager of the property is also the owner.[128] Even at first sight, the two requirements of article 5 of LD 92 make the chances of a sanction very limited. For instance, a landlord of an estate that provides shelter for illegal immigrants allocates the management of the property to a business that s/he owns. The company is the estate manager (not the owner) of the property and so article 5 of LD 92 does not apply to the landlord.

Once it is assumed that, firstly, rules such as article 5 of LD 92 are intended to change the behaviours of unscrupulous landlords/ladies who protect illegal immigrants, and secondly, that the reasons for article 5 becoming a law of the Italian republic were not a manifestation of parliamentary absentmindedness, then LD 92 should be considered an example of anthropomorphic mimicry typical of a political system based on patronage. The structure of the anti-illegal immigration law, it is reasonable to suggest, is one example of Lega Nord's rhetoric of 'getting tough on illegal immigration'. The political narrative shows a commitment to the rule of law, but in practice, the policy *de jure* protects Northern middle-class entrepreneurs who provide the bulk of the votes for the Lega Nord and who prosper by employing cheap illegal labour.[129]

It could be suggested that the Lega Nord represents a missed opportunity for the Italian political system as it channelled the middle-class interest in having an open and efficient political system into a network of clientele that mimics the existing Italian patrimonial model.[130] However, the Lega Nord had two indirect processes for constitutional reforms that had the potential to alter the Italian system of governance in a way that might have increased the level of efficiency in territorial government.[131] The first one is constitutional law no. 1 1999, which, among other aspects, allowed for the direct election of the president of the region and the possibility of altering the regional constitution without receiving the

---

128 Legislative Decree no. 92 2008.

129 'Ministero Dell'Interno, Archivio Storico Delle Elezioni – Camera Del 13 Aprile 2008' http://elezionistorico.interno.it/index.php?tpel=C&dtel=13/04/2008&tpa=I&tpe=I&lev0=0&levsut0=0&lev1=2&levsut1=1&ne1=2&es0=S&es1=S&ms=S (accessed 1 May 2015).

130 Sargiacomo and others (n 119).

131 Constitutional Law no. 3 18.10.2001 (n 60).

assent of central government regional representatives.[132] The second constitutional reform introduced fiscal federalism (constitutional law no. 3 2001). The new law, supported among others by the Lega Nord, radically altered the system of legislative competences of Italian regular regions.[133]

In the current system, the central state, as in other federal systems considered in this book, has a defined list of exclusive legislative competences, and the regions have all the remaining heads of power.[134] Furthermore, the newly inserted comma 3 of article 117 of the constitution lists 23 concurring central state–regional competences. These competences could also be allocated to a region. Each region, in relation to its distinctive set of legislative competences, must have fiscal autonomy.[135] In other words, the regions can collect a share of the territorial fiscal resources necessary for 'unloading' the legislative and administrative policies set in their own regional statute.[136] Until 2014, each region had the opportunity to set its own budgetary criteria. The loophole which allowed regions to validate their own yearly financial plans and with it, to hide corruption,[137] was eventually covered by the Constitutional Court.[138]

Thus, constitutional law no. 1 (1999) and constitutional law no. 3 (2001) had a combined effect. Any of the ordinary regions can change their own legislative prerogatives that are not listed in article 117, and once that has been done, the same region can also collect fiscal resources to support its new heads of power. This is a radical level of flexibility for a former unitary/regional system of governance.

It is reasonable to suggest that a range of new territorial administrative and legislative arrangements should have increased the competition between the regions in providing services. That was not the case. Antonini, for instance, suggests that the anxiety around delivering rapid reform by a government that had collapsing parliamentary support was one of the main reasons for the uncompleted and wicked ('scellerata' is

---

132 Constitution of the Italian Republic (n 1).

133 Antonini (n 2).

134 Constitutional Law no. 3 18.10.2001 (n 60) Article 3; Constitution of the Italian Republic (n 1) Article 117 [3–4].

135 Constitutional Law no. 3 18.10.2001 (n 60) Article 5; Constitution of the Italian Republic (n 1) Article 119.

136 Constitutional Law no. 3 18.10.2001 (n 60) Article 5; Constitution of the Italian Republic (n 1) Article 119.

137 Sargiacomo and others (n 119) 94.

138 *Decision no. 29 2014* (n 18).

the term used) constitutional reform.[139] Scellerata/o: 'Act, thought, behavior, which comes from [an] evil heart or which [has] a criminal end'.[140] This is a rare stance from a leading Italian constitutional academic and one of the leading government advisers on federalism. However, there are sufficient indications in the text of the reform that unionist political parties approved it with the intention of reducing the impetus of regionalist movements such as the Lega Nord and, perhaps more importantly, of enhancing their ability to collect public resources for their regional clientele networks.[141] For instance, in the 1980s, the construction of the motorway between Salerno and Reggio Calabria was the catalyst for the development of a local organized crime syndicate called 'ndrangheta' in the areas surrounding Naples.[142] In the past three decades, the ndrangheta has developed into the largest criminal syndicate in Italy and has been held accountable for thousands of homicides.[143]

In the five-year period that followed the constitutional law no. 3 reforms, the number of investigations into corruption declined, by way of comparison with the preceding five years, by 90 per cent.[144] This might induce a perception that corruption was in decline, but studies suggest that a process of decentration facilitated the hiding of an increased level of corruption.

In response to 'corruption in government' as a problem, government officials appear to have begun a deterritorialization that is effectively a reterritorialization. Politicians, anxious about public opinion and eager to appear active on the anticorruption front, created new authorities and instruments designed to minimize corruption. However, at the same time, they neutered any supporting infrastructure that would have made it possible to effectively investigate and prosecute corrupt politicians.[145]

---

139 Antonini (n 2) 12, 165, 2779.

140 Antonin considers the wording of article 117 'scellerato' which literally translated means 'wicked'. Antonini (n 2) 165. The Italian definition from a dictionary adds a criminal qualification: 'Act, thought, behavior, which comes from evil heart or which has a criminal end'. 'Scellerato'(n 17).

141 Sargiacomo and others (n 119).

142 Fukuyama (n 38) 90; Ginsborg (n 118) 5–6.

143 Direzione Nazional Antimafia, 'Relazione Annuale Sulle Attività Svolte Dal Procuratore Nazionale Antimafia e Dalla Direzione Nazionale Antimafia Nonché Sulle Dinamiche e Strategie Della Criminalità Organizzata Di Tipo Mafioso Nel Periodo 1° Luglio 2013–30 Giugno 2014' 12 http://www.stampoantimafioso.it/wp-content/uploads/2015/05/Relazione%20DNA%202013-2014.pdf (accessed 17 June 2015); Di Martino, Felice and Vasta (n 14).

144 Sargiacomo and others (n 119) 93.

145 Sargiacomo and others (n 119) 94.

The two constitutional reforms allocate resources to regional institutions which, in turn, pass legislation that can spare large sections of the regional budget from external, independent financial reviews, thus seriously impacting on the possibility of ever flagging up irregularities (and corruption).[146]

Consequently, the reform of the Italian constitution, indirectly promoted by the Lega Nord, failed. It did not increase the legislative power of the North nor the openness of the civil sector that would have satisfied the Lega Nord's clientele.[147] The reform had the opposite effect. It favoured the inefficient civil sector in the South and penalized it in the efficient North.[148]

Lega Nord regional governments, such as the one in Veneto, accepted the limitations of constitutional law no. 3 and focused on increasing their regional political powers.[149] For instance, in 2017, and after a consultative referendum in Veneto and Lombardy, the regional governments commenced a process of negotiation aimed at transferring the legislative competences shared with the central state to their respective regions.[150] The official process commenced with the approval of the regional statute that set out the conditions of the referendum.[151] The constitutional soundness of the Venetian proposal was also tested by the Constitutional Court.[152] Decision no. 118 purged, for instance, the regional law of several technical mistakes.[153] The Constitutional Court repealed, for instance, commas of the regional law in which Veneto tried to force the terms of the forthcoming negotiation.[154] The Court also considered

---

146 *Decision no. 39 2014* (n 18).

147 Legislative proposal, pursuant to Section 2 [2] of the Regional Law of the 19th June 2014, no. 15: 'Modalities and Contents for the Recognition for the Increase of Specific Forms of Autonomy for the Veneto Region, pursuant to the third paragraph of Article 116 of the Constitution' (n 113).

148 Ibid; Luca Antonini, *Federalismo all'italiana* (Marsilio 2013).

149 Legislative proposal, pursuant to Section 2 [2] of the Regional Law of the 19th June 2014, no. 15: 'Modalities and Contents for the Recognition for the Increase of Specific Forms of Autonomy for the Veneto Region, pursuant to the third paragraph of Article 116 of the Constitution' (n 113).

150 Ibid; Lillo Montalto Monella, 'Monitoraggio Autonomia – Lombardia e Veneto, Cosa Succede Dopo Il Voto' (*euronews*, 23 November 2017) http://it.euronews.com/2017/11/23/monitoraggio-autonomia-lombardia-e-veneto-cosa-succede-dopo-il-referendum (accessed 14 December 2017).

151 Regional Law no. 15 19.06.2014.

152 *Decision no. 118 2015.*

153 Ibid paras 1.1–2, 7, 8.6–8.7.

154 Ibid.

unconstitutional the suggestion that a negotiation based on article 116 could change the status of the region form normal to a special autonomous region such as South Tyrol.[155] These qualifications helped to maintain the appearance of legitimacy, by way of comparison with the events that unfolded during the 2017 Catalonian referendum, of the 2017 Venetian referendum.[156] It is, however, clear that the aim of the 2017 referendum was not to pursue the protection of an identity group, rather, it was an attempt to collect and retain public resources.

DRIVER OF CHANGE: IDENTITY-BASED CONSTITUTIONAL CLAIMS IN A PATRIMONIAL SYSTEM

It could be argued that, in theory, Italy had an ideal constitutional framework for the recognition of identity-based constitutional demands. Title V of the Italian constitution appears to have the advantages of parliamentarism that foster ad hoc systems of governance such as the one in Britain and New Zealand, and the benefits of an entrenched federal system that ensures equanimity and protects rights.[157] As in the Westminster Model, the Italian constitution allows minority groups that represent a majority in a limited geographical area to engage the central institutions and, if arguments are perceived to be of merit, to obtain the transfer of the political power needed to protect and promote cultural diversity.[158] In Italy, the possibility of altering the system of territorial governance is, in theory, available to all identity groups that manage to channel their demands through a political party, yet this institutional structure is

---

[155] Ibid paras 1.2, 8.

[156] Legislative proposal, pursuant to Section 2 [2] of the Regional Law of the 19th June 2014, no. 15: 'Modalities and Contents for the Recognition for the Increase of Specific Forms of Autonomy for the Veneto Region, pursuant to the third paragraph of Article 116 of the Constitution' (n 113).

[157] Vernon Bogdanor, *Devolution in the United Kingdom* (updated and reissued, Oxford University Press 2001); Dominic O'Sullivan, 'Needs, Rights and "One Law for All": Contemporary Debates in New Zealand Maori Politics' (2008) 41 Canadian Journal of Political Science/Revue canadienne de science politique 973; John Borrows, *Recovering Canada: The Resurgence of Indigenous Law* (University of Toronto Press 2002).

[158] Great Britain: Parliament: House of Commons: Scottish Affairs Committee, *The Sewel Convention: The Westminster Perspective; Fourth Report of Session 2005–06; Report, Together with Formal Minutes, Oral and Written Evidence* (The Stationery Office 2006).

normally used to funnel resources (for example, public-sector jobs) towards a clientele network that supports local politicians.

For instance, in Sicily, where the patrimonial political system has been particularly efficient in funnelling national resources into a network of political supporters, there are 13 230 regional employees for 5 million inhabitants at a cost of 1.7 billion Euros.[159] The rest of the Italian regions (that provide similar and, in most cases, better services to 55 million inhabitants) do so with 12 566 employees and at a lesser cost.[160] It is reasonable to argue that Italian politics, notwithstanding the noble aspirations of its constitutional document, continues to function as a patrimonial state.

More specifically, Italian politics shows signs of the isomorphic mimicry of a neo-patrimonial system.[161] In a neo-patrimonial system, politicians might refer to general principles of good government such as the endorsement of the freedom of enterprise or the pursuit of the cost-effective delivery of key public services, but in practice, these aspirations are formally reproduced, that is, by mimicking statutory and regulatory provisions, whilst the majority of the population expects that politicians and civil servants will use their prerogative for personal benefits and for the benefit of their respective clientele.[162] The political ventures of a media magnate called Silvio Berlusconi, who used politics to delay criminal charges and to promote his business interests, are often used as an example of the hindering effects of neo-patrimonialism in the Italian political system.[163] Berlusconi's flamboyant stewardship of the Italian government is, as Fukuyama points out, only a manifestation of Italian patrimonialism.[164]

The practice of clientelism, which originated in rural societies, included an informal vertical power relation between the power holder (for example, the patron/landowner) and many inferiors (for example, seasonal workers). However, the new Italian clientelism is horizontal and

---

[159] Antonini (n 2) 2680.

[160] Ibid.

[161] Yves-Andre Faure, 'Jeitinho and Other Related Phenomena in Contemporary Brazil' in Daniel Bach and Mamoudou Gazibo (eds), *Neopatrimonialism in Africa and Beyond* (Routledge 2013) 5, 198. The distinction between patrimonial and neo-patrimonial is also given in Fukuyama (n 38) 4.

[162] Faure (n 161) 5, 198; Vito Breda, 'Constitutional Patriotism' in Mortimer Sellers and Stephan Kirste (eds), *Encyclopedia of the Philosophy of Law and Social Philosophy* (Springer Netherlands 2017).

[163] Fukuyama (n 38) 98; Breda (n 43).

[164] Fukuyama (n 38) 100.

might include a nationwide network of individuals who exchange tangible favours such as jobs, public contracts and political votes at the national level.[165]

The patronage system invests in all areas of the public sector. For instance, from a qualitative analysis of Italian academia, Morano-Foadi provides a pungent description of the Italian job market for academics:

> Almost all the scientists interviewed referred to an unofficial, internal practice indicated as a 'law' that favours a less competent person over someone better qualified merely because the former has been working in the same group for a long period of time. This 'law', described as a feudal-like practice, requires the researcher to be present at all times, obey orders given by a powerful professor and then wait for a proper employment opportunity to come.[166]

It is also improbable that state policies that seek to reform such a practice might have the effect of diminishing its pervasiveness. Studies on this type of relationship network indicate that perfunctory reforms might be ineffective or might even work against the desired outcome.[167]

One of the reasons in support of the resilience of Italian patrimonialism is its ability to foster a stable system of relationships that reacts against reforms.[168] The large geographical variations of the effect of patrimonialism in Italy are well documented.[169] Sicily, the Neapolitan region and Puglia are also linked to rackets that historically provided services such as security, which are normally associated with the state.[170] The economic implications of the competition between the state and organized crime in a patrimonial system do not need to be explored in this book, but their perceived effect on the overall performance of the

---

165 Mario Caciagli, 'The Long Life of Clientelism in Southern Italy' in Junichi Kawata (ed), *Comparing Political Corruption and Clientelism* (Ashgate 2006) 159.

166 Morano-Foadi (n 45); Scuola (n 46); 'Firenze, Concorsi Truccati: "E" Il Vile Commercio Dei Posti' (n 46).

167 Caciagli (n 165); Bauman (n 53).

168 Di Martino, Felice and Vasta (n 14); Felice (n 42).

169 Jane Schneider (ed), *Italy's 'Southern Question': Orientalism in One Country* (Berg 3PL 1998).

170 Annelise Anderson, 'Organised Crime, Mafia and Governments' in Sam Peltzman and Gianluca Fiorentini (eds), *The Economics of Organised Crime* (Cambridge University Press 1997).

Italian public helped to promote the development of identity-based constitutional demands in the Northern regions.[171]

The resilience of patrimonialism in modern societies, which Fukuyama associated with Italian and Greek politics, has been a past historical feature of both the USA and of the UK.[172] What is distinctive of Italy is, perhaps, that patrimonialism and, as a corollary, the Italian public sector, were not reformed in ways that are analogous to the UK political system between 1854 and 1871.[173] The American system was reformed in 1883.[174] The modernization of the British political system, for instance, which followed the 1854 Northcote–Trevelyan report, was prompted by the middle classes and elites who had grown impatient with the process that allocated public resources to nobles.[175]

In the Italian political system, there are strong indications that the middle classes in the industrialized North might have an interest in having similar reforms, yet the Lega Nord's contribution has been more symbolic than substantial.[176] Reforms such as the one in constitutional law no. 3 had, for instance, the effect of entrenching patrimonialism even further within the political system.[177] This is not an unexpected response. The initial hope that a constitutional reform of the system of governance could channel the aspirations of a meritocracy and the efficiency of the Italian legal system were misplaced. The Lega Nord has brought a new narrative to Italian politics, but its claims of reforming Italian politics have led to a simulated legalism.

CONCLUSION

In this chapter, I sketched the process of the constitutional recognition of identity-based constitutional claims in Italy. The Italian system of governance is highly articulate and it mirrors a complex multinational society. There are 12 officially recognized national minorities (the

---

[171] Gianluca Fiorentini and Sam Peltzman, *The Economics of Organised Crime* (Cambridge University Press 1997); Di Martino, Felice and Vasta (n 14) 8–13; Felice (n 42).

[172] Fukuyama (n 37) 100.

[173] Oxford University Act 1854 (c 81); Cambridge University Act 1856 (c 88); Universities Tests Act 1871 (c 26).

[174] Pendleton Civil Service Reform Act 1883 (c 27).

[175] Stafford Northcote and Charles E Trevelyan, 'The Northcote–Trevelyan Report'. Fukuyama (n 37) 129.

[176] Cento Bull (n 16).

[177] Anderson (n 170); Caciagli (n 165); Sargiacomo and others (n 119).

Friulian, the German, the Ladin, the Sardinian, the French, the Occitan, the Franco-Provençal, the Arberesh, the Slovenian, the Croatian, the Catalan and the Greek). The chapter focused on the process of recognition of such a diverse society by two political parties: the SVP in South Tyrol and the Lega Nord in northern Italy. Notwithstanding the allegation of a possible dark legacy, the SVP managed to lead a process of recognition and accommodation of German, Ladin and Italian identities.[178] The current setting of this ongoing process of accommodation is a mindbogglingly complex system of territorial governance. Ad hoc parliamentary institutions such as the South Tyrol–Italian government Standing Committee dynamically ensure that central state and regional policies do not hinder the development of regional identities. The result of the relentless bargaining process is a minutely defined system of territorial governance. A system for the accommodation of identity claims that is aptly referred to as 'tolerance through law'. South Tyrol communities economically and socially thrived, whilst experiencing, by way of comparison with most of the identity groups considered in this book, very limited constitutional litigation.[179] The South Tyrol model cannot easily be replicated, but it gives an indication that negotiations and rules do help with the process of the constitutional integration of very different identity groups.[180]

This conclusion, albeit for very different reasons, cannot be drawn in relation to the Lega Nord and its constitutional claims. The Lega Nord carries the votes and the perceptions of many Northern Italian residents who consider the South of Italy corrupt, violent and economically depressed.[181] The Lega Nord Party, as part of a coalition partner, was in government for most of the past two decades and had the specific aim of promoting the identity of the Northern regions. However, it promoted policies that had little to do with the aim of increasing the efficiency of the civil sector.[182] Constitutional law no. 3 2001, which introduced fiscal federalism in Italy, was indirectly promoted by the Lega Nord. It could be described, perhaps, as a constitutional reform that reacted to (rather than engaged with) the increasing secessionist claims. Anyway, in the new federal system of governance, regions do have all the legislative competences and financial prerogatives which have not explicitly been

---

178 Grote (n 27).
179 Palermo (n 104).
180 Wolff (n 108).
181 Di Martino, Felice and Vasta (n 14).
182 Fukuyama (n 37).

allocated to the central state.[183] The reform had limited success. The combined effects of allocating resources on precarious assumptions (for example, historical expenditures) with the possibility of increasing the yearly expenditure by approving unchecked regional budgets has allowed regional politicians to consolidate the patrimonial system and has helped in bringing Italy to the very edge of bankruptcy. Patrimonialism, in the South of Italy, remains widely used as a political practice and politicians are expected to provide resources to their clientele.[184]

One of the positive aspects of the constitutional law no. 3 reform is the introduction of the central government–regional negotiation process. Regions can negotiate with the government over the allocation of the central state's concurrent legislative competences and, if an agreement is found, they can obtain the fiscal allocation related to the new heads of power. The advantage of the process is increased dynamic control over how a territory is managed. Central and regional institutions negotiate bespoke institutional arrangements with the aim of increasing the connection between regional and central institutions and their citizens. Unfortunately, this process is set up in, and perhaps for, the benefit of a patrimonial political system where the commonwealth of a political clientele only occasionally overlaps with national or regional interests.

---

[183] Constitution of the Italian Republic (n 1) Article 117.
[184] Di Martino, Felice and Vasta (n 14); Fukuyama (n 37) 100.

5. Canada: a multinational constitution and the obligation to negotiate

INTRODUCTION: A DIVERSIFIED SOCIETY AND ITS CONSTITUTION

The Canadian federation includes 10 provinces and three territories: the Northwest Territories, Nunavut and Yukon.[1] Recently, Peter Oliver, in his reflection on 150 years of the Canadian federation, noted that 'Canada was formed as a federation 150 years ago because no other model would have been acceptable to French Canadians, a minority in British North America but a majority in what was to become Quebec'.[2] Canada does not have a codified constitution and the British North America Act 1867 (UK) is historically considered the starting point of the modern Canadian federation.[3] In the following section, I will explain the effect of three drivers of change (Quebec liberal nationalism, the incremental jurisprudence of the Supreme Court and the escalating requirement of the amendment process) on Canadian constitutional negotiations, but a series of elements of these analyses should be engaged as part of a preliminary debate.

Firstly, the Canada Act 1982 (UK) repatriated the Canadian constitution. It is an ordinary British statute that had the effect of rescinding the

---

[1] British North America Act 1867 (C3) part II, V–IX, XI. Peter Oliver, Patrick Macklem and Nathalie Des Rosiers, *The Oxford Handbook of the Canadian Constitution* (Oxford University Press 2017) op IV; Peter W Hogg, *Constitutional Law of Canada* (Carswell 2009) pt II; Peter W Hogg, 'Canada: From Privy Council to Supreme Court' in Jeffrey Goldsworthy (ed), *Interpreting Constitutions: A Comparative Study* (Oxford University Press 2007) 55.

[2] 'Peter Oliver: Canada @ 150' https://ukconstitutionallaw.org/2017/11/02/peter-oliver-canada-150/ (accessed 2 November 2017).

[3] British North America Act 1867 (n 1); Alain-G Gagnon and Xavier Dionne, 'Historiographies et Fédéralisme Au Canada' [2009] Revista d'estudis autonòmics i federals 10, 12; Alain-G Gagnon, 'Québec-Canada's Constitutional Dossier', *Quebec* (University of Toronto Press 2004) 127–128, http://www.jstor.org/stable/10.3138/j.ctt2tv5rx.10.

authority of the UK parliament over Canada. The (Canadian) Constitution Act 1982, which is schedule B to the Canada Act 1982 (UK), 1982, c 11, organized the textual material that is the bulk of the current Canadian constitution.[4] In this chapter, the Constitution Act 1982, schedule B to the Canada Act 1982 (UK), 1982, c 11, will be referred to as the Constitution Act 1982.[5] The organization of the legal material includes implicit principles (for example, federalism) and treaties with Aboriginal Peoples that have been constitutionalized by section 35 of the Constitution Act 1982. The Constitution Act 1982 recognizes its constituency as a multinational polity composed of the 'Aboriginal Peoples of Canada',[6] and albeit indirectly, of French-speaking minorities.[7]

Secondly, the province of Quebec has a distinctive and problematic historical status within the Canadian federation. The Treaty of Paris 1763 transferred New France to the British Crown.[8] In the areas that were formally controlled by the Imperial House of France, a combination of English common law and pre-codification French civil law was, with an

---

[4] The Constitution Act 1982. The Constitution Act 1982 is the Schedule B of the Canada Act 1982 (UK). The Constitution of Canada includes: the Canada Act 1982, a list of 30 acts and orders in the schedule of the Constitution Act 1982, and the future amendments. Hogg, *Constitutional Law of Canada* (n 1) 7.

[5] The Constitution Act 1982 (n 4) Sections 38–42; Stephen Tierney, 'Popular Constitutional Amendment: Referendums and Constitutional Change in Canada and the United Kingdom' (2015) 41 Queen's Law Journal 41, 42; Richard Albert, 'The Theory and Doctrine of Unconstitutional Constitutional Amendment in Canada' (2015) 41 Queen's Law Journal 176.

[6] Hogg, *Constitutional Law of Canada* (n 1) pt I; The Constitution Act, 1982, being Schedule B to the Canada Act 1982 (UK), 1982, c 11 Official Languages: 16–23, Aboriginal Peoples of Canada, 35, 35.1. Sharon Mascher and Simon Young, 'Rights-Based "Recognition": The Canadian Experience' in Simon Young, Jennifer Nielsen and Jeremy Patrick (eds), *Constitutional Recognition of First Peoples in Australia: Theories and Comparative Perspectives* (Federation Press 2016); James Tully, 'Introduction' in James Tully and Alain Gagnon (eds), *Multinational Democracies* (Cambridge University Press 2001) 6, 14; Michael Keating, 'So Many Nations, so Few States: Territory and Nationalism in the Global Era' in James Tully and Alain Gagnon (eds), *Multinational Democracies* (Cambridge University Press 2001); Vito Breda, 'A European Constitution in a Multinational Europe or a Multinational Constitution for Europe?' (2006) 12 European Law Journal 330; James Tully, *Strange Multiplicity: Constitutionalism in an Age of Diversity* (Cambridge University Press 1995) 15–16, 57, 63.

[7] The Constitution Act 1982 (n 4).

[8] King of Great Britain and King of France, 'The Definitive Treaty of Peace and Friendship between His Britannick Majesty, the Most Christian King, and the King of Spain (The Treaty of Paris)'.

exclusion owing to a brief hiatus, applied.[9] The Constitution Act 1791 institutionally separated the French and predominantly English-speaking communities of Quebec.[10] The Act of Union 1840, instead, unified the provinces in the province of Canada, yet English and French private law continued to have different applications along the borders set by the two linguistic communities.[11] The British North American Act 1867 established the dominion of Canada by uniting the geographical areas covered by the province of Canada with Nova Scotia and New Brunswick, but Quebec and Ontario were divided again.[12]

Later in this chapter, I will discuss the effect of Quebec nationalism in the process of the accommodation of regionalist demands, but by way of an introduction, it is important to note that, in the middle of the twentieth century, during a transformative period for the Quebec national identity which is normally called the Quiet Revolution, Quebec nationalism started a process of debunking sectarian narratives that normally associated French speakers with conservative Catholicism.[13] Furthermore, from 1968, the Partí Québécois has taken a leading, yet not exclusive, role as being representative of Québécois identity.[14]

The change in direction of Quebec nationalism during the Quiet Revolution supported a recasting of the partnership between Quebec and federal institutions.[15] In the 1980s, a consultative referendum which aimed, among other aspects, at assessing the support of Quebec residents to consider Quebec as a nation, and negotiating the repartition of legislative and fiscal competences between the central government and

---

[9] The Quebec Act 1774 14 Geo III c 83 section 8.

[10] Constitutional Act 1791 131 Geo 3 c 31 section II.

[11] Hogg, *Constitutional Law of Canada* (n 1) 42; Act of Union 1840 (officially British North America Act 1840) 3 & 4 Victoria, c 35 2017.

[12] The Constitution Act, 1867, 30 & 31 Vict, c 3 (renamed from the British North America Act 1867 by the Constitution Act 1982 section 53 (2)).

[13] Garth Stevenson, *Parallel Paths: The Development of Nationalism in Ireland and Quebec* (McGill-Queen's University Press 2006) 14, 258, 267; Michael Keating, 'Stateless Nation-Building: Quebec, Catalonia and Scotland in the Changing State System' (1997) 3 Nations and Nationalism 689, 695, 697–698. Gagnon (n 3) 131–138.

[14] Bloc Québécois and the Quebec Liberal Party also had, and still have, significant roles in promoting Quebec national identity. Stevenson (n 13) 14; Keating (n 13) 695, 697–698.

[15] Stevenson (n 13) 3101–307; Government of Quebec, 'Québec-Canada: A New Deal. The Québec Government Proposal for a New Partnership Between Equals: Sovereignty-Association – Independence of Québec'.

Quebec, failed to collect enough votes.[16] The federal government commenced a series of constitutional reforms that resulted in the aforementioned Constitution Act 1982. The act recognized the statutory material which is currently considered part of the Canadian federal constitution, yet, quite remarkably, did not recognize Quebec either as a nation or as a distinctive society.[17]

The 1987 Meech Lake Accord and the 1992 Charlottetown Accord which tried, among other aims, to respond positively to the demands for recognition of the Quebec government, could not reach the level of political support necessary for a constitutional amendment.[18] The Meech Lake Accord failed to obtain the support in all of the provincial assemblies.[19] The Charlottetown Accord was instead rejected by a consultative national referendum.[20] The repeated failures to amend the constitution in a way that recognized Quebec's distinctive society were the proxy for increased frustration among Quebec residents and the Indigenous Peoples of Canada.[21]

---

[16] 'The referendum question is available in several outlets: the Government of Quebec has made public its proposal to negotiate a new agreement with the rest of Canada, based on the *equality of nations*; this agreement would enable Quebec to acquire the exclusive power to make its laws, levy its taxes and establish relations abroad – in other words, sovereignty – and at the same time to maintain with Canada an economic association including a common currency; any change in political status resulting from these negotiations will only be implemented with popular approval through another referendum; on these terms, do you give the Government of Quebec the mandate to negotiate the proposed agreement between Quebec and Canada?' [My emphasis.] Stephen Tierney, *Constitutional Referendums: The Theory and Practice of Republican Deliberation* (Oxford University Press 2012) 268.

[17] Gagnon (n 3) 138–139. The political recognition arrived later in 2006; HC Deb 27 November 2006 vol 141, col 1245–1250.

[18] 'Constitutional Accord (Meech Lake Accord)'; Mary Dawson, 'From the Backroom to the Front Line: Making Constitutional History or Encounters with the Constitution: Patriation, Meech Lake, and Charlottetown' (2012) 57 McGill Law Journal/Revue de droit de McGill 955; 'Consensus Report on the Constitution: Final Text (Charlottetown Accord)'; Hogg, *Constitutional Law of Canada* (n 1)74, 674. Mascher and Young (n 6) 185.

[19] Manitoba and New Brunswick did not approve the accord. Dawson (n 18) 979.

[20] Referendum Act, SC 1992, c 30; Dawson (n 18) 996; Hogg, *Constitutional Law of Canada* (n 1) 76.

[21] Dawson (n 18) 998; Hogg, *Constitutional Law of Canada* (n 1) 674; Mascher and Young (n 6) 185; Keating (n 13) 698.

One of the political responses to the two consecutive failed accords was the 1995 Quebec government-sponsored referendum over Quebec's secession.[22] The referendum result favoured those who denied secession, but a legal challenge to the validity of the referendum reached the Supreme Court.[23] The *Reference Re Secession* case is one of the best-known cases in the area of comparative public law and its implications are analysed in multiple outlets, but in short, the Supreme Court decided that Quebec's plan for unilateral secession was unconstitutional.[24] However, in an articulated obiter, it was stated that if a 'clear majority' of the Quebec population were to favour independence from Canada, the federal government would have an 'obligation to negotiate' secession in 'good faith' with Quebec.[25] The effects of the decision, it is reasonable to suggest, have influenced secessionist movements in Spain and in Great Britain.[26] The *Reference Re Secession* was followed by the legislative activity of the Canadian parliament and the Quebec Assembly,

---

22 Prime Minister of Quebec, Draft Bill on the Sovereignty of Quebec 1995.

23 *Reference Re Secession of Quebec [1998] 2 SCR 217* [1998] 217.

24 Susanna Mancini, 'Secession and Self-Determination' in Michel Rosenfeld and András Sajó (eds), *The Oxford Handbook of Comparative Constitutional Law* (Oxford University Press 2012) 497.

25 *Reference Re Secession of Quebec [1998] 2 SCR 217* (n 23) para 98, 130.

26 *Asunto: 5830-2014*; Paul Williams and others, 'The Legitimacy of Catalonia's Exercise of Its Right to Decide' (2017); W J Norman, *Negotiating Nationalism: Nation-Building, Federalism, and Secession in the Multinational State* (Oxford University Press 2006); David Haljan, *Constitutionalising Secession* (Hart 2013); Germa Bel, *Disdain, Distrust and Dissolution: The Surge of Support for Independence in Catalonia* (Sussex Academic Press 2015); Stephen Tierney, 'Reclaiming Politics: Popular Democracy in Britain after the Scottish Referendum' (2015) 86 Political Quarterly 226; Tierney (n 5); Javier García Oliva, 'Javier Garcia Oliva: The Referendum on Catalonian Independence: The Position of the Spanish Authorities' https://ukconstitutionallaw.org/2017/10/03/javier-garcia-oliva-the-referendum-on-catalonian-independence-the-position-of-the-spanish-authorities/ (accessed 4 January 2018); Elisenda Casanas Adam, 'The Referendum on Catalonian Independence: The Position of the Catalan Authorities' https://ukconstitutionallaw.org/2017/10/03/elisenda-casanas-adam-the-referendum-on-catalonian-independence-the-position-of-the-catalan-authorities/ (accessed 4 January 2018); Gavin W Anderson and others, 'Gavin Anderson et al: The Independence Referendum, Legality and the Contested Constitution: Widening the Debate' http://ukconstitutionallaw.org/2012/01/31/gavin-anderson-et-al-the-independence-referendum-legality-and-the-contested-constitution-widening-the-debate/ (accessed 24 November 2012).

respectively,[27] yet the idea that sub-state and central institutions share an obligation to negotiate elements of their partnership has inspired other constitutional systems considered in this book.[28]

Thirdly, the Indigenous Peoples of Canada are recognized by treaties and by imperial declarations. King George III's Royal Proclamation granted, for instance, protection of Indian land ownership.[29] The Aboriginal Peoples of Canada are also explicitly recognized in the Constitution Act 1982.[30] However, the 1763 Royal Proclamation, continuing the Cristoforo Colombo misnomer, recognized Canadian Indians, and the Constitution Act 1867 allocates legislative competences over Indians and over land allocated to Indian reserves to federal institutions.[31] The

---

27 An Act to Give Effect to the Requirement for Clarity as Set out in the Opinion of the Supreme Court of Canada in the Quebec Secession Reference, SC 2000, c 26 2000; An Act Respecting the Exercise of the Fundamental Rights and Prerogatives of the Québec People and the Québec State, CQLR c E-20.2 2001.

28 Vernon Bogdanor, *Devolution in the United Kingdom* (Oxford University Press 1999); Constitution of the Italian Republic 1948 section 116 (3); Luca Antonini, *Federalismo all'italiana* (Marsilio 2013); Vito Breda, 'Indigenous Australians and the Constitutional Reform: Learning from a Very British Experience' in Simon Young, Jennifer Nielsen and Jeremy Patrick (eds), *Constitutional Recognition of First Peoples in Australia: Theories and Comparative Perspectives* (Federation Press 2016).

29 King George III, 'Royal Proclamation, 1763 (UK), No. 1', para 11.

30 '35(1) The existing aboriginal and treaty rights of the aboriginal peoples of Canada are hereby recognized and affirmed.

(2) In this Act, "aboriginal peoples of Canada" includes the Indian, Inuit and Métis peoples of Canada.

(3) For greater certainty, in subsection (1) "treaty rights" includes rights that now exist by way of land claims agreements or may be so acquired.

(4) Notwithstanding any other provision of this Act, the aboriginal and treaty rights referred to in subsection (1) are guaranteed equally to male and female persons.

35.1 The government of Canada and the provincial governments are committed to the principle that, before any amendment is made to Class 24 of section 91 of the "Constitution Act, 1867", to section 25 of this Act or to this Part,

(a) a constitutional conference that includes in its agenda an item relating to the proposed amendment, composed of the Prime Minister of Canada and the first ministers of the provinces, will be convened by the Prime Minister of Canada; and

(b) the Prime Minister of Canada will invite representatives of the aboriginal peoples of Canada to participate in the discussions on that item. The Constitution Act 1982 (n 4).'

31 King George III (n 29); British North America Act 1867 (n 1) Section 92.

recognition was a manifestation of sociological Darwinism and the policies of physical genocide were alternated by a series of treaties which had the effect of attempting cultural genocide.[32] The final report of the Truth and Reconciliation Commission of Canada describes the colonization process in a succinct narrative.

> In its dealing with Aboriginal people, Canada did all these things [attempting physical and cultural genocides]. Canada asserted control over Aboriginal land. In some locations, Canada negotiated Treaties with First Nations; in others, the land was simply occupied or seized. The negotiation of Treaties, while seemingly honourable and legal, was often marked by fraud and coercion, and Canada was, and remains, slow to implement their provisions and intent.[33]

However, in the past decades, an articulate and pragmatic process of reconciliation between 'white' Canada and the Indigenous Peoples of Canada has fostered new treaties and land settlements,[34] which aimed at

---

[32] 'In 1876, the Parliament of Canada facilitated the construction of the deep structure of racial hierarchy that rested on a belief in white racial superiority with the enactment of the Indian Act, 9 which deviated from imperial treaties with First Nations and Aboriginal legal traditions. The federal act defined "Indian" as not a "person"'. James Youngblood Henderson, 'Dialogical Governance: A Mechanism of Constitutional Governance' (2009) 72 Saskatchewan Law Review 29, 32; Glen Sean Coulthard, *Red Skin, White Masks: Rejecting the Colonial Politics of Recognition* (University of Minnesota Press 2014) 1–9. See also Jill St Germain, *Broken Treaties* (University of Nebraska Press 2009). More generally, Howard Zinn, *A People's History of the United States* (reissue edition, Harper 2017) Ch 1.

[33] [My emphasis.] Truth and Reconciliation Commission of Canada, *Honouring the Truth, Reconciling for the Future: Summary of the Final Report of the Truth and Reconciliation Commission of Canada.* (2015) 1. For a comparative historical analysis of the process and its reason see Henry Reynolds, *An Indelible Stain?: The Question of Genocide in Australia's History* (Penguin 2001); Nan Seuffert, *Jurisprudence of National Identity: Kaleidoscopes of Imperialism and Globalisation from Aotearoa New Zealand* (Ashgate 2006); Haunani-Kay Trask, *From a Native Daughter: Colonialism and Sovereignty in Hawaii* (revised edition, University of Hawai'i Press 1999); Patrick Vinton Kirch and Jean-Louis Rallu, *The Growth and Collapse of Pacific Island Societies: Archaeological and Demographic Perspectives* (University of Hawai'i Press 2007); A Dirk Moses, *Genocide and Settler Society: Frontier Violence and Stolen Indigenous Children in Australian History*, vol 6 (Berghahn Books 2004).

[34] For instance: Government of Canada; Indigenous and Northern Affairs Canada; Communications Branch, 'Statement of the Government of Canada on

protecting indigenous heritage and promoting an indigenous commonwealth within the Canadian federation.[35]

The rolling back of paternalism has been a gradual process and the Supreme Court of Canada has played a significant role in extending Aboriginal rights recognized in section 35, land entitlement and the related obligations of Canadian provincial and federal institutions.[36]

Indian Policy (The White Paper, 1969)' (2008) report, http://www.aadnc-aandc.gc.ca/eng/1100100010189/1100100010191 (accessed 13 October 2017); Canadian Parliament Special Committee on Indian Self-Goverment, 'Indian Self-Government of Canada, Report of the Special Committee on Indian Self-Government (The Penner Report)' http://www.metismuseum.ca/resource.php/148890 (accessed 8 October 2017); 'Statement of Apology to Former Students of Indian Residential Schools' (3 November 2008) http://www.aadnc-aandc.gc.ca/eng/1100100015644/1100100015649 (accessed 10 October 2017); Government of Canada; Indigenous and Northern Affairs Canada; Communications Branch, 'The Government of Canada's Approach to Implementation of the Inherent Right and the Negotiation of Aboriginal Self-Government' (3 November 2008) http://www.aadnc-aandc.gc.ca/eng/1100100031843/1100100031844 (accessed 11 October 2017); Ministry of Aboriginal Relations and Reconciliation, 'Reconciliation & Other Agreements – Province of British Columbia' http://www2.gov.bc.ca/gov/content/environment/natural-resource-stewardship/consulting-with-first-nations/first-nations-negotiations/reconciliation-other-agreements (accessed 13 October 2017); Truth and Reconciliation Commission of Canada (n 33).

[35] Government of Canada, 'First Ministers and National Aboriginal Leaders Strengthening Relationships and Closing the Gap Document (Kelowna Accord)'; Government of Canada, 'Sustaining Momentum: The Government of Canada's Fourth and Final Report in Response to the Kelowna Accord Implementation Act 2011–12'; Law Commission of Canada and British Columbia Treaty Commission (Canada) (eds), *Speaking Truth to Power: A Treaty Forum* (Law Commission of Canada; British Columbia Treaty Commission 2001); Coulthard (n 32); The Constitution Act 1982 (n 4) sections 35, 25.

[36] The research material on the role of the Supreme Court of Canada is extensive. For a general overview see Mascher and Young (n 6); Hogg, *Constitutional Law of Canada* (n 1) Ch 28; *Tsilhqot'in Nation v British Columbia* [2014] SCC 34986, 2 SCR 257; *Daniels v Canada (Indian Affairs and Northern Development)* [2016] SCC 35945, 1 SCR 99; *Haida Nation v British Columbia (Minister of Forests)* [2004] SCC 29419, 3 SCR 511; *St Catharines Milling and Lumber Co v R* (C); *Delgamuukw v British Columbia* [1997] C 23799, 3 SCR 1010; *R v Van der Peet* [1996] C 23803, 2 SCR 507; *R v Pamajewon* [1996] C 24596, 2 SCR 821; *R v Sparrow* [1990] C 20311, 1 SCR 1075; *Hamlet of Baker Lake v Canada (Indian Affairs and Northern Development)* (C); *Calder et al v Attorney-General of British Columbia* (SC); *Attorney General of Canada v Lavell* (C); *Kanatewat et al v James Bay Development Corp et al* (1973) 1 SCR 48 (C). Contra: Hogg, 'Canada: From Privy Council to Supreme Court' (n 1) 71.

Section 35 of the Constitution Act explicitly recognizes a right to self-government for Aboriginal Peoples.[37] This process included the aforementioned Meech Lake Accord in 1987 and the Charlottetown Accord in 1993 by the federal and provincial governments.[38] The accords intended to reform the Constitution Act 1982 in a way that recognized the Aboriginal Peoples of Canada and, as discussed earlier, Quebec's distinctive society.[39]

Fourthly, the development of the obligation on the regional and central institutions to negotiate amendments to the system of governance did not occur in a theoretical vacuum. In 1995, Will Kymlicka's 'Multicultural Citizenship' explained, in a persuasive narrative, the connection between communal minority rights and liberal democracy.[40] In the same year, James Tully published 'Strange Multiplicity: Constitutionalism in the Age of Diversity', which among other aspects, explains the dynamic nature of identity-based constitutional claims and the limits of current constitutional perceptions.[41] In 2001, Alain Gagnon and James Tully edited 'Multinational Democracies', which reported the recent transformation of identity politics and the implications for a constitutional multinationalism as a newly established theoretical stance.[42]

---

37 The Constitution Act 1982 (n 4) section 35 (1).

38 'Constitutional Accord (Meech Lake Accord)' (n 18); 'Consensus Report on the Constitution: Final Text (Charlottetown Accord)' (n 18).

39 'Constitutional Accord (Meech Lake Accord)' (n 18) section 2, 3. 101A (2): 101C (3): 16; 'Consensus Report on the Constitution: Final Text (Charlottetown Accord)' (n 18) section I, A (2–3), II A (9), B (20), C (22); Hogg, *Constitutional Law of Canada* (n 1) 73–78; 674; Mascher and Young (n 6) 185–188; Keating (n 13) 698.

40 Will Kymlicka, *Multicultural Citizenship: A Liberal Theory of Minority Rights* (Clarendon Press 1995) Ch 3.

41 Tully, *Strange Multiplicity: Constitutionalism in an Age of Diversity* (n 6).

42 Alain Gagnon and François Boucher, in Alain-G Gagnon and Brian Tanguay (eds), *Canadian Parties in Transition, Fourth Edition* (fourth edition, University of Toronto Press, Higher Education Division 2016); Alain-G Gagnon and James Tully (eds), *Multinational Democracies* (Cambridge University Press 2001). Gagnon is one of the most prolific and engaged observers of Canadian constitutionalism and much of this chapter is based on his observations: Alain-G Gagnon, 'Political Dynamics in Quebec: Charting Concepts and Imagining Political Avenues' in David R Cameron and Richard Albert (eds), *Canada in the World: Comparative Perspectives on the Canadian Constitution* (Cambridge University Press 2017); Xavier Dionne and Alain-G Gagnon, *L'évolution Des Relations Fédérales-Provinciales Au Canada*, ed. Alain-G Gagnon (Presses de l'Université du Québec 2014); Alain-G Gagnon and Brian Tanguay (eds), *Canadian Parties in Transition, Fourth Edition* (4th edition, University of

Fifthly, the Canadian Supreme Court never established the idea of dependent nations which is discussed in the US chapter, nor did it construct the principle of formal equality in a way that greatly reduces the recognition of distinctive minority rights.[43] In addition, Canadian federal and provincial institutions, by way of comparison with US institutions, continue to sign treaties with representatives of the Indigenous Peoples of Canada.[44]

DRIVER OF CHANGE: QUEBEC AND ITS LIBERAL NATIONALISM

The obligation to negotiate identity claims in good faith is one of the innovative principles developed by the Canadian Supreme Court and, in the next section, I will argue that such a development in the Canadian constitutional system has been part of a process of incremental jurisprudential recognition of identity-based claims promoted by, among others, the Indigenous Peoples of Canada. This section focuses, however, on the role of Quebec's nationalism and the political parties that, over the years, have sought recognition of the role of French-speaking communities in the Canadian constitutional system. In particular, it will be argued that, post the Quiet Revolution, Quebec's nationalism acknowledged the diversity of Quebec's society and of a distinctive balance between the protection of individual and community rights.

Toronto Press, Higher Education Division 2016); Alain-G Gagnon and José María Sauca, *Negotiating Diversity Identity, Pluralism and Democracy* (PIE Peter Lang 2014); Luc Turgeon and Alain-G Gagnon, 'The Representation of Ethnic and Linguistic Groups in the Federal Civil Service of Belgium and Canada' (2013) 56 Canadian Public Administration 565; Gagnon and Dionne (n 3); Gagnon, 'Québec-Canada's Constitutional Dossier' (n 3); Jocelyn Maclure, Alain-G Gagnon and McGill University (eds), *Repères En Mutation: Identité et Citoyenneté Dans Le Québec Contemporain* (Québec Amérique 2001).

43 Hope M Babcock, 'A Civic-Republican Vision of Domestic Dependent Nations in the Twenty-First Century: Tribal Sovereignty Re-Envisioned, Reinvigorated, and Re-Empowered' (2005) 2005 Utah Law Review 443; Frank Pommersheim, 'At the Crossroads: A New and Unfortunate Paradigm of Tribal Sovereignty' (2010) 55 South Dakota Law Review 48; David H Getches, 'Beyond Indian Law: The Rehnquist Court's Pursuit of States' Rights, Color-Blind Justice and Mainstream Values' (2001) 86 Minnesota Law Review 267.

44 Reconciliation (n 34); Albert (n 5) 158; Dawson (n 18); St Germain (n 32); John T Cross and Kristin M Lomond, 'The Civil Rights of the Aboriginal Peoples of the United States and Canada' (1993) 10 Arizona Journal of International and Comparative Law 253, 266.

As discussed in Chapter 1, regional and state nationalism have a qualifying role in the development of multinational constitutional systems.[45] Regional nationalism tends, for instance, to put forward claims that alter the allocation of resources and it is also often associated with the protection of sociological aspects that define a community such as a minority language or the use of national symbols on public buildings.[46] The Canadian constitutional system had, since its inception, recognized the existence of a dual identity – French and Anglo-Saxon – of its polity. However, two of the 'founding fathers' of the Canadian constitutional system, George-Étienne Cartier and John A. Macdonald, have been referred to as the starting points of two diverging historical interpretations of the British North America Act 1867.[47]

Macdonald favoured a unifying conception of the state and of the Canadian nation, whereas Cartier preferred a multinational association.[48] Whilst there is general agreement on some implicit effects of recognizing the French-speaking community (for example, the role of federalism as the chosen system of governance),[49] there is a persistent dual perception of the role that the British North America Act 1867 should have within the constitutional system.[50] Dionne and Gagnon argue, for instance, that the 1982 Charter of Rights created the conditions for the political use of constitutional principles that favoured those who supported the role of federal over provincial institutions in a way that is antithetical to Cartier's intention.[51] Individual rights allocated by the Charter of Rights displaced identity-based prerogatives such as the protection of minority languages

---

45 Robert Hazell, *Constitutional Futures Revisited: Britain's Constitution to 2020* (Palgrave Macmillan 2008); Dominique Arel, 'Political Stability in Multinational Democracies', in Alain Gagnon and James Tully (eds), *Multinational Democracies* (Cambridge University Press 2001).

46 John Hutchinson and Anthony D Smith, 'Introduction' in John Hutchinson and Anthony D Smith (eds), *Nationalism* (Oxford University Press 1994) 10; Anthony D Smith, 'The Origins of Nations' in John Hutchinson and Anthony D Smith (eds), *Nationalism* (Oxford University Press 1994) 154.

47 Gagnon and Dionne (n 3) 12.

48 Ibid 13; 37.; Hogg, *Constitutional Law of Canada* (n 1) 116.

49 'Peter Oliver: Canada @ 150' (n 2).

50 Jaime Lluch, *Visions of Sovereignty, Nationalism and Accommodation in Multinational Democracies* (University of Pennsylvania Press 2014) 67.

51 'Le discours des droits individuels s'est superposé aux droits collectifs et est venu légitimer l'intervention fédérale'. [The debate over individual rights is over imposed communal rights and imposed a federal intervention on areas which were considered covered by provincial competences.] Gagnon and Dionne (n 3) 35.

which were implicitly or explicitly allocated to Quebec by the British North American Act 1867.[52]

Whilst the Charter has reduced the potential extent of identity-based constitutional demands, the majority of Quebec nationalist demands are considered to be in tune with liberal values.[53] That is, the range of claims supported by political parties such as the Partí Québécois and the Bloc Québécois are normally considered within the range of political aspirations accepted in a society that cares for the protection of liberal rights and at the same time acknowledges cultural diversity.[54] Consequently, the current manifestation of Quebec might still show signs of associations with religious beliefs, but they are formulated, in the majority of instances, as a manifestation of distinctive cultural features such as the desire to use and protect French as an official language.[55]

What is distinctive of Quebec is the interplay between the representation of the (imagined ethnic) nation and Canadian public institutions that is currently anchored to administrative territorial borders.[56] As expected in most multinational constitutional systems, Quebec's nationalism seeks recognition in the activity of provincial institutions whereas the Anglo-Saxon Canadian identity appears to lean towards federal politics.[57] However, provincial institutions were not established with the intention of giving a voice to national minorities, nor do Quebec's politics appear to show strong indications of the consociative politics found, for instance, in Northern Ireland and South Tyrol.[58] Quebec's nationalism is, by way

---

[52] 'Le discours des droits individuels s'est superposé aux droits collectifs et est venu légitimer l'intervention fédérale'. [The debate over individual rights is over imposed communal rights and imposed a federal intervention on areas which were considered covered by provincial competences.] Ibid. The reference here is to *AG (Que) v Quebec Protestant School Boards* [1984] C 17821, 2 SCR 66.

[53] Stevenson (n 13) 269; Anthony D Smith, *Ethnicity and Nationalism* (Brill 1992) 60; Anthony D Smith, *Theories of Nationalism* (Duckworth 1971) 171; Smith (n 46) 154.

[54] Stevenson (n 13) 276.

[55] Ibid.

[56] Michael Keating, 'Par Delà La Souveraineté. La Démocratie Plurinationale Dans Un Monde Post-Souverain', in Jocelyn Maclure and Alain-G Gagnon (eds), *Repères en Mutation: Identité et Citoyenneté dans le Québec Contemporain* (Québec Amérique 2001) 72, 85.

[57] Stefan Wolff, 'The Institutional Structure of Regional Consociations in Brussels, Northern Ireland, and South Tyrol' (2004) 10 Nationalism and Ethnic Politics 387.

[58] Stevenson (n 13) 351, 360.

of comparison with other nationalist movements considered in this book, distinctively liberal.[59]

That is not to say that ethnic and sectarian narratives are not still part of the fabric of Quebec's nationalism, but these stances are supported by a minority.[60] It is, instead, the acceptance of the liberal virtues, combined with the multifarious nature of modern polities and a commitment to liberal ideals, that normally leads to Quebec's nationalism being compared with the Scottish nationalism of Neil MacCormick.[61] The recognition of cultural diversity also has the effect of distinguishing Quebec's nationalism from its ethnic and sectarian manifestations recorded in Northern Ireland and in the Balkan regions.[62]

For a long period, Quebec's nationalism might have followed a parallel path to Northern Irish nationalism,[63] but a series of political cycles in the 1960s and 1970s allowed the Quebec Liberal Party to implement modernizing economic and socio-political reforms. French became the language of the professional and cultural elites. It was the time of the Quiet Revolution, which commenced as a cultural movement a decade earlier with the development of French-speaking TV and radio broadcasts. The economic results of liberal policies were mixed but, on a general level, a new image and a new nationalist political party emerged

---

[59] Colin Williams, 'Recognition of National Justice for Quebec: A Canadian Conundrum' in Steve Fenton and Stephen May (eds), *Ethnonational Identities* (Palgrave Macmillan 2002) 25, 29; Lindsay Paterson, 'Sources of Support for the SNP' in Catherine Bromley and others (eds), *Has Devolution Delivered?* (Edinburgh University Press 2006); Bel (n 26); Marco Brunazzo and Mark Gilbert, 'Insurgents against Brussels: Euroscepticism and the Right-Wing Populist Turn of the Lega Nord since 2013' (2017) 22 Journal of Modern Italian Studies 624.

[60] Williams (n 59) 44. See, in general, Roger Gibbins and Guy Laforest (eds), *Beyond the Impasse: Towards Reconciliation* (McGill-Queen's University Press 1998). In particular, Will Kymlicka, 'Multinational Federalism in Canada; Rethinking the Partnership' in Roger Gibbins and Guy Laforest (eds), *Beyond the Impasse: Towards Reconciliation* (McGill-Queen's University Press 1998).

[61] Stevenson (n 13) 341; Neil MacCormick, *Questioning Sovereignty Law, State and Nation in the European Commonwealth* (Oxford University Press 1999); Keating (n 56).

[62] Stevenson (n 13) 284; Michael Ignatieff, *The Warrior's Honor: Ethnic War and the Modern Conscience* (Vintage 1999); Michael Ignatieff, *Blood & Belonging: Journeys into the New Nationalism* (Vintage 1994).

[63] Stevenson (n 13) Chs 8–9; Brendan O'Leary, 'Debating Consociational Politics: Normative and Explanatory Arguments' in Sidney John Roderick Noel (ed), *From Power Sharing to Democracy: Post-Conflict Institutions in Ethnically Divided Societies* (McGill-Queen's University Press); Wolff (n 57).

from the period of transformation.[64] In 1967, a group of liberals formed the Partí Québécois from a split branch of the Quebec Liberal Party.[65] The period of the Quiet Revolution also saw the progressive reduction in the role of the Catholic church and, albeit unrelatedly, the development and collapse of political violence.[66] Quebec's nationalism emerged from the Quiet Revolution as a new quasi-secular sociological phenomenon with liberal political aspirations that were, and still are, similar to other modern democracies' regionalist movements.[67]

All was not well, so to speak. Even during the period covered by the Quiet Revolution, one of the most contentious issues was the use of official languages. The federal government enacted, for instance, the Official Languages Act (1969), which allowed French speakers to obtain official documents in French and that established bilingual districts in administrative areas that had more than 10 per cent of the population as minority French or English speakers.[68] The Quebec government, perhaps as a response, passed its Official Language Act of 1974 (hereafter, Bill 101) and that had the consequence, among others, of preventing immigrants from accessing English-speaking schools.[69] The use of languages remains hotly debated in Canada, but it is the 1980 consultative referendum over the possibility of sovereignty association (between Quebec and the rest of Canada) that has become one of the most influential factors in the history of the interplay between federal Canada and Quebec.

The theoretical underpinning of the referendum, which saw the Quebec nationalists defeated, was prepared during 1970.[70] The referendum was intended to ask whether the majority of Quebec residents considered the sovereign association as the best form of political government for Quebec. However, the question was cumbersome and the result, as mentioned earlier, favoured the status quo. It could have been a storm in a tea cup. Another identity group had failed to convince the majority of a constituency that an identity is worth protecting, yet one of the tangential

64 Stevenson (n 13) 260–263.
65 Ibid 267.
66 Ibid 263–270.
67 Hutchinson and Smith (n 46) 5–9; Gagnon and Dionne (n 3) 18.
68 Official Languages Act (1969) 1970, R.S.C, Ch. 0–2 ss 9, 19–34.
69 Stevenson (n 13) 276.
70 Government of Quebec (n 15).

effects of the campaign was a perceived mandate on the Canadian government to reform the Canadian constitutional system.[71]

The Constitution Act 1982 was the final result of the process of systematization of the constitutional system promoted by the federal government of Pierre Trudeau, who perceived Quebec's nationalism as an idiosyncratic social aspect of Canadian society.[72] The political stance that abased Quebec nationalism is reflected in the text of the Constitution Act, which tilted the Canadian constitutional system towards a federal and homogenous conception of the Canadian polity which, albeit incidentally, weakened the idea of a multinational constitutional polity. The Quebec government, led by the Partí Québécois, tried to veto the application, but the Supreme Court explained that such a power was not inserted in the constitution.[73]

The application of the Constitution Act 1982 had almost immediate implications for Quebec.[74] In 1984, for instance, the Supreme Court interpreted the Charter of Rights in a way that restricted Quebec's legislative prerogative in selecting the type of language school for English-speaking children whose parents were immigrants.[75] The issue, among others, engaged by the Court, was related to section 71 and 73 of Bill 101 (as amended by the Language Act 1974) and their compatibility with section 23 of the Charter of Rights, which lists a series of minority language rights.[76] '[c]hildren of immigrants, even English-speaking immigrants from other parts of Canada or from foreign countries, are not to be admitted into English schools in Quebec'.[77] The Court acknowledged that Quebec was the only province in which the Charter of Rights was not in force,[78] yet declared the restriction on the prerogative to select

[71] Peter W Hogg, 'Canadian Constitutional Law: Presentation to the Annual Conference of International Association of Law Libraries' (2013) 41 International Journal of Legal Information 58, 74; Hogg, *Constitutional Law of Canada* (n 1) 74–75.

[72] Lluch (n 50) 74.

[73] *Reference re: Amendment to the Canadian Constitution* [1982] C 16904, 2 SCR 791.

[74] Gagnon and Dionne (n 3) 21, 31; Hogg, *Constitutional Law of Canada* (n 1) 59, 73–79.

[75] *A.G. (Que.) v. Quebec Protestant School Boards* (n 52); The Constitution Act 1982 (n 4) section 23.

[76] *A.G. (Que.) v. Quebec Protestant School Boards* (n 52).

[77] Ibid 76.

[78] 'To begin with, the fact that Quebec is the only province in Canada in which, by virtue of section 59(1) and (2) of the Constitution Act, 1982, section 23(1)(a) of the Charter is not yet in force and cannot be brought into force

the type of institution that parents might choose for their children incompatible with section 23 of the Charter of Rights.[79] The *A.G. (Que.) v Quebec Protestant School Boards* decision is well articulated and it is, within a margin of discretion, ethnically unbiased, yet it had political repercussions on the nationalists who perceived it as a manifestation of an attempt at indirect cultural homogenization.[80]

Furthermore, the failure to accommodate Quebec's political aspirations in the newly reformed constitutional system had a series of political and constitutional implications.[81] For instance, in 1985, Quebec's government, led by the Liberal Party, demanded a series of amendments to the constitution, which included the recognition of Quebec as a distinctive society and the insertion of a veto power on future constitutional amendments which altered, directly or indirectly, Quebec's system of territorial governance.[82] The Meech Lake Accord was devised to accommodate Quebec's demands but failed because two provincial legislatures (Manitoba and Newfoundland) did not approve it within the term imposed by the amendment process.[83] A subsequent accord in Charlottetown required a consultative national referendum, which could have, if it were to show the support of a majority of voters, helped to form a strong case for amending the federal constitution in the provincial legislatures.

The Charlottetown Accord was perceived as controversial. Hogg describes the Charlottetown Accord with his pawky clarity: 'There was something in the package to annoy just about everyone'.[84] The accord included, for instance, an explicit recognition of Quebec as a distinct society and a prerogative for the government of Quebec to 'preserve and promote' such distinctiveness.[85] The accord also comprised a reference to Quebec's reserved quotas within the House of Commons and the

---

without the consent of Quebec, indicates clearly that the framers of the Constitution had Quebec specially in mind when they enacted section 23 of the Charter.' Ibid 82.

[79] Ibid 91.

[80] Gagnon and Dionne (n 3) 32; Hogg, 'Canada: From Privy Council to Supreme Court' (n 1) 69.

[81] Hogg, *Constitutional Law of Canada* (n 1) 73.

[82] Ibid 74–75.

[83] The Constitution Act 1982 (n 4) section 41; Hogg, 'Canada: From Privy Council to Supreme Court' (n 1) 57; Gagnon, 'Québec-Canada's Constitutional Dossier' (n 3) 140.

[84] Hogg, 'Canada: From Privy Council to Supreme Court' (n 1) 57.

[85] 'Consensus Report on the Constitution: Final Text (Charlottetown Accord)'. (n 18) section 2(c), 3.

possibility of setting provincial–federal agreements over immigration.[86] However, the result of the consultative referendum supported the status quo.[87]

Two successive failed attempts to amend the constitution in a way that was clearly multinational persuaded most Canadian politicians of the quixotic nature of sweeping constitutional reforms.[88] 'The failures of the Meech Lake Accord and the Charlottetown Accord have persuaded Canadian politicians that constitutional amendments are not a career enhancing activity. One must conclude that significant amendments to the Constitution of Canada are, at least for the foreseeable future, impossible'.[89] Politicians seldom like to be associated with risky initiatives and the strict requirements of the Canadian constitutional amendment process substantially reduce the possibility of successful constitutional reform. The lesson learnt, so to speak, from the two failed accords, is that the Canadian constitution recognized a French linguistic minority but would not recognize Quebec as a nation.[90]

The frustration for the repeated failed attempts to recognize Quebec as a distinctive society, combined with a change of helm in Quebec's government, prepared the conditions for the 1995 consultative referendum over the secession.[91] In the case of Quebec, as was the case for Scotland in 2014 and Catalonia in 2017, nationalist parties collected an electoral mandate during a regional election and acted on the basis of an expression of popular will (albeit territorially restricted). The result of Quebec's referendum in 1995 was again in favour of the status quo, but it reaffirmed a demarked distinction between Quebec's nationalists who supported independence and Quebec's French speakers who supported recognition within Canada.[92]

One of the best-known effects of the 1995 referendum was a judicial qualification in the *Reference Re Secession* case of the right to secession from the rest of Canada.[93] The Supreme Court asserted that a clear majority of Quebec's residents can trigger a negotiation process with the

---

86 Ibid 21, 27.

87 Stevenson (n 13) 314.

88 Hogg, 'Canada: From Privy Council to Supreme Court' (n 1) 57.

89 Ibid. There were, since 1982 a series (less than 10) of small amendments which affected parliament or single provinces.

90 Gagnon, 'Québec-Canada's Constitutional Dossier' (n 3) 139–140.

91 Ibid 143.

92 Williams (n 59) 27.

93 *Reference Re Secession of Quebec [1998] 2 SCR 217* (n 23).

rest of Canada which might lead to secession.[94] In the aftermath of *Reference Re Secession*, the federal parliament passed legislation that tried to clarify the concept of a clear majority,[95] recognized Quebec as a distinctive society[96] and introduced a Quebec regional veto over government-sponsored constitutional reforms.[97]

These initiatives formally recognized, in relation to Quebec, that Canada is a multinational society, yet they had the effect of pausing the process of recognition of such diversity. For instance, given that constitutional reforms are perceived as Panglossian,[98] Quebec French speakers increasingly perceived Quebec institutions as vessels through which 'their' national identity should be manifested.[99] Similarly, the rest of Canada appears appeased by the idea that federal institutions are 'their' institutions. Thus, the current arrangements justify institutional, stable territorial nationalism that is partially unhinged from the dynamic nature expected from modern national-identity groups.[100]

DRIVER OF CHANGE: AN INCREMENTAL JURISPRUDENTIAL RECOGNITION OF IDENTITY-BASED CLAIMS

Canada is a multinational society and that has fostered a type of distinctively liberal territorial nationalism. What is also distinctive of

---

[94] Ibid para 86; Hogg, *Constitutional Law of Canada* (n 1) 148.

[95] An Act to Give Effect to the Requirement for Clarity as Set out in the Opinion of the Supreme Court of Canada in the Quebec Secession Reference, SC 2000, c 26 (n 27).

[96] The motion agreed by the House of Commons read as follows: '*That this House recognize that the Québécois form a nation within a united Canada*'. 'Debates (Hansard) No. 87 – November 27, 2006 (39-1) – House of Commons of Canada'.

[97] An Act respecting Constitutional Amendments, SC 1996, c 1.

[98] Hogg, 'Canada: From Privy Council to Supreme Court' (n 1) 57.

[99] Williams (n 59) 44; Quebec Government, 'Quebecers Our Way to Be Canadians [2017]' sections 3.2, 3.4; Keating (n 56).

[100] Gagnon, 'Québec-Canada's Constitutional Dossier' (n 3) 146; Smith, *Theories of Nationalism* (n 53); Z Bauman, 'Identity: Then, Now, What For?' in M Kempny and A Jawlowska (eds), *Identity in Transformation: Postmodernity, Postcommunism, and Globalization* (Praeger 2002).

Canada is the role that the judiciary has taken in recognizing identity-based constitutional claims. In this section, I will focus on the obligations regarding two distinctive elements of the Canadian jurisprudential qualifications on the role of identity-based constitutional claims. Firstly, I will explain that the Supreme Court has elaborated, over the years, an obligation on representatives of identity groups and central institutions to negotiate demands in good faith.[101] Secondly, the recognition of agreements over identity-based constitutional demands should be, I argue, considered part of a transgenerational relationship between identity groups and institutions that cannot be expected to be settled indefinitely.[102]

Consequently, this section focuses on a series of landmark decisions that firstly altered the interplay between Aboriginal Peoples and Canadian institutions and subsequently inspired the qualifications of Quebec's secessionist aspirations.[103] The recent *Tsilhqot'in Nation v British Columbia* is one of the latest qualifications of the line of authority that both recognized and limited Aboriginal Peoples' land claims which might have commenced in 1973 with the cases of *Calder et al v Attorney-General of British Columbia* and *Kanatewat et al v James Bay Development Corp. et al.*[104]

---

[101] *Reference Re Secession of Quebec [1998] 2 SCR 217* (n 23) para 88. *R. v. Sparrow* (n 36) 1004–1008; *Guerin v The Queen* [1984] C 17507, 2 SCR 335.

[102] *Delgamuukw v. British Columbia* (n 36) p. 1066; *R. v. Van der Peet* (n 36) p. 263; James Tully, 'Introduction' in Law Commission of Canada and British Columbia Treaty Commission (Canada) (eds), *Speaking Truth to Power: A Treaty Forum* (Law Commission of Canada; British Columbia Treaty Commission 2001) 11, 13.

[103] Branch, 'Statement of the Government of Canada on Indian Policy (The White Paper, 1969)' (n 34). *Tsilhqot'in Nation v British Columbia* [2014] SCC 34986, 2 SCR 257; *Daniels v Canada (Indian Affairs and Northern Development)* [2016] SCC 35945, 1 SCR 99; *Haida Nation v British Columbia (Minister of Forests)* [2004] SCC 29419, 3 SCR 511; *St Catharines Milling and Lumber Co v R* (C); *Delgamuukw v British Columbia* [1997] C 23799, 3 SCR 1010; *R v Van der Peet* [1996] C 23803, 2 SCR 507; *R v Pamajewon* [1996] C 24596, 2 SCR 821; *R v Sparrow* [1990] C 20311, 1 SCR 1075; *Hamlet of Baker Lake v Canada (Indian Affairs and Northern Development)* (C); *Calder et al v Attorney-General of British Columbia* (C); *Attorney General of Canada v Lavell* (C); *Kanatewat et al v James Bay Development Corp et al* (1973) 1 SCR 48 (C).

[104] *Tsilhqot'in Nation v. British Columbia* (n 36). Richard Frank Salisbury, *A Homeland for the Cree: Regional Development in James Bay, 1971–1981* (McGill-Queen's University Press 1986); Liz Cassell, 'Some Reflections on Hydroelectric Development and the Land Rights of the Innu Who Live in Quebec and Those Who Live in Labrador' (2013) 1 Journal of Human Rights in

The 1974 *James Bay Development Corporation* case is an appeal case against an injunction, known as Malouf's judgment, that recognized Aboriginal rights over land.[105] Judge Malouf considered *Calder et al v Attorney-General of British Columbia* and accepted the claims of, among others, the Cree peoples. The injunction is unreported and lasted only a few days, but it signalled a change in the judicial stance towards Aboriginal Peoples' struggle for recognition.[106] For instance, the injunction was one of the factors that led to the 1975 James Bay and Northern Quebec Agreement. The agreement recognizes (and compensates for) the loss of traditional land and its resources and allocates a level of self-governance to a selection of Aboriginal Peoples of Canada.[107] The point is made explicit in the text of the agreement: 'No paternalism [...] we must recognize the needs of the native peoples, the Crees and the Inuit, who have a different culture and a different way of life from those of other peoples of Quebec'.[108] The James Bay and Northern Quebec Agreement, whilst it might be considered as a 'sell out' to some, is one of the first of recent treaties that does not openly intend to assimilate Canadian Aboriginal cultures.[109]

The signing of the James Bay and Northern Quebec Agreement was the harbinger of a change of attitude towards the Aboriginal Peoples. It was preceded by the White Paper on Indian Policy, which explicitly recognized the role that the original inhabitants of Canada should have in a Canadian multinational society.[110] The government proposes to negotiate with the provinces and conclude agreements under which Indian people would participate in and be served by the full programmes of the provincial and local systems. Equitable financial arrangements would be sought to ensure that services could be provided in full measure commensurate with needs. The negotiations must seek agreements to end discrimination whilst ensuring that no harm is inadvertently done to Indian interests.

---

the Commonwealth 3–17; *Gros-Louis et autres c La Société de développement de la Baie James et autres, [1974] RP 38.*

[105] *Gros-Louis et autres c. La Société de développement de la Baie James et autres, [1974] R.P. 38* (n 104).

[106] Cassell (n 104). A copy of the decision was published by Gagnon. Andre Gagnon (ed), *La Baie James* (Editions du Jour 1973).

[107] Prime Minister of Quebec and others, 'James Bay and Northern Quebec Agreement' sections 10, 11, 26–30.

[108] Ibid 9–10.

[109] Cassell (n 104) 11.

[110] Branch, 'Statement of the Government of Canada on Indian Policy (The White Paper, 1969)' (n 34).

The effect of the 1969 White Paper on the judiciary is a matter of speculation,[111] yet its publication was followed by a series of decisions such as the ones by Judge Malouf and the one found in *Calder*.[112] In *Calder et al. v Attorney-General of British Columbia*, the Supreme Court accepted the argument that land ownership pre-existed the Royal Proclamation of 1763. Judge Hall recognized, for instance, the pre-Columbian existence of the Nishgas's claims over their land in a clear narrative: 'The Nishgas were never conquered nor did they at any time enter into a treaty or deed of surrender as many other Indian tribes did throughout Canada and in southern British Columbia'.[113] Hall dissented and the final decision was inconclusive (the judges did not reach a majority over the issue of the extinction of the land claim), but the key element in *Calder* is the acknowledgement that, short of a treaty or a military conquest that might extinguish land ownership, Aboriginal communal land ownership is part of modern Canada.[114]

Given the limited effects of Malouf's judgment, *Calder* is normally considered the first in the line of authority to have considered (in a way that is unbiased by Darwinism) Aboriginal Peoples' claims over their land and the management of their resources. Again, land claims are not squarely engaged in this book,[115] but *Calder* is considered because it had the effect of a 'legal irritant' in the debate over self-government.[116] Legal irritants, as Teubner explains, unsettle perceptions and might trigger unexpected processes.[117] The reasoning in the *Calder* case indeed had the effect of recasting the relationship between the Aboriginal Peoples of

---

[111] The White Paper was withdrawn in 1971.

[112] *Gros-Louis et autres c. La Société de développement de la Baie James et autres, [1974] R.P. 38* (n 104); *Calder et al. v. Attorney-General of British Columbia* (n 36); Mascher and Young (n 6) 180.

[113] *Calder et al. v. Attorney-General of British Columbia* (n 36) 345; *Haida Nation v. British Columbia (Minister of Forests)* (n 36) para 25.

[114] Andree Lajoie, 'What Constitutional Law Doesn't Want to Hear about History' in Law Commission of Canada and British Columbia Treaty Commission (Canada) (eds), *Speaking Truth to Power: A Treaty Forum* (Law Commission of Canada; British Columbia Treaty Commission 2001) 20; Hogg, *Constitutional Law of Canada* (n 1) 634; Mascher and Young (n 6) 189.

[115] For a general review see Hogg, *Constitutional Law of Canada* (n 1) Ch 28. A comparative update of native titles between Canada and Australia is provided in Mascher and Young (n 6).

[116] Gunther Teubner, 'Legal Irritants: Good Faith in British Law or How Unifying Law Ends up in New Divergences' (1998) 61 The Modern Law Review 11.

[117] Ibid 12.

Canada and the federal and provincial governments.[118] Tully argued, for instance, that representatives of the Aboriginal Peoples of Canada were expected to have equal standing in front of government negotiators, and described the ideal interaction between the parties as a quasi-diplomatic interaction that accepted narratives in the spirit of reconciliation.[119] Furthermore, he explained that a negotiation process is an aspect of the dynamic interplay between fluctuating (Canadian and Aboriginal) identities and should not be considered as a permanent solution to changing social interaction.[120]

The general implications of fluctuating interactions between identity groups and politics is well described in Bauman,[121] yet Tully and Keating explain the implications of considering the effects of constitutional recognition as a process of permanent discussion and evolution (rather than as a definitive solution to a problem).[122] In the *Van der Peet* case, for instance, the court reminded the parties that Aboriginal self-government is one of the results of recognizing Aboriginal traditional land rights. A further dimension of Aboriginal title is the fact that it is held communally. Aboriginal title cannot be held by individual Aboriginal persons; it is a collective right to land held by all members of an Aboriginal nation. Decisions with respect to that land are also made by that community. This is another feature of Aboriginal title which is *sui generis* and distinguishes it from orthodox doctrine on property rights.[123]

There is, it could be argued, a direct connection between recognizing traditional communal ownership, the allocation of self-governing prerogatives and the ongoing process of reconciliation between nations. In considering *Delgamuukw v British Columbia*, for instance, the court reiterated the beneficial effect of reconciliation between cultures.[124] One of the key aspects of *Delgamuukw* is a description of the 'right to hold

---

118 Tully (n 102) 6.

119 Ibid; Tully, *Strange Multiplicity: Constitutionalism in an Age of Diversity* (n 6).

120 Tully (n 102) 10–13.

121 Z Bauman, 'Living in the Era of Liquid Modernity' (2001) 22 Cambridge Anthropology 1; Vito Breda, 'Constitutional Identities in a Liquid Society' in Jiri Priban (ed), *Liquid Society and its Law* (Routledge 2007); Bauman (n 100).

122 Tully (n 102) 14; Keating (n 6).

123 *Delgamuukw v. British Columbia* (n 36) para 115.

124 Ibid 1066; *R. v. Van der Peet* (n 36) 263; Tully, 'Introduction' (n 102) 11, 13. For one of the most insightful analyses of the interplay between identity and constitutional law see Tully, *Strange Multiplicity: Constitutionalism in an Age of Diversity* (n 6); James Tully, 'Struggles over Recognition and Distribution' (2000) 7 Constellations 469.

the land for a variety of purposes which fostered the development of the subsequent Aboriginal Peoples' claim to self-governance'.[125] Again, *Delgamuukw* qualified the reference to a process of reconciliation which can be found in *Van der Peet*[126] and in *R. v Pamajewon*, in which the Court curtailed, by rejecting the appeal, the right to self-government derived from section 35 of the Constitution Act 1982.[127] *Tsilhqot'in Nation v British Columbia* is, instead, one of the latest cases that shows an indication of the incremental stance of Canadian jurisprudence.[128] In *Tsilhqot'in Nation v British Columbia*, the Supreme Court confirmed that Aboriginal title includes 'the right to proactively use and manage the land',[129] but such a prerogative has to balance with, among other limits, the effects that current land management might have on future generations.[130] Furthermore, the Court reaffirmed the legal obligation on the Crown to negotiate a settlement in good faith.[131]

The analysis of the jurisprudential qualification of the Aboriginal Peoples' land claims and the related recognition of administrative autonomy can continue but, I think, the analysis has shown sufficient evidence that 'the obligation to negotiate, in good faith, identity-based constitutional claims' has been influential in the development of the Supreme Court's jurisprudence.

An obligation to negotiate identity-based constitutional claims in good faith is also one of the defining criteria in the well-known *Reference Re Secession* case that engaged the legitimacy of the unilateral secession of Quebec.[132] In *Reference Re Secession*, the Supreme Court answered a series of queries which had the effect of evaluating the legitimacy of the 1995 Quebec referendum over unilateral secession. The Supreme Court's response to the issue is paramount to the development of a constitutional negotiation for several reasons, but there are two key contributions to the

---

125 *Delgamuukw v. British Columbia* (n 36) para 117; *Tsilhqot'in Nation v. British Columbia* (n 36) para 77.

126 *R. v. Van der Peet* (n 12) 263

127 *R. v. Pamajewon* (n 36) 823; The Constitution Act 1982 (n 4) section 35.

128 *Tsilhqot'in Nation v. British Columbia* (n 36); Nigel Bankes, 'The Implications of the Tsilhqot'in (William) and Grassy Narrows (Keewatin) Decisions of the Supreme Court of Canada for the Natural Resources Industries' (2015) 33 Journal of Energy & Natural Resources Law 188; Mascher and Young (n 6) 196.

129 *Tsilhqot'in Nation v. British Columbia* (n 36) para 73.

130 Ibid 74.

131 *Tsilhqot'in Nation v. British Columbia* (n 36) para 17, 78–80.

132 *Reference Re Secession of Quebec [1998] 2 SCR 217* (n 23).

debate over the recognition of regional identity.[133] Firstly, unilateral secessions are constitutionally illegitimate.[134] In particular, the Supreme Court stated that, in a modern liberal and democratic society, a regional secession which is not explicitly recognized by the constitution has to be considered illegitimate. A state, whose government represents the whole of the people or peoples who are resident within its territory, on a basis of equality and without discrimination, and that respects the principles of self-determination in its own internal arrangements, is entitled to the protection under international law of its territorial integrity.[135]

Secondly, in the case that a majority of regional residents, in this case Quebec's residents, express the political desire to secede from the rest of Canada, the federal government would have an obligation to negotiate in good faith over the procedures and the implications of a provincial secession.

The federalism principle, in conjunction with the democratic principle, dictates that the clear repudiation of the existing constitutional order and the clear expression of the desire to pursue secession by the population of a province would give rise to a reciprocal obligation on all parties to the confederation to negotiate constitutional changes to respond to that desire.[136]

There are still substantial doubts over the amendment procedure listed in section 35.[137] It is interesting that an obligation to negotiate and the modality of such a negotiation are inferred by the Supreme Court from an analysis of the Canadian constitutional system. It is mentioned in, for instance, *R v. Sparrow*, and was derived 'implicitly' from a reading of the *Guerin* case.[138] Indeed, Hogg questioned whether it ever existed.[139] Independently from the rather foggy genesis and Hogg's unfettered evaluation, the obligation to negotiate between provinces is not casuistry. Regions that are politically controlled by a party (which aspires to

---

133 It discusses, for instance, the possibility of a *de facto* unilateral secession. Ibid para 97, 106. In a stance that echoes Kelsen's analysis of the constitutional effect of successful revolution, the Supreme Court recognized the possibility of a *de facto* provincial secession and international recognition, but did not speculate over the implications for the rest of Canada. Hans Kelsen, *Pure Theory of Law* (Lawbook Exchange 2005) 215. It is outside of the scope of this book to discuss the implications of a *de facto* secession.

134 *Reference Re Secession of Quebec [1998] 2 SCR 217* (n 23) para 130.

135 Ibid para 130. Williams and others (n 26).

136 *Reference Re Secession of Quebec [1998] 2 SCR 217* (n 23) para 88.

137 Hogg, *Constitutional Law of Canada* (n 1) 150.

138 *R. v. Sparrow* (n 36) 1004–1008; *Guerin v. The Queen* (n 101).

139 Hogg, *Constitutional Law of Canada* (n 1) 146.

promoting that regional nationalist interest) and central government are expected to negotiate changes to their partnership in Canada and in other legal systems considered in this book.

The UK devolution, for instance, has several interring processes in which devolved and central institutions negotiate potential bordering issues.[140] The document that allowed Scotland to have a consultative referendum was based on the consultative procedures set in section 30 (2) of the Scotland Act 1998. The reform of the Italian constitution, instead, included the prerogative to negotiate regional competences, and the 2017 referendum in the Venetian region and Lombardy is considered, at least for the regions that organized it, part of the negotiation process inserted in the Italian constitution.[141] There is no indication, as far as I know, of a direct link between the establishment of the principle of constitutional negotiation by the Supreme Court in the *Reference Re Secession* case and either the UK devolution of 2001 or the Italian constitutional reform. However, it is important to consider the effect that the obligation to negotiate had in legal systems such as the Canadian, the British and the Italian systems, for the development of a dynamic conception of territorial governance.

There are, by logical deduction, two general implications. Firstly, unilateral secession (and unilateral annexation) is perceived as constitutionally and internally illegal. Secondly, once a majority[142] of the residents in the regional community has shown a clear and free political indication that it intends to negotiate the balance of political powers between its representative institutions and the representative institutions of the central state, representatives of both parties should conduct negotiations over the issue(s) raised. These issues might be perceived as radical in their nature. They might, for instance, be related to the extent of the right to self-determination of the nation. Yet all representatives have to act in good faith. Thus, a political stance that refuses to negotiate might induce a form of political power not dissimilar from the one of 'imperial dominium' that is considered illegitimate by the international

---

[140] The UK Government and The Government of Ireland, 'The Belfast Agreement: An Agreement Reached at the Multi-Party Talks on Northern Ireland 1998. CM 3883 (the Belfast Agreement)' Strand 2–3.

[141] Constitution of the Italian Republic (n 28); Guido Corso and Vincenzo Lopilato, *Il diritto amministrativo dopo le riforme costituzionali. Parte generale* (Giuffrè Editore 2006) 167.

[142] Williams and others (n 26); 'I·CONnect – Catalonia: Is There a "Right" to Secession?' http://www.iconnectblog.com/2017/10/catalonia-is-there-a-right-to-secession/ (accessed 21 October 2017); García Oliva (n 26).

community, and it allows us to question the normative connection between popular will and constitutional norms.[143]

In the recent *Kahkewistahaw First Nation v Taypotat*, the Supreme Court of Canada assessed the obligation to act in good faith. The Crown, the Court asserted, has the task of protecting the present and future generations' interests of the Indigenous Peoples of Canada.[144] Again *Sparrow* was referred to by the Supreme Court: 'The special trust relationship and the responsibility of the government vis-à-vis aboriginal people must be the first consideration in determining whether the legislation or action in question can be justified'.[145] In short, the legislation should not anthropomorphically mimic the intended effect of a treaty.

This is only a succinct commentary on the role that the Supreme Court had, and it is likely to continue to have, on defining the limits of the recognition of Quebec's distinctive society and the right to self-government of the Aboriginal Peoples of Canada. The historical overview, in particular, shows strong evidence that principles such as federalism, proportionality, the obligation to negotiate in good faith and the consideration of future generations set in cases such as *Reference Re Secession* and *Delgamuukw* are the manifestations of an incremental and critical analysis of the interplay between a modern multinational society and its constitutional system. It could be argued that, historically, Canadian courts such as the Supreme Court could have done much more to support the Aboriginal Peoples of Canada's aspiration for self-governance.[146] This is the narrative supported in Lajoie's article. It is difficult to speculate on how judicial narratives could have expedited the current process of recognition. Hogg perceived the historical intervention of the Supreme Court as legally questionable.[147]

It is relatively clear that, by way of comparison with the stance taken by the US Supreme Court[148] or by the Australian High

---

143 Williams and others (n 26); García Oliva (n 26); Casanas Adam (n 26).

144 *Kahkewistahaw First Nation v Taypotat* [2015] SCC 35518, 2 SCR 548.

145 *R. v. Sparrow* (n 36) [12].

146 Lajoie (n 114).

147 Hogg, 'Canada: From Privy Council to Supreme Court' (n 1) 71.

148 *Johnson v M'Intosh* [1823] US LEXIS 293 (US Supreme Court); *Cherokee Nation v Georgia 30 US 1 (1831)* 30 US 1; *Worcester v State of Georgia* (1831) 31 US 515. R Stephen McNeill, 'In a Class by Themselves: A Proposal to Incorporate Tribal Courts into the Federal Court System without Compromising Their Unique Status as Domestic Dependent Nations The Washington and Lee Law Alumni Association Student Notes' (2008) 65 Washington and Lee Law

Court,[149] Canadian jurisdictions helped in recasting the role of Aboriginal Peoples in Canadian society.[150] Foster, for instance, acknowledges that cases such as *Delgamuukw* substantially contributed to the process of the accommodation of Aboriginal claims in Canada.[151] Foster also suggests that future treaties should not seek to reduce the prerogative to challenge agreements between Aboriginal Peoples and provincial and federal institutions.[152] The courts, in other words, appear to be perceived as a bearer of equanimity in the process of the accommodation of identity-based constitutional claims. It is worth mentioning as a conclusive note for this section that the Supreme Court has not endorsed the narrow views of the US Indian jurisprudence discussed at length in the US chapter. In *Andrews v Law Society of British Columbia*, the Court qualified the concept of a 'differential impact' in sections of the population but did not engage the concept of an ethnic group.[153]

Review 283; Caprice L Roberts, 'A Desert Grows between Us – The Sovereignty Paradox at the Intersection of Tribal and Federal Courts The Washington and Lee Law Alumni Association Student Notes' (2008) 65 Washington and Lee Law Review 347; Frank Pommersheim, *Braid of Feathers: American Indian Law and Contemporary Tribal Life* (University of California Press 1997); Joseph P Kalt and Joseph William Singer, 'Myths and Realities of Tribal Sovereignty: The Law and Economics of Indian Self-Rule' (Social Science Research Network 2004) SSRN Scholarly Paper ID 529084 https://papers.ssrn.com/abstract=529084 (accessed 21 April 2017).

[149] George Williams, 'Removing Racism from Australia's Constitutional DNA' (2012) 37 Alternative Law Journal 151.

[150] John Borrows, 'Questioning Canada's Title to Land: The Rule of Law, Aboriginal Peoples and Colonialism' in Law Commission of Canada and British Columbia Treaty Commission (Canada) (eds), *Speaking Truth to Power: A Treaty Forum* (Law Commission of Canada; British Columbia Treaty Commission 2001); John Borrows, *Freedom and Indigenous Constitutionalism* (University of Toronto Press, Scholarly Publishing Division 2016).

[151] Hamar Foster, 'Getting There' in Law Commission of Canada and British Columbia Treaty Commission (Canada) (eds), *Speaking Truth to Power: A Treaty Forum* (Law Commission of Canada; British Columbia Treaty Commission 2001) 165, 173.

[152] Ibid 168.

[153] Cross and Lomond (n 44) 278–279.

DRIVER OF CHANGE: THE ESCALATING REQUIREMENTS OF THE AMENDMENT PROCESS AND THE FAILED CONSTITUTIONAL ACCORDS

In the previous section, I explained the effect that the Supreme Court's incremental jurisprudence has on the recognition of identity-based constitutional claims. Over the years, the Court clarified the interplay between communal land ownership and the self-government of the Aboriginal Peoples of Canada, and in relation to Quebec, also explains an obligation to negotiate political demands that have constitutional implications. This process happened, or perhaps was induced, in an exceptionally complex constitutional amendment procedure.[154]

The Constitution Act 1982 includes five amendment procedures and, in the case of a government-supported plan to alter the constitution, the proposal might need to meet specific statutory requirements.[155] In addition, the Supreme Court of Canada inserted a series of constitutionally implied requirements such as the respect of the principle of federalism and, in the case of identity-based constitutional claims supported by a clear majority, the obligation to negotiate in good faith.[156]

In describing the Canadian constitutional amendment system, Albert Richard uses the term 'formal escalation' to define the progressive increase in the level of procedural difficulty and political support that a proposal might need to pass in order to change a distinctive aspect of the Canadian constitution.[157] For instance, the so-called general amendment procedure is explained in section 38 and it requires the approval of the federal parliament, the support of two thirds of the provinces and 50 per

---

[154] Albert (n 5); The Constitution Act 1982 (n 4) sections 38–45; Peter W Hogg, 'Formal Amendment of the Constitution of Canada' (1992) 55 Law & Contemporary Problems 253; Hogg, *Constitutional Law of Canada* (n 1) 78; Hogg, 'Canada: From Privy Council to Supreme Court' (n 1) 104.

[155] The Constitution Act, 1982, being Schedule B to the Canada Act 1982 (UK), 1982, c 11 (n 6); An Act respecting Constitutional Amendments, SC 1996, c 1 (n 97). The procedure that approved the Constitution Act 1982 was then adopted to amend the British North America Act 1867.

[156] *Reference Re Secession of Quebec [1998] 2 SCR 217* (n 23); Jean Leclair, 'Judicial Review in Canadian Constitutional Law: A Brief Overview' (2004) 36 The George Washington International Law Review 543; Jean Leclair, 'Canada's Unfathomable Unwritten Constitutional Principles' (2001) 27 Queen's Law Journal 389; Albert (n 5) 170.

[157] Albert (n 5) 159.

cent of the population.[158] However, internal changes to the rules regulating the executive government of Canada require an ordinary legislative procedure,[159] but an alteration in the norms regulating bilingualism demands the support of all provincial legislative assemblies.[160]

Demanding a stringent requirement to change a perceived crucial aspect of a constitutional system is not unique to Canada.[161] Article 89 of the French constitution prevents the continuation of an amendment that might have the effect of altering the 'integrity of the national territory'.[162] Distinctive to the Canadian amendment system are, perhaps, the implications that such a set of stringent requirements might have for the recognition and development of a multinational Canada.

For instance, the proposed amendment that resulted from the Meech Lake Accord required the unanimous support of all Canadian provinces.[163] In the case of the Meech Lake Accord, quite remarkably, the final document found for the support of the Senate, the House of Commons and all provincial governments. However, during the time that was required for its approval, several provincial governments ran out of their respective electoral mandate and two of the new administrations refused to honour the commitment of the previous governments. The proposed amendment failed.[164] This level of complexity has a negative implication for the recognition of Quebec's nationalism.[165] One of the effects of the failure of the Meech Lake Accord, the Charlottetown Accord and the 1995 Quebec referendum was the introduction of the Quebec veto over constitutional

---

[158] The Constitution Act 1982 (n 4); Hogg, *Constitutional Law of Canada* (n 1) 81.

[159] The Constitution Act 1982 (n 4).

[160] Ibid 43 (d).

[161] Constitution of the Italian Republic (n 28) section 117; The Australian Constitution section 128; Spanish Constitution 1978 pt X; Hogg, *Constitutional Law of Canada* (n 1) 79.

[162] French Constitution 1958 (as revised 23 July 2008) Article 83 (3).

[163] The Constitution Act, 1982, being Schedule B to the Canada Act 1982 (UK), 1982, c 11 (n 6) Section 38(3). A province that opts out of an approved amendment might be compensated. These limits reduce the possibility that financial incentives are used to force provinces to accept constitutional amendments.

[164] Hogg, *Constitutional Law of Canada* (n 1) 107; Dawson (n 18); 'Constitutional Accord (Meech Lake Accord)' (n 18).

[165] Hogg, *Constitutional Law of Canada* (n 1) 73.

reforms which might affect the province.[166] The Act Respecting Constitutional Amendments allows, for instance, a number of provinces, and that includes French-speaking Quebec, to veto government-supported motions to change the constitution.[167]

The Act Respecting Constitutional Amendments is a statutory and not a constitutional requirement and therefore it prevents only Ministers of the Crown from proposing a motion that triggers an amendment procedure.[168] It could be speculated, for instance, that an amendment process might be commenced within the Canadian parliament by an MP who might try to convince the majority of colleagues to support a motion. MPs tend to follow political party lines, which, in exchange, help them during their electoral campaign.[169] It is also unlikely that an MP who is also a member of a government political party will try to start a constitutional amendment procedure by skirting around the limit imposed on the government.[170]

Equally articulate is the requirement to discuss a proposal to amend the constitution in cases in which Aboriginal Peoples are affected. If the amendment were to affect the rights of the Aboriginal Peoples of Canada, the First Minister should convene a constitutional conference consisting of first ministers and representatives of the Aboriginal Peoples.[171] The Supreme Court, as discussed in the previous section, has also added some qualifications to the modality of the negotiation process between the

---

[166] An Act respecting Constitutional Amendments, SC 1996, c 1 (n 97); 'Debates (Hansard) No. 87 – November 27, 2006 (39-1) – House of Commons of Canada' (n 96) (Québécois nation motion).

[167] An Act respecting Constitutional Amendments, SC 1996, c 1 (n 97).

[168] The Governor General cannot issue a proclamation within one year of the adoption of the resolution which formally commenced the amendment process and the process, from the same date, should not take more than three years. The Constitution Act 1982 (n 4) section 39.

[169] It is even more unlikely, for analogous reasons, that such an eventuality would be successful if it were triggered by an independent MP.

[170] Please recall that in 2006 the so-called Québécois nation motion was approved by the House of Commons that 'Québécois form a nation within a united Canada' but it had no legal or constitutional implications. 'Debates (Hansard) No. 87 – November 27, 2006 (39-1) – House of Commons of Canada' (n 96) 5375.

[171] The Constitution Act 1982 (n 4).

government and minorities.[172] In particular, in the *Reference Re Secession*, the Court introduces a list of unwritten constitutional principles such as federalism and the obligation to negotiate in good faith.[173]

This is, again, a concise analysis, but there is enough evidence of the distinctive constraint of the Canadian amendment process. The 'escalating' requirement of the multiple procedures inserted in the Constitutional Act 1982 ensures the relative stability of the constitutional text and the continuity of the federation.[174] The flip side of the stability is a legally imposed social immovability, like Joshua's sun over Gibeon, which might frustrate both Quebec nationalists[175] and the Aboriginal Peoples of Canada.[176]

CONCLUSION

In the past few decades, Canadian constitutional law and the jurisprudence of the Supreme Court have been considered at the forefront of constitutional scholarship and jurisprudential analysis.[177] This chapter explained that such perceptions are supported by a review of multiple factors. The progressive and incremental activity of the Supreme Court, for instance, qualified and developed a process of the accommodation of

---

172 *Reference re Senate Reform* [2014] SCC 35203, 1 SCR 704; *Reference Re Secession of Quebec [1998] 2 SCR 217* (n 23).

173 *Reference Re Secession of Quebec [1998] 2 SCR 217* (n 23); Leclair, 'Judicial Review in Canadian Constitutional Law' (n 156); Leclair, 'Canada's Unfathomable Unwritten Constitutional Principles' (n 156); Albert (n 5) 170, 197.

174 Albert (n 5).

175 Jocelyn Maclure, *Quebec Identity: The Challenge of Pluralism* (McGill-Queen's University Press 2014) Ch 4.

176 Branch, 'The Government of Canada's Approach to Implementation of the Inherent Right and the Negotiation of Aboriginal Self-Government' (n 34).

177 Stephen Tierney, 'Constitutional Referendums: A Theoretical Enquiry' (2009) 72 The Modern Law Review 360; Mancini (n 24); Michel Rosenfeld, 'Constitutional Identity' in Michel Rosenfeld and András Sajó (eds), *The Oxford Handbook of Comparative Constitutional Law* (Oxford University Press 2012); Nicholas Aroney and James Allan, 'An Uncommon Court: How the High Court of Australia Has Undermined Australian Federalism' (2008) 30 Sydney Law Review 245; Antonini (n 28); Richard Price, 'New Zealand's Interim Treaty Settlement and Arrangements – Building Blocks of Certainty' in Law Commission of Canada and British Columbia Treaty Commission (Canada) (eds), *Speaking Truth to Power: A Treaty Forum* (Law Commission of Canada; British Columbia Treaty Commission 2001).

constitutional demands purported by Canadian Aboriginal Peoples and, to a lesser extent, by Quebec French speakers.[178] A series of remarkable general principles emerged from this activity. The obligation to negotiate claims supported by a clear majority, and the idea that a majority within a constituency cannot trump another majority in a larger constituency and vice versa, have been firmly inserted in the Canadian constitutional system.[179] The obligation to negotiate has been inserted in other constitutional systems considered in this book such as the British and Italian systems.[180]

Whilst it is difficult to support, via deductive reasoning, the existence of legal transplants and it is necessary to accept that comparative analyses are bound by simplifications and emphases, it is also reasonable to suggest that Canada's constitutional law and the theoretical stances that supported it inspired legal systems in Europe and in the Pacific region.[181] Kymlicka, for instance, might not have invented 'minority rights', but has provided one of the most articulate explanations of the interplay between cultural diversity and liberal democracy.[182] Similar in the level of contribution, albeit with different conclusions, is Tully's analysis of the role of constitutional rules and procedures in modern democracy.[183] Furthermore, political and sociological changes such as the Quiet Revolution, which greatly reduced the sectarian undertones of Quebec's nationalism, and the process of reconciliation between 'white' Canada and the Aboriginal Peoples auspicated in the 1960s, moved in parallel, so to speak, with the development of political and legal theories.

---

[178] Hogg, 'Canada: From Privy Council to Supreme Court' (n 1).

[179] Hogg, 'Canadian Constitutional Law' (n 71); Mancini (n 24).

[180] Tierney (n 178); Antonini (n 28); *Asunto: 5830-2014* (n 26); Williams and others (n 26); Norman (n 26); Haljan (n 26); Bel (n 26); Tierney, 'Reclaiming Politics' (n 26); Tierney, 'Popular Constitutional Amendment' (n 5); García Oliva (n 26); Casanas Adam (n 26); Anderson and others (n 26).

[181] Tony Angelo, 'To Be or Not to Be [...] Integrated, That is the Problem of Islands' [2002] Revue Juridique Polynésienne 87; Aroney and Allan (n 177).

[182] Kymlicka (n 40); Anthony Simon Laden, *Reasonably Radical: Delibertive Liberalism and the Politics of Identity* (Cornell University Press 2001).

[183] James Tully, 'The Unfreedom of the Moderns in Comparison to Their Ideals of Constitutional Democracy' (2002) 65 Modern Law Review 204; James Tully, 'Diversity's Gambit Declined' in Curtis Cook (ed), *Constitutional Predicament: Canada after the Referendum of 1992* (McGill-Queen's University Press 1994); James Tully, 'The Challenge of Reimagining Citizenship and Belonging in Multicultural and Multinational Societies' in Catriona McKinnon and Iain Hampsher-Monk (eds), *The Demands of Citizenship* (Continuum 2000).

Quebec's nationalism and the process of the jurisdictional accommodation of Aboriginal Peoples' claims were selected as one of the most important drivers of change in the process of the negotiation of constitutional demands.[184] An additional driver of change considered the internal structure of the Canadian constitution. It was argued, for instance, that the Canadian sociological and political changes considered in this chapter took place in a constitutional system that has a very articulated and extremely rigid amendment system.[185] It is reasonable to suggest that a combination of the rigidity of the amendment process combined with consistent support for the status quo manifested in recent Canadian referenda had the effect of reducing the speed of development of Canadian constitutional law.

---

[184] Roberta Lexier, 'Two Nations in Canada: The New Democratic Party, the Waffle Movement and Nationalism in Quebec/Deux Nations Au Canada: Le Nouveau Parti Démocrate, Le "Waffle" et Le Nationalisme Au Québec' (2017) 30 British Journal of Canadian Studies 1; Jose Santiago, 'Religion, Secularisation and Nationalism in Quebec and the Basque Country: A Comparative Approach' (2015) 21 Nations and Nationalism 120; Stevenson (n 13); Gagnon, 'Québec-Canada's Constitutional Dossier' (n 3); Gagnon and Tanguay (n 42); Tully (n 102); Lajoie (n 114); Borrows, 'Questioning Canada's Title to Land: The Rule of Law, Aboriginal Peoples and Colonialism' (n 150).

[185] Albert (n 5); Hogg, 'Canada: From Privy Council to Supreme Court' (n 1); Hogg, 'Formal Amendment of the Constitution of Canada' (n 154).

6. The USA: constitutional negotiations and peripheral nationalism

INTRODUCTION: A SKELETON ANALYSIS OF THE LEGAL CONTEXT AND PRELIMINARY DEBATES

The USA is considered the first truly modern, multiethnic, federal constitutional democracy. The US constitution is also considered one of the best examples of a stable constitutional text.[1] A successful constitutional amendment requires a two-thirds majority in both houses of parliament, the so-called super-majority, or a convention requested by two-thirds of the states. In addition, the proposals must be rectified by three-quarters of the state legislatures or by state conventions.[2] Congress decides on the types of ratification procedures and normally sets a time limit within which state conventions or legislatures must ratify the proposed amendment. There have only been 27 amendments and some, like the one that prompted the prohibition era, were repealed.[3]

The USA has, by way of comparison with other legal systems considered in this book, the most complex and perhaps the most analysed

[1] Walter Dellinger, 'The Legitimacy of Constitutional Change: Rethinking the Amendment Process' (1983) 97 Harvard Law Review 386, 388; András Sajó and Claude Klein, 'Constitution-Making; Progress and Substance' in Michel Rosenfeld and András Sajó (eds), *The Oxford Handbook of Comparative Constitutional Law* (Oxford University Press 2012) 439; Richard Albert, 'The Structure of Constitutional Amendment Rules' (2014) 49 Wake Forest Law Review 913, 921, 927; Xenophōn I Kontiadēs (ed), 'Constitutional Change Engineering', *Engineering Constitutional Change: A Comparative Perspective on Europe, Canada and the USA* (Routledge 2013) 2; Rosalind Dixon and Richard Holden, 'Constitutional Amendment Rules: The Denominator Problem' (2011) 4.

[2] U.S. Const. Article V.

[3] Sajó and Klein (n 1) 439; Michael D Thomas, Diana W Thomas and Nicholas A Snow, 'Rational Irrationality and the Political Process of Repeal: The Women's Organization for National Prohibition Reform and the 21st Amendment' (2013) 66 Kyklos 130.

system of territorial governance.[4] The US system of governance includes a federal system with a two-tier legislative sovereignty system that regulates the interaction between central institutions and 50 US states,[5] an ad hoc territorial administration for the District of Columbia,[6] the constitutional recognition of a distinctive system of governance for American Indian Nations,[7] a series of bespoke statutory settlements for five inhabited territories and three free-associated sovereign nations.[8] The list of the five territories includes American Samoa, the Virgin Islands of the United States (hereafter the US Virgin Islands), Guam, the Commonwealth of the Northern Mariana Islands (hereafter, Northern Mariana Islands) and the Commonwealth of Puerto Rico (hereafter, Puerto Rico).[9] The list of countries in free association with the USA includes the Federated States of Micronesia, the Marshall Islands and Palau.[10] The

---

[4] Tom Ginsburg and Eric A Posner, 'Subconstitutionalism' (2010) 62 Stanford Law Review 1583, 1602.

[5] U.S. Const. Adm. X (Federal Reserved Powers – Residual State Legislative Powers); U.S. Const. Adm. XVI (Application of Federal Law); U.S. Const. Article V (Constitutional Amendment Process); U.S. Const. Article VI (Conflicts between Federal and State laws), U.S. Const. Article I, §8 (Dorman Commerce Clause and Trade with Indian Nations); U.S. Const. Article I, §8 (Congress Legislative Power – Necessary and Proper Cause); U.S. Const. Article I and U.S. Const. Adm. XIV (Limits on State Legislative Sovereignty). Ginsburg and Posner (n 4).

[6] U.S. Const. Article I §17.

[7] Frank Pommersheim, *Broken Landscape: Indians, Indian Tribes, and the Constitution* (Oxford University Press 2009); Frank Pommersheim, 'At the Crossroads: A New and Unfortunate Paradigm of Tribal Sovereignty' (2010) 55 South Dakota Law Review 48; Frank Pommersheim, 'The Crazy Horse Malt Liquor Case: From Tradition to Modernity and Halfway Back' (2012) 57 South Dakota Law Review 42; Vicki C Jackson, 'The (Myth of Un)Amendability of the US Constitution and the Democratic Component of Constitutionalism' (2015) 13 International Journal of Constitutional Law 575; Hope M Babcock, 'A Civic-Republican Vision of Domestic Dependent Nations in the Twenty-First Century: Tribal Sovereignty Re-Envisioned, Reinvigorated, and Re-Empowered' (2005) 2005 Utah Law Review 443; Clare Boronow, 'Closing the Accountability Gap for Indian Tribes: Balancing the Right To Self-Determination with the Right to a Remedy' (2012) 98 Virginia Law Review 1373; David H Getches, 'Beyond Indian Law: The Rehnquist Court's Pursuit of States' Rights, Color-Blind Justice and Mainstream Values' (2001) 86 Minnesota Law Review 267; Gary Lawson and Guy Seidman, *The Constitution of Empire* (Yale University Press 2004).

[8] U.S. Const. Article IV §3.

[9] 'Developments in the Law – The U.S. Territories' (2016) 130 Harvard Law Review 1616, 1616.

[10] Lawson and Seidman (n 7) 117. The procedure that might result in a free association agreement between a national minority and the central state is

Federated States of Micronesia, the Marshall Islands and Palau are in a free association with the USA. An analysis of free association is discussed in the chapter that analyses the Realm of New Zealand and will not be covered in this chapter. The constitution also provides the criteria for the territorial organization and the allocation of legislative powers to federal and state institutions.[11] Individuals who reside in the US territories have, by way of comparison with US citizens, limited rights.[12]

These are just a part of a series of general assertions and there is a dazzling amount of literature that engages the US constitutional system from multiple 'angles'. Whilst acknowledging the inevitable simplifications and selections implicit in any comparative evaluation, this chapter will focus on a range of driving factors for the process of the recognition and accommodation of identity claims in the US constitutional system. For instance, it analyses the recent series of events that might foster a transition of status for Puerto Rico from territory to statehood and perhaps recognize Puerto Rico as a distinctive society.[13] Hawaii has already obtained statehood and also a distinctive system of governance of the archipelago's public land resources which are designated to support Native Hawaiians.[14] The Alaska Native Claims Settlement Act allocated land to a list of Alaska Native regional corporations managed by shareholders.[15] Given the limited scope of this book and the specific

---

discussed in the analysis of Basque Country and Tokelau's United Nations sponsored decolonization process. Michael Keating and Zoe Bray, 'Renegotiating Sovereignty: Basque Nationalism and the Rise and Fall of the Ibarretxe Plan' (2006) 5 Ethnopolitics 347; Antony Hooper, 'Tokelau: A Sort of "Self-Governing" Sort of "Colony"' (2008) 43 The Journal of Pacific History 331.

[11] Lawson and Seidman (n 7).

[12] Ibid 191, 197.

[13] Congressional Research Service, 'Political Status of Puerto Rico: Options for Congress (2017)'.

[14] In this chapter I will use the terms 'Indian Tribes', and Native Hawaiian (liberally translated from the term Kanaka Maoli) in a way that is analogous of Australian 'Aboriginal Peoples' and 'Maori Peoples or Maori Tribes'.

[15] Martha Hirschfield, 'The Alaska Native Claims Settlement Act: Tribal Sovereignty and the Corporate Form' (1992) 101 The Yale Law Journal 1331, 1333; Christian G Vazquez, 'A Business Entity by Any Other Name: Corporation: Community and Kinship' (2016) 33 Alaska Law Review 353, 355; Elizaveta Barrett Ristroph, 'Traditional Cultural Districts: An Opportunity for Alaska Tribes to Protect Subsistence Rights and Traditional Lands' (2014) 31 Alaska Law Review 211; Peter Metcalfe, *A Dangerous Idea: The Alaska Native Brotherhood and the Struggle for Indigenous Rights* (University of Alaska Press

private nature of the arrangement, the Alaska Native Claims Settlement will not be discussed in this chapter.

The recognition of Native Hawaiians' aspirations for statehood and the current Puerto Rican attempt to join the US federation as a state do not occur in an institutional and political vacuum. There are a series of drivers of change that set out a distinctive American process of the negotiation and accommodation of identity-based constitutional claims.[16] As for the rest of this book, the term 'driver of change' in the process of the negotiation of identity claims includes factors that might resist a change in the status quo.

CONSTITUTIONAL PATRIOTISM AND A DISPERSED CIVIC NATIONALISM

In the process of the recognition of identity claims, American civic nationalism has multiple implications. As I mentioned in Chapter 1, Smith's idea of polycentric nationalism suggests that modern nationalism within a liberal democracy tends to combine a system of values of liberal polity and ethnic nationalism.[17] The priority of values over peoplehood is manifested in daily activities such as the recital of the Pledge of Allegiance in schools,[18] and on the assertion of contra-majoritarian effects that constitutional norms have in judicial debates within elite institutions.[19] The manifestation of reverence to the constitutional text is

---

2014) Ch 7; ANCSA, Pub. L. 92-203,85 Stat. 688 (1971) (codified as amended at 4 3U.S.C. §§ 1601–1629h (2012)).

[16] Robert Hazell, *Constitutional Futures: A History of the next Ten Years* (Oxford University Press 1999); Robert Hazell, *Constitutional Futures Revisited: Britain's Constitution to 2020* (Palgrave Macmillan 2008); Vito Breda, 'Constitutional Futures Revisited: Britain's Constitution to 2020 Edited by Robert Hazell [Book Review]' [2011] Public Law 446.

[17] Anthony D Smith, *Ethnicity and Nationalism* (Brill 1992); John E Smith, *Quasi-Religions: Humanism, Marxism, and Nationalism* (Macmillan 1994).

[18] Grace Y Kao and Jerome E Copulsky, 'The Pledge of Allegiance and the Meanings and Limits of Civil Religion' (2007) 75 Journal of the American Academy of Religion 121.

[19] James B Thayer, 'The Origin and Scope of the American Doctrine of Constitutional Law' (1893) 7 Harvard Law Review 129, 130, 137–139; Mark Tushnet, 'Policy Distortion and Democratic Debilitation: Comparative Illumination of the Countermajoritarian Difficulty' (1995) 94 Michigan Law Review 245; Jan-Werner Müller, *Constitutional Patriotism* (Princeton University Press 2007) 7. For a comparison between US Nationalism, Canadian Federalism and

sometimes defined as one of the expressions of a daily plebiscite that, according to Renan, is distinctive of a national community.[20] For example, in *Roper v Simmons*, Justice Anthony Kennedy describes how citizens and the US Supreme Court honour the American constitution as an expression of a communal endeavour. Kennedy explains this process as follows:

> The document sets forth, and rests upon, innovative principles original to the American experience such as federalism; a proven balance in political mechanisms through separation of powers; specific guarantees for the accused in criminal cases; and broad provisions to secure individual freedom and preserve human dignity. These doctrines and guarantees are central to the American experience and remain essential to our present-day self-definition and national identity. Not the least of the reasons we honor the Constitution, then, is because we know it to be our own. It does not lessen our fidelity to the Constitution or our pride in its origins to acknowledge that the express affirmation of certain fundamental rights by other nations and peoples simply underscores the centrality of those same rights within our own heritage of freedom.[21]

This is, as worded by Justice Kennedy, a manifestation of a sociological attachment, let us call it a patriotic attachment, made by the members of an elite institution to the universal values manifested in the American constitutional system.[22] Whilst carefully worded, the passage does not cover the tension between the universal values protected by the US constitution (that in *Roper v Simmons* spared Mr Christopher Simmons from being unfairly executed) and the reference to the constitution as a distinctive asset of the American nation. At a conceptual level, individual freedoms and human dignity are influential aspects in the development of modern democracy, but, as such, are considered 'universal'.[23] From Kennedy's narrative, it is reasonable to subsume that, firstly, the US Supreme Court perceived those universal values as belonging to a

---

Quebecois identity see Garth Stevenson, *Parallel Paths: The Development of Nationalism in Ireland and Quebec* (McGill-Queen's University Press 2006) 364.

[20] 'A nation's existence is (please excuse the metaphor) a daily plebiscite, just [...] metaphysical than divine right and less brutal than so-called law of history'. Ernest Renan, 'What Is a Nation?' (Presses-Pocket 1882) 10.

[21] *Roper v Simmons* (2005) 543 US 551 (US Supreme Court) 578.

[22] This narrative is also in Vito Breda, 'Constitutional Patriotism' in Mortimer Sellers and Stephan Kirste (eds), *Encyclopedia of the Philosophy of Law and Social Philosophy* (Springer Netherlands 2017).

[23] James Tully, 'The Unfreedom of the Moderns in Comparison to Their Ideals of Constitutional Democracy' (2002) 65 Modern Law Review 204.

national heritage, and, secondly, their interpretation is an exclusive element of American institutional history.

The narrative in the US Supreme Court is both a manifestation and a validation by a final appellate institution of the sense of national ownership of the values expressed in the constitutional text. The sense of communal ownership is associated with the so-called normative spill-over (or normative surplus) of a process aimed at clarifying the current significance of the constitutional text.[24] In particular, the American veneration for its constitution is sometimes defined as a form of thick constitutional patriotism.[25] The 'bundle' of explicit and implicit constitutional values (such as freedom and equality) is perceived by strong constitutional patriots as a vessel through which individuals who are strangers to one another form a communal bond.[26]

Thick constitutional patriotism is normally considered to be the middle ground between thin constitutional patriotism and ethnic nationalism.[27] By way of comparison, constitutional patriots, whose attachment is to the deliberative process that forms political consensus, think that constitutional patriots are attached to the substantive values manifested in the constitution.[28] In contrast with ethnic nationalists, who define their identity through blood and belonging, strong constitutional patriotism is instead originally anchored to an enlightened project that promotes human dignity, justice and fairness.[29]

---

[24] Müller (n 19) 49, 125, 147; Jean-Werner Müller, 'A General Theory of Constitutional Patriotism' (2008) 6 International Journal of Constitutional Law 72, 76–77; Breda (n 22).

[25] Jan-Werner Müller, 'A "Thick" Constitutional Patriotism for the EU? On Morality, Memory and Militancy' [2006] 2006; Law and Democracy in the Post-National Union, CIDEL Report, Oslo: Arena 375; Matthias Kumm, 'Idea of Thick Constitutional Patriotism and its Implications for the Role and Structure of European Legal History' (2005) 6 German Law Journal 319; Vito Breda, 'Constitutional Patriotism: Redux', in Mitja Sardoc (ed), *Handbook of Patriotism* (2018); Vito Breda, 'Constitutional Identities in a Liquid Society' in Jiri Priban (ed), *Liquid Society and its Law* (Routledge 2007); Vito Breda, 'The Incoherence of the Patriotic State: A Critique of Constitutional Patriotism' (2004) 10 Res Publica 247.

[26] For the most comprehensive analysis of the recent evolution of the US constitutional identity see Michel Rosenfeld, *The Identity of the Constitutional Subject* (Routledge 2010).

[27] Dora Kostakopoulou, 'Thick, Thin and Thinner Patriotisms: Is This All There Is?' (2006) 26 Oxford Journal of Legal Studies 73.

[28] Breda, 'Constitutional Patriotism: Redux' (n 25); Kumm (n 25).

[29] Müller (n 19) 7, 139; Z Bauman, 'Soil, Blood and Identity' in C Mongardini and M Ruini (eds), *Europa, nazione e stato alla vigilia del XXI*

The sense of attachment to a system of values is not, at least in theory, associated with a specific national identity. However, America's colonial heritage left behind a distinctive Anglo-Saxon influence.[30] Members of a national identity, including those who, like in the USA, endorse a thick patriotism as a bounding element of a polity, are 'glued together', among other aspects by such things as a communal language, or by the manifestation of a shared system of beliefs.[31] The system of beliefs, Smith explains, defines the distinctive element of the national group and, in most liberal democracies, includes the endorsement of basic human values and the recognition of other nation groups.[32] As discussed in Chapter 1, outside a general agreement over the ideological underpinning of the concept of a nation, within the sociological literature, there is no clear distinction between civic, dispersed and ethnic national groups.[33]

The US Supreme Court has acknowledged such an indeterminacy by considering the idea of a nation as a political concept. In *Mancari*, for

---

secolo (Rome 1993); Michael Ignatieff, *Blood & Belonging: Journeys into the New Nationalism* (Vintage 1994); Jan-Werner Müller, 'Seven Ways to Misunderstand Constitutional Patriotism' (2009) 25 Notizie di Politeia 20.

[30] Alexis de Tocqueville, *Democracy in America*, JP Mayer ed, George Lawrence trans, Harper Perennial Modern Classics edition (Harper Perennial Modern Classics 2006) pt II; Donald S Lutz, *Colonial Origins of the American Constitution* (Liberty Fund 1977) http://ebookcentral.proquest.com/lib/usq/detail.action?docID=3327341 (accessed 27 November 2017); Donald S Lutz, 'Toward a Theory of Constitutional Amendment' (1994) 88 The American Political Science Review 355, 355; Kenneth D Stern, 'John Locke and the Declaration of Independence' (1966) 15 The Cleveland State Law Review 186; David L Wardle, 'Reason to Ratify: The Influence of John Locke's Religious Beliefs on the Creation and Adoption of the United States Constitution' (2002) 26 Seattle University Law Review 291; John Locke, *The Second Treatise on Civil Government* (Prometheus Books 1986). Racism, discrimination, and slavery were also among some historical factors that have shaped the present process of recognition of identity based constitutional claims. Amílcar Antonio Barreto, 'American Identity, Congress, and the Puerto Rico Statehood Debate' (2016) 16 Studies in Ethnicity and Nationalism 100.

[31] Smith, *Ethnicity and Nationalism* (n 17) 60; Breda, 'Constitutional Identities in a Liquid Society' (n 25); Breda, 'Constitutional Patriotism: Redux' (n 25); Maciej Hułas and Stanisław Fel (eds), *Intricacies of Patriotism: Towards a Complexity of Patriotic Allegiance* (Peter Lang 2015).

[32] Chapter 2 of this book; Anthony D Smith, *Theories of Nationalism* (Duckworth 1971); Ernest Gellner, *Nations and Nationalism* (Basil Blackwell 1983).

[33] Smith's analyses persuasively have argued so. Smith, *Ethnicity and Nationalism* (n 17); Anthony D Smith, *Nationalism: Theory, Ideology, History* (Polity Press/Blackwell 2001).

instance, the Court acknowledged that a rational criterion must be adopted to differentiate the treatment of individuals who, for whatever sociological reason, are perceived to be a part of a distinctive polity.[34] A reading of the case of *Alaska Chapter, Associated General Contractors of America v Pierce* reiterated the political nature of the definition of the Indian Nation by considering a series of institutional qualifications relating to being a member of an Indian tribe.[35] The list includes the definition of 'any person recognized as being an Indian or Alaskan Native by a tribe, the Government, or any state' from the Department of Housing and Urban Development's regulation as well as the requirement of being, by blood, one-quarter Indian in *Mancari*.[36] The variation in the criteria shows that a public law definition of a nation is, in the Court's words, political:

> In Alaska, where the Natives' situation is distinctly different from that of other American Indians, the use of blood quantum as one factor in defining which persons are to be included as Indians and subject to the statutory benefits is helpful in identifying the defined group and does not detract from the *political nature* of the classification.[37]

The Court, it is reasonable to suggest, conceived that individuals do define themselves as members of a nation and it is an internal prerogative of the community to regulate its membership criteria. Furthermore, by conceding that it is outside its prerogative to define national minorities, the Court directed its cognitive activity towards the issue of whether policies that single out a specific group in a positive way are based on rational explanations that appease the principle of formal equality.[38]

In the following sections, I will return to discussing the interaction between the distinctive implications of formal equality, American dispersed nationalism and Indian tribes, but suffice to say that such an

---

[34] *Morton v Mancari 417 US 535 (1974)* 555. An analysis of the rational basis criterion is provided in Jon M Van Dyke, 'The Political Status of the Native Hawaiian People' (1998) 17 Yale Law & Policy Review 95, 131–133; John T Cross and Kristin M Lomond, 'The Civil Rights of the Aboriginal Peoples of the United States and Canada' (1993) 10 Arizona Journal of International and Comparative Law 253, 274.

[35] *Alaska Chapter, Associated General Contractors of America v Pierce, 694 F2d 1162 (9th Cir 1982).*

[36] Ibid 8.

[37] My emphasis, ibid 10.

[38] *Morton v. Mancari 417 U.S. 535 (1974)* (n 34).

interaction has conditioned the recognition and negotiation of identity-based claims at state and federal level.[39] However, before closing this section, it is important to say that the idea of 'dispersed nationalism' and the thick constitutional patriotism manifested in the jurisprudence of the US Supreme Court might not be the most efficient of interactions between ethnic groups and federal institutions in, for instance, a hypothetical, newly accepted state of Puerto Rico.

The Puerto Rican population is, according to official data, almost exclusively Hispanic or Latino and Puerto Rican nationalism is analogous to that found in European nations and national minorities.[40] The Puerto Rican level of ethnic uniformity (in the 2010 census, 99 per cent of the population chose to be classified as Latino or Hispanic) is, by way of comparison with other states and US territories, distinctive. Even the isolated territory of American Samoa does not reach the level of represented ethnic uniformity of Puerto Rico.[41] It is a matter of speculation as to how the combination of present US dispersed nationalism and constitutional patriotism might affect the accommodation of localized national minorities in the near future, such as the one distinctive of Puerto Rico. It is, however, reasonable to suggest that an institutional attachment that is part of US distinctive constitutional patriotism will continue to alter the process of the negotiation and accommodation of identity-based constitutional claims at state level, as is the case for Native Hawaiians, and at federal level.[42]

---

39 Ginsburg and Posner (n 4).

40 Amílcar Antonio Barreto, 'American Identity, Congress, and the Puerto Rico Statehood Debate' (2016) 16 Studies in Ethnicity and Nationalism 100; Arlene M Dávila, *Sponsored Identities: Cultural Politics in Puerto Rico* (Temple University Press 1997); David A Rezvani, 'The Basis of Puerto Rico's Constitutional Status: Colony, Compact, or "Federacy"?' (2007) 122 Political Science Quarterly 115. Some 99% of the population define themselves as Hispanic or Latino. US Census Bureau: Department of Commerce, Economics and Statistics Administration, 'U.S. Census Bureau QuickFacts Selected: Puerto Rico' https://www.census.gov/quickfacts/table/PST045216/72 (accessed 20 June 2017).

41 Central Intelligence Agency, 'The World Factbook: American Samoa' https://www.cia.gov/library/publications/the-world-factbook/geos/aq.html (accessed 20 June 2017).

42 Ginsburg and Posner (n 4); Alex Schwartz, 'Patriotism or Integrity? Constitutional Community in Divided Societies' (2011) 31 Oxford Journal of Legal Studies 503.

DRIVER OF CHANGE: INDIAN TRIBES' IDENTITY CLAIMS AND THE PRINCIPLE OF FORMAL EQUALITY

The combination of a rigid constitution left the judiciary with the task of modernizing the American constitutional system.[43] In this section, it will be argued that the process of balancing the principle of formal equality and the recognition of the Indian tribes gives an indication of the ability of the US constitutional system to recognize and to adapt, within the limit of reasonableness, to the demands of identity-based constitutional claims.[44] I have called this driver of change the 'constitutional ductility of the Supreme Court jurisprudence'. The US constitutional system is, as with the Canadian system, colour blind.[45] Discriminatory policies based on statutes are, by assumption, unconstitutional. However, a disparity in the treatment of individuals on the basis that they belong to ethnic communities that are economically depressed might be rationally justified. It is in this process that the US Supreme Court has shown the ability to adapt a colour-blind constitution to a multinational society.[46] I use the term 'jurisprudential ductility' to define the US Supreme Court's practice of adapting constitutional references and the interpretation of the Indian treaties to current demands without sudden ruptures in the lines of authority. Given the historical implications of my analysis, it is important to say, as a foreword, that such a process had a historically negative implication for the process of the recognition of American Indians. For instance, the development of the concept of dependent nations that are

---

[43] For a general analysis of the diversity/equality debate, see for instance Courtenay W Daum and Eric Ishiwata, 'From the Myth of Formal Equality to the Politics of Social Justice: Race and the Legal Attack on Native Entitlements' (2010) 44 Law & Society Review 843; Cross and Lomond (n 34) 271; Leslie F Goldstein, *The U.S. Supreme Court and Racial Minorities: Two Centuries of Judicial Review on Trial* (Edward Elgar 2017).

[44] U.S. Const., Article, I §2 cl. 3, U.S. Const., Article, I §8 cl. 3, U.S. Const., Amend., XIV §2 cl. 1; Getches (n 7) 269.

[45] The Equal Protection Clause (U.S. Const., Amend., XIV) might apply only to state governments. U.S. Const., Amend. V is routinely referred to in order to enforce the Equal Protection Clause on the Federal Government. Cross and Lomond (n 34) 272.

[46] Ibid 273.

cared for by Congress had been used both to restrain Indian sovereignty vis-à-vis states and, more recently, to expand states' prerogatives.[47]

Within the US mainland there are 326 federal reservations and tribes associated with pre-Columbian inhabitants.[48] The total number of pre-Columbian residents, including those who claim multiple ethnic heritages, represent 2 per cent of the US population.[49] The small perceptual number of American Indians per head of population is combined with a limited, by way of comparison with Native Hawaiians in the state of Hawaii, per-state density.[50] This data, as is the case with Australian Aboriginals, has a significant impact on a political system with a uninominal voting system where successful politicians tend to lean their policy towards 'the middle' and to ignore minorities.[51]

It is also relevant to this debate that the current and future development of the Native Indian system of governance is affected by a past

---

[47] Babcock (n 7); R Stephen McNeill, 'In a Class by Themselves: A Proposal to Incorporate Tribal Courts into the Federal Court System without Compromising Their Unique Status as Domestic Dependent Nations The Washington and Lee Law Alumni Association Student Notes' (2008) 65 Washington and Lee Law Review 283; Frank Pommersheim, *Braid of Feathers: American Indian Law and Contemporary Tribal Life* (University of California Press 1997); Pommersheim, 'The Crazy Horse Malt Liquor Case' (n 7).

[48] US Census Bureau: Department of Commerce, Economics and Statistics Administration, 'FFF: American Indian and Alaska Native Heritage Month: November 2015' https://www.census.gov/newsroom/facts-for-features/2015/cb15-ff22.html (accessed 14 June 2017). Similar data, albeit with some variations, is reproduced in Caprice L Roberts, 'A Desert Grows between Us – The Sovereignty Paradox at the Intersection of Tribal and Federal Courts The Washington and Lee Law Alumni Association Student Notes' (2008) 65 Washington and Lee Law Review 347, 349; Pommersheim, *Braid of Feathers* (n 47) 7.

[49] US Census Bureau: Department of Commerce, Economics and Statistics Administration, 'FFF' (n 48).

[50] '14.3% The proportion of Alaska's population identified as American Indian and Alaska Native, alone or in combination, in 2013, the highest share for this race group of any state. Alaska was followed by Oklahoma (7.5 percent), New Mexico (9.1), South Dakota (8.5 percent) and Montana (6.8 percent).' Ibid.

[51] Alain-G Gagnon and José María Sauca, *Negotiating Diversity Identity, Pluralism and Democracy* (Peter Lang 2014) 108; Ron Levy and Graeme Orr, *The Law of Deliberative Democracy* (Routledge 2016); Daniel J Elazar, 'Religious Diversity and Federalism' (2001) International Social Science Journal 3; Australian Government – Referendum Council, 'Final Report' 1–10; David A Dulio and James A Thurber, 'America's Two-Party System: Friend or Foe?' (2000) 52 Administrative Law Review 769; Ian Marsh, 'Beyond the Two Party System: New Zealand and Australia? [Address to The Sydney Institute, 11 June 1996.]' (1996) 8 Sydney Papers 40.

interaction which has been far from ideal. As discussed in other sections of this book, European colonization had an overall negative impact on original inhabitants.[52] Past injustices have been recognized by Congress.[53] In addition, this section of the book is not intended to provide a comprehensive analysis of multifarious relationships between complex sociological entities and the US institutions, nor is it intended to suggest a potential solution to the debate over the role of tribal sovereignty in the American constitutional system.[54] The aim of this chapter is, instead, to show how past institutional engagements with identity-based claims might inform the process of the recognition and negotiation of distinctive territorial governance for, for instance, Native Hawaiians or, in the future, Puerto Ricans.[55]

The source of pre-Columbian populations' constitutional claims is the US constitution and the series of statutes that stemmed from it.[56] In addition, US Supreme Court jurisprudence has devised key principles of

---

52 Howard Zinn, *A People's History of the United States: 1492–Present* (Kindle Edition) (HarperCollins 2003) Ch 1; Jared Diamond, *Guns, Germs and Steel. A Short History of Everybody in the Last 13,000 Years* (Kindle Edition Vintage 2005) Ch 18. See, for instance, the reports of the effect of first contacts with European settlers: Donna L Akers, 'Choctaw' in Richard Schaefer, *Encyclopedia of Race, Ethnicity, and Society* (SAGE 2008); Arieahn Matamonasa-Bennett, 'Cherokee' in Richard Schaefer, *Encyclopedia of Race, Ethnicity, and Society* (SAGE 2008); Pommersheim, 'Broken Landscape' (n 7) Ch 1.

53 Pub. L. 111-118 – S.J. Res. 14 – 111th Congress (2009–2010): A joint resolution to acknowledge a long history of official depredations and ill-conceived policies by the Federal Government regarding Indian tribes and offer an apology to all Native Peoples on behalf of the United States. 2009; Committees: Indian Affairs – Congress U.S., 'S. Rept. 108–310 – To Acknowledge a Long History of Official Depredations and Illconceived Policies by The United States Government Regarding Indian Tribes and Offer an Apology to All Native Peoples on Behalf of The United States' 108–310 https://www.congress.gov/congressional-report/108th-congress/senate-report/310/1 (accessed 15 June 2017).

54 Babcock (n 7); Joseph William Singer, 'Property and Coercion in Federal Indian Law: The Conflict between Critical and Complacent Pragmatism Symposium on the Renaissance of Pragmatism in American Legal Thought: Comments' (1989) 63 Southern California Law Review 1821; Pommersheim, *Braid of Feathers* (n 47); Cross and Lomond (n 34).

55 Ginsburg and Posner (n 4).

56 U.S. Const., Article, I §2 cl. 3, U.S. Const., Article, I §8 cl. 3, U.S. Const., Amend., XIV §2 cl. 1; Cross and Lomond (n 34) 261; Getches (n 7) 269. For an example of statute that engages the accommodation of rights see Indian Civil Rights Act of 1968, 82 Stat. 73.

the system of governance for American tribes.[57] The distinctive role of American Indians within the American constitutional system is recognized in the 1789 constitution and from the eighteenth-century jurisprudence of the Supreme Court.[58] There are a series of debates over the nature of the recognition and the extension of American Indian judicial autonomy.[59] However, it is reasonable to suggest that American Indians directly and indirectly influenced the drafting of the constitution.[60] In addition to constitutional textual references, the interaction between American institutions and tribes has been heavily dependent on the Supreme Court's jurisprudence. Early cases such as *Johnson v M'Intosh*, *Cherokee Nation v Georgia* and *Worcester v State of Georgia* defined the long-lasting relationship between Americans and Indian tribes.[61] *Johnson v M'Intosh* is a land-law case that qualified the federal prerogative to

---

[57] U.S. Const., Article, I §2 cl. 3, U.S. Const., Article, I §8 cl. 3, U.S. Const., Amend., XIV §2 cl. 1, *Cherokee Nation v Georgia 30 US 1 (1831)* 30 US 1; *Worcester v State of Georgia* (1831) 31 US 515, 530, 545; *Johnson v M'Intosh* [1823] US LEXIS 293 (US Supreme Court); *U S v Kagama* [1886] US 375 (United States Supreme Court) 385; *US v Winans* (1905) 371 US 375 (Supreme Court of the United States) 382. The controversial nature of the land ownership original title originated in *Johnson v. M'Intosh* will not be discussed in this book. Pommersheim, 'Broken Landscape' (n 7) Ch 3.

[58] U.S. Const., Article, I §2 cl. 3, U.S. Const., Article, I §8 cl. 3, U.S. Const., Amend., XIV §2 cl. 1, *Cherokee Nation v. Georgia 30 U.S. 1 (1831)* (n 57); *Worcester v. State of Georgia* (n 57); *Johnson v. M'Intosh* (n 57); *U S v. Kagama* (n 57) 385; *U.S. v. Winans* (n 57) 382. The controversial nature of the land ownership original title originated in Johnson v. M'Intosh (n 57) will not be discussed in this book. Pommersheim, 'Broken Landscape' (n 7) Ch 3; Robert J Miller, 'American Indian Constitutions and Their Influence on the United States Constitution' [2016] https://papers.ssrn.com/sol3/papers.cfm?abstract_id=2739936 (accessed 4 October 2017).

[59] Babcock (n 7); Pommersheim, 'Broken Landscape' (n 7) Ch 8; Gregory Ablavsky, '"With the Indian Tribes": Race, Citizenship, and Original Constitutional Meanings (Stanford Public Law Working Paper – Stanford Law Review) 2018 –' https://papers.ssrn.com/abstract=3082038 (accessed 2 January 2018).

[60] These sovereign-to-sovereign concerns are most distinctly reflected in the federal–state and state–state context by the Interstate Commerce Clause, the Supremacy Clause, the Full Faith and Credit Clause, the Tenth Amendment, and Eleventh Amendment, and in the federal–tribal context by the Indian Commerce Clause and the treaty-making power. Pommersheim, 'Broken Landscape' (n 7) 34.

[61] *Johnson v. M'Intosh* (n 57); *Cherokee Nation v. Georgia 30 U.S. 1 (1831)* (n 57); *Worcester v. State of Georgia* (n 57). McNeill (n 47) 283; Roberts (n 48); Pommersheim, *Braid of Feathers* (n 47); Joseph P Kalt and Joseph William Singer, 'Myths and Realities of Tribal Sovereignty: The Law and Economics of

manage land titles and prepared the basis for the US doctrine of the so-called *terra nullius*.[62]

The line of authority set by Chief Justice Marshall in *M'Intosh* was further qualified by *Cherokee Nation v Georgia.* The case concerned the prerogative of the state of Georgia to legislate in areas controlled by the Cherokees. The Cherokees had, as a sovereign foreign nation, signed a series of treaties with the USA which granted the control of land that was included in the state of Georgia.[63] The acceptance of Cherokee sovereignty was, however, curtailed by the qualification of their relation with the federal government:

> They [the Cherokees] occupy a territory to which we assert a title independent of their will, which must take effect in point of possession when their right of possession ceases. Meanwhile they are in *a state of pupillage*. Their relation to the United States resembles that of *a ward to his guardian.*[64]

The idea of federal institutions as the trustees of the tribes provides substance to the so-called domestic dependent nation which, again, Chief Justice Marshall defined in the opening section of the case: 'It may well be doubted whether those tribes which reside within the acknowledged boundaries of the United States can, with strict accuracy, be denominated foreign nations. They may more correctly, perhaps, be denominated domestic dependent nations.'[65] The paternalist stance manifested in the idea of a

---

Indian Self-Rule' (Social Science Research Network 2004) SSRN Scholarly Paper ID 529084 https://papers.ssrn.com/abstract=529084 (accessed 21 April 2017).

[62] 'However, the tribes of Indians inhabiting this country were *fierce savages*, whose occupation was war, and whose subsistence was drawn chiefly from the forest. To leave them in possession of *their country, was to leave the country a wilderness*; to govern them as a distinct people, was impossible, because they were as brave and as high spirited as they were fierce, and were ready to repel by arms every attempt on their independence.' [My emphasis.] *Johnson v. M'Intosh* (n 57) 590.

[63] By those treaties, the bill asserts, the Cherokee Nation of Indians are acknowledged and treated as sovereign and independent states, within the boundary arranged by those treaties, and that the complainants are, within the boundary established by the treaty of 1719, sovereign and independent, with the right of self-government, without any right of interference with the same on the part of any State of the United States. *Cherokee Nation v. Georgia 30 U.S. 1 (1831)* (n 57).

[64] [My emphasis.] Ibid 17.

[65] Ibid 2.

domestic 'dependent nation', whose interests were to be managed by federal institutions, projected a long shadow on the jurisprudence of the Supreme Court. In *Lone Wolf v Hitchcock*, for instance, the Supreme Court established that, whilst bound by the doctrine of good faith, the US Congress has plenary authority over the Indian tribes.[66] In addition, the US Congress has the power to act for the benefit of an inferior and has a duty of care for those who are deemed unable to look after themselves.[67]

The implications of this paternalist stance have been almost exclusively negative.[68] For instance, it relegates the role of the Indian court within reservations to Indians: 'Because Congress has done little to disrupt these decisions, the Supreme Court has almost single-handedly created the modem framework for tribal court jurisdiction, while simultaneously limiting tribal sovereignty'.[69] So, the Supreme Court has further curtailed the role of Indian identity-based constitutional claims by reducing the effect of federal prerogatives to care for Indian tribes, but without giving those prerogatives back. In 1959, for instance, the Supreme Court allowed state legislation in areas of law that were not previously covered by federal law to be effective within Indian reservations.[70] States can regulate areas of law within the reservations that were not explicitly covered by federal legislation and therefore had the consequence of transferring *in absentia*, so to speak, the federal duty of care to the states. Unfortunately, states tend to have a vested interest in managing resources on Indian reservation lands that are owned by or leased to non-tribal members.[71]

---

[66] 'It is to be presumed that in this matter the United States would be governed by such considerations of justice as would control a Christian people in their *treatment of an ignorant and dependent race* [...] Plenary authority over the tribal relations of the Indians has been exercised by Congress from the beginning, and the power has always been deemed a political one, not subject to be controlled by the judicial department of the government.' [My emphasis.] *Lone Wolf v Hitchcock 187 US 553 (1903)* 566.

[67] 'These Indian tribes are the wards of the nation'. Ibid 567; Babcock (n 7) 501.

[68] Babcock (n 7) 502.

[69] McNeill (n 47) 289.

[70] 'Essentially, absent governing Acts of Congress, the question has always been whether the state action infringed on the right of reservation Indians to make their own laws and be ruled by them'. *Williams v Lee 358 US 217 (1959)* 458.

[71] Marietta L Baba, 'Anthropology and Transnational Migration: A Focus on Policy' (2013) 51 International Migration 1, 502.

The negative implications, including the recent twists and turns in the dependant nation's jurisprudence, do not need to be explored further. This short overview of the Supreme Court's engagement with identity-based constitutional claims shows sufficient indications of its ability to engage a rather limited amount of lexical references in the US constitution and in the treaties to form a very articulated analysis of the role of the American Indian tribes in the current US constitutional system.

The recognition of an American Indian national sovereignty, by way of comparison with state sovereignty, had been subdued. Indian autonomy has been limited to Indians.[72] There is, however, an increase in the theoretical awareness of the limits of the line of authority that seeks to reduce the autonomy of Indian tribes.[73] Both the negative implications, and they are more than a few, and the positive aspects of the jurisprudence set a reference point for the process of the recognition and negotiation of Indians' identity-based constitutional claims for other American identity groups who have a distinctive claim for self-governance based on a historical narrative. That would be the case, with the opportune distinctions that such analogies should have, for the Natives Hawaiians and Puerto Ricans.

It is the distinctive ability to engage limited, by way of comparison with other legal systems considered in this book, textual material and to develop a ductile line of authority that make US Supreme Court jurisprudence one of the current (and future) drivers of change in an analysis of the process of the recognition and negotiation of identity-based claims.

DRIVER OF CHANGE: HAWAIIAN SUBCONSTITUTIONALISM

American Indian Nations, as discussed, have a privileged status within the rigid USA and the ductility of the Supreme Court's jurisprudence on Indian tribes qualified the interplay between the principle of formal equality and Indian constitutional claims. In this section, I will continue to discuss the role of territorial minorities by considering Native Hawaiians who make self-governance claims within the US federal system. These claims do not have, as the Indian tribes' claims do, a privileged US constitutional status. They are negotiated and recognized in the state

---

72 Kalt and Singer (n 61).

73 Getches (n 7) 273; Pommersheim, 'Broken Landscape' (n 7); Pommersheim, 'The Crazy Horse Malt Liquor Case' (n 7).

constitution, yet the legitimacy of the 'deals' are subject to constitutional review.[74] Ton Ginsburg and Eric Posner call the processes of negotiation and recognition that occur at state level 'subconstitutional'.[75] The main concern of Ginsburg and Posner's article is to show the economic command/control implications of subconstitution in a system of governance;[76] in this section, I will show instead how identity claims are negotiated into the state constitution. In particular, I will focus on the effects of the aforementioned ductile constitutional jurisprudence of the Supreme Court, the possibility of Native Hawaiians conveying votes in state and national elections, and the existence of a distinctive communal land regulatory system.

A distinctive historical element of the Hawaiian colonization was the appropriation of over half a million acres of Hawaiian public and Crown land by the US government.[77] A large section of the ironically named 'ceded land' had to be held in a trust by the US government for the benefit of Native Hawaiians.[78] Before the US occupation, the Hawaiian archipelago was organized as an internationally recognized kingdom and the invasion was motivated by a request from an unofficial government.[79]

---

[74] Kimberly A Costello, 'Rice v. Cayetano: Trouble in Paradise for Native Hawaiians Claiming Special Relationship Status Notes' (2000) 79 North Carolina Law Review 812.

[75] Ginsburg and Posner (n 4).

[76] Ibid 1588.

[77] Hawaiian Homes Commission Act (Act of July 9, 1921, c 42, 42 Stat 108) 2011. Melody Kapilialoha MacKenzie, 'Ke Ala Loa – The Long Road: Native Hawaiian Sovereignty and the State of Hawai'i' (2012) 47 Tulsa Law Review 621, 627; Jennifer M L Chock, 'One Hundred Years of Illegitimacy: International Legal Analysis of the Illegal Overthrow of the Hawaiian Monarchy, Hawai'i's Annexation, and Possible Reparations' (1995) 17 University of Hawai'i Law Review 463.

[78] Pub. L 56-339: An Act To provide a government for the Territory of Hawaii (1900) 599.

[79] Van Dyke (n 34) 95; Tom Coffman, *The Island Edge of America: A Political History of Hawai'i* (University of Hawai'i Press 2003) 7–8; Haunani-Kay Trask, *From a Native Daughter: Colonialism and Sovereignty in Hawaii* (revised ed, University of Hawai'i Press 1999) 7; MacKenzie (n 77) 625; Kathryn Nalani Setsuko Hong, 'Understanding Native Hawaiian Rights: Mistakes and Consequences of Rice v. Cayetano' (2008) 15 Asian American Law Journal 9, 11; Department of the Interior and Department of Justice, 'From Mauka To Makai: The River of Justice Must Flow Freely Report on the Reconciliation Process between the Federal Government and Native Hawaiians' 1 https://www.doi.gov/sites/doi.gov/files/migrated/ohr/library/upload/Mauka-to-Makai-Report-2.pdf (accessed 14 June 2017).

The tales of physical genocide by alien diseases,[80] sometimes spread by individuals with honourable intentions such as missionaries, and duly signed international treaties that were, once the colonies were established, quickly brushed aside, are stable elements of the Hawaiian colonization process.[81]

Distinctive of the Hawaiian colonization process is, perhaps, that it arrived relatively later than most Colonial Era campaigns.[82] Hawaii was militarily occupied in 1893 and was declared as annexed in 1898 by the Joint Resolution to Provide for Annexing the Hawaiian Islands to the USA.[83] The recognition of relatively recent past injustices has been central to the recent process of reconciliation.[84] As is the case for the Indian tribes, the recognition of Native Hawaiians and US institutions has been conditioned by the aforementioned jurisprudence of the Supreme Court. Cases such as *Rice v Cayetano* and *Hawaii v Office of Hawaiian Affairs* had the effect, among others, of showing the limits within which Hawaiian identity claims and future identity claims by, for instance, Puerto Ricans, can be accommodated via the distinctive American principle of formal equality.[85]

In the case of *Rice*, for instance, the issue was whether article XII of the state constitution, which prevented non-Native Hawaiians from voting for the election of trustees who administered public land for the benefit of Native Hawaiians, was incompatible with the Fourteenth and Fifteenth

---

[80] Trask (n 79) 9; Jon M Van Dyke, *Who Owns the Crown Lands of Hawaii?* (University of Hawai'i Press 2008) 21.

[81] A review of the historical implication of Treaty of Waitangi, discussed in this book is provided in: Anthony Angelo, *Constitutional Law in New Zealand* (Kluwer Law International 2011) 154. For a general review of the Imperial Era see Daniel R Headrick, 'The Tools of Imperialism: Technology and the Expansion of European Colonial Empires in the Nineteenth Century' (1979) The Journal of Modern History 231; Eric Hobsbawm, *Age Of Empire: 1875–1914* (Hachette UK 2010); Francis Fukuyama, *The Origins of Political Order: From Prehuman Times to the French Revolution* (Profile Books 2012).

[82] Hobsbawm (n 81) location 1241.

[83] 7 July 1898, 30 Stat. 750. Coffman (n 79) Ch 2.

[84] Pub. L 103-150 (S.J. Res. 19 – 103rd Congress; 1993–1994): A joint resolution to acknowledge the 100th anniversary of the January 17, 1893 overthrow of the Kingdom of Hawaii, and to offer an apology to Native Hawaiians on behalf of the United States for the overthrow of the Kingdom of Hawaii (1993) 103–150; Department of the Interior and Department of Justice (n 79).

[85] *Rice v Cayetano 528 US 495 (2000)*; Costello (n 74); *Hawaii v Office of Hawaiian Affairs 556 US 163 (2009)*; MacKenzie (n 77) 637.

Amendments.[86] The Supreme Court considered the preferential treatment in terms of voting rights given to Native Hawaiians incompatible with the Fifteenth Amendment that prevents discriminatory practices in ring-fencing the voting franchise.[87] In *Rice*, the Supreme Court also distinguished the line of authority set in *Morton v Mancari* in which it discussed the different treatment of American Indian employees. The *Morton v Mancari* case was over the qualification of the equal treatment clause set in the Fourteenth Amendment and was not over the prohibition to reduce the electoral franchise on the basis of race.[88]

Native Hawaiians were indeed designed as the beneficiaries of the public trust which was inserted in the Hawaii Admission Act 1959.[89] Given the clear indications of the beneficiaries and the objective criteria of the types of activities that the trust would support, it would be reasonable to assume that the ethnicity of the trustees, and of those who elected them, ought to be inconsequential. However, it is common for multinational societies, Wolff explains, to have ethnic groups which bear a reciprocal mistrust.[90]

The issue of 'who is entitled' to and 'how' to manage public land commenced before annexation.[91] The Hawaiian Crown estate was partitioned, following Western land-law principles, during the 1848 Māhele

---

[86] Hawaii. Const. Art. XII, Para 6. *Rice v. Cayetano 528 U.S. 495 (2000)* (n 85).

[87] The legal syllogism is expressed in a lucid three stages narrative. 'The purpose and command of the Fifteenth Amendment are set forth in language both explicit and comprehensive. The National Government and the States may not violate a fundamental principle: They may not deny or abridge the right to vote on account of race. […] The voting structure now before us is neither subtle nor indirect. It is specific in granting the vote to persons of defined ancestry and to no others […] Ancestry can be a proxy for race. It is that proxy here.' Ibid 511–514.

[88] *Morton v. Mancari 417 U.S. 535 (1974)* (n 34). For critical review of the relationship between the two cases see Kathryn Nalani Setsuko Hong, 'Understanding Native Hawaiian Rights: Mistakes and Consequences of Rice v. Cayetano' (2008) 15 Asian American Law Journal 9.

[89] Pub. L 86-3 An Act to provide for the admission of the State of Hawaii into the Union. (Hawaii Admission Act) 1959 s 5 (f). Pub. L 86-3 makes a direct reference to the Hawaiian Homes Commission Act (Act of July 9, 1921, c 42, 42 Stat 108) (n 77).

[90] Stefan Wolff, 'The Institutional Structure of Regional Consociations in Brussels, Northern Ireland, and South Tyrol' (2004) 10 Nationalism and Ethnic Politics 387.

[91] Van Dyke (n 80) Ch 4.

land reform.[92] The Māhele reform was promoted, among others, by the landowners of European and American ancestors who found the mediaeval common Crown lease systems economically inefficient for the development of large plantations.[93] The Crown public land was, following the US annexation, transferred to different US institutions.[94] In 1920, and in response to the deterioration in living conditions, by way of comparison with other groups, of the Native Hawaiians, a section of Crown land and government land (circa 203 500 acres) was given in trust to the Hawaiian Homes Commission. The Commission has the task of using the land for the benefit of Native Hawaiians.[95]

Following the 1959 statehood process, which was favoured by the majority of Native Hawaiians, large sections of the land ceded to the USA were returned to the state of Hawaii and, as a requirement of admission, the Hawaiian Homes Commission Act was inserted in the Hawaii constitution.[96] However, the Hawaiian state received only the so-called naked title and the obligation to manage it in trust for the betterment of Native Hawaiians.[97] Finally, in 1978, the constitutional

---

[92] Ibid 42; Stuart Minor Benjamin, 'Equal Protection and the Special Relationship: The Case of Native Hawaiians' (1996) 106 The Yale Law Journal 537, 549; Van Dyke (n 34) 102.

[93] MacKenzie (n 77) 625. The Māhele, literally partition, allowed private ownership of the divided land wanted by foreign farmers but also allocated a third of the partitioned land to be held in trust for the benefits of Native Hawaiians. Hong (n 79) 12; Van Dyke (n 80) Ch 4.

[94] Pub. L 56-339: An Act to Provide a Government for the Territory of Hawaii. (n 78).

[95] Hawaiian Homes Commission Act (Act of July 9, 1921, c 42, 42 Stat 108) (n 77); Van Dyke (n 34) 104.

[96] Hong (n 79) 13. Van Dyke (n 62) 257, Hawaii Constitution, Section 4. The lands granted to the State of Hawaii by Section 5(b) of the Admission Act and pursuant to Article XVI, Section 7, of the State Constitution, excluding therefrom lands defined as 'available lands' by Section 203 of the Hawaiian Homes Commission Act, 1920, as amended, shall be held by the State as a public trust for native Hawaiians and the general public [Add Const Con 1978 and election Nov 7, 1978]. Some areas remained controlled by the US Navy.

[97] 'Lands and the income therefrom, shall be held by said State as a public trust for the support of the public schools and other public educational institutions, for the betterment of the conditions of native Hawaiians, as defined in the Hawaiian Homes Commission Act, 1920, as amended, for the development of farm and home ownership on as widespread a basis as possible for the making of public improvements, and for the provision of lands for public use.' Pub. L 83-3: An Act to provide for the Admission of the State of Hawaii into the Union (The Admission Act) 1959 s 5 (e).

reform established the Office of Hawaiian Affairs with a board of trustees elected, in its initial design, by a franchise that included only Native Hawaiians.[98]

Given such a controversial history, the reluctance of Native Hawaiians to include non-natives in the process that managed their newly acquired ancestral land is understandable. However, these types of narratives are negatively considered in *Rice v Cayetano*. The supporting reason for deciding *Rice* is both simple and formally persuasive.[99] The recognition of the implausibility of racial categorization in a way that discriminates the allocation of a universal right to participate in an election appears reasonable.[100] However, regarding the management and access to land, there is a historical context which explains the mistrust that Native Hawaiians have vis-à-vis those who are not natives.[101] The reduction of the electoral franchise on the basis of racial categorization was therefore unfortunate but not dissimilar from the de facto sectarian limits of the process that selected the appointees to the office of First Minister and her/his Deputy in the Northern Irish government.[102] *Rice* is, largely, about who is managing public resources and the Good Friday Agreement is about who should benefit from those resources, yet *Rice* shows a limit to the idea that subconstitutionalism should be considered only from an allocation of rights' perspective.[103] In particular, *Rice* also sets a clear limitation on the state constitution that negotiates identity claims, and overall, on the US constitutional system. The justifications for allocating the management of resources to a minority cannot, the Court suggests, be historical.[104] Native Hawaiian communities are, by way of comparison

---

98 The trust had to be manged in a way that was analogous to a private trust. *Ahuna v Dept of Hawaiian Home Lands 640 P2d 1161 (1982).*

99 The purpose and command of the Fifteenth Amendment are set forth in language both explicit and comprehensive. 'The National Government and the States may not violate a fundamental principle: They may not deny or abridge the right to vote on account of race. [...] The voting structure now before us is neither subtle nor indirect. It is specific in granting the vote to persons of defined ancestry and to no others [...] Ancestry can be a proxy for race. It is that proxy here'. (My emphasis.) *Rice v. Cayetano 528 U.S. 495 (2000)* (n 85). pp 511–515.

100 J Kehaulani Kauanui, 'The Politics of Blood and Sovereignty in Rice v. Cayetano' (2002) 25 Political and Legal Anthropology Review 110, 100; Tully (n 23).

101 Wolff (n 90).

102 Northern Ireland (St Andrews Agreement) Act 2006 c. 53 pt 8 (4, 5).

103 Ginsburg and Posner (n 4) 1588.

104 Costello (n 74).

with other Hawaiian ethnic communities, economically depressed and that might be linked to the illegal annexation which interfered with the traditional land-management system.[105]

Furthermore, and as mentioned in the discussion on Indian tribes, the idea that a group has privileged status is already part of American constitutionalism, yet historical narratives which indeed shaped the current perception of Native Hawaiian national identity cannot be, according to the Supreme Court, constructed in a way that justifies derogations to the Fifteenth Amendment. This is unfortunate because the concern over the protection of a direct link between the popular will and its statutory manifestation that the Fifteenth Amendment seeks to protect might be considered truncated. A majority cannot insert a management system that protects a historically underprivileged minority. Again, the refusal to accept that majorities with minority status might adopt, for historical reasons, a distinctive system of values (that is negotiated into a state constitution)[106] appears to be missing in the jurisprudence of the Supreme Court. In *Tuaua v United States*, for instance, the Court of Appeal of the District of Columbia Court accepted the derogation of the principle of formal equality on the ground that such a derogation was supported by the majority of democratically elected representatives of Samoa.[107] In relation to Hawaii, the Supreme Court does not give weight to the fact that a land-management arrangement was an effect of the negotiation process that was democratically supported and that followed a historically unfair appropriation of common land.[108]

The discrepancy between the treatment of the two Pacific nations can be explained by the different territorial arrangements (one is a territory

---

[105] Van Dyke (n 34) 96; Hong (n 79) 16–20; Pub. L 103-150 (S.J. Res. 19 – 103rd Congress; 1993–1994): A joint resolution to acknowledge the 100th anniversary of the January 17, 1893 overthrow of the Kingdom of Hawaii, and to offer an apology to Native Hawaiians on behalf of the United States for the overthrow of the Kingdom of Hawaii (n 84); US Census Bureau: Department of Commerce, Economics and Statistics Administration, 'Native Hawaiian and Other Pacific Islander Alone or in Combination with One or More Other Races (500–599) & (100–299) or (300, A01–Z99) or (400–999)' https://factfinder.census.gov/faces/tableservices/jsf/pages/productview.xhtml?src=bkmk (accessed 16 June 2017).

[106] Pub. L 86-3 An Act to provide for the admission of the State of Hawaii into the Union. (Hawaii Admission Act) (n 90). See, in general, Ginsburg and Posner (n 4).

[107] *Tuaua v United States 788 F 3 d (DC Cir 2015).*

[108] Pub. L 86-3: An Act to provide for the admission of the State of Hawaii into the Union. (Hawaii Admission Act) (n 89).

and the other is a state), but it also gives an indication that courts might, as they did in the past, continue to dynamically change the process of evaluation of identity-based constitutional claims.

DRIVER OF CHANGE: COLLABORATION BETWEEN IDENTITY GROUPS IN A TWO-PARTY SYSTEM

In the previous sections, I discussed the limits that identity-based constitutional claims and negotiation over their accommodation might encounter in the US constitutional system. I explained that, whilst the jurisprudence of the US Supreme Court is ductile, the principle of formal equality is deeply entrenched in the US narrative in a way that makes a deviation from orthodox constitutional narratives theoretically possible yet quite improbable. It is within this highly structured set of narratives, which has only been sketched out in the previous section, that identity-based constitutional claims can aspire to be inserted in state constitutions and indirectly into the US constitutional system.[109] In this section, I will explain that, at the political level, the two-party system of identity-based claims from a minority requires the external support of voters who are not part of the group. This support might come from other ethnic communities or from a political party such as the Democratic Party, for example. For instance, first- and second-generation Japanese immigrants to Hawaii have historically supported Native Hawaiians' demands for institutional recognition.[110] As is the case for other general drivers of change, the requirement of an alliance with other groups might act as a catalyst in the process of recognition and also as a limitation, since it requires claims to be mediated by a political process.

The Native Hawaiian struggle for recognition of their land claims has, as mentioned, received the support of other Hawaiian demographically significant ethnic groups such as the Japanese first- and second-generation immigrants who are currently US citizens.[111] The collaboration between ethnic groups of the archipelago might not be without tensions,[112] but in the recent past, this multi-identity collaboration

[109] Ginsburg and Posner (n 4).

[110] Van Dyke (n 34) 108; Kerry Lee Haynie and Jane Junn, *New Race Politics in America* (Cambridge University Press 2008) 74–87.

[111] The first evidence of collaboration between ethnic groups was during the 1920 strikes. Judy Rohrer and Josie Herr, *Haoles in Hawai'i* (University of Hawai'i Press 2010) 354.

[112] Ibid 2, 3.

between ethnic groups has been an effective strategy for obtaining the recognition of political claims.[113] The Japanese American community included, for instance, by way of comparison with other identity groups, a higher number of statehood supporters.[114] This point is delicate. There are, it is important to add, strong indications taken from the demographic and sociological analyses that most of the population of Hawaii adopts a form of American dispersed nationalism, but that their dispersed nationalism is distinctive of the East Asian and Oceania communities.[115]

Native Hawaiians' collaboration with the Democratic Party and the American Japanese, for instance, allowed significant inputs into the 1978 constitutional reform.[116] 'In its Hawaiian Amendments, the Convention made the Hawaiian language an official language of the state, reinstalled the right of free access to the ocean and religious spaces, and established the Office of Hawaiian Affairs'.[117] On a more general level, during the last few decades, there have been clear signs that Hawaii's partnership between the Democratic Party, the Asian waves of immigration and Native Hawaiians has continued to shape Native Hawaiian identity-based political claims.[118] The analysis of Hawaii's subconstitution shows, on a more general level, that the process of collaboration between ethnic communities and national political parties is one of the drivers of change for the US recognition process for identity groups that move in sync with, rather than against, the idea of an American constitutional patriotism.

Two-party systems tend to marginalize minorities at the national level.[119] That is, for instance, the case in Canada and in the UK, but they might also create situations in which minor political parties, which associate with identity groups, have the role of king makers in the

---

[113] Alan Trench, 'Scotland and Wales: The Evolution of Devolution' in Robert Hazell (ed), *Constitutional Futures Revisited: Britain's Constitution to 2020* (Palgrave Macmillan 2008); Rohrer and Herr (n 111) 339.

[114] Coffman (n 79) 290.

[115] Judith Schachter and Albrecht Funk, 'Sovereignty, Indigeneity, Identities: Perspectives from Hawai'i' (2012) 18 Social Identities 399.

[116] Coffman (n 79) 304–5.

[117] Schachter and Funk (n 115) 404.

[118] Coffman (n 79) 330–348, 354.

[119] Dulio and Thurber (n 51); Marsh (n 51); Darrell West and Zev Chafets, 'Is America's Two-Party System Broken?' (2012) 144 New York Times Upfront 22; Judith Brett, *The Australian Liberals and the Moral Middle Class* (Cambridge University Press 2003).

national political arena.[120] For instance, in the 2017 UK election, the normal cycle of the two-party system has been interrupted by a coalition between the Conservative Party and one of the Northern Irish nationalist parties called the Democratic Unionist Party.[121] The Democratic Unionist Party, in exchange for political support within the UK parliament, managed to obtain substantial economic and institutional concessions for its constituency.[122] The example of the Democratic Unionist Party might be, by way of comparison with the US national political arena, extreme, yet the point is that American national minorities might collaborate with other political entities in a way that substantially changes the process of negotiation between regional and central institutions. This is, in other words, a general driver of change that does affect Native Hawaiians and other US localized identity groups such as the Puerto Rican nation.[123]

The historical collaboration (or indeed antagonism) between one of the two large political parties and regional ethnic groups has implications for the territorial management of that state. Collaboration is only one of the selected drivers of change, a part of the complex interactions that had to be respectful of the qualification of the principle of formal equality. The principle has developed diverging implications in the qualifications given by the Supreme Court for the management of Indian reservations and Native Hawaiians' land. It is reasonable to suggest, again within the limits of reasonableness, that the negotiation of identity claims within the US federation has, by way of comparison with the other legal systems considered in this book, a narrow scope.

---

[120] Jonathan J Bean, *Race and Liberty in America* (University Press of Kentucky 2009) Ch 7; Haynie and Junn (n 110) 167.

[121] Jonathan Tonge, 'Supplying Confidence or Trouble? The Deal Between the Democratic Unionist Party and the Conservative Party' (2017) 88 The Political Quarterly 412.

[122] Ibid 415.

[123] J Font-Guzmán, *Experiencing Puerto Rican Citizenship and Cultural Nationalism* (Springer 2016).

REFLECTING ON THE EFFECTS OF FLEXIBLE CONSTITUTIONAL ARRANGEMENTS: THE CONGRESSIONAL PLENARY POWER TO REGULATE IDENTITY-BASED CONSTITUTIONAL CLAIMS IN AMERICAN TERRITORIES

In the previous sections, I discussed the political and constitutional drivers of change. I reviewed the limiting factors that a rigid amendment process and the application of the principle of formal equality had in the process of the recognition and negotiation of identity-based constitutional claims at federal and state level. In the following sections, I will evaluate the process of the accommodation of identity-based claims in the US-inhabited territories.[124] In these territories, Congress has a statutory prerogative to accommodate identity claims that might, if sufficient reasons are given, trump the individual rights and qualifications of these rights by the US Supreme Court. There is an obvious sinister implication to such power, but the larger legislative power also provides an opportunity to test one of the claims defended in this book. That is, a flexible constitutional setting allows for the accommodation, within the limit of reasonableness, of identity claims and the protection of cultural diversity.

Before an analysis of identity-based claims in the US territories can begin, a series of general qualifications is necessary. Firstly, the US constitutional system, as mentioned earlier in this chapter, extends sovereignty claims over a series of territories, but only five of these are inhabited: American Samoa, the Commonwealth of the Northern Mariana Islands, Guam, the US Virgin Islands and Puerto Rico. Distinctive of these five territories is the existence of politically significant linguistic groups that are ethnically linked to a territory.[125] They should be considered as ethnic nations in a way that is comparable with, for instance, European national minorities, Quebec, or the nation islands administrated by the Realm of New Zealand.[126] There is also, at least in

---

[124] *Late Corp. of the Church of Jesus Christ of Latter-Day Saints v United States, 136 US 1, 42 (1890)*, 42. A recent general analysis of the territorial governance of US territories is provided in Lawson and Seidman (n 7) pt II.

[125] John Kincaid, 'Territorial Neutrality and Cultural Pluralism in American Federalism: Is the United States the Archenemy of Peripheral Nationalism?' (2016) 22 Swiss Political Science Review 565, 577.

[126] Michael Keating, 'So Many Nations, so Few States: Territory and Nationalism in the Global Era' in James Tully and Alain Gagnon (eds), *Multinational Democracies* (Cambridge University Press 2001); Stevenson

theory, a congressional prerogative to allocate special protections – in terms of the preservation of cultural assets such as establishing an official language and traditions – to these national groups, which might be contrary to the general principle of formal equality as qualified by the Supreme Court.[127] The congressional prerogative, for instance, includes the power to delegate legislative and administrative prerogatives to institutions operating within a US territory.[128]

Secondly, the constitutional power granted to Congress to legislate in the territories does not include, as mentioned earlier, an automatic allocation of constitutionally protected rights. This qualification is, again, controversial, but only tangential to the debate over the recognition of identity-based constitutional claims discussed in this book.[129] The issue of whether some of the fundamental rights (e.g. no person can be deprived of life, liberty, or property without the due process of law) have been granted to all residents of a territory is part of the debate over the legislative prerogatives given to Congress.[130]

However, this book discusses how identity-based constitutional claims are negotiated and inserted into a system of governance in a way that tunes an ethnic community's perception of fairness with the value protected in the constitution. For instance, Native Hawaiians' management of public land has altered the general administration of public resources in a way that favours an ethnic group. In the case of the territories, the debate over the allocation of rights is relevant in an examination of the process that recognizes minorities only insofar as those rights are demanded by an identity group and the request is associated with a level of territorial self-governance.[131] The question is engaged, among others, in the Insular Cases' jurisprudence of the US

(n 19); Tony Angelo, 'To Be or Not to Be […] Integrated, That is the Problem of Islands' [2002] Revue Juridique Polynésienne 87; Wolff (n 90).

[127] 'The power of Congress over the Territories of the United States is general and plenary, arising from and incidental to the right to acquire the Territory itself, and from the power given by the Constitution to make all needful rules and regulations respecting the Territory or other property belonging to the United States.' *Late Corp. of the Church of Jesus Christ of Latter-Day Saints v United States, 136 US 1, 42 (1890)* 42. A recent general analysis of the territorial governance of US territories is provided in Lawson and Seidman (n 7) pt II. Jorge Duany, *Puerto Rico: What Everyone Needs to Know* (Oxford University Press 2017) 152.

[128] Ibid 128–134.

[129] Ibid 7.

[130] 'Developments in the Law – The U.S. Territories' (n 9) 1618.

[131] Costello (n 74).

Supreme Court.[132] However, identity-based claims discussed in this book are part of political endeavours that seek the recognition of cultural diversity. In other words, identity-based claims are requests by a political group 'to be treated differently' for whatever reason by way of comparison with other political groups; the debate over the limited constitutional rights of those who reside in a territory is based on individual requests to be treated in exactly the same way as any other US citizen. For instance, in *Tuaua v United States*, a group of Samoan nationals, some of whom were US veterans, sought to extend the effect of the status of being a US citizen to American Samoan nationals.[133] The legal challenge was, however, opposed by the government of American Samoa that considered the effects of enlarging the US system of rights to the islands of Samoa as potentially hindering the cultural independence of the Samoans.[134]

Thirdly, the US territories have been managed in a way that is distinctive of other historically acquired US territories. For instance, the expansion of the US federation to include the Louisiana Purchase was perceived as inevitable.[135] Randolph argued, for instance, that the status of a territory such as the Philippines, which was at the time controlled by the USA, had to be temporary.[136] The different stances in relation to what to do with the new territories, so to speak, were typical of the era. Some of the narratives were squarely racist and inflammatory.[137] However, the prevailing stance, which informed the subsequent jurisprudence of the

---

[132] There is a rich and articulated literature on the so-called Insular Cases that discusses the constitutional limits of, for instance, rights to US Citizen and US Nationals who reside in the US Territories. In general see: *DeLima v Bidwell 182 US 1 (1901)*; *Goetze v United States 182 US 221 (1901)*; *Dooley v United States 182 US 222 (1901)*; *Armstrong v United States 182 US 243 (1901)*; *Downes v Bidwell 182 US 244 (1901)*; *Huus v New York & Porto Rico Steamship Co 182 US 392 (1901)*. For instance, see the qualification of this issue in *Balzac v Porto Rico 258 US 298 (1922)* 312–313.

[133] *Tuaua v. United States 788 F. 3 d (D.C. Cir 2015)* (n 107).

[134] Ibid 310.

[135] 'Developments in the Law – The U.S. Territories' (n 9) 1618; Carman F Randolph, 'Constitutional Aspects of Annexation' (1898) 12 Harvard Law Review 291, 313; Christopher Columbus Langdell, 'The Status of Our New Territories' (1899) Harvard Law Review 365; Simeon E Baldwin, 'The Constitutional Questions Incident to the Acquisition and Government by the United States of Island Territory' (1899) Harvard Law Review 393.

[136] Randolph (n 135) 313.

[137] In reference to the new possessions he used this qualifier: 'The presence of an alien and inferior race'. James Bradley Thayer, 'Our New Possessions' (1899) 12 Harvard Law Review 464, 474.

US Supreme Court, is inspired by Langdell. In the constitution and its amendments,

> it is declared that the same persons shall be citizens of the State in which they reside, and this shows that the authors of the amendment contemplated only States, for, if they had contemplated Territories as well, they certainly would have said citizens of the State or Territory in which they reside.[138]

Thus, the US constitution recognizes the power of Congress to rule the territories but it does not extend, to those residing in these lands the same rights enjoyed by US citizens in their homeland.[139] Distinctive of Langdell's stance, by way of comparison with Thayer's, is the possibility that territories can be ruled by Congress for a long period of time without necessarily assuming that they will be incorporated into the USA or, for instance, ceded to another country.[140]

Again, the historical repercussions on individuals of Langdell's position and his rendering by the US Supreme Court have been significant, yet that debate is only incidental to the demand to alter the system of government of the territories on the basis of a perception of fairness.[141] It is relevant to our discussion that these territories are autonomous and self-governing political entities. The American Samoan constitution includes a Bill of Rights and it is a self-governed territory.[142] Guam is an autonomous territory which hosts, by way of comparison with other territories, a large military area,[143] and it is considered by the UN as a non-self-governing territory.[144] The US Virgin Islands is a US territory currently without a constitution and it is also considered, as is Guam, non-self-governing by the Special Committee on the Situation with Regard to the Implementation of the Declaration on the Granting of

---

[138] Langdell (n 135) 376.

[139] 'Developments in the Law – The U.S. Territories' (n 9) 1618.

[140] *Downes v. Bidwell 182 U.S. 244 (1901)* (n 132).

[141] 'Developments in the Law – The U.S. Territories' (n 9) 1617–1622.

[142] American Samoa Constitution (copy provided by the American Samoa Bar Association).

[143] Frank Quimby, 'Fortress Guåhån: Chamorro Nationalism, Regional Economic Integration and US Defence Interests Shape Guam's Recent History' (2011) 46 The Journal of Pacific History 357.

[144] United Nations General Assembly, 'Question of Guam: Draft Resolution Submitted by the Chair Special Committee on the Situation with Regard to the Implementation of the Declaration on the Granting of Independence to Colonial Countries and Peoples 2017 A/AC.109/2017/L.18' https://www.un.org/press/en/2017/gacol3313.doc.htm (accessed 10 July 2017).

Independence to Colonial Countries and Peoples.[145] Puerto Rico is currently considered a self-governing commonwealth.[146]

Fourthly, with the exception of Puerto Rico, which has a credible claim to statehood, Guam, the Commonwealth of the Northern Mariana Islands, the US Virgin Islands and American Samoa have a limited population. So, if four territories (except Puerto Rico) want to become fully incorporated into the USA, they might only have the option of becoming part of a state. For instance, American Samoa has a population of less than 56 000.[147] The smallest US state, by way of comparison with American Samoa, is the state of Wyoming, yet it has a population of over 585 000.[148] Similar reasoning does apply to other territories.[149] It is important to note that size is relevant only because it is perceived as such. European microstates such as San Marino and the Vatican state are fully recognized sovereign entities and have a population which is a fraction of that of American Samoa or of the Commonwealth of the Northern Mariana Islands.[150] It is, again, outside the scope of this book to discuss the appropriate size for a region, a state or a sovereign nation.

The Commonwealth of Puerto Rico

In 2017, the Puerto Rican government sponsored a consultative referendum in which the majority of the votes supported the proposal of the country becoming a US state. The result and the negotiations that might follow are likely to substantially alter the role of the Spanish-speaking

---

145 Pub. L 83-517 Revised Organic Act of the Virgin Island 1954 Pub. L 83-517.

146 'Developments in the Law – The U.S. Territories' (n 9) 1623.

147 Central Intelligence Agency, 'The World Factbook: American Samoa' (n 41); US Census Bureau: Department of Commerce, Economics and Statistics Administration, 'U.S. Census Bureau Releases 2010 – Census Population Counts for American Samoa' https://www.census.gov/2010census/news/releases/operations/cb11-cn177.html (accessed 22 July 2017).

148 US Census Bureau: Department of Commerce, Economics and Statistics Administration, 'State Population Totals Tables: 2010–2016 – Nation, States, Counties, and Puerto Rico Population.' https://www.census.gov/data/tables/2016/demo/popest/state-total.html (accessed 22 July 2017).

149 The narrative is also provided in Joseph E Horey, 'The Right of Self-Government in the Commonwealth of the Northern Mariana Islands' (2003) 4 Asian-Pacific Law & Policy Journal 180, 222.

150 NationMaster.com, 'Encyclopedia: Demographics of San Marino' (2004) http://www.nationmaster.com/encyclopedia/Demographics-of-San-Marino (accessed 2 May 2018).

minority in the American constitutional system and perhaps the self-perception of what constitutes the American national identity. Puerto Rico might, for instance, within all the limits that a comparative analysis might require, take on the role that Quebec has for the Canadian sense of identity. Whether US constitutional patriotism might tilt towards a Canadian multinational nationalism is not for this book to forecast. What is argued in this section is that the size of Puerto Rico as a state and the large population of Spanish speakers might push the process of US constitutional accommodation of minority claims into untested territory.

Puerto Rico is the largest and most populated of the American territories.[151] Distinctive of Puerto Rico is, as mentioned in the previous section, the possibility of changing the constitutional status of the island in a way that is correspondent to the perceived identity of the majority of Puerto Ricans. Whilst the analysis is not intended to predict future developments in a way that is analogous to the 'Constitutional Futures' project,[152] it is reasonable to suggest that the most likely alteration to Puerto Rico's system-of-governance status might be associated with US statehood.[153] In this section, I will explain that the driving factors, among several, in the process of the accommodation of Puerto Rican identity-based claims are currently accommodated by the legislative activity of Congress. The assumption is that such a practice might affect the future process of the accommodation of constitutional claims.[154]

The Commonwealth of Puerto Rico was acquired, like Guam, as a result of the Spanish American War via the Treaty of Paris.[155] It is considered a self-governing territory by the UN[156] and it includes a

---

151 US Census Bureau: Department of Commerce, Economics and Statistics Administration, 'State Population Totals Tables' (n 148).

152 Hazell, *Constitutional Futures* (n 16); Hazell, *Constitutional Futures Revisited: Britain's Constitution to 2020* (n 16).

153 Congressional Research Service (n 13).

154 Pew Research Center, 'The Parties on the Eve of the 2016 Election: Two Coalitions, Moving Further Apart – Party Affiliation among Voters: 1992–2016'.

155 'Treaty of Peace (Treaty of Paris) 30 Stat. 1754 Treaty Series 343 Signed 12/10/1898, Rectified 11/3/1899' s II.

156 Special Committee on the Situation with regard to the Implementation of the Declaration on the Granting of Independence to Colonial Countries and Peoples, 'List of Non-Self-Governing Territories: The United Nations and Decolonization. Data Is from United Nations Secretariat 2017 Working Papers on Non-Self-Governing Territories (NSGTs), and for Western Sahara, from UNdata (Data.Un.Org), a Database by the United Nations Statistics Division of the Department of Economic and Social Affairs, United Nations.' http://www.un.org/en/decolonization/nonselfgovterritories.shtml (accessed 2 August 2017).

population of around 3.7 million inhabitants, the majority of whom are Spanish speakers.[157] Following the 1992 Presidential Memorandum on the Commonwealth of Puerto Rico, all federal administrative departments interact with Puerto Rican administrations as if they were US state administrations,[158] yet the level of administrative autonomy of Puerto Rican institutions is still heavily dependent on Congress's delegation of power.[159]

The 2007 President's Task Force report on Puerto Rico's status notes that US Congress still retains a very large legislative discretion on matters related to Puerto Rico. The recently approved Puerto Rico Oversight, Management, and Economic Stability Act 2016, which allocates large administrative powers over the island institutions to an appointed committee, is evidence of such legislative power.[160] However, the most interesting aspect of the 2007 President's Task Force report is its analysis of a potential change in the system of governance for Puerto Rico. The idea of a 'quasi' constitutionally entrenched US 'New Commonwealth' in which Congress would allocate, for instance, some legislative powers to Puerto Rican institutions is considered implausible. Such a category is not contemplated in the current US constitutional system.[161] It is also implausible to expect that constitutional amendments might allocate a special status to Puerto Rico as a

---

[157] US Census Bureau: Department of Commerce, Economics and Statistics Administration, 'State Population Totals Tables' (n 148); T Alexander Aleinikoff, 'Puerto Rico and the Constitution: Conundrums and Prospects' (1994) 11 Constitutional Commentary 15, 15.

[158] The US President, 'Memorandum for the Heads of Executive Departments and Agencies Regarding Puerto Rico'. https://www2.pr.gov/agencias/FederalFunds/Puerto_Rico_Guidance/Documents/Federal%20Regulations/Memorandum%20for%20the%20Heads%20of%20Executive%20Departments%20and%20Agencies%20regarding%20Puerto%20Rico%20Eligibility.pdf (accessed 7 August 2017).

[159] Task Force on Puerto Rico's Status, 'Report by the Task Force on Puerto Rico's Status' 5–6 http://charma.uprm.edu/~angel/Puerto_Rico/reporte_status.pdf (accessed 3 August 2017).

[160] Pub. L 114-187 48 U.S.C. § 2101 et seq Puerto Rico Oversight, Management, and Economic Stability Act or PROMESA 2016.

[161] *National Bank v County of Yankton 101 US 129 (1879)* 133; Task Force on Puerto Rico's Status (n 159) 3; Task Force on Puerto Rico's Status, 'Report by the Task Force on Puerto Rico's Status' 5 http://charma.uprm.edu/~angel/Puerto_Rico/reporte_status.pdf (accessed 3 August 2017).

US state.[162] These types of limitations, as mentioned elsewhere, are unfortunate.[163]

The remaining two options that are worth considering in the President's Task Force report are independence and statehood.[164] Independence is, however, problematic for the millions of Puerto Ricans who live on the US mainland. What is more probable is the inclusion of Puerto Rico in the constitution as a US state.[165] The report stresses, however, that a change of status must be linked to a manifestation of people's wishes.[166]

> The democratic will of the Puerto Rican people is paramount for determining the future status of the territory. To this end, the 2005 Task Force Report recommended a two-stage plebiscite to determine whether the Puerto Rican people wish to retain the status quo, and if not, which of the two available options they prefer.[167]

The report recommended a two-stage referendum process that was concluded in 2017 with a referendum that showed strong support for statehood.

The Puerto Rican desire, as manifested in the referendum results, to become a state might be impeded by the effects that its large population might have on presidential and national elections.[168] Furthermore, US voters with a Hispanic ethnic background have, in the past decades, shown a strong tendency to vote for the Democratic Party.[169] Given that Congress is the ultimate decider on the status of Puerto Rico, it is unlikely that Puerto Rico will obtain statehood without a Congress comfortably controlled by the Democratic Party. However, the US

---

162 *National Bank v. County of Yankton 101 U.S. 129 (1879)* (n 161); Task Force on Puerto Rico's Status (n 159) 3; Task Force on Puerto Rico's Status (n 161) 5. See, for a general analysis of the US amendment system, Lutz, 'Toward a Theory of Constitutional Amendment' (n 30). For an empirical comparison see Albert (n 1).

163 Dellinger (n 1); Thomas M, Thomas D and Snow (n 3).

164 Task Force on Puerto Rico's Status (n 159) 6.

165 Ibid 7; Jorge Duany, *Puerto Rico: What Everyone Needs to Know* (Oxford University Press 2017) 152.

166 Task Force on Puerto Rico's Status (n 159) 11.

167 Ibid 10.

168 Pub. L 64-368: Puerto Rican Federal Relations Act of 1917 (Foraker Act) s 5.

169 Pew Research Center (n 154); 1615 L. Street and others, 'Hispanics' http://www.pewresearch.org/data-trend/society-and-demographics/hispanics/ (accessed 8 August 2017).

political arena tends to have cycles, and thus, it is plausible to suggest that Puerto Rican statehood aspirations are likely to be accommodated in the medium future.[170] The federal aid policies that followed the 2017 hurricane Maria are unlikely to change close relations between Puerto Ricans and the Democratic Party.

In the past decades, a series of referenda sought to clarify Puerto Ricans' political views, but the results have been controversial.[171] Even the last two-stage unbinding plebiscite indicates that the majority of those who voted preferred statehood as the way forward for the system of governance of the island, yet only a relatively small minority of the electoral franchise bothered to vote. The last two-stage referendum was promoted by the government controlled by the New Progressive Party which historically had a long history of promoting statehood. The result of the 2017 two-part plebiscite indicated that the majority of the voters (97.2 per cent) would prefer to change the status of Puerto Rico from a commonwealth to a US state.

However, in 2017, only 23 per cent of those eligible to vote decided to go to the ballot boxes.[172] The low turnout in the elections and the referenda is a general trend in modern liberal democracies.[173] The so-called over-involvement has, it is argued, the effect of disfranchising voters with the political process.[174] Independently from a low turnout, the government, according to proposals approved by the Puerto Rican

---

170 Barreto (n 40).

171 Kincaid (n 125) 577.

172 Congressional Research Service (n 13) 10. The PROMESA Act introduced a special financial regime for Puerto Rican public institutions. S. 2328 – 114th Congress (2015–2016) (n 160).

173 Christopher Kirkland and Matthew Wood, 'Legitimacy and Legitimization in Low Turnout Ballots' (2017) 52 Government and Opposition 511, 512–517; Lawrence LeDuc, 'Referendums and Deliberative Democracy' (2015) 38 Electoral Studies 139, 142; Daniel Bochsler and Simon Hug, 'How Minorities Fare under Referendums: A Cross-National Study' (2015) 38 Electoral Studies 206; John H Aldrich, 'Rational Choice and Turnout' (1993) 37 American Journal of Political Science 246; Stephen Tierney, 'Giving with One Hand: Scottish Devolution within a Unitary State', (2007) 5 International Journal of Constitutional Law 4.

174 Kirkland and Wood (n 173) 512–517; LeDuc (n 173) 142; Bochsler and Hug (n 173); Aldrich (n 173); Tierney (n 173).

Assembly, intends to ask Congress to apply the so-called Tennessee plan, in which Puerto Rico declares itself a US state and asks US Congress to agree.[175]

Indeed, the recent referendum appears to have met most of the requirements set by Congress. A successful request for recognition normally needs three prerequisites: 'its inhabitants were committed to democratic governance, a clear majority favoured statehood, and the proposed state needed a sufficient population'.[176] Whether that request is accepted depends very much, as mentioned above, on the composition of Congress.[177] The effects of the recent hurricane have shown the level of economic dependence of the Puerto Rican economy on US federal subsidies, but that is only the latest in a series of events that commenced an economic crisis. The island institutions, which used the bond market to subsidize their finance, struggled to recover from the 2008 financial crisis.[178] It is a matter of speculation as to whether statehood might, in the long term, be economically and socially beneficial to Puerto Rico, but it is relatively clear that economic evaluations do affect voting behaviours.

The dire economic state of the Puerto Rican public institutions combined with the effect of recent natural disasters are likely to be referred to by those within Congress who might oppose a bid for statehood. It is, however, unlikely that the racist narratives used in the past would be used during a potential congressional debate over a Puerto Rican bid for statehood.[179] Again, Hispanic voters are part of one of the fastest growing political/ethnic communities in the USA. Moreover, large sections of the state constituencies have, according to the census, a

---

[175] Ley no. 7 2/2/2017 Ley para la descolonizazion Immedista de Puerto Rico 13; Congressional Research Service (n 13) 1.

[176] Barreto (n 40) 105.

[177] Jorge Duany, *The Puerto Rican Nation on the Move: Identities on the Island & in the United States* (University of North Carolina Press 2002) 2–6, 124.

[178] Mary Williams Walsh, 'How Puerto Rico is Grappling with a Debt Crisis', *The New York Times* (16 May 2017) https://www.nytimes.com/interactive/2017/business/dealbook/puerto-rico-debt-bankruptcy.html (accessed 4 August 2017).

[179] Jacqueline N Font-Guzmán, 'Confronting a Colonial Legacy: Asserting Puerto Rican Identity by Legally Renouncing US Citizenship' (2013) 25 Centro: Journal of the Center for Puerto Rican Studies 25; Roger Smith, 'The Bitter Roots of Puerto Rican Citizenship', in Christina Duffy Burnett and Burke Marshall (eds), *Foreign in a Domestic Sense: Puerto Rico, American Expansion, and the Constitution* (Duke University Press 2001).

majority of Spanish speakers.[180] The most likely debates would be on the protection of the official language in a state in which over 90 per cent of the population would perceive themselves as Latino or Hispanic.[181] It is because of this debate over the role of the minority language that the US constitutional system might be driven into unexplored territory.[182] It is also safe to say that a discussion over Puerto Rican statehood might provide an opportunity to discuss specific systems of territorial governance based on this historical distinctiveness of its polity. These types of discussions are, for instance, part of the constitutional narratives found in Canada in relation to Quebec's status.

American Samoa

Puerto Rico might become a state and, if that were to be the case, it is reasonable to suggest, based on the experience of Canada, that the negotiation process might alter the role played by the former Spanish colony in the US constitutional system. Negotiations over the status of American Samoa are, by way of comparison with Puerto Rico, less consequential. However, the recent case of *Tuaua v United States* gives an indication of the potential benefits, for a community that seeks the recognition of its cultural diversity, of less formally restricted systems of governance in the US territories. In particular, *Tuaua* recognized the democratic prerogative of territories to restrict the rights of their residents in a way that protects a perception of national identity supported by the majority of the island's residents.[183]

American Samoa is an autonomous US territory with a distinctive legal system and that is considered non-self-governing.[184] However, the level of indeterminacy of its status, by way of comparison with other territories and the US states, and Congress's prerogatives to allow such an indeterminacy to persist helped in the preservation of a traditional system of governance. The establishment of self-government in American Samoa happened in a 'disorderly manner'. US self-governing territories are normally governed by an organic law. This is not the case for American

---

180 Kincaid (n 125) 577.

181 Barreto (n 40).

182 Ibid 107.

183 *Tuaua v. United States 788 F. 3 d (D.C. Cir 2015)* (n 128).

184 United Nations General Assembly, 'American Samoa (A/AC.109/2017/i). The Special Committee on the Situation with Regard to the Implementation of the Declaration on the Granting of Independence to Colonial Countries and Peoples'.

Samoa. In 1951, an executive order transferred administrative responsibility to a self-governing institution expecting the enactment of a constitution.[185] A constitution was approved, via a constitutional convention, by the US Secretary of the Interior. In 1983, the US Congress finally passed a statute restricting further amendments to the constitution which had the effect of transforming de jure the American Samoan constitution into the Organic Act.[186]

The level of self-government combined with Samoa's remoteness allowed both traditional and modern forms of government to exist in parallel, so to speak.[187] There is no nationalist political party analogous to European regionalist movements; however, the national distinctiveness of Samoa is manifested in the social structure of its society.[188] Family chiefs, called 'matai', are the kingpins of Samoan societal structure 'fa'a Samoa'.[189] Furthermore, as was the case for Native Hawaiians before annexation, America has a system of management for common land which is enshrined in the American Samoan constitution.[190]

The management of the common land was perceived as potentially endangered by an attempt to extend, via judicial procedure, US citizenship to American Samoans. National American Samoans are non-citizen nationals, and this is considered one of the elements that has helped in the protection of American Samoan identity.[191] However, the current legislation and related regulations were challenged in *Tuaua v United States*.[192] A small number of Samoan nationals, some of whom were US veterans, challenged the legitimacy of the Department of State Foreign Affairs Manual, which prevents Samoan nationals from automatically obtaining US citizenship. The legal challenge required the District Court to reconsider the Insular Cases' jurisprudence, but, more importantly for

---

185 Exec. Order no. 10,264, 3 C.F.R. 447 (Supp. 195 1).

186 Act of Dec. 8, 1983, Pub. L 98-213, § 12, 97 Stat.

187 Eni FH Faleomavaega, 'Brief of the Honorable Eni F.H. Faleomavaega as Amicus Curiae in Support of Defendants – Civil Action No. 12-1143-RJL', 5 http://www.asbar.org/images/legal_issues/citizenship/tuaua%20v%20%20us%20faleomavaega%20amicus%20brief.pdf (accessed 24 July 2017).

188 Arnold H Leibowitz, 'American Samoa: Decline of a Culture' (1980) 10 California Western International Law Journal 220.

189 Ibid.

190 Faleomavaega (n 187) 5.

191 'Developments in the Law – The U.S. Territories' (n 9) 1684. US Department of State, Foreign affairs Manual §1125. i(b) (1996).

192 *Tuaua v. United States 788 F. 3 d (D.C. Cir 2015)* (n 107).

our analysis of the identity-based constitutional claims, gave the opportunity to the American Samoan government to clarify its position in relation to the allocation of rights to Samoan nationals.[193]

The Samoan government considers the extension of US citizenship rights and, in particular, the application of formal equality as potentially disadvantageous for American Samoans.[194] The DC Circuit evaluated the implications of accepting the veterans' claims that were refused by a democratic assembly and answered in the negative: '[T]o impose citizenship by judicial fiat – where doing so requires us to override the democratic prerogatives of the American Samoan people'.[195] *Tuaua and others'* application was rejected at district level and, in 2016, the US Supreme Court denied *certiorari*.[196] In short, in *Tuaua*, the Court accepts that formal equality cannot be constructed in a way that trumps the normative connection between popular will and statutory legitimacy.

Again, it is a matter of speculation whether *Tuaua* will aid in the development of a line of authority that helps, for instance, Puerto Rican institutions' intention to protect the use of Spanish colonial history. *Tuaua* should, however, be considered a remarkable decision since it shows again a manifestation of the ability of the US jurisprudence to adapt its narrative in a way that balances identity demands (supported by the majority of minority groups) with the concept of formal equality.

Commonwealth of the Northern Mariana Islands and Guam

The Northern Mariana Islands is a Pacific archipelago, without Guam, which covers an area of 464 km^2. The population is less than 60 000 and it includes a demographic mosaic of Pacific Islanders and peoples of Asian ancestry.[197] The relationship between US institutions and the archipelago's institutions is regulated by the 1975 Covenant to Establish a Commonwealth of the Northern Mariana Islands in Political Union

193 Faleomavaega (n 187).

194 United Nations General Assembly, 'American Samoa (A/AC.109/2017/i). The Special Committee on the Situation with Regard to the Implementation of the Declaration on the Granting of Independence to Colonial Countries and Peoples' (n 184) 7.

195 *Tuaua v. United States 788 F. 3 d (D.C. Cir 2015)* (n 107).

196 'Order List: 579 U.S Supreme Court June 13, 2016' https://www.supremecourt.gov/orders/courtorders/120715zor_6j37.pdf (accessed 24 July 2017).

197 Central Intelligence Agency, 'The World Factbook: Australia–Oceania: Northern Mariana Islands' https://www.cia.gov/library/publications/the-world-factbook/geos/cq.html (accessed 28 July 2017).

(hereafter, the Covenant).[198] The Northern Mariana Islands are self-governing. The USA maintains theoretically extensive legislative sovereignty;[199] however, there is a general assumption that the US Congress will not legislate in a way that is perceived to be in contrast to powers allocated to the Northern Mariana Islands by the Covenant.[200] The Covenant regulates, for instance, the allocation of US citizenship and allows a distinctive regime for immigration to the island outside of the US general rules. More importantly, it allows the Northern Mariana Islands' judicial institutions the prerogative of suspending the application of US statutory measures that are considered outside the remit of the Covenant.[201] The higher level of autonomy set in the Covenant, by way of comparison with other territories, had a direct effect on identity-based constitutional claims. It allows, for instance, strict control to be maintained over the management of land ownership, which is a common cause of attrition between Native Oceania Islanders and other residents.[202]

Guam is the largest of the islands of the Mariana archipelago and was one of the territories that Spain ceded to the USA in the Treaty of Paris.[203] The current system of governance is derived from the 1950 Organic Act which set up the conditions of democratic self-government and some basic rights for the island's residents.[204] Like the rest of the Mariana Islands, its population is made up of individuals of Pacific and

---

[198] Approved by Congress. Pub. L 94-241, § 1, Mar. 24, 1976, 90 Stat. 263. Reprinted in 48 U.S.C. § 1801.

[199] Horey (n 149) 182–186. Section 103 set the principle of self-governance and Section 105 the principle of limited US legislative sovereignty; Covenant to Establish a Commonwealth of the Northern Mariana Islands in Political Union as Approved by Congress. Pub. L 94-241, § 1, Mar. 24, 1976, 90 Stat. 263. Reprinted in 48 U.S.C. § 1801.

[200] Quimby (n 143) 360.

[201] Horey (n 149) 201, 240.

[202] Jon M Van Dyke, Carmen Di Amore-Siah and Gerald W Berkley-Coats, 'Self-Determination for Nonself-Governing Peoples and for Indigenous Peoples: The Cases of Guam and Hawai'i' (1996) 18 University of Hawai'i Law Review 623, 683; Rose Cuison Villazor, 'Blood Quantum Land Laws and the Race versus Political Identity Dilemma' (2008) 96 California Law Review 801, 807.

[203] 'Treaty of Peace (Treaty of Paris) 30 Stat.1754 Treaty Series 343 Signed 12/10/1898, Ractified 11/3/1899' (n 155) s II.

[204] 48 U.S.C. H§ 142I-24b (2012).

Asian ancestry.[205] The Chamorros are the largest of the Pacific Islander groups who reside in Guam, but, like Native Hawaiians, they do not constitute a majority of the population.[206]

Chamorros nationalism has, for several decades, demanded increased autonomy for the island in a way that is inspired by the system of governance of the Commonwealth of the Northern Mariana Islands, as well as promoting civil rights.[207] However, the process of decolonization and the related recognition of identity-based constitutional claims have to be balanced with a series of legal and pragmatic considerations that make the change of Guam's status, independently from the level of flexibility of the US constitutional system, very difficult.[208] Firstly, Chamorros nationalism has been one of the driving factors in the process of Guam's decolonization.[209] However, as is the case with all the identity-based groups, the community is 'fractured' regarding both the type and the extent of constitutional demands. Both Perez's and Quimby's analyses show, for instance, that on the crucial issue of land management,[210] there are profound disagreements among the Chamorros families over the best accommodation of the island's aspiration for autonomy, how land which is currently on lease to the US Navy ought to be reallocated and on the US economic and military interests in the East Pacific.[211]

Secondly, it remains unclear for the majority of Guam's population, as is discussed in the case of Tokelau, what the potential implications of a

---

[205] Central Intelligence Agency, 'The World Factbook: Australia–Oceania: Guam' https://www.cia.gov/library/publications/the-world-factbook/geos/gq.html (accessed 29 July 2017).

[206] Ibid; Quimby (n 143) 357.

[207] Quimby (n 143) 358. A historical analysis is provided in Penelope Bordallo Hofschneider, *A Campaign for Political Rights on the Island of Guam, 1899–1950* (CNMI Division of Historic Preservation 2001). An analysis of cultural effects of colonization is provided in Camilla Fojas, *Islands of Empire: Pop Culture and U.S. Power* (University of Texas Press 2014) Ch 5.

[208] United Nations General Assembly, 'Question of Guam: Draft Resolution Submitted by the Chair Special Committee on the Situation with Regard to the Implementation of the Declaration on the Granting of Independence to Colonial Countries and Peoples 2017 A/AC.109/2017/L.18' (n 144).

[209] Michael P Perez, 'Colonialism, Americanization, and Indigenous Identity: A Research Note on Chamorro Identity in Guam' (2005) 25 Sociological Spectrum 571; Michael P Perez, 'Pacific Identities beyond US Racial Formations: The Case of Chamorro Ambivalence and Flux' (2002) 8 Social Identities 457; Quimby (n 143).

[210] Commission on Self-Determination, 'The Draft of Guam Commonwealth Act' para 1001.

[211] Perez, 'Colonialism, Americanization, and Indigenous Identity' (n 209).

change of status would be.[212] The recent Commission on Decolonization for the Implementation and Exercise of Chamorro Self-Determination has taken on the task of increasing the level of knowledge related to the process of decolonization. The activity of the Commission on Decolonization is partly financed by the US federal institutions and one of the many educational issues that it has to grapple with is the interplay between the US citizenship allocated automatically to Guam residents, which many perceive as a valuable asset, and the demands for increased autonomy.[213]

Thirdly, the plan to change the current legal status of Guam is strongly linked to the Guam Commonwealth Act which has been repeatedly submitted as a bill to the US Congress.[214] The Guam Commonwealth Act, if it were approved by Congress, would substantially change the nature of the partnership between Guam's institutions and the USA.[215] One of the most consequential and controversial aspects of the bill is the adoption of the concept of mutual consent between Congress and the Guam Legislative Assembly for a series of legislative activities.[216] The principle of mutual consent has direct repercussions for the US Congress's legislative sovereignty over the island and it is considered one of the stumbling blocks for Congress approval.[217] As is the case for Puerto Rico, even after approval by Congress, a new hypothetical Guam organic law cannot create a new category, let us call it 'territory plus', in the US constitution.[218] Furthermore, the issue of how to manage public land which is currently on lease to the US Navy and the US Airforce overlaps both the debate over the expanding US military activities in the Pacific

---

[212] United Nations General Assembly, 'Question of Guam: Draft Resolution Submitted by the Chair Special Committee on the Situation with Regard to the Implementation of the Declaration on the Granting of Independence to Colonial Countries and Peoples 2017 A/AC.109/2017/L.18' (n 144) 4, point 3; Quimby (n 143) 380.

[213] Quimby (n 143) 378.

[214] Commission on Self-Determination (n 210); Perez, 'Colonialism, Americanization, and Indigenous Identity' (n 209) 572.

[215] T Alexander Aleinikoff, 'Securing Tribal Sovereignty: A Theory for Overturning Lone Wolf Symposium – Lone Wolf v. Hitchcock: One Hundred Years Later' (2002) 38 Tulsa Law Review 57; *Lone Wolf v. Hitchcock 187 U.S. 553 (1903)* (n 66).

[216] Commission on Self-Determination (n 210) paras 103, 104, 202, 302.

[217] Perez, 'Colonialism, Americanization, and Indigenous Identity' (n 209) 5723; Quimby (n 143).

[218] Task Force on Puerto Rico's Status (n 159).

and the debate over the role that the Chamorros wish to have in relation to property rights.[219]

Fourthly, Guam is an important US military hub for the North-East Pacific. Large sections of the island are controlled by the US Navy and by the US Airforce, which, in the past have been unsupportive of the islanders' aspiration for self-determination.[220] Even without considering the current international tensions generated by North Korea's regime, the economic development of South-East Asia has increased the importance of trade routes to and from the US mainland. Currently, the military presence in Guam is likely to increase.[221]

Thus, Guam's process of the recognition of its identity-based constitutional claims is, in comparison with the one that is affecting the Commonwealth of the Northern Mariana Islands, more complex. The process that approved the Guam Commonwealth Act and its submission to Congress shows a level of dissatisfaction with the current arrangements. The driving factor of the process of the recognition of Chamorros national identity is balanced with the concern over the potential destabilizing effect that such a change might have in the region. It is logical to deduce that a larger level of legislative discretion for Congress or a more flexible constitution might not help to qualify the political aspirations of the Chamorros.

US Virgin Islands

The US Virgin Islands is a Caribbean archipelago with limited self-governing prerogatives and it is currently listed as one of the territories, like Guam and American Samoa, that should benefit from a process of decolonization.[222] The insular system of governance is based on the 1954 Revised Organic Act of the Virgin Islands.[223] Several attempts have been

---

[219] Commission on Self-Determination (n 210) para 1001.

[220] Quimby (n 143).

[221] Perez, 'Pacific Identities beyond US Racial Formations' (n 209) 458; 'U.S. to Start Moving Okinawa-Based Marines to Guam in 2024' *The Japan Times Online* (27 April 2017) http://www.japantimes.co.jp/news/2017/04/27/national/politics-diplomacy/u-s-start-moving-okinawa-based-marines-guam-2024/ (accessed 29 July 2017).

[222] United Nations General Assembly, 'United States Virgin Islands (A/AC.109/2017/16). The Special Committee on the Situation with Regard to the Implementation of the Declaration on the Granting of Independence to Colonial Countries and Peoples'.

[223] Revised Organic Act of the Virgin Islands Pub.L 83-517, 68 Stat. 497 1954.

made to approve an American Virgin Islands constitution which, it is reasonable to suggest, would have increased the level of self-government of the Caribbean community.

The last attempt to approve a new version of the constitution ended with a US Congress joint resolution.[224] The new proposed constitution does not recognize US sovereignty and includes restrictions on the ability to buy land on the basis of official residency or ancestry.[225] These defective points, among many others, were noted during the oversight hearing before the Subcommittee on Insular Affairs, Oceans, and Wildlife of the Committee on Natural Resources.[226] The reasons for submitting such a bold, at the limit of the quixotic, proposal to Congress is a matter for speculation, but during the oversight hearing, the Territory of the Virgin Islands' Delegate in Congress argued that such views were representative of the electorate of the US Virgin Islands.[227] Again, there

---

[224] Whereas the Department of Justice concluded that several features of the proposed constitution warrant analysis and comment, including: (1) the absence of an express recognition of United States sovereignty and the supremacy of Federal law; (2) provisions for a special election on the territorial status of the United States Virgin Islands; (3) provisions conferring legal advantages on certain groups defined by place and timing of birth, timing of residency, or ancestry; (4) residence requirements for certain offices; (5) provisions guaranteeing legislative representation of certain geographic areas; (6) provisions addressing territorial waters and marine resources. Pub. L 111-194: To provide for the reconsideration and revision of the proposed constitution of the United States Virgin Islands to correct provisions inconsistent with the Constitution and Federal law.

[225] Ibid. *The Proposed Virgin Islands Constitution from the Fifth Constitutional Convention: Oversight Hearing before the Subcommittee on Insular Affairs, Oceans, and Wildlife of the Committee on Natural Resources, U.S. House of Representatives, One Hundred Eleventh Congress, Second Session, Wednesday, March 17, 2010* (Washington: 2010) http://hdl.handle.net/2027/mdp.39015090407241>.

[226] Pub. L 111-194: To provide for the reconsideration and revision of the proposed constitution of the United States Virgin Islands to correct provisions inconsistent with the Constitution and Federal law (n 224). *The Proposed Virgin Islands Constitution from the Fifth Constitutional Convention: Oversight Hearing before the Subcommittee on Insular Affairs, Oceans, and Wildlife of the Committee on Natural Resources, U.S. House of Representatives, One Hundred Eleventh Congress, Second Session, Wednesday, March 17, 2010* (n 225).

[227] *The Proposed Virgin Islands Constitution from the Fifth Constitutional Convention: Oversight Hearing before the Subcommittee on Insular Affairs, Oceans, and Wildlife of the Committee on Natural Resources, U.S. House of Representatives, One Hundred Eleventh Congress, Second Session, Wednesday, March 17, 2010* (n 225).

is no connection between the reference by the Delegate in Congress to the majority will and the 2015 *Tuaua* case.[228] It is plausible, from all that has been said throughout the chapter, that arguments reducing the principle of formal equality need to be better supported.[229] The failure is not, in other words, an exclusion *tout court* of the possibility that Congress might recognize other proposals that were supported by the majority of the US Virgin Islands' residents.

CONCLUSION

This chapter discussed a selection of identity-based claims and the process of mediation associated with it within the American constitutional system. The narrative was divided into two sections. The first considered the process of the negotiation and accommodation of identity-based claims that reside within one of the states. I argued, for instance, that the possibility that identity-based claims might be inserted into the US constitutional system is dependent on the ability of a national identity to persuade one or both of the two large political parties which dominate American politics that such rights are part of a fair allocation of resources. The US Supreme Court might also evaluate whether such a distinctive treatment might be considered a political prerogative to respond to a reasoned need or desire of a political community or to a violation of the principle of formal equality as entrenched in the US constitution. The US Supreme Court has developed a well-established jurisprudence in relation to the status of American Indians that indirectly influences all demands for recognition. The line of authority allows for a level of reasonable ductility. That is, the ability to 'bend the meaning' of the constitution without breaking away from its original aspirations.[230]

The second section of the chapter discussed the asymmetric system of governance that distinguishes US territories. Congress has general and plenary legislative sovereignty over the territories and that allows, by way of comparison with the states, the development of clusters of systems of governance. For instance, the Mariana Islands have developed a level of autonomy that allows for the continuation of traditional government by

---

[228] *Tuaua v. United States 788 F. 3 d (D.C. Cir 2015)* (n 128).

[229] Pub. L 111-194: To provide for the reconsideration and revision of the proposed constitution of the United States Virgin Islands to correct provisions inconsistent with the Constitution and Federal law (n 224).

[230] Costello (n 74).

chiefs. The US Virgin Islands instead struggled to formalize a constitution via Congress. The current development of Puerto Rico is among the most dynamic of those analysed in this chapter. Following the results of the latest two-stage referendum, the Puerto Rican government might have met most of the requirements necessary for demanding statehood. Again, the process requires the support of Congress, which might arrive at the end of the current political cycle. These large variations are also supported, within the limits of reasonableness, by the courts. If that were the case, Puerto Rico's linguistic and sociological status within the US federation would be analogous to that of French-speaking Quebec in English-speaking Canada.

As for the rest of the analyses proposed in this chapter, it is a matter of speculation as to whether the US would consider Puerto Rico as a distinctive society (which might have different legislative prerogatives). Yet it is reasonable to suggest that the level of flexibility granted by Article V to Congress has allowed for the development of a cluster of systems of governance that is dynamically tuned to the polity it intends to regulate.

7. New Zealand: the Westminster Model and meso-governance

INTRODUCTION

New Zealand's constitution is uncodified, flexible and adopts an asymmetric system of governance.[1] As was the case with the UK parliament before the adoption of the European Community Act[2] (which introduced a new legal hierarchy positioned alongside the UK constitutional system), a New Zealand parliament, cannot bind its successor.[3] Section 17 of the Constitution Act 1986 and some of the sections of the Electoral Act 1993 introduced a formal exception to the unbound power of the sovereign in right of New Zealand parliament yet its effectiveness is considered partial.[4] The New Zealand constitution has adopted an ad hoc Westminster Model that includes a constitutional amendment procedure for its constitutional acts, but it is considered flexible.[5] As is the case for the UK constitutional system, the stability of the New Zealand constitution is linked to the self-restraint of its parliament and its institutions.[6] This self-restraint is manifested, for instance, in a network of parliamentary

---

1 Anthony Angelo, *Constitutional Law in New Zealand* (Kluwer Law International 2011) 17; Richard Albert, 'The Structure of Constitutional Amendment Rules' (2014) 49 Wake Forest Law Review 913, 939.

2 European Communities Act 1972 (UK) (c 68).

3 Angelo (n 1) 51; Albert Venn Dicey, *The Law of the Constitution* (John Allison ed, Oxford University Press 2013) Ch 2; John Allison, *The English Historical Constitution: Continuity, Change and European Effects* (first edition, Cambridge University Press 2007) 123–158.

4 Angelo (n 1) 18.

5 Albert (n 1) 972.

6 Vito Breda, 'Lingering with Intent: The UK Constitutional Review' in Miodrag A Jovanovic (ed), *Constitutional Review and Democracy* (Eleven International 2015); Angelo (n 1) 37, 43; Kd Ewing, 'The Human Rights Act and Parliamentary Democracy' (1999) 62 The Modern Law Review 79.

and independent committees that ensure the respect of democratic principles and of the rule of law.[7]

Over the past century, the combination of a high degree of parliamentary discretion through the Westminster Model and the restraint in the use of parliamentary sovereignty fostered the development of an articulated system of governance which includes the Ross Dependency in the Antarctic,[8] free association with the Cook Islands and Niue, respectively, the de jure self-governing territory of Tokelau[9] and the administration of the South Island and North Island, which are considered 'New Zealand proper'.[10]

The large variations in the systems of governance at the territorial periphery of the Realm of New Zealand had little effect in 'New Zealand proper'. New Zealand includes the North and South Islands of New Zealand, the Chatham Islands, the Campbell Islands and Raoul Island. These geographical areas are administered as territorial administrative units of a unitary state.[11] In New Zealand, however, Maori Peoples who were recognized in the Treaty of Waitangi went through a process of reconciliation with the rest of New Zealand which allowed for the settling of land claims.[12] The process of the constitutional accommodation of the Maori Peoples, as with the process of the negotiation of the demands of the Cook Island, Niue and Tokelau residents, remains open ended.

---

[7] The activity of the Human Rights Commission is one of the examples of an institutional soft control on the activity of Parliament. Human Rights Commission and others, 'Human Rights in New Zealand Today' [2004] Wellington: Human Rights Commission; Justice Wallace, 'New Zealand Human Rights Commission' (1989) 58 Nordic Journal of International Law 155. The UK has a similar system of control on the activity of Parliament. Breda (n 6).

[8] Angus Ross, *New Zealand Aspirations in the Pacific in the Nineteenth Century* (Clarendon Press 1964).

[9] Kelihiano Kalolo, 'Tokelau' (2007) 19 The Contemporary Pacific 256.

[10] Angelo (n 1) 126.

[11] Ibid.

[12] Treaty of Waitangi Act 1975 N. 114 1975; Treaty of Waitangi (State Enterprises) Act 1988 N. 105; Dominic O'Sullivan, 'The Treaty of Waitangi in Contemporary New Zealand Politics' (2008) 43 Australian Journal of Political Science 317.

DRIVER OF CHANGE: MAORI CONSTITUTIONAL IDENTITY AND THE TREATY OF WAITANGI

Before an international match, the New Zealand national rugby team normally performs for the audience and for the other team a 'Haka'.[13] Maori warriors performed a similar coordinated routine to intimidate their opponents before battle, and in the rugby union international matches, the Haka has lost most, but not all, of its functions. It is, however, one of the most visible reminders to all of those who follow rugby that New Zealand is a multinational society that is, within the limit of reasonableness, proud of its precolonial traditions.[14]

Maori heritage is also part of the New Zealand constitutional system.[15] The statutory recognition of the Treaty of Waitangi in the Treaty of Waitangi Act 1975,[16] and its successive amendments such as the Treaty of Waitangi (State Enterprises) Act 1988, the Claim Settlements[17] and the related case law are the most notable manifestations of the legal recognition and accommodation of Maori identity claims.[18] In 2017, the government estimated that there were 734 200 Maoris and that they made up over 15 per cent of the population.[19] Maori Peoples' social identity is composed of a mosaic of distinctive self-perceptions that have been

---

[13] 'The Haka | Allblacks.Com | Allblacks.Com' (*All Blacks*) http://www.allblacks.com/Teams/Haka (accessed 27 November 2017).

[14] Jared Diamond, *Guns, Germs and Steel. a Short History of Everybody in the Last 13,000 Years* (Kindle edition) (Vintage 2005) section 841.

[15] Treaty of Waitangi Act 1975 N. 114 (n 12).

[16] Ibid.

[17] Treaty of Waitangi (State Enterprises) Act 1988 N. 105 (n 12); 'New Zealand Legislation: List of Amendments Incorporated of the Treaty of Waitangi Act 1975 (Including Claims Settlement)' http://www.legislation.govt.nz/act/public/1975/0114/latest/versions.aspx (accessed 3 February 2016).

[18] *New Zealand Maori Council v Attorney-General* (1987) 1 NZLR 641 (Court of Appeal); *Te Runanga o Wharekauri Rekohu Inc v Attorney General* (1992) 2 NZLR 301 (Court of Appeal).

[19] Government of New Zealand – Stats, 'National Population Estimates: At 30 June 2017' http://www.stats.govt.nz/browse_for_stats/population/estimates_and_projections/NationalPopulationEstimates_HOTPAt30Jun17.aspx (accessed 27 November 2017). Government of New Zealand – Stats, 'Māori Population Estimates: At 30 June 2017 – Tables' http://www.stats.govt.nz/browse_for_stats/population/estimates_and_projections/MaoriPopulationEstimates_HOTPAt30Jun17.aspx (accessed 27 November 2017).

adapted to modern society.[20] There is, as expected in polities with a large minority such as New Zealand and Canada,[21] an ongoing debate over the role that identities should (and should not) have within national politics.[22] Distinctive of New Zealand's politics is, however, the reserved allocation of Maori Peoples' seats given in the House of Representatives.[23]

Before colonization, Maori tribes formed a highly evolved society based on ownership of land rights, forestry, agriculture and, like mediaeval European kingdoms, organized warfare.[24] With the arrival of European powers in the South Pacific, some Maori tribes were more skilful than others in exploiting the technological advances brought in by the Europeans.[25] On 19 November 1835, a Maori raid on the Mariori Peoples based on navigational information given to the Maoris by Europeans resulted in the entire Mariori population being either enslaved or executed.[26] However, the cultural and technological interchange between European settlers and the Maori tribes contributed to a distinctive sociological context which was the proxy for the signing of the 1840 Treaty of Waitangi.[27]

With the Treaty of Waitangi, the signatory Maori tribes and the British imperial representatives sought to guarantee a civil coexistence between the settlers and the chiefs of New Zealand.[28] There are a series of quarrels attached to the original text, its translations and its legal

---

20 Karyn Paringatai, 'Maori Identity Development Outside of Tribal Environments' (2014) 26 Aotearoa New Zealand Social Work 47, 49; Carla A Houkamau and Chris G Sibley, 'The Revised Multidimensional Model of Māori Identity and Cultural Engagement (MMM-ICE2)' (2015) 122 Social Indicators Research 279, 281; Dominic O'Sullivan, 'Needs, Rights and "One Law for All": Contemporary Debates in New Zealand Maori Politics' (2008) 41 Canadian Journal of Political Science/Revue canadienne de science politique 973, 978.

21 O'Sullivan (n 20); Jean-François Caron, 'The Exclusive Nature of Quebec's Contemporary Nationalism: The Pitfalls of Civic Nationalism' (2014) 47 International Journal of Canadian Studies 221.

22 O'Sullivan (n 20) 974, 982.

23 Ibid 980.

24 Diamond (n 14) sections 843–845; Claudia Orange, *The Treaty of Waitangi* (Bridget Williams 2015) 4.

25 Diamond (n 14) section 827; Orange (n 24) 4; R D Crosby and Michael King, *The Musket Wars: A History of Inter-Iwi Conflict 1806–45* (Raupo 1999).

26 Diamond (n 14) section 827.

27 Orange (n 24) 254; Nan Seuffert, *Jurisprudence of National Identity: Kaleidoscopes of Imperialism and Globalisation from Aotearoa New Zealand* (Ashgate 2006) 12–17.

28 A English translation of the Treaty is in the Schedule 1. Treaty of Waitangi Act 1975 N. 114 (n 12).

implications.[29] The historical controversy over the text of the treaty is related, among other aspects, to the unparalleled translations between the English and Maori versions of the document, and to their relative jurisprudential interpretations which focused on the English translation.[30] The differences between the Maori and English translations underpinned the perception of an intent to deceive the Maori tribes, which has just recently, and only partially, been remedied.[31]

The date 6 February 1840 is considered to be when the bulk of tribal chiefs signed the Treaty of Waitangi with the British Crown. More tribal leaders, but not all, signed after that date.[32] The current popular perception of the nature of the document remains divided, but it is reasonably clear that, at the time of its signature, the British Crown intended to amalgamate (and to extinguish) the tribal tradition that dominated the North and the South Islands.[33] The intention of the Crown representatives not to be bound by the treaty can be inferred from the textual differences between the English and Maori versions of the signed document, but it did not become apparent to the Maori tribes until 1860. However, even in the contested English version, there are indications of a shared intention to establish a harmonious society.

> Her Majesty therefore being desirous to establish a settled form of Civil Government with a view to avert the evil consequences which must result from the absence of the necessary Laws and Institutions alike to the native population and to Her subjects has been graciously pleased [...] to invite the confederated and independent Chiefs of New Zealand to concur in the following Articles and Conditions.[34]

Unfortunately, there is little to distinguish the colonization of New Zealand from that of other European colonies. Imperialism brought to New Zealand cultural genocidal policies, which are currently perceived as repulsive and unbecoming for modern liberal democracy, yet, at the time, they were perceived as a manifestation of the cultural evolutionism

---

[29] Angelo (n 1) 153–156; Seuffert (n 27) 17–28; Orange (n 24) 91; O'Sullivan (n 20) 977; O'Sullivan (n 12) 321.

[30] Seuffert (n 27) 17.

[31] Angelo (n 1) 153–156; Seuffert (n 27) 17–28; Orange (n 24) 91.

[32] Tony Angelo, 'To Be or Not to Be [...] Integrated, That is the Problem of Islands' [2002] Revue Juridique Polynésienne 87, 152; Orange (n 24) vi.

[33] Orange (n 24) viii; O'Sullivan (n 12).

[34] Schedule 1 Treaty of Waitangi Act 1975 N. 114 (n 12).

which underpinned British, American and European imperialistic policies.[35] For instance, in 1901, at the time of the ratification of the Australian constitution, the possibility of racial discrimination was explicitly inserted in section 127[36] and eugenics was 'in vogue' in the USA and most European countries.[37]

The Treaty of Waitangi was signed 60 years before the enactment of the Australian constitution and, thus, it is not surprising that it aimed at ensuring the pacific transition of the tribal system whilst ensuring the safety of the small, by way of comparison with the Maoris, population of European settlers.[38] It is also important to remember that, before 1840, the Maori tribes were able to sell land to settlers, preventing the de jure establishment of the *terra nullius* jurisprudence, and to obtain, in exchange, a significant number of firearms which partly reduced the impact of British genocidal policies.[39]

Between 1840 and 1860, the British administration continued to comply with the terms of the treaty. In *R v Symonds*, for instance, the Supreme Court reiterated the Crown's commitment to complying with the treaty.[40] However, after 1860, the progressive expansion of the colony combined with the proportional reduction in the Maori's military ability

---

[35] Diamond (n 14); Eric Hobsbawm, *Nations and Nationalism since 1780: Programme, Myth, Reality* (Cambridge University Press 1992) 101; Howard Zinn, *A People's History of the United States: 1492–Present* (Kindle edition) (HarperCollins 2003); Frank Pommersheim, *Broken Landscape: Indians, Indian Tribes, and the Constitution* (Oxford University Press 2009); Laura R Graham and H Glenn Penny, 'Performing Indigeneity: Emergent Identity, Self-Determination, and Sovereignty' in Laura R Graham and H Glenn Penny (eds), *Performing Indigeneity: Global Histories and Contemporary Experiences* (University of Nebraska Press 2014).

[36] Geoffrey Sawer, 'Australian Constitution and the Australian Aborigine', (1966) 2 Federal Law Review 17, 17; Commonwealth of Australia Constitution Act 1900 section 127.

[37] For a chilling comparative review see Gunnar Broberg and Nils Roll-Hansen, *Eugenics and the Welfare State: Norway, Sweden, Denmark, and Finland* (Michigan State University Press 2005) https://muse.jhu.edu/book/40871 (accessed 1 December 2017).

[38] Orange (n 24) viii, 154.

[39] Crosby and King (n 25); Andree Lajoie, 'What Constitutional Law Doesn't Want to Hear about History' in Law Commission of Canada and British Columbia Treaty Commission (Canada) (eds), *Speaking Truth to Power: A Treaty Forum* (Law Commission of Canada; British Columbia Treaty Commission 2001).

[40] *Charles Hunter McIntosh v John Jeremyn Symonds* [1847] NZSC 1, NZPCC 388.

to resist a British expansion prepared the ground for disentangling the Crown from the commitment set in the Treaty of Waitangi. For instance, by 1858, British military technological advances, which were field tested during the Indian Mutiny, made those muskets sold in the previous decades to Maori tribes obsolete.[41] In 1860, a conference of chiefs organized by the British administrators sought to unify the interpretation of the Treaty in a way that maintained a peaceful acceptance, but in the same year, in *Wi Parata v Bishop of Wellington*, many of the effects of the Treaty of Waitangi were considered not binding for the Crown.[42] In particular, the traditional ownership of the land of an uncivilized nation was not considered as legally enforceable by the British common law.[43] *Wi Parata v Bishop of Wellington* commenced a line of authority that had long-term repercussions for the current Maori minority.[44]

The effects of *Wi Parata v Bishop of Wellington* were partially mitigated by the Maori Representation Act 1867 that allocated four seats to Maori representatives in the parliament of New Zealand (at the time, it was referred to as the General Assembly).[45] After 1996 and the adoption of the mixed-member proportional representation system, the number of Maori seats increased to six.[46] Maoris can also, and do, contest general seats, but Maori MPs elected using the normal system appear less concerned with the representation of Maori issues.[47]

In 1970, the Maori Peoples benefitted from a cultural and political revival and sought the recognition of their status and their communal rights asserted in the Treaty of Waitangi. A statutory recognition of the Treaty is in schedule 1 of the Treaty of Waitangi Act 1975. The Treaty of Waitangi Act 1975 includes, in chapter 1, an English version of the Treaty of Waitangi and sets out the basis of the partnership between the state and Maori Peoples.[48] Again, this is a statutory recognition that

---

[41] Daniel R Headrick, 'The Tools of Imperialism: Technology and the Expansion of European Colonial Empires in the Nineteenth Century' (1979) The Journal of Modern History 231, 251.

[42] *Wi Parata v Bishop of Wellington [1877] 3 NZ Jur (NS) 72.*

[43] *Wi Parata v Bishop of Wellington* (n 42) 78.

[44] Treaty of Waitangi Act 1975 N. 114 (n 12).

[45] Maori Representation Act 1867 (31 Victoriae 1867 N. 47) 1867; The New Zealand Constitution Act 1852 c. 72 1852.

[46] Electoral Act 1993 N. 87 1993 section 47, 76–79. Please note that MPs of Maori ancestry manage to obtain seats in Parliament outside the Maori seats.

[47] Te Hau White, 'A Difference of Perspective? Māori Members of Parliament and Te Ao Māori in Parliament' (2016) 68 Political Science 175, 176.

[48] Treaty of Waitangi Act 1975 N. 114 (n 12); O'Sullivan (n 12) 320.

could be amended but it is unlikely to be fully repealed.[49] For instance, the Treaty of Waitangi (State Enterprises) Act was the proxy of a series of amendments of the Treaty of Waitangi Act which manifested the parliament's commitment to protecting the Maori tribes and an intention to redress some of their claims.[50] The change of attitude was acknowledged by the court. In *Council v Attorney-General*, section 9 of the Treaty of Waitangi was interpreted in a way that limited the ability of the Crown to sell state-owned enterprises.[51] Again, parliament intervened quickly and established an ad hoc tribunal (which initially had very limited jurisdictional roles) that, over time, contributed to reducing the perplexity, and perhaps the popular mistrust, towards the process of the recognition of Maori claims.[52]

In short, since the approval of the Treaty of Waitangi Act 1975, successive governments have continued to implement policies aimed at settling Maori claims.[53] In 2014 the Crown allocated legal personality to a traditional land called Te Urewera. One of the latest was signed on 18 December 2015. The Minister for the Treaty of Waitangi Negotiations, who acted as the representative of the Crown, signed the deed which

---

[49] Angelo (n 1) 109.

[50] Richard Mulgan and Peter Aimer, *Politics in New Zealand* (Auckland University Press 2013) Ch 6.

[51] *New Zealand Maori Council v Attorney-General* (n 18) section 9. 'Nothing in this Act shall affect in any way the right of any person to petition the House of Representatives for the redress of any grievance, or the jurisdiction of any committee or other body set up by the House of Representatives to deal with a petition to the House of Representatives'. Treaty of Waitangi Act 1975 N. 114 (n 12).

[52] Angelo (n 32) 156–160; Jacinta Ruru and Anna Crosbie, 'Key to Unlocking Landlocked Maori Land: The Extension of the Maori Land Court's Jurisdiction' (2004) 10 Canterbury Law Review 318; O'Sullivan (n 12); Richard Price, 'New Zealand's Interim Treaty Settlement and Arrangements – Building Blocks of Certainty' in Law Commission of Canada and British Columbia Treaty Commission (Canada) (eds), *Speaking Truth to Power: A Treaty Forum* (Law Commission of Canada; British Columbia Treaty Commission 2001); O'Sullivan (n 20).

[53] Greg Hamilton, 'Our 2014 Election Policies, Maori Affairs (National Party)' https://www.national.org.nz/docs/default-source/PDF/2014/policy/maori-affairs-policy.pdf (accessed 3 February 2016).

settled the Ngatikahu ki Whangaroa's claim over their ancestral land.[54] This Ngatikahu ki Whangaroa Deed aims at compensating for the economic loss[55] and the historical disregard of a cultural identity relating to the violation of article 2 of the Treaty of Waitangi.[56]

The textual analysis of the Treaty of Waitangi should be inserted in a specific context.[57] This is particularly the case for the Treaty of Waitangi as it is currently perceived as one of the key constitutional elements of an uncodified constitution, and at the same time, as a historical contested document which recognized a distinctive set of rights for Maori tribes such as the Ngatikahu ki Whangaroa.[58] Furthermore, the Tribunal of Waitangi had the function, among others, of hearing Maori claims against the Crown[59] and the exclusive interpretation of the Treaty itself. The Tribunal of Waitangi had some jurisdictional implications, but its statutory nature was a direct manifestation of the political intention to change the role of the Maori identity and of the Treaty within the national constitutional system. The Waitangi Tribunal proceedings were in Maori and, in one of the first reports, the Tribunal found the Crown responsible for a violation of fishing rights protected in the Treaty.[60]

The limited number of complaints, for instance, and the reduced scope of the demands also had the effect of reassuring the majority of the population that Maori identity claims might re-balance some aspects of New Zealand economy by allocating resources to original owners, but that this was not an excessive economic burden for the national

[54] The Crown (NZ) and Ngatikahu ki Whangaroa, 'Deed of Settlement (Ngatikahu Ki Whangaroa's Claim)' https://www.govt.nz/dmsdocument/6281.pdf (accessed 3 February 2016); National Party (NZ), 'Press Release: Deed of Settlement Signed with Ngatikahu Ki Whangaroa' https://www.national.org.nz/news/news/media-releases/detail/2015/12/20/Deed-of-Settlement-signed-with-Ngatikahu-ki-Whangaroa (accessed 3 February 2016). A Geddis and J Ruru, 'Places as Persons: Creating a New Framework for Māori-Crown Relations' (speech to biennial Public Law Conference, Melbourne 2018).

[55] The Crown (NZ) and Ngatikahu ki Whangaroa (n 54) section 5.

[56] Ibid 3.

[57] Ran Hirschl, *Comparative Matters: The Renaissance of Comparative Constitutional Law* (Oxford University Press 2014) 15, 151–190.

[58] Angelo (n 32) 158; O'Sullivan (n 12); O'Sullivan (n 20).

[59] Treaty of Waitangi Act 1975 N. 114 (n 12).

[60] The Waitangi Tribunal, 'Report of the Waitangi Tribunal on Yhe Motunui – Waitara Claim' (1983) http://www.justice.govt.nz/tribunals/waitangi-tribunal/Reports/wai0006/06title (accessed 28 January 2016).

economy.[61] It is important to mention that economic compensation and formal apologies might be perceived by Maoris as a form of economic commodification of past genocidal policies and as unfair for the rest of New Zealand population.[62] For instance, the Foreshore and Seabed Act 2004 sparked a controversy over the use of public coastal areas and the seabed.[63] Economic access to shores and the seabed has important economic implications for the national economy. Reports by the UN Human Rights Commission and by the Tribunal of Waitangi recommended a repeal of the Act in a way that considered its cultural implications.[64]

The foreshore and seabed controversy revealed the limits of the overreliance on an economic bargaining process as the principal method of accommodation for identity-based claims.[65] These are, however, tuning issues related to any policy that alters the public allocation of resources. Similar narratives, albeit with the opportune qualifications necessary for any comparative evaluation, emerged from the process of the accommodation of land claims in the USA and Canada.[66] Again, in the foreshore and seabed controversy, the parliament played a pivotal role by allowing the dynamic changes required by the recognition process for Maori identity claims.[67]

It is plausible to suggest that one of the reasons for the recognition of the Maori cultures, in comparison with, for instance, the Australian

---

[61] New Zealand Election Study, '2005 Mass Survey. Most Important Issue? Major Categories' http://www.nzes.org/exec/show/freq_2005a (accessed 3 February 2016); O'Sullivan (n 12); O'Sullivan (n 20).

[62] Seuffert (n 27) 87–94; O'Sullivan (n 12) 322.

[63] Foreshore and Seabed Act 2004 N. 93 (repealed by the Marine and Coastal Area (Takutai Moana) Act 2011 N. 3 2004); Angelo (n 1) 157–158.

[64] Rodolfo Stavenhagen, 'Commission on Human Rights: Report of the Special Rapporteur on the Situation of Human Rights and Fundamental Freedoms of Indigenous People. Addendum: Mission to New Zealand' para 192; New Zealand (ed), *Report on the Crown's Foreshore and Seabed Policy* (Legislation Direct 2004) 138.

[65] Kerensa Johnston, 'Maori Legal Developments' (2017) New Zealand Law Review 131; O'Sullivan (n 12) 318.

[66] Peter Metcalfe, *A Dangerous Idea: The Alaska Native Brotherhood and the Struggle for Indigenous Rights* (University of Alaska Press 2014); Vance A Sanders, 'A Tribal Advocate's Critique of Proposed ANCSA Amendments: Perpetuating a Broken Corporate Assimilationist Policy' (2016) 33 Alaska Law Review 303; Hamar Foster, 'Getting There' in Law Commission of Canada and British Columbia Treaty Commission (Canada) (eds), *Speaking Truth to Power: A Treaty Forum* (Law Commission of Canada; British Columbia Treaty Commission 2001); Price (n 52).

[67] Price (n 52).

process of constitutional recognition of the Aboriginal Peoples and Torres Strait Islanders, is the wider prerogative given to parliament by adopting the Westminster system.[68] It is, for instance, a prerogative of New Zealand parliament to monitor the effect of the Treaty of Waitangi Act 1975 and, if the political perception of the fairness of its implications is engaged, to intervene and tune its effects with regard to popular perceptions.[69] The Treaty of Waitangi Act 1975 is not entrenched.[70] It can be amended (as it was on different occasions) by an ordinary statute in a way that dynamically follows societal changes related to Maori self-perceptions of their identity and the idea of the fair accommodation of these perceptions in New Zealand society.[71]

DRIVER OF CHANGE: CONSTITUTIONAL FLEXIBILITY AND TERRITORIAL HETEROGENEITY

The previous section discussed the processes involved in the negotiation and accommodation of Maori Peoples in New Zealand. These processes would not have been possible without a substantial change in the political and social attitudes towards a minority that was, for a period, brutally discriminated against.[72] I explained that the Westminster Model helped government negotiators and Maori representatives to manage the process of the reconciliation and recognition of a minority. Self-perceptions of identity groups fluctuate, and so the process of negotiation and accommodation is not, and should not be considered, completed.[73] In this section, I continue to show the beneficial aspects of having a flexible constitutional system that allows for the recognition of identities at the territorial periphery of New Zealand system of territorial governance. The Realm of New Zealand includes a large variety of landmasses which stretch from the Cook Islands' archipelago in the middle of the Pacific, via New Zealand to the territorial claims of the Ross Dependency in the

---

68 Angelo (n 1) 17; Albert (n 1) 939.

69 Price (n 52); O'Sullivan (n 12).

70 Treaty of Waitangi Act 1975 N. 114 (n 12); Treaty of Waitangi (State Enterprises) Act 1988 N. 105 (n 12).

71 Albert (n 1).

72 O'Sullivan (n 12); Price (n 52).

73 Z Bauman, 'Identity: Then, Now, What For?' in M Kempny and A Jawlowska (eds), *Identity in Transformation: Postmodernity, Postcommunism, and Globalization* (Praeger 2002); Z Bauman, 'Identity in the Globalising World' (2001) 9 Social Anthropology 121.

South Pole. The geographical variations are matched (with the exclusion of the Ross Dependency) by a similar level of ethnic diversity.

Niue and the Cook Islands

Niue and the Cook Islands are part of the Realm of New Zealand but they are considered associated states.[74] The definition of a free association can be retrieved from General Assembly resolution 1541.[75] In particular, principle VII of the annex of the resolution stated that a free-associated state can determine its own constitution and should not be in a position of arbitrary subjugation from any other states (principle IV).[76] In other words, a free association between states is an arrangement in which two constitutionally sovereign states agree to share some of the aspects of their policies such as defence and their international standing. For instance, the Cook Islands retain the possibility of asking for the military protection of New Zealand.[77]

The international and internal status of a free association is normally part of the decolonization process.[78] However, the current tendency towards decentralization within multinational states such as the UK, Spain and Italy has increased the interest in the possibility of adopting a free association as a mode of governance.[79] The Basque government, for instance, tried to establish a free association with Spain by altering its current Statute of Autonomy.[80] The attempt was, as explained in the Spanish chapter, part of a simulated-politics strategy.

---

[74] Alison Quentin-Baxter, 'New Zealand Model of Free Association: What Does It Mean for New Zealand' (2008) 39 Victoria University Wellington Law Review 607.

[75] United Nations General Assembly, 'General Assembly Resolution Defining the Three Options for Self-Determination General Assembly Resolution 1541 (XV)'.

[76] Ibid.

[77] Cook Islands Constitution Act 1964 no. 69 section 5.

[78] United Nations, 'The United Nations and Decolonization: Non-Self-Governing Territories (United Nations Secretariat 2015 Working Papers on NSGTs)' http://www.un.org/en/decolonization/nonselfgovterritories.shtml (accessed 5 February 2016).

[79] Luca Antonini, *Federalismo all'italiana* (Marsilio 2013); Michael Keating, *Rescaling the European State: The Making of Territory and the Rise of the Meso* (first edition, Oxford University Press 2013).

[80] Basque Government, Propuesta Estatuto político de la Comunidad de Euskadi 2003 [127/000001]; Michael Keating and Zoe Bray, 'Renegotiating Sovereignty: Basque Nationalism and the Rise and Fall of the Ibarretxe Plan'

In the case of New Zealand, there are two landmasses in free association with the Realm. The Cook Islands are situated in the middle of the Pacific and cover an area of 232 km^2 of land and 1.8 million km^2 of sea belonging to the state.[81] Niue is a 260 km^2 island located 2400 km from New Zealand.[82] The economic differences between the three states allowed for some interdependencies to be established. For instance, the Cook Islands and Niue citizens are automatically New Zealand citizens, but New Zealanders are not Niue or Cook Islands citizens.[83] There is, however, an expectation that both governments do protect analogous citizen rights.[84]

In the case of the Cook Islands, the Cook Islands Constitution Act 1964 is considered the founding document of the Cook Islands' constitutional monarchy.[85] The act, in section 1, explicitly asserts the self-governing prerogative of the Cook Islands' institutions and, in section 5, allocates shared competence for international affairs and defence with New Zealand. New Zealand interventions for the Cook Islands' archipelagos on defence and foreign relations are, however, dependent on the assent of the Cook Islands' government. The Head of State is the Queen of New Zealand, who is appointed in accordance with the Royal Succession Act 2013.[86] In short, the Cook Islands are an independent state that shares a series of policies with a larger self-governing nation.[87]

This form of partnership is not unusual between large European states and microstates such as Jersey and the UK, Monaco and France, and San Marino and Italy. The distinctive aspect of the connection of the associated state of the Cook Islands (as defined by the UN) is a complete constitutional independence combined with an asymmetric citizenship

---

(2006) 5 Ethnopolitics 347; S Acierno, 'The Order of the Spanish Constitutional Court on the Proposal to Convert the Basque Country into a Freely Associated Community: Keeping Hands off Constitutional Politics' (2005) 3 International Journal of Constitutional Law 687; *Ley Orgánica 3/1979, de 18 de diciembre, de Estatuto de Autonomía para el País Vasco, 1979.*

[81] Angelo (n 1) 129; Central Intelligence Agency, 'The World Factbook: Cook Islands' https://www.cia.gov/library/publications/the-world-factbook/geos/print_cw.html (accessed 2 January 2016).

[82] Central Intelligence Agency, 'The World Factbook: Niue' https://www.cia.gov/library/publications/the-world-factbook/geos/ne.html (accessed 2 January 2016).

[83] Angelo (n 1) 130.

[84] Quentin-Baxter (n 74) 631.

[85] Cook Islands Constitution Act 1964 no. 69 (n 77); Angelo (n 1) 131.

[86] Royal Succession Act 2013 N. 149; Quentin-Baxter (n 74) 613.

[87] Quentin-Baxter (n 74) 631.

which, in turn, fosters a tendency for the uniform protection of individual rights. For instance, in 1978, New Zealand rectified the International Covenant on Economic, Social and Cultural Rights which extended the protection of the Covenant to the Cook Islands' citizens.[88]

The ratification of the Covenant on Economic, Social and Cultural Rights had two correlated effects on the free association. Firstly, it augmented the expectation that Cook Islanders held regarding the Cook Islands' institutions, because they anticipated that there would be an equivalence between the level of service provided by the Cook Islands' institutions and New Zealand's institutions. Secondly, New Zealand's public institutions that transferred financial resources to Cook Islands' institutions requires that such a support must be properly accounted for.[89] That expectation includes a public auditing of government accounts.[90] In short, the ratification of the Covenant on Economic, Social and Cultural Rights altered the relation between the two states in a way that sought a levelling of individual expectations.[91]

The dynamics of the interaction between the Cook Islands and New Zealand that resulted from the International Covenant on Economic, Social and Cultural Rights is, perhaps, a distinctive form of what Keating calls the 'meso' level of governance.[92] The aspirations of smaller regions are modelled around the interaction between the protection of rights (which includes cultural rights) and the pragmatic limitations that public institutions have in implementing policies.[93] UN has also influenced the process of accommodation of national minorities in New Zealand, but the parliament has been particularly responsive. Again, it is a matter of speculation as to whether such interaction would have been possible in a more rigid constitutional system. It is, however, reasonable to suggest

---

88 Ministry of Justice (New Zealand), 'International Covenant on Economic, Social and Cultural Rights' http://www.justice.govt.nz/policy/constitutional-law-and-human-rights/human-rights/international-human-rights-instruments/international-human-rights-instruments-1/international-covenant-on-economic-social-and-cultural-rights (accessed 5 February 2016); United Nations General Assembly, 'General Assembly Resolution no. 2200A (XXI) International Covenant on Economic, Social and Cultural Rights'.

89 Quentin-Baxter (n 74) 622.

90 Ibid.

91 Ibid 628.

92 Keating and Bray (n 80); Michael Keating, 'So Many Nations, so Few States: Territory and Nationalism in the Global Era' in James Tully and Alain Gagnon (eds), *Multinational democracies* (Cambridge University Press 2001); Angelo (n 32).

93 Keating (n 92).

that having an executive power that is 'fused' with the legislative power helped the process of the negotiation and accommodation of the Cook Islands' claims.

It is worth mentioning that such an arrangement might be perceived as a form of colonial control by proxy, yet in the case of the Cook Islands (and Niue), public institutions actively try to maintain control over the use of public money by using independent auditors and by appointing, for instance, retired New Zealand High Court judges as independent advisors.[94] Furthermore, the commitment to upholding standards of good governance in both governments is perceived as a method of consolidating cooperation between two states and not as a manifestation of a dominion. Nevertheless, the Cook Islands (and Niue) have sovereign state prerogatives and the cooperation can be unilaterally rescinded.[95]

The Curious Case of Tokelau's UN-Sponsored Referenda: The Archipelago That does not Want to be Freed

In this section of the chapter, I will consider the pragmatic limits of referenda as elements of a negotiation process between New Zealand central government and Tokelau residents. In the previous section, I argued that the Cook Islands' free association with New Zealand is one of the shades of the gamut of systems of governance that allow multinational political systems to act, if both communities perceive that as appropriate, as a single entity or, in case they have different perceptions of what is acceptable, to take diverging paths. This level of flexibility is helped by having a flexible constitutional system that allocates a larger, by way of comparison of rigid constitutional systems like the one adopted in Spain and Australia, discretion to the government.[96] This section will focus on the limits to referenda as elements of a decentralization process. In particular, this section will discuss the limited success of the UN-sponsored referenda aimed at altering Tokelau's system of governance.

In 2006 and then in 2007, the registered voters of Tokelau had the opportunity to vote in two successive UN-sponsored referenda which, if approved, would have changed the status of Tokelau from an autonomous

[94] *Controller and Auditor-General v Sir Ronald Davison (CA 226/95)* [1996] NZLR 278 (Court of Appeal) 88.

[95] Keating (n 79) Ch 1, 5; Neil Walker, 'The Idea of Constitutional Pluralism' (2002) 65 The Modern Law Review 317.

[96] Albert (n 1).

region within the Realm of New Zealand.[97] The referendum question asked whether to accept or reject the following proposal: 'That Tokelau become a self-governing state in free association with New Zealand on the basis of the Constitution and the Treaty'.[98] The two-thirds majority support necessary to change the system of governance of Tokelau was not achieved in either of the two referenda. The process indicated, in particular, that even in ideal conditions of well-planned and extremely well-resourced information campaigns, large sections of voters would find it extremely difficult to predict and evaluate the pragmatic implications of the proposed change to a system of governance.

Tokelau is an isolated Pacific archipelago, which includes three islands and has a population of over 1300 individuals.[99] The islands, after two decades of structural investments, have just developed the infrastructure necessary to sustain the free association. In 1926, New Zealand took over the role of Britain as the colonial power, and in 1948, the status of Tokelau was changed by the Tokelau Act 1948. Section 3 of the Tokelau Act 1948 officially included the archipelago in the Realm and section 5 of the same act set out the legislative prerogatives of the Tokelau Assembly (called the 'General Fono' or simply 'Fono').[100] The process of institutional development started in the 1990s and included, among others, structural development for the establishment of Tokelau's self-government institutions. This was structural development in compliance with the UN Special Committee of 24 and it was aimed at reducing the dependence of Tokelau on external financial aid.[101]

---

97 Andrew Townend, 'Tokelau's 2006 Referendum on Self-Government' (2007) 5 New Zealand Journal of Public and International Law 127; David Marrani, 'Will New Caledonia Be Another Tokelau?' (2006) 31 Alternative Law Journal 102; Kalolo (n 9); Judith Huntsman, *The Future of Tokelau: Decolonising Agendas, 1975–2006* (Auckland University Press 2013).

98 Government of Tokelau, 'Referendum Commission, Self Determination Package, Voting Procedure'. http://www.tokelau.org.nz/About+Us/Government/Self+Determination+Package.html (accessed 12 January 2016).

99 Central Intelligence Agency, 'The World Factbook: Tokelau' https://www.cia.gov/library/publications/the-world-factbook/geos/tl.html (accessed 2 January 2016).

100 Tokelau Act 1948 N. 24 (as at 20 September 2007).

101 UN Visiting Mission to Tokelau, 1986 (ed), *Report of the United Nations Visiting Mission to Tokelau, 1986* (UN 7); Tokelau Government and New Zealand Government, 'Joint Statement of The Principles Of Partnership Between New Zealand and Tokelau' http://www.tokelau.org.nz/About+Us/Government.html (accessed 14 January 2016).

The archipelago has a population that is both ethnically and linguistically distinct from the Maoris, and is of predominately Polynesian ancestry with the European population representing less than 1 per cent of the inhabitants.[102] The most common spoken languages are Tokelau and English. English is spoken as a second language by less than 60 per cent of the population and all official documents are translated.[103]

As a de jure self-governing territory, Tokelau has an assembly, a government and a territorial division based on the three villages that make up its entire landmass.[104] Since the enactment of the Tokelau Act 1948, the General Fono has been the main legislative institution for the archipelago.[105] The Head of State is the Queen of New Zealand, and the role of First Minister is taken in rotation by the chiefs of the three main villages.[106] Since 1996, the national government of Tokelau has been representing the region within New Zealand and in international meetings.[107] The economy is subsidized directly and indirectly by the New Zealand Government.[108] Financial aid makes up the bulk of the direct support, whereas civil servant employment (paid for by the New Zealand government) supports the economy indirectly. Remissions from emigrants, the large majority of whom reside within the North and South Islands, constitute a substantive help to the local economy.[109]

Since its establishment, the UN Special Committee of 24 continued to promote an increased level of independence for Tokelau from New Zealand.[110] In one of the most recent meetings, the UN Special Committee of 24 approved the Draft Resolution on Tokelau and the Vice-Chair

---

102 Central Intelligence Agency, 'The World Factbook: Tokelau' (n 99).

103 Ibid; Anthony Payne and Paul Sutton, 'Towards a Security Policy for Small Island and Enclave Developing States' in Anthony Payne and Paul Sutton (eds), *Size and Survival* (Routledge 2014).

104 Tokelau Government and New Zealand Government (n 101).

105 Angelo (n 1) 127; Antony Hooper, 'Tokelau: A Sort of "Self-Governing" Sort of "Colony"' (2008) 43 The Journal of Pacific History 331, 332.

106 Kalolo (n 9) 257.

107 Ibid.

108 Hooper (n 105) 331.

109 Ibid.

110 Official Name: United Nations Special Committee on the Situation with Regard to the Implementation of the Declaration on the Granting of Independence to Colonial Countries and Peoples 'The United Nations and Decolonization' http://www.un.org/en/decolonization/specialcommittee.shtml (accessed 9 January 2016). The activity of the Committee is in pursuant of the United Nations General Assembly, 'General Assembly Resolution no. 1514 Declaration on the Granting of Independence to Colonial Countries and Peoples'.

Pedro Núñez Mosquera stated that the number of non-self-governing territories such as Tokelau 'has to be reduced wherever possible'.[111]

This commitment was, perhaps ironically, perceived as a manifestation of cultural imperialism. For instance, the Fiji Minister of Foreign Affairs considered the Tokelau–New Zealand relationship as a model of cooperation and praised the care that Tokelauan and New Zealand institutions have for the development of Tokelau's social and economic interests: '[The diplomat acting for the Fijian Minister of Foreign Affairs] acknowledged the decision to defer any act of self-determination and instead emphasize development, which showed that, while it was critical to strive for political independence, it was also important to focus on the social and economic needs in Non-Self-Governing Territories'.[112] The need to balance the social–economic needs of post-colonial communities and the overarching desire to establish a level of institutional development to reduce the lingering effects of a dark colonial past was indeed one key issue voiced in the pre-referenda debates.

However, this is a difficult task for most of the Pacific territories.[113] Firstly, international organizations, such as the UN Special Committee of 24, might not be perceived as friendly actors in the process of constructing a new system of governance,[114] yet the good faith intentions of the UN Special Committee of 24 are, in regard to Tokelau's referenda, relatively uncontested.[115] Secondly, it has become common practice to use referenda to validate a decolonization process.[116] However, the complexity of the process to change territorial governance can seldom be explained in a way that is both accurate and easily transmitted. The recent Scottish and Welsh referenda have shown the limits of the level of

---

[111] Fiji Minister of Foreign Affairs (as per Mr Luke Daunivalu), 'Special Committee on Decolonization Concludes Session with Approval of Draft Resolution on Tokelau, Another Containing Report on Organizational Matters | Meetings Coverage and Press Releases' http://www.un.org/press/en/2011/gacol3227.doc.htm (accessed 9 January 2016); Townend (n 97) 121.

[112] Fiji Minister of Foreign Affairs (as per Mr Luke Daunivalu) (n 111).

[113] Angelo (n 32) 89–91.

[114] Zoran Oklopcic, 'Constitutional (Re) Vision: Sovereign Peoples, New Constituent Powers, and the Formation of Constitutional Orders in the Balkans' (2012) 19 Constellations 81; Zoran Oklopcic, 'The Territorial Challenge: From Constitutional Patriotism to Unencumbered Agonism in Bosnia and Herzegovina' (2012) 13 German Law Journal 23.

[115] Huntsman (n 97) Ch 1.

[116] Angelo (n 32) 89. Deborah Z Cass, 'Re-Thinking Self-Determination: A Critical Analysis of Current International Law Theories' (1992) 18 Syracuse Journal of International Law & Commerce 21, 30.

information that can be presented to the voters and the effect that such information might have on their voting preferences. Jones and Scully, for instance, explain that only a minority of the population understood the reasons for the Welsh 2010 referendum.[117] Similar conclusions could be drawn over the preparatory work of the 2014 Scottish referendum and the 2017 Catalonian referendum.[118]

In the case of Tokelau, the issue of missing information was acknowledged by Tokelau residents, the UN and the New Zealand government. The process of educating the Tokelau residents had, by way of comparison with a large constituency such as Italy or Australia, the benefit of dealing with a small group of people. For instance, all Tokelau registered voters had the possibility of attending communal interactive meetings in which both supporters and sceptics could discuss the benefits and drawbacks of a free association with New Zealand. This communal process had the support of the UN Special Committee of 24 that had several decades of expertise on decolonization issues. Furthermore, the New Zealand government, which was one of the main stakeholders in the referendum, was committed to dispelling the lingering image of it being

---

[117] Richard Wyn Jones and Roger Scully, *Wales Says Yes: Devolution and the 2011 Welsh Referendum* (University of Wales Press 2012) Ch Introduction.

[118] The Scottish Executive, 'Choosing Scotland's Future, a National Conversation' (2007); Scottish Government, 'List of Contributions, Scotland's Future: A National Conversation' (2012) http://www.scotland.gov.uk/Topics/a-national-conversation/NC-contributions-inds-org (accessed 1 January 2012); The Scottish Government, 'A National Conversation – Your Scotland Your Voice' (The Scottish Government 2009); Rachel Minto and others, 'A Changing UK in a Changing Europe: The UK State between European Union and Devolution' (2016) 87 Political Quarterly 179; Stephen Tierney, 'Popular Constitutional Amendment: Referendums and Constitutional Change in Canada and the United Kingdom' (2015) 41 Queen's Law Journal 41; Hannah Strange, 'Spain's Constitutional Court Suspends Catalan Referendum Law' *The Telegraph* (7 September 2017) http://www.telegraph.co.uk/news/2017/09/07/catalonias-independence-referendum-intolerable-act-disobedience/ (accessed 4 January 2018); Javier García Oliva, 'Javier Garcia Oliva: The Referendum on Catalonian Independence: The Position of the Spanish Authorities' https://ukconstitutionallaw.org/2017/10/03/javier-garcia-oliva-the-referendum-on-catalonian-independence-the-position-of-the-spanish-authorities/ (accessed 4 January 2018); Germa Bel, *Disdain, Distrust and Dissolution: The Surge of Support for Independence in Catalonia* (Sussex Academic Press 2015); Elisenda Casanas Adam, 'The Referendum on Catalonian Independence: The Position of the Catalan Authorities' https://ukconstitutionallaw.org/2017/10/03/elisenda-casanas-adam-the-referendum-on-catalonian-independence-the-position-of-the-catalan-authorities/ (accessed 4 January 2018).

a colonial power which it inherited only because territories were allocated to it by the British Empire.[119]

For instance, the New Zealand government sponsored a series of projects aimed at developing the administrative skills necessary to an independent Tokelau. In particular, key aspects of the political administration of the archipelago, self-governance, the building of institutions and economic sustainability were developed with the help of New Zealand institutions.[120] In addition, a series of training initiatives aimed at increasing the skills of Tokelau administrators and political institutions was directly sponsored by the New Zealand public sector. The list of interventions cannot be replicated here, but Hooper provides a snapshot of the most significant schemes.[121] He argued, for instance, that by the end of 2001, each of the islands' 1300 residents had been through workshops devoted to management training (led by New Zealand public-sector management consultants), financial management (led by an official from the New Zealand Audit Department) and policy training analysis (led by analysts from the New Zealand Department of Labour). Along with these activities, there were audits and reviews of education, health, telecommunications, finances and information technology.[122]

The training of Tokelau's administrators was combined with a reduction in the presence of New Zealand officials within the political institution and, by 2004, the Tokelau Assembly, the Fono, did not include any representatives of the New Zealand government.[123] The reduction in New Zealand interference in the administration of the self-governing territory was coupled with an increase in financial support. In 2003, Tokelau received over $2 million (US) per year in direct and indirect New Zealand economic support, and by the end of 2009, that amount increased to over $7 million (US) per year.[124] In 2004, an international trust fund was established to offer an independent source of revenue.[125] The trust currently holds a deposit of $37 million (US). Recall that Tokelau's population is less than 2000 and so these are extravagant per-head public money allocations.[126]

---

[119] Ross (n 8); Hooper (n 105) 333.

[120] Hooper (n 105) 334.

[121] Ibid.

[122] Ibid.

[123] Tokelau Government and New Zealand Government (n 101).

[124] Hooper (n 105) 335.

[125] 'Deed Concerning the Tokelau International Trust Fund (Wellington)'.

[126] David Rea, 'Government Expenditure and Revenue in New Zealand: A Brief Overview' 5 Policy Quarterly 58.

A reduction in the central state contribution to decentralized systems is again a relatively common aspect of the decentralization process,[127] and both from the financial and constitutional perspectives, Tokelau's administration is one of many manifestations of the meso level of governance which is discussed elsewhere in this book.[128] For instance, the prerogatives of the national government of Tokelau and the legislative prerogative in areas such as fisheries and tourism might be compared with those of the Scottish parliament, the South Tyrol Assembly or the Basque government.[129] In short, the possibility of altering the status of Tokelau from self-government to a free association had the advantage of stabilizing the level of New Zealand public spending,[130] and of complying with the decolonizing aspiration policies suggested by the UN Special Committee of 24.

The process of informing voters of the 2006 referendum and of its implications in case of a victory by the free-association campaign was recommended by the UN General Assembly, which 'Calls upon New Zealand and Tokelau to consider developing an education programme to inform the population of Tokelau about the nature of self-determination, including the three options of integration, free association and independence, so that it may be better prepared to face a future decision on this matter'.[131] The call was substantiated by the distribution of a series of documents that explained the constitutional history of Tokelau, the referendum question and a brief overview of the implications of the free association with New Zealand.[132] The range of information was reasonably clear and engaged a series of issues that were perceived as important for the voters. For instance, the economic support that Tokelau would receive in the case of Tokelauans voting in favour of free association would not be changed, and the rights of those Tokelauans who lived abroad would not be affected by the outcome of the referendum.[133]

---

[127] Helen Holden, 'The Commission on Scottish Devolution – The Calman Commission' (2010) 29 Scottish Affairs http://researchbriefings.files.parliament.uk/documents/SN04744/SN04744.pdf (accessed 10 January 2016).

[128] Keating (n 79).

[129] Scotland Act 1998 (UK) (c 46); *Ley Orgánica 3/1979, de 18 de diciembre, de Estatuto de Autonomía para el País Vasco* (n 80).

[130] Government of Tokelau (n 98).

[131] United Nations General Assembly, 'General Assembly Resolution no. 57/137. Question of Tokelau' pt 19.

[132] Government of Tokelau (n 98).

[133] A treaty would make the current 3 years understanding on economic support a secure arrangement for the future. The treaty would give Tokelau greater protection against policy changes in New Zealand. Ibid.

Again, the intervention of a third party or an international organization is not unusual in a decentralization process. The UN helped in the process of normalization for the Italian South Tyrol.[134] The Council of Europe, the Republic of Ireland and the USA participated in the process that led to the Belfast Agreement which started Northern Ireland's devolution process.[135] It is, however, distinctive of the Tokelau process of decentralization that referenda were considered officially as part of a long-standing decolonization process. For instance, in 1976, as elements of a visit of an envoy from the UN Special Committee of 24, the island institutions were asked whether they would be willing to move to self-government, free association or independence. On that occasion, Tokelauan institutions (the representatives of three villages) declined all three options.[136]

The UN Special Committee of 24 perceived that a campaign aimed at increasing awareness might change Tokelauans' public perceptions. It was as part of the plan to increase the level of awareness of the benefits of the decolonization process that the UN Special Envoy sponsored the Modern House of Tokelau project which aimed at increasing the level of information regarding the referendum over free association with New Zealand.[137] Kelihiano Kalolo argues, for instance, that The Modern House Transition Teams had, by the year 2000, established a functioning training programme for political leaders and scheduled a series of meetings aimed at informing residents.[138] However, the programme had limited success.[139] Public consultations in 2005, for instance, revealed a

---

[134] United Nations, 'Article 14, Analytical Summary of Practice – Resolutions 1497 (XV) and 1661 (XVI) 31/10/1960 346-357' http://legal.un.org/repertory/art14/english/rep_supp3_vol1-art14_e.pdf (accessed 5 July 2015); Georg Grote, *The South Tyrol Question, 1866–2010: From National Rage to Regional State* (Peter Lang 2012); Jens Woelk, Francesco Palermo and Joseph Marko, *Tolerance Through Law: Self Governance and Group Rights in South Tyrol* (Brill 2007); Emma Lantschner, 'History of the South Tyrol Conflict and its Settlement' in Jens Woelk, Francesco Palermo and Joseph Marko (eds), *Tolerance Through Law: Self Governance and Group Rights in South Tyrol* (Brill 2007); Rolf Steininger, *South Tyrol: A Minority Conflict of the Twentieth Century* (Transaction 2003).

[135] The UK Government and The Government of Ireland, 'The Belfast Agreement: An Agreement Reached at the Multi-Party Talks on Northern Ireland 1998. CM 3883 (the Belfast Agreement)'.

[136] Kalolo (n 9) 257.

[137] Ibid 258.

[138] Ibid.

[139] Ibid.

level of anxiety over the implications of the referendum for the island residents and for those Tokelauans who lived and worked abroad.[140] A series of public consultations also indicated that large parts of the population had a limited level of understanding of general constitutional principles such as self-determination, democracy, good governance and accountability.[141]

Public understanding of constitutional principles such as divided state and federal sovereignty are normally misunderstood.[142] If we were, for instance, to consider a cohort of first-year undergraduate law students at the start of public law courses as somehow representative of the general population, most public law professors would agree that only a limited number of students would understand the practical implications of the constitutional principles. Even among experts, concepts such as national self-determination and sovereignty tend to generate debates over their taxonomy and pragmatic implications.[143] For instance, the 2014 Scottish referendum was preceded by a debate over the sovereignty of the Scottish parliament and the legitimacy of the agreement between the UK government and the Scottish government.[144] In the case of the Scottish referendum and by comparison with the case of Tokelau, the debate among academics attracted a large number of world-leading constitutional experts such as Joseph Weiler (at the New York University Law

140 Ibid 260.

141 Ibid 258.

142 Keating and Bray (n 80).

143 Vito Breda, 'An Odd Partnership: Identity-Based Constitutional Claims in Modern Democracy' in Fiona Jenkins, Mark Nolan and Kim Rubenstein (eds), *Allegiance and Identity in a Globalised World* (Cambridge University Press 2014).

144 'Debate: J. H.H. Weiler: Scotland and the EU: A Comment' http://ukconstitutionallaw.org/2014/09/10/debate-j-h-h-weiler-scotland-and-the-eu-a-comment/ (accessed 13 August 2015); 'Debate: Jo Murkens: Scotland and the EU: A Comment' http://ukconstitutionallaw.org/2014/09/10/debate-jo-murkens-scotland-and-the-eu-a-comment/ (accessed 13 August 2015); 'Debate: Sionaidh Douglas-Scott: Why the EU Should Welcome an Independent Scotland' http://ukconstitutionallaw.org/2014/09/10/debate-sionaidh-douglas-scott-why-the-eu-should-welcome-an-independent-scotland/ (accessed 13 August 2015); Gavin W Anderson and others, 'Gavin Anderson et al: The Independence Referendum, Legality and the Contested Constitution: Widening the Debate' http://ukconstitutionallaw.org/2012/01/31/gavin-anderson-et-al-the-independence-referendum-legality-and-the-contested-constitution-widening-the-debate/ (accessed 24 November 2012).

School) and Douglas-Scott (at Oxford University). Whilst the contributions of these experts and many others enriched the understanding of the potential effects of the referendum, it also indicated the limits of analyses aiming at assessing the pragmatic implications of a change in the system of governance.[145] Analogous conclusions might be drawn in relation to the campaign of information that preceded the Tokelau referenda.

It is reasonable to expect that, for instance, preparatory activities for the Tokelau referenda left Tokelauans anxious over the effects of the referendum (and the constitutional implications of the free association). The first referendum took place in 2006 and the result failed to reach the 67 per cent necessary to approve the switch from de facto self-governance to a free association with New Zealand. After an active campaign of information, a second referendum (with the same question as the 2006 referendum) took place in October 2007 and the result for those in favour of free association with New Zealand improved but it was still short of the required majority.[146]

There is a distinctive lack of empirical data associated with the referendum. Again this is a common occurrence since neither the winners nor the losers have a political interest in lingering over the reasons for their victory or, even worse, their defeat.[147] Kalolo argues, for instance, that the most common answer given by the Tokelau residents for rejecting the free association was '"Ko au e he malamalama" (I do not understand)'.[148] It might be tempting to take a Eurocentric perspective and consider the lack of understanding of the implications of free associations by Tokelau's population as related to, for instance, the relatively low level of wealth and education of the population, yet complex constitutional change, such as that discussed for the Ibarretxe

---

[145] 'Debate: Sionaidh Douglas-Scott: Why the EU Should Welcome an Independent Scotland' (n 144); 'Debate: J. H.H. Weiler: Scotland and the EU: A Comment' (n 144).

[146] Hooper (n 105) 331; United Nations Secretary-General, 'Secretary-General Gratified by Conduct Of Tokelau's Self-Determination Referendum' http://www.un.org/press/en/2007/sgsm11238.doc.htm (accessed 13 January 2016); Government of Tokelau (n 98).

[147] Vito Breda, 'A European Constitution in a Multinational Europe or a Multinational Constitution for Europe?' (2006) 12 European Law Journal 330; Marina Dekavalla, 'Framing Referendum Campaigns: The 2014 Scottish Independence Referendum in the Press' [2016] Media, Culture & Society 0163443715620929.

[148] Kalolo (n 9) 259.

plan or for the Scottish referendum over independence is seldom associated with a high level of comprehension.[149] For instance, Keating's empirical analysis of individual perceptions of the effect of the Ibarretxe plan (which intended to change the system of governance of the Basque region towards a free association with Spain) found those perceptions to be based on emotional assumptions and few referenced, in their interviews, any elements of the plan.[150] In the case of Tokelau, Kalolo reports similar results. Residents, when asked about the reasons for voting 'no' answered that they did not understand the implications of moving from self-government to a free association. The lack of a clear understanding of the potential effects of the referendum convinced a substantial segment of Tokelauans to vote for the status quo.[151]

This would have been a logical decision; however, by 2007, the New Zealand government had already delegated almost all the administrative and legislative powers, short of independence, to Tokelauan institutions. The delegation of administrative powers reached its climax in 2003 with the signing of the Joint Statement of the Principles of Partnership between New Zealand and Tokelau.[152] The joint statement formally recognized the right of determination of Tokelau (point 2), it established a principle of no surprises in developing common administrative activities (point 1), the allocation of citizenship (point 4) and the principle of consultation on matters of defence and international obligations (points 9 and 10).[153] The Joint Statement of the Principles of Partnership between New Zealand and Tokelau also includes a joint commitment to increase the level of administrative autonomy for Tokelau whilst New Zealand pledged to maintain the same level of economic support (point 6). The New Zealand parliament cannot bind its successor, and so it could be argued that Tokelau might be unilaterally deprived of its autonomy. This is a very unlikely event. As is the case with the UK parliament, once New Zealand parliament has allocated powers to a devolved institution, only an exceptional event such as civil unrest or war might provide the

---

[149] Keating and Bray (n 80); Geoffrey Evans and Dafydd Trystan, 'Why Was 1997 Different?' in Bridget Taylor and Katarina Thomson (eds), *Scotland and Wales Nations Again?* (University of Wales Press 1999) http://search.ebscohost.com/login.aspx?direct=true&scope=site&db=nlebk&db=nlabk&AN=27094 (accessed 14 June 2013); Wyn Jones and Scully (n 117).

[150] Keating and Bray (n 80) 361; Dekavalla (n 147).

[151] Kalolo (n 9) 259.

[152] Tokelau Government and New Zealand Government (n 101); Huntsman (n 97).

[153] Tokelau Government and New Zealand Government (n 101).

conditions to relocate those powers to a central institution.[154] It is important to remember that, since the approval of the Tokelau Act 1948, New Zealand statutes would apply to Tokelau only if they were specifically mentioned. This is a rare occurrence.[155] It is, therefore, reasonable to assume that many of the debates that took place after the first referendum over the implications of the free association were, de jure, not relevant. The Tokelauan Executive Council, the General Fono and the Village Councils had already received all the legislative, administrative and financial powers that New Zealand government could have given (short of formal independence).

The debates and the popular concerns related to the effects of the 2006 and 2007 referenda show that, in a small and exceptionally well-founded referenda campaign, individual perceptions of the implications of a change in the system of governance will remain vague. On a general level, Tokelau's referenda could be considered a small-scale testbed in which theoretical assumptions (such as the one developed by supporters of communicative democracy) are evaluated.[156] Habermas, for instance, argues that in an ideal communicative democracy which includes open discussion and the equality of the speakers, individuals might reach shared normative solutions.[157] However, large-scale initiatives such as the European Commission's Plan D for Dialogue, Democracy and Debate, which investigated, among other activities, public perceptions after the

---

[154] T Hadden and K Boyle, 'Northern Ireland: Conflict and Conflict Resolution' in K Rupesinghe (ed), *Ethnic Conflict and Human Right* (United Nations University Press 1988); Stefan Wolff, 'The Institutional Structure of Regional Consociations in Brussels, Northern Ireland, and South Tyrol' (2004) 10 Nationalism and Ethnic Politics 387.

[155] Tokelau Act 1948 N. 24 (as at 20 September 2007) (n 100); Angelo (n 1) 127.

[156] James Tully, 'The Imperialism of Modern Constitutional Democracy' in Martin Loughlin and Neil Walker (eds), *The Paradox of Constitutionalism: Constituent Power and Constitutional Form* (Oxford University Press 2007); Jürgen Habermas, 'Popular Sovereignty as Procedure' in William Rehg (ed), *Deliberative Democracy: Essays on Reason and Politics* (The MIT Press 1997); Jürgen Habermas, *The Structural Transformation of the Public Sphere: An Inquiry into a Category of Bourgeois Society* (The MIT Press 1991).

[157] Jürgen Habermas, 'On the Relation Between the Nation, the Rule of Law and Democracy' in Pablo De Greiff and Ciaran Cronin (eds), *The Inclusion of the Other: Studies in Political Theory* (The MIT Press 2000).

failed referenda over a European constitution, shows that open deliberative arenas are not the proxy for normative solutions.[158] Tokelau's experimentation with an open deliberative arena and direct democracy also revealed the explicative limits of open debates over complex constitutional issues. A similar consideration was reported in Jones and Scully with regard to the 2010 Welsh referendum, and by Keating with regard to the public perception of a plan to establish a free association between the Basque Country and Spain.[159] Referenda are, it appears, a procedural aspect of the negotiation process, but are weak as ratification devices.

CONCLUSION

Earlier in this chapter, I mentioned the 'Haka', which is perhaps one of the best-known international projections of Maori culture, and discussed the historical controversies surrounding the Treaty of Waitangi that is perceived as the formal expression of the constitutional recognition of the Maori Peoples in the constitutional system. New Zealand cultural heterogeneity is also manifested in its system of governance, which, over the years, has accommodated a large variation of identity-based constitutional demands. Some of these were the results of the process of decolonization. This was the case for the free association with the Cook Islands and Niue. Others were the expression of a popular perception of legitimacy. The two recent UN-sponsored referenda confirmed, for instance, the intention of its residents to maintain a self-governing legislative assembly in Tokelau without moving to a free association with New Zealand.

The New Zealand constitutional system, it was argued in this chapter, had adapted its system of governance to accommodate a large spectrum of identity-based constitutional claims and the current statutory measures show an articulated meso-governance system. Over the past four decades, there has been increased legislative and administrative territorial autonomy for the Polynesian residents of the Cook Islands, Niue and Tokelau. There is an express constitutional recognition of the Maori Peoples in the constitution system.

---

158 Committee of the Regions, 'EU Communication Policy and Plan D'; Michael O'Neill, *The Struggle for the European Constitution: A Past and Future History* (Routledge 2008) 439. For a general analysis of the failed Constitution for Europe project see, for instance Breda, 'A European Constitution in a Multinational Europe or a Multinational Constitution for Europe?' (n 147).

159 Wyn Jones and Scully (n 117); Keating and Bray (n 80).

The perception of the legitimacy of such demands among New Zealanders with European and Asian ancestry has also changed. This is the case even if the current political situation might show indications of a 'push back'. The Treaty of Waitangi, which in 1840 might have been one of the expedients chosen by the Crown to control and pacify Aboriginals, is currently considered one of the cornerstones of New Zealand multinational constitutional system. The change in the perception of legitimacy of Maori claims over fishing, forestry and land has received, albeit limited, jurisdictional protection by the Waitangi Tribunal.

The relative dynamism of New Zealand, and other flexible constitutional systems such as the British system, and the increased level of positive attitudes among the general population towards minorities have shifted the debate over principles to the pragmatic implications of the process of reconciliation and the accommodation of cultural diversity.[160]

[160] O'Sullivan (n 20); Hans-Peter Erb and others, 'Processing Minority and Majority Communications: The Role of Conflict with Prior Attitudes' (2002) 28 Personality and Social Psychology Bulletin 1172.

8. Australia: the recognition of Aboriginal Peoples and Torres Strait Islanders

INTRODUCTION

The Australian constitution recognized the Australian federation as having a new political entity.[1] The British statute established a federal,[2] rigid,[3] asymmetric,[4] and codified constitutional system.[5] Two statutes, the Australia Act 1986 (UK) and the Australia Act 1986 Commonwealth curtailed the UK prerogative to legislate for Australia.[6] Before the colonization process began, a jigsaw of nations with their distinctive rules and customs, currently defined as the Aboriginal Peoples and Torres Strait Islanders, lived and ruled the landmass that makes present-day Australia.[7] As was the case for other original inhabitants of the former colonies such as in Canada and the USA, there were commercial and

[1] Commonwealth of Australia Constitution Act 1900 (hereafter Australian Constitution); Jennifer Clarke and others (eds), *Hanks Australian Constitutional Law: Materials and Commentary* (9th edition, LexisNexis Butterworths 2013).

[2] Australian Constitution (n 1); Clarke and others (n 1) 51.

[3] Australian Constitution (n 1) S. 128; Clarke and others (n 1) 142. There were 44 attempts to amend the Australian Constitution. Only eight attempts were successful. Richard Albert, 'The Structure of Constitutional Amendment Rules' (2014) 49 Wake Forest Law Review 913, 927.

[4] Australian Constitution (n 1); Clarke and others (n 1) 14, Ch 3–6.

[5] Australian Constitution (n 1). For a general introduction on Australian Constitutional Law see, for instance, Clarke and others (n 1).

[6] Australia Act 1986 Commonwealth section 1; Australia Act 1986 c. 2 section 1.

[7] Jennifer Nielsen, 'Breaking the Silence: The Importance of Constitutional Change' in Simon Young, Jennifer Nielsen and Jeremy Patrick (eds), *Constitutional Recognition of First Peoples in Australia: Theories and Comparative Perspectives* (Federation Press 2016) 3–4; Vito Breda, 'Indigenous Australians and the Constitutional Reform: Learning from a Very British Experience' in Simon Young, Jennifer Nielsen and Jeremy Patrick (eds), *Constitutional Recognition of First Peoples in Australia: Theories and Comparative Perspectives* (Federation Press 2016).

sporadic encounters with people from other nations, including Europeans.[8] However, Captain Cook is normally considered the first individual of European ancestry to have firmly inserted Australia into European imperial maps.[9] Following 'discovery', from an Eurocentric perspective, the first of the penal colonies was established in 1828.[10] The population consisted of convicts and their minders ruled by governors with almost unlimited power.[11] No treaties were signed with Aboriginal Peoples and Torres Strait Islanders and none of the legal systems that existed before the establishment of the British penal colonies were subsequently recognized.[12] From the Aboriginal Peoples' and Torres Strait Islanders' perspective, that first colony was the harbinger of a forced invasion.[13]

The present constitution was approved by the UK imperial parliament in 1900 and its text was the result of a multistage articulated process that included referenda and a constitutional convention. The six states (New South Wales, Queensland, South Australia, Tasmania, Victoria and West Australia) benefit from a repartition of legislative competences that guarantees a two-tier allocation of parliamentary sovereignty.[14] The list

---

[8] Nielsen (n 7) 3; Andree Lajoie, 'What Constitutional Law Doesn't Want to Hear about History' in Law Commission of Canada and British Columbia Treaty Commission (Canada) (eds), *Speaking Truth to Power: A Treaty Forum* (Law Commission of Canada; British Columbia Treaty Commission 2001); Glen Sean Coulthard, *Red Skin, White Masks: Rejecting the Colonial Politics of Recognition* (University of Minnesota Press 2014) 1; Henry Reynolds, *An Indelible Stain?: The Question of Genocide in Australia's History* (Penguin 2001).

[9] Nielsen (n 7) 4; Clarke and others (n 1) 34.

[10] Clarke and others (n 1) 34, 155, 181; Henry Reynolds, *Dispossession: Black Australians and White Invaders* (second edition, Allen & Unwin 1996) 11; Nielsen (n 7) 4–5; Ambelin Kwaymullina, 'Recognition, Referendums and Relationships: Indigenous Worldviews, Constitutional Change, and the "Spirit" of 1967' in Simon Young, Jennifer Nielsen and Jeremy Patrick (eds), *Constitutional Recognition of First Peoples in Australia: Theories and Comparative Perspectives* (Federation Press 2016) 33.

[11] Clarke and others (n 1) 34, 155, 181; Reynolds (n 10) 11; Nielsen (n 7) 4–5; Kwaymullina (n 10) 33.

[12] Clarke and others (n 1) 33; Nielsen (n 7) 4–7; Australian Parliament, Joint Select Committee on Constitutional Recognition of Aboriginal and Torres Strait Islander Peoples, *Final Report* (2015) 4, 17.

[13] Australian Government – Referendum Council, 'Final Report 1'; Clarke and others (n 1) 191.

[14] Clarke and others (n 1) Ch 3; Ciaran O'Faircheallaigh, 'Aborigines, Mining Companies and the State in Contemporary Australia: A New Political

of territories includes the Australian Capital Territory and the Northern Territory.[15] They are autonomous political regions.[16] There are no territorial minorities that democratically control a geographical area such as with French speakers in Quebec, and in 2015, after a federal bailout, the only autonomous regional parliament, on Norfolk Island, had its administrative autonomy revoked.[17] Western Australia, perhaps in analogy with the state of Texas in the USA, has a lingering claim of independence, yet its relatively moderate political support and the rigid structure of the Australian constitution greatly reduce the plausibility of a negotiated Western Australia secession. The claim and the debates generated by it will not be discussed in this chapter. This chapter will focus instead on the demands for recognition by Aboriginal Peoples and Torres Strait Islanders which consist of 649 200 people and who represent 2.8 per cent of the Australian population.[18]

Australia, in comparison with other legal systems considered in this book, does not have a territorial identity-based constitutional claim or a set of treaties that acknowledge the historical existence of its precolonial multinational legal systems.[19] The direct references to race in the 1900 constitution have been interpreted in a way that had almost exclusively negative effects for the population of Aboriginal Peoples and Torres Strait Islanders.[20] In the constitution, there were three original references to race and two of the three are still in the text.[21] The first reference is in

---

Economy or "Business as Usual"?' (2006) 41 Australian Journal of Political Science 1.

[15] Clarke and others (n 1) Ch 4.

[16] Australia includes 10 territories including the Australian Antarctic Territory and a series of islands. Ibid 4.1.

[17] Ibid 707.

[18] Commonwealth of Australia – Australian Bureau of Statistics, 'Census: Aboriginal and Torres Strait Islander Population' http://www.abs.gov.au/ausstats/abs@.nsf/MediaRealesesByCatalogue/02D50FAA9987D6B7CA25814800087E03?OpenDocument (accessed 12 December 2017).

[19] Sharon Mascher and Simon Young, 'Rights-Based "Recognition": The Canadian Experience' in Simon Young, Jennifer Nielsen and Jeremy Patrick (eds), *Constitutional Recognition of First Peoples in Australia: Theories and Comparative Perspectives* (Federation Press 2016); Nielsen (n 7); Richard Price, 'New Zealand's Interim Treaty Settlement and Arrangements – Building Blocks of Certainty' in Law Commission of Canada and British Columbia Treaty Commission (Canada) (eds), *Speaking Truth to Power: A Treaty Forum* (Law Commission of Canada; British Columbia Treaty Commission 2001); Clarke and others (n 1) Ch 2 , p. 35.

[20] Nielsen (n 7) 7.

[21] Marcia Langton, 'Indigenous Exceptionalism and the Constitutional "Race Power"' [2013] Space, Place and Culture 1; Nicholas Pengelley, 'The

section 25. Section 25 prevents, if the state's statutory measures allow for an alteration in a census, individuals of Aboriginal ancestry from voting in federal elections.[22] The second reference is in section 51 (xxvi). It is normally called 'the race power' and it allocates a legislative competence to parliament to make laws with race as a discriminant. The third reference is in section 127, and it imposed the exclusion of individuals of Aboriginal ancestry from the federal franchise.[23] Section 127 was repealed via the constitutional amendment process included in the 1967 referendum.[24] The same referendum altered the wording of section 51 (xxvi) in a way that might have prevented, it was wrongly assumed, discriminatory policies against Aboriginal Peoples and Torres Strait Islanders.[25]

As in the other colonization processes, such as the ones in New Zealand and Canada, the initial British settlers had relatively amicable relations with the original inhabitants but ever growing immigration combined with unfounded Darwinist assumptions of social evolution were the proxy for the expansion of settlements and the relocation of original inhabitants.[26] The idea that colonization might foster human

---

Hindmarsh Island Bridge Act: Must Laws Based on the Race Power Be for the "benefit" of Aborigines and Torres Strait Islanders?' (1998) 20 Sydney Law Review, 144; Esther Pearson, '2014 Essay Winner: "Constitutionally Speaking We Are Still Basically White Australia, However Much We Boast That We Have Changed", Says Former High Court Justice Michael Kirby. Do You Agree? Does the Constitution Need to Be Changed? If so How?' (2014) 8 Indigenous Law Bulletin 31; Shireen Morris, 'Indigenous Constitutional Recognition, Non-Discrimination and Equality before the Law: Why Reform Is Necessary' (2011) 7 Indigenous Law Bulletin 7.

[22] 'For the purposes of the last section, if by the law of any State all persons of any race are disqualified from voting at elections for the more numerous House of the Parliament of the State, then, in reckoning the number of the people of the State or of the Commonwealth, persons of that race resident in that State shall not be counted'. Australian Constitution section 25.

[23] 'In reckoning the numbers of the people of the Commonwealth, or of a State or other part of the Commonwealth, aboriginal natives shall not be counted'. Australian Constitution (n 1) S. 127.

[24] Nielsen (n 7) 14.

[25] Australian Constitution section 51 (xxvi); George Williams, 'Removing Racism from Australia's Constitutional DNA' (2012) 37 Alternative Law Journal 151, 151; Kwaymullina (n 10) 29, 32.

[26] For a general review of the Imperial Era see Daniel R Headrick, 'The Tools of Imperialism: Technology and the Expansion of European Colonial Empires in the Nineteenth Century' (1979) The Journal of Modern History 231; Eric Hobsbawm, *Age of Empire, 1875–1914* (Kindle edition, Vintage 1989);

progress by an elite group chosen by natural selection or deity was a part of the ideological underpinnings of the European imperialist policies which justified the rapid assimilation of Australia.[27] Even before the colonization, imperialism had little philosophical support.[28] However, the fallacies of a superior right to land informed the expansion of European colonies in the rest of the world.[29] It is worth mentioning that, from the sixteenth century onward, the continued expansion of European nation-states and the lack of technological development of the populations met by the European explorers also solidified a perception of the racial superiority of European white races.[30] When the technological advances brought by warfare in a competitive environment, in comparison with other human communities, reached the point of organized efficient intercontinental travels, European nations used their respective military apparatus and their inherited resilience to contagious diseases to their own advantage.[31]

> The importance of lethal microbes in human history is well illustrated by Europeans' conquest and depopulation of the New World. Far more Native Americans died in bed from Eurasian germs than on the battlefield from European guns and swords. Those germs undermined Indian resistance by killing most Indians and their leaders and by sapping the survivors' morale.[32]

Francis Fukuyama, *The Origins of Political Order: From Prehuman Times to the French Revolution* (Profile Books 2012); Reynolds (n 10).

[27] Reynolds (n 10) 120; Eric J Hobsbawm, *The Age of Revolution, 1789–1848* (New American Library 1962) 170; Hobsbawm (n 26) location 517.

[28] '[B]ecause originally no one had a greater right to any region of the hearth than anyone else'. Immanuel Kant, *To Perpetual Peace: A Philosophical Sketch* (Ted Humphrey transl, Hackett 2003) 16.

[29] Mark D Walters, 'Histories of Colonialism, Legality, and Aboriginality' (2007) 57 University of Toronto Law Journal 819, 94.

[30] Senate Standing Committe – Legal and Constitutional Affairs, *Unfinished Business: Indigenous Stolen Wages* (Senate Standing Committee on Legal and Constitutional Affairs 2006) 54; Jared Diamond, *Collapse: How Societies Choose to Fail or Succeed: Revised Edition* (Penguin 2011).

[31] Australian Parliament – Human Rights and Equal Opportunity Commission, *Bringing Them Home: Report of the National Inquiry into the Separation of Aboriginal and Torres Strait Islander Children from Their Families* (Human Rights and Equal Opportunity Commission 1997) 14; Diamond (n 30) Ch 11.

[32] Diamond (n 30) 210.

In Australia, the imperial policies found little resistance and entrenched racist assumptions which continued well into the second half of the twentieth century.[33]

It is difficult to estimate the combined effects of these policies. There is, in relation to Aboriginal Peoples and Torres Strait Islanders, a distinct lack of consensus on the estimate of the size of the original Australian population and thus is difficult to guess the negative effect of colonization.[34] However, accurate analyses such as those provided by Bain Atwood that focused on Tasmania give an anecdotal indication of the scale of the genocide of the Aboriginal Peoples and Torres Strait Islanders.[35] The reduction in size of the resident population coupled with an assumption that Aboriginals could not hold land titles allowed the 1778 land settlement which, despite a few judicial challenges, considered the legal basis of the land acquisition by the British Empire.[36] The Torres Strait Islands were annexed by the Queensland colony in 1879.[37]

The Australian experience with its First Nations is not unique. As is discussed in the Canadian, US and New Zealand chapters, European expansions found a convenient justification based on Darwinian ideological assumptions.[38] The timing of the process and enactment of the Australian constitution coincided with the late stage of imperialism and the increased popularity of eugenics.[39] Sawer, in explaining the negative implications of racism in the Australian constitution, summarizes the narratives that supported the decision to ignore Aboriginal communities with a chilling clarity: 'Firstly, there were no reliable counts of the aboriginal population then available and contemporary guesses grossly

---

33 Williams (n 25); Reynolds (n 10) 9; Nielsen (n 7) 5.

34 Bain Attwood, *Telling the Truth About Aboriginal History* (Allen & Unwin 2005) Ch 4.

35 Ibid.

36 Australian Parliament, Joint Select Committee on Constitutional Recognition of Aboriginal and Torres Strait Islander Peoples (n 12) 19; Nielsen (n 7) 4; *Mabo v Queensland (No 2)* [1992] HCA 23.

37 Clarke and others (n 1) Ch 4.1.

38 Hobsbawm (n 26) locations 1572, 5328. 'What made eugenics "scientific" was precisely the rise of the science of genetics after 1900, which appeared to suggest that environmental influences on heredity could be absolutely excluded, and that most or all traits were determined by a single gene, i.e. that the selective breeding of human beings along Mendelian lines was possible'. Ibid location 5328. Reynolds (n 10) 9, 96–122; Frank Pommersheim, *Broken Landscape: Indians, Indian Tribes, and the Constitution* (Oxford University Press 2009); Attwood (n 34); Price (n 19); Lajoie (n 8); Kwaymullina (n 10).

39 Reynolds (n 10) 120; Clarke and others (n 1) 156–158.

underestimated their probable numbers, and secondly it was widely thought that the aborigines *were a dying race* whose future was unimportant'.[40] The racist assumptions which underpinned, for instance, the race power of the Australian constitution have been discredited, yet their effects were lingering until the 1970s.[41]

For instance, the Pacific Island Labourer Act 1901 and the Immigration Restriction Act 1901 entrenched the White Australia immigration policy which continued until 1973.[42] 1973 is also the year in which Aboriginal Peoples and Torres Strait Islanders could emigrate without previous authorization.[43] Again, the Australian Constitution Act 1900 did not explicitly affirm the superiority of the white race, but it prevented, for instance, Aboriginal Peoples and Torres Strait Islanders from being included in the census, and it gave a prerogative to parliament to enact legislation that discriminated between individuals on the basis of their race.[44] It could be argued, by lexical extrapolation, that with section 51 (xxvi), 'white Europeans' could have been interpreted in a way that discriminates against white Australians. Given that the Australian parliament has been dominated by white individuals of European stock, the race power has been used primarily to discriminate against Aboriginal Peoples and Torres Strait Islanders.[45]

However, the 1960s were also the years in which Aboriginal Peoples and Torres Strait Islanders, like other native groups around the world that

---

[40] My emphasis. Geoffrey Sawer, 'Australian Constitution and the Australian Aborigine' (1966) 2 Federal Law Review 17, 18.

[41] Williams (n 25); Reynolds (n 8) Ch 4; Kwaymullina (n 10) 33; Nielsen (n 7) 9–17; Clarke and others (n 1) 153–156.

[42] Australian Government. Department of Immigration and Border Protection, 'Fact Sheet – Abolition of the "White Australia" Policy' http://www.border.gov.au/about/corporate/information/fact-sheets/08abolition (accessed 6 December 2017). Pacific Island Labourers Act 1901; Immigration Restriction Act 1901.

[43] Migration Act; Clarke and others (n 1) 151.

[44] Sawer (n 40); The Australian Constitution (n 161); Australian Parliament, Joint Select Committee on Constitutional Recognition of Aboriginal and Torres Strait Islander Peoples (n 12); Pengelley (n 21); Anne Twomey, 'The Race Power – Its Replacement and Interpretation' (2012) 40 Federal Law Review 413; Langton (n 21).

[45] Williams (n 25); Attwood (n 34) 21, 133; Clarke and others (n 1) 161, 203–209; United Nations Committee on the Elimination of Racial Discrimination, 'Concluding Observations on the Eighteenth to Twentieth Periodic Reports of Australia'.

had been victimized by the colonization process,[46] achieved a mature sense of cultural and political self-awareness.[47] In 1967, the references to race in section 51 of the constitution were amended. 'The people of any race, for whom it is deemed necessary to make special laws'.[48] Section 127 was also repealed: 'the numbers of the people of the Commonwealth, or of a State or other part of the Commonwealth, aboriginal natives shall not be counted'.[49] The proposed amendments were approved by a referendum in which 90.77 per cent of the voters demonstrated their intention of ending discriminatory policies.[50] In 1975, parliament passed the Racial Discrimination Act that aims, among other objectives, to protect Aboriginal Peoples and Torres Strait Islanders from overt discrimination, and in 1992, the High Court decided *Mabo v Queensland* (no. 2). *Mabo* established the doctrine of native titles in the Australian legal system.[51] However, in 1997, parliament interpreted section 51 (xxvi) as giving the prerogative to pass a statute,[52] which had the effect of hindering the Kartinyeri tribe's right to protect a culturally sensitive site.[53] The unexpected revival of the negative use of the race power, that is, drafting a statute that has racist implications for a group that was historically discriminated against, was one of the elements that promoted the current process of constitutional recognition.[54] The two drivers of change that are considered in this chapter, among the multifarious elements that distinguish the Australian constitutional system, are the revival of the Aboriginal Peoples' and Torres Strait Islanders' demands for recognition and the limiting effect of High Court jurisprudence.

---

46 Hobsbawm (n 26).

47 Australian Parliament, Joint Select Committee on Constitutional Recognition of Aboriginal and Torres Strait Islander Peoples (n 12) 19.

48 Australian Constitution section 51 (xxvi).

49 Australian Constitution section 127.

50 Nielsen (n 7) 15.

51 *Mabo v Queensland (No 2)* (n 36).

52 Hindmarsh Island Bridge Act 1997.

53 *Kartinyeri v Commonwealth* [1998] HCA 22, 195 CLR 337; Pengelley (n 21).

54 Simon Young, Jennifer Nielsen and Jeremy Patrick, 'Preface' in Simon Young, Jennifer Nielsen and Jeremy Patrick (eds), *Constitutional Recognition of First Peoples in Australia: Theories and Comparative Perspectives* (Federation Press 2016); Megan Davis, 'Political Timetables Trump Workable Timetables: Indigenous Constitutional Recognition and the Temptation of Symbolism over Substance' in Simon Young, Jennifer Nielsen and Jeremy Patrick (eds), *Constitutional Recognition of First Peoples in Australia: Theories and Comparative Perspectives* (Federation Press 2016).

Before I qualify my analysis, a series of narratives must be inserted as a preliminary debate. Firstly, many of the ideas that informed this chapter were collected and discussed at the colloquium titled '2015 Indigenous Australian and the Constitution' organized by the University of Southern Queensland School of Law and Justice and the University of the Southern Cross.[55] The list of presenters included international scholars and stakeholders.[56] One of the presenters at the colloquium was Mick Gooda, who is the Aboriginal and Torres Strait Islanders' Social Justice Commissioner and a member of the Gangulu people.[57] Professor Megan Davis, a member of the Prime Minister's Expert Panel on Recognition,[58] was also one of the contributors, and John McVeigh, who is the Federal Minister for Regional Development, participated in one of the morning sections.[59]

Secondly, the community of nations that is defined by the term 'Aboriginal Peoples and Torres Strait Islanders' is made up of a kaleidoscope of cultures that have distinctive social characteristics and a range of political aspirations. The term 'Aboriginal Peoples and Torres Strait Islanders' is used in this chapter, but I acknowledge that it is reductive of a very complex phenomenon.[60] Thirdly, given the limited scope of this book, this chapter will focus on the process of constitutional recognition in the Australian federal constitution. Australian states have, in different ways, already recognized the contributions that Aboriginal Peoples and Torres Strait Islanders have made to their polities.[61] Fourthly, parts of the political movement that seek recognition of Aboriginal Peoples and Torres Strait Islanders also demand 'sovereignty'.[62] The idea of a

---

55 Breda (n 7).

56 Young, Nielsen and Patrick (n 54).

57 Ibid ix.

58 P L Dodson and others, 'Recognising Aboriginal and Torres Strait Islander Peoples in the Constitution: Report of the Expert Panel' (Department of Families, Housing, Community Services & Indigenous Affairs 2012) 15.

59 Davis (n 54).

60 Australian Government – Referendum Council (n 13) 10. Kwaymullina (n 10) 29–32.

61 See for instance, Constitution Amendment (Recognition of Aboriginal People) Act 2015 (WA); Constitution (Preamble) Amendment Act 2010 (QLD) (3); Constitution Amendment (Recognition of Aboriginal People) Act 2010 (NSW) 2010.

62 Australian Government – Referendum Council (n 13) 11–12; Australian Parliament, Joint Select Committee on Constitutional Recognition of Aboriginal and Torres Strait Islander Peoples (n 12) Ch 7; James Allan, 'The Document We Have Sure Ain't Broken, so Why Change It?' (Sydney, 30 January 2014)

multilayered expression of legislative sovereignty is embedded into all federal systems, and that includes the Australian constitutional system.[63] However, the recognition of Aboriginal Peoples and Torres Strait Islanders as sovereign or the setting up of a system of treaties between the federal government and Aboriginal Peoples and Torres Strait Islanders is highly unlikely.[64] The treaty system that might recognize some or all Aboriginal Peoples and Torres Strait Islanders is strongly opposed by the National Liberal Party.[65] Given that a successful reform of Australia's constitution de facto requires the support of both political parties, a debate over the recognition of Aboriginal sovereignty is improbable and will not be discussed in this chapter.[66]

DRIVER OF CHANGE: THE ABORIGINAL PEOPLES AND TORRES STRAIT ISLANDERS SEEKING RECOGNITION

In this section, I will discuss the role of Aboriginal Peoples and Torres Strait Islanders and the civic society groups that support the idea of a multinational Australia. In particular, this section will focus on the process that seeks to have the Aboriginal Peoples and Torres Strait Islanders recognized in the Australian constitution.[67] It will be argued that the current constitutional identity-based constitutional demands of the Aboriginal Peoples and Torres Strait Islanders are regrettably out of tune with popular perceptions and that makes their constitutional recognition improbable.[68]

---

http://www.theaustralian.com.au/opinion/the-document-we-have-sure-aint-broken-so-why-change-it/story-e6frg6zo-1226813351770 (accessed 18 April 2016).

63 Neil MacCormick, *Questioning Sovereignty Law, State and Nation in the European Commonwealth* (Oxford University Press 1999).

64 Law Commission of Canada and British Columbia Treaty Commission (Canada) (eds), *Speaking Truth to Power: A Treaty Forum* (Law Commission of Canada; British Columbia Treaty Commission 2001); Mascher and Young (n 19); Price (n 19).

65 Judith Brett, *The Australian Liberals and the Moral Middle Class* (Cambridge University Press 2003) 146; Australian Parliament, Joint Select Committee on Constitutional Recognition of Aboriginal and Torres Strait Islander Peoples (n 12) Ch 7.

66 Australian Parliament, Joint Select Committee on Constitutional Recognition of Aboriginal and Torres Strait Islander Peoples (n 12) 86; Davis (n 54).

67 Australian Government – Referendum Council (n 13).

68 Davis (n 54).

The 1967 constitutional referendum is perceived as the watershed point in the history of Australian institutional racism. The combination of the striking out of the words from section 51, the complete repeal of section 127 and the end of the White Australia policy was perceived as the starting point of a new multicultural society and, at the same time, the acceptance of the Aboriginal Peoples and Torres Strait Islanders as the national communities that preceded colonization.[69] The success of the 1967 referendum and subsequent policies was due, at least in part, to the determined activity of multiple entities that represented Aboriginal Peoples and Torres Strait Islanders and concerned citizens.[70] Public opinion was also particularly receptive.[71] The 1967 referendum was linked to limited reforms and the social perceptions that informed politics in the 1960s have since dynamically changed.[72] The current process of recognition appears to receive strong support from a limited section of the population.[73]

Political support for any constitutional reform might be transient and might be affected by multifarious external elements. In a two-party political system, like the Australian one, minority claims seldom receive support.[74] The marginalization of Aboriginal Peoples and Torres Strait Islanders is particularly unfortunate in Australia where a constitutional amendment requires the support of voters in a referendum in the majority of states and overall in the federal franchise.[75] In practice, Aboriginal Peoples and Torres Strait Islanders, representing a minute part of the voting franchise, have to convince both of the two large political parties

---

69 Nielsen (n 7) 14–17.

70 Brett (n 65) 146.

71 Nielsen (n 7) 14.

72 Zygmunt Bauman, 'Identity: Then, Now, What For?' in M Kempny and A Jawlowska (eds), *Identity in Transformation: Postmodernity, Postcommunism, and Globalization* (Praeger 2002); Zygmunt Bauman, *In Search of Politics* (Polity 1999).

73 Davis (n 54); United Nations Committee on the Elimination of Racial Discrimination (n 45).

74 Brett (n 65) 126, 146, 192; Ian Marsh, 'Beyond the Two Party System: New Zealand and Australia? [Address to The Sydney Institute, 11 June 1996]' (1996) 8 Sydney Papers 40, 42–43; Jean-François Godbout and Monika Smaz, 'Party Development in the Early Decades of the Australian Parliament: A New Perspective' (2016) 51 Australian Journal of Political Science 478, 493.

75 Australian Constitution (n 1) section 128.

that a reform is needed and that a referendum might be successful.[76] However, there is a larger, in comparison with Aboriginal Peoples and Torres Strait Islanders, group of Australians that bear indirect and direct racial bias towards Aboriginal Peoples and Torres Strait Islanders.[77] These negative public perceptions do affect political strategies and, as a result, make a successful constitutional recognition of the Aboriginal Peoples and Torres Strait Islanders improbable.[78]

This is, again, lamentable, because the present constitutional arrangements are perceived as out of tune with an Australian multi-ethnic society.

> When the Constitution was drafted, the exclusion of Aboriginal and Torres Strait Islander peoples was unremarkable for the time, as Aboriginal and Torres Strait Islander peoples were not considered citizens and had minimal rights and protections. However, the continued constitutional silence maintained by this exclusion is remarkable. That our Constitution allows a state to ban a race from voting is remarkable. That in our Constitution there are more references to lighthouses than to the first peoples of this nation is remarkable. That constitutional recognition has not occurred already is remarkable.[79]

The final report to the parliament by the Joint Select Committee on Constitutional Recognition of Aboriginal and Torres Strait Islander

---

[76] Dodson and others (n 58) 71; Newspoll, 'Recognition of Aboriginal and Torres Strait Islander Peoples in the Australian Constitution – National Survey' 7, https://www.dss.gov.au/sites/default/files/documents/08_2012/11_12_039_foi_3.pdf; United Nations Committee on the Elimination of Racial Discrimination (n 45).

[77] Anne Pedersen and others, 'Attitudes toward Aboriginal Australians in City and Country Settings' (2000) 35 Australian Psychologist 109; Mir Rabiul Islam and Mirna Jahjah, 'Predictors of Young Australians' Attitudes Toward Aboriginals, Asians And Arabs' (2001) 29 Social Behavior and Personality: An International Journal 569; Bruce Petty and Australia Office of the Minister for Aboriginal and Torres Strait Islander Affairs, *Rebutting the Myths: Some Facts about Aboriginal and Torres Strait Islander Affairs* (Australian Government Publishing Service 1994); David Mellor, 'Contemporary Racism in Australia: The Experiences of Aborigines' (2003) 29 Personality and Social Psychology Bulletin 474; Conrad Gershevitch, Amy Lamoin and Cassandra Dawes, 'Racism in Australia: Is Denial Still Plausible?' (2010) 3 Race/Ethnicity: Multidisciplinary Global Contexts 229.

[78] Davis (n 54); Australian Parliament, Joint Select Committee on Constitutional Recognition of Aboriginal and Torres Strait Islander Peoples (n 12) xiii, 73. See recommendation no. 2.

[79] Australian Parliament, Joint Select Committee on Constitutional Recognition of Aboriginal and Torres Strait Islander Peoples (n 12) v.

Peoples describes succinctly the current shortcomings of the constitution. However, and as expected, there are a range of opinions on 'how to fix it'.[80]

It is reasonably clear, for instance, that Aboriginal Peoples and Torres Strait Islanders must be involved in a process of recognition, but there is little common ground on the type of inputs that representatives of the hundreds of representatives of Aboriginal Peoples and Torres Strait Islanders might have.[81] There are also many diverging opinions on the scope of recognition.[82] If the recognition were not strictly symbolic, as expected by the majority of Aboriginal Peoples and Torres Strait Islanders,[83] there is a concern that allocating a distinctive set of rights to a minority might open and increase the level of litigation, which might be antithetical to the reconciliation process.[84] However, there is a general agreement among experts that Aboriginal Peoples' and Torres Strait Islanders' constitutional recognition might not be improved by a mere formal acknowledgement.[85] The final report of the Referendum Council, after a National Constitutional Convention which was attended by 600 Aboriginal Peoples' and Torres Strait Islanders' representatives, dismissed the idea of a mere formal constitutional acknowledgement.[86]

The recognition, in other words, must include the substantive allocation of rights and political prerogatives.[87] The range of proposals considered by the Referendum Council and Joint Select Committee on Constitutional Recognition of Aboriginal and Torres Strait Islander Peoples cannot be reproduced here. The proposal for the recognition of First Nation sovereignty was considered but perceived as premature.[88] The most interesting, in relation to the aims of a book on constitutional negotiations, is the proposal to establish an Indigenous Advisory Council which acts as a consultative committee within parliament.[89] The proposal for a consultative institution within parliament was supported by the

80 Ibid xiv; Australian Government – Referendum Council (n 13) 15.

81 Australian Parliament, Joint Select Committee on Constitutional Recognition of Aboriginal and Torres Strait Islander Peoples (n 12) xiv–xvii; Breda (n 7) 240–242.

82 Australian Government – Referendum Council (n 13) 15.

83 Ibid.

84 Breda (n 7) 246.

85 Young, Nielsen and Patrick (n 54) x; Davis (n 54); Breda (n 7) 246.

86 Australian Government – Referendum Council (n 13) 10, 15.

87 Australian Parliament, Joint Select Committee on Constitutional Recognition of Aboriginal and Torres Strait Islander Peoples (n 12) 10, 25–31.

88 Ibid 7.

89 Ibid 35.

Cape York Institute and the Yothu Yindi Foundation.[90] The existence of a consultative institution within parliament would have the advantage of giving voice to a minority without imposing an excessive burden on the legislative process. Furthermore, in case of a reform that allocates rights to the recognition of Aboriginal Peoples and Torres Strait Islanders, an Indigenous Advisory Council might help in the reduction of litigation. The Council might operate in a way similar to consultative institutions such as the Joint Ministerial Committee, which discussed the potential bordering issues of UK legislation in Scotland.[91] The Joint Ministerial Committee, in the case that contentious issues are flagged at committee level, seeks to draft unbinding concordats in which the parties commit to solving potential disputes without the use of litigation.[92] By modelling its activity in a way that is analogous to the Joint Ministerial Committee, the Indigenous Advisory Council that includes federal government representatives could provide an interface between federal and Aboriginal Peoples' and Torres Strait Islanders' delegates. The aim of such an interface would be to facilitate dialogue and to reduce tensions over the potential economic implications of allocating rights.[93]

Constitutional recognition might also include the possibility of protecting against discrimination. This should prevent the passing of statutory measures that discriminate directly and indirectly against Aboriginal Peoples' and Torres Strait Islanders' assets.[94] It is important to note that aspirations manifested in the National Constitutional Convention seek a substantive recognition of Australian First Peoples and not equality and civil rights.[95] The 1967 reforms, which intended to purge the constitution from some of its racist assumptions, saw the cooperation of multiple organizations that represented Aboriginal Peoples and Torres Strait Islanders such as the Federal Council for the Advancement of Aborigines with representatives of civic societies such as the Australian Council of Trade Unions.[96] The present demands for recognition focus instead on the allocation of resources and their management, protection against

---

90 Ibid.

91 Breda (n 7) 242.

92 Scotland Act 1998 c 46 section 30.

93 Breda (n 7).

94 Aboriginal and Torres Strait Islander Heritage Protection Act no. 79 1984; Hindmarsh Island Bridge Act 1997; Pengelley (n 21); Nielsen (n 7); Australian Parliament, Joint Select Committee on Constitutional Recognition of Aboriginal and Torres Strait Islander Peoples (n 12) vi, 47–50.

95 Nielsen (n 7) 13.

96 Ibid.

discrimination, public acknowledgement of past wrongs and the possibility of being heard by national political institutions.[97]

However, a series of quantitative and qualitative analyses of 'white Australian attitudes' shows strong indications that the majority of Australians hold a negative perception towards Aboriginal Peoples.[98] These negative perceptions are shared by city and countryside dwellers.[99] For instance, a recent study, conducted by Pedersen, Bishop, Contos, Walker and Griffiths, shows that 60 per cent of the interviewed residents of Perth, the 1.2 million capital of West Australia, and over 60 per cent of the residents of Kalgoorlie, a 30 000 inhabitant country town, show markers of prejudice against Aboriginal Peoples.[100] The study also indicates that 25 per cent of those interviewed in Perth and 23 per cent of those interviewed in Kalgoorlie hold a series of perceptions that are consistent with ethnocentric racial prejudice. The data reveals, for example, open support for racial segregation.[101] However, the most significant result of this study is the large scale of negative attitudes that are classified as 'modern prejudice': 52 per cent of Perth's residents and 70 per cent of Kalgoorlie's residents show a level of intolerance towards

---

[97] Australian Parliament, Joint Select Committee on Constitutional Recognition of Aboriginal and Torres Strait Islander Peoples (n 12); Australian Government – Referendum Council (n 13); Davis (n 54); Nielsen (n 7) 23; Shireen Morris, 'Re-evaluating Mabo: The Case for Native Title Reform to Remove Discrimination and Promote Economic Opportunity' (2012) 5 Land, Rights, Laws: Issues of Native Title 1; Native Title Act 1993; *Mabo v Queensland (No 2)* (n 36).

[98] United Nations Committee on the Elimination of Racial Discrimination (n 45); Islam and Jahjah (n 77); Pedersen and others (n 77); Petty and Australia Office of the Minister for Aboriginal and Torres Strait Islander Affairs (n 77); Mellor (n 77); Gershevitch, Lamoin and Dawes (n 77); Australian Human Rights Commission, *National Anti-Racism Strategy Consultation Report July 2012* (Australian Human Rights Commission 2012) 12 http://www.rwi.lu.se/NHRIDB/Asia/Australia/NationalAnti-racismStrategyConsultationReportJuly2012.pdf (accessed 11 December 2017).

[99] Pedersen and others (n 77). The data of the Pedersen and others study was independently assessed and it adopted internationally recognized standards for gathering and evaluating empirical information. Kaine Grigg and Lenore Manderson, 'Developing the Australian Racism, Acceptance, and Cultural-Ethnocentrism Scale (RACES)' (2015) 32 The Australian Educational and Developmental Psychologist 1, 72; Grigg and Manderson, 'The Australian Racism, Acceptance, and Cultural-Ethnocentrism Scale (RACES): Item Response Theory Findings' (2016) 15 International Journal for Equity in Health 49.

[100] Pedersen and others (n 77) 112.

[101] Ibid 111.

Aboriginal political and legal claims.[102] A large part of the sample believes that 'Aborigines are getting too demanding in their push for land rights'.[103] Similar results are replicated across age groups and across Australian states and territories.[104]

Even by comparison with other ethnic groups, Aboriginal Peoples and Torres Strait Islanders appear to have the most negative perceptions held against them from among those who perceive themselves as white Australians.[105] For instance, 51 per cent of the sample of adults in New South Wales who defined themselves as white Anglo-Saxon Australians hold a negative and misinformed perception of Aboriginal Peoples.[106] The negative perceptions are also confirmed regarding discriminatory behaviours by public and private institution studies.[107] For instance, in a study on the experience of racism among Queensland Aboriginal residents, 91 per cent had the experience of having had a public service refused (e.g. a pre-booked hotel room or a table at a restaurant) after a manager realized that such a service had been promised to an individual of Aboriginal appearance.[108] The recurrence of these events contributes to increasing the level of mistrust between white multicultural Australians and Aboriginal and Torres Strait Islander Peoples.[109]

It is a matter of speculation as to whether such a set of misinformed beliefs might change in the future. In December 2017, the Concluding Observations on the Eighteenth to Twentieth Periodic Reports of Australia by the UN Committee on the Elimination of Racial Discrimination reported an increase in racism in Australia: 'expressions of racism, racial discrimination, and xenophobia, including in the public sphere and political debates as well as the media, are on the rise [...] Indigenous Peoples are particularly affected by racist hate speech and violence'.[110] In 2014, for instance, *The Australian*, which is the only national broadsheet newspaper, published over 21 articles that directly or indirectly criticized the current constitutional reform aimed at recognizing Aboriginal Peoples

---

102 Ibid.

103 Ibid.

104 Grigg and Manderson, 'Developing the Australian Racism, Acceptance, and Cultural-Ethnocentrism Scale (RACES)' (n 99).

105 Islam and Jahjah (n 77) 572.

106 Ibid 574.

107 Mellor (n 77) 480.

108 Ibid.

109 Dodson and others (n 58) 70; Newspoll (n 76).

110 United Nations Committee on the Elimination of Racial Discrimination (n 45) 3.

and Torres Strait Islanders and none in favour.[111] A few of these analyses are well argued. Professor James Allan, one of the most eminent voices against the reform, expresses concern for the potential judicial implications of the proposed amendments.[112] Allan suggests, in short, that the 'Constitution ain't broken'.[113] Again, the UN Committee on the Elimination of Racial Discrimination and several of the experts mentioned in this chapter disagree with Allan, but it appears that such a view struggles to reach the media in a way that might inform potential voters in a constitutional referendum.[114] It is, indeed, *The Australian*'s editorial team's prerogative, and a manifestation of freedom of speech, to allow academics to voice concerns, but these views are published next to editorial opinions which might be an example of modern racial bias.[115] Barry Maley's editorial in *The Australian*, for instance, argues that racial discrimination has a legitimate role in modern constitutional systems:

> In denying the [c]ommonwealth and the states power to discriminate 'on the grounds of race, colour or ethnic or national origin', it is conceivable that those authorities would be deprived of the power to act, when necessary, for purposes of national defence, border protection, immigration, the management of civil disorder, international sanctions, or measures such as the recent Northern Territory intervention into Aboriginal settlements.[116]

Similar media responses followed the *Mabo* case which recognized some of the Aboriginal Peoples' and Torres Strait Islanders' land claims against the Crown.[117] The issue here is not whether Maley's narrative is in tune

---

[111] Allan (n 62); Australian Indigenous Leadership Centre, 'Submission to Joint Select Committee on Constitutional Recognition of Aboriginal and Torres Strait Islander Peoples, Australian Indigenous Leadership Centre' (Australian Indigenous Leadership Centre 2014) 062.

[112] Allan (n 62); 'Submission to Joint Select Committee on Constitutional Recognition of Aboriginal and Torres Strait Islander Peoples, Australian Indigenous Leadership Centre' (n 12).

[113] Allan (n 62).

[114] United Nations Committee on the Elimination of Racial Discrimination (n 45); Young, Nielsen and Patrick (n 54); Nielsen (n 7); Davis (n 54); Breda (n 7).

[115] Grigg and Manderson, 'The Australian Racism, Acceptance, and Cultural-Ethnocentrism Scale (RACES)' (n 99).

[116] Barry Maley, 'Abandon Change to Constitution' (2014) The Australian 10.

[117] *Mabo v Queensland (No 2)* (n 36); Simone C Muller and Gary D Meyers, 'Mabo – Through the Eyes of the Media (Part II): The Land Fund Legislation' (1995) 2 Deakin Law Review 99; Native Title Act 1993.

with the modern rendering of the concept of equality and freedom of speech, or whether his views are compatible with international treaties.[118] The problem is rather this: bigotry is relayed in the only truly national broadsheet which also tends to pass more articulated and objective analyses (such as the one proposed by Allan), and that has the effect of misapprehending opinions with legal assessments. In August 2014, a few weeks after Maley's article, the First Minister announced that he would postpone the referendum to 2017; in August 2015, he faced a cabinet rebellion over his support for the referendum, and the following month he was forced to resign.[119] The current First Minster has implemented the previous administration's plan for the Referendum Council which delivered its final report in June 2017 but has so far made no declaration regarding the government support for the recognition of Aboriginal Peoples and Torres Strait Islanders.[120]

DRIVER OF CHANGE: AN UNCOMMON HIGH COURT JURISPRUDENCE AS A LIMIT TO THE PROCESS OF CONSTITUTIONAL RECOGNITION OF ABORIGINAL PEOPLES AND TORRES STRAIT ISLANDERS

In the previous section, I discussed the constitutional aspirations of Aboriginal Peoples and Torres Strait Islanders. Aboriginal Peoples' and Torres Strait Islanders' constitutional claims are articulated and in tune with the expectations of international organizations but, at this stage, have not collected the political support necessary for a constitutional reform.[121] In this section, I will discuss the role of the High Court of Australia as a limiting element to the process of constitutional recognition of Aboriginal Peoples and Torres Strait Islanders. It will be argued that an excessive use of textual formalism by the High Court, which normally has the effect of reducing ideological narratives in interpreting

---

[118] United Nations Committee on the Elimination of Racial Discrimination (n 45).

[119] Anna Henderson and Eliza Borrello, 'Abbott Facing Internal Rebellion on Indigenous Recognition Push' (*ABC News*, 20 August 2015) http://www.abc.net.au/news/2015-08-20/abbott-facing-rebellion-on-indigenous-recognition/6711708 (accessed 19 April 2016).

[120] Australian Government – Referendum Council (n 13). The stance has been confirmed in 2018 in the relation to the 2017 Uluru Statement.

[121] Davis (n 54); Australian Government – Referendum Council (n 13).

constitutional texts,[122] resulted in an unstable line of authority that increased the level of uncertainty over the potential implications of constitutional reforms.[123] The potential instability had negative effects on the process of constitutional reforms, like the one proposed by Aboriginal Peoples and Torres Strait Islanders, which aimed at introducing new protections for an economically depressed Aboriginal and Torres Strait Islander minority.[124]

The High Court tendency to endorse a literal approach has a detrimental effect on the process of recognition of Aboriginal Peoples and Torres Strait Islanders because, by refusing to consider the pragmatic implications of its interpretation, the Court might extend or reduce the pragmatic effect of constitutional reforms.[125] This level of unpredictability has the effect of increasing the concern of all those involved in a constitutional reform. For instance, the Joint Select Committee on Constitutional Recognition of Aboriginal and Torres Strait Islander Peoples recommended against inserting in the constitutional reform narratives such as: 'advancement of Aboriginal and Torres Strait Islander peoples'.[126] The term 'advancement' might be interpreted as giving a paternalist legislative prerogative to parliament that might be used to hinder Aboriginal and Torres Strait Islander freedoms and rights.[127]

Allan and Aroney qualify the High Court's jurisprudence as uncommon.[128] The two authors argue that the High Court tends to construct narrow literal interpretations of constitutional norms that, in turn, might deliver unforeseeable decisions for the drafter. Again, the issue in Allan and Aroney is not that courts have a prerogative to interpret text, but the quasi-randomness of the judicial outcomes. They deliver such a conclusion in a pungent narrative:

> [The reasons why] the High Court of Australia has done this are perhaps unique, for they have rested upon a rather unlikely foundation: a certain kind of textual formalism, the professed motivating reason for which has been the

---

122 Antonin Scalia, *A Matter of Interpretation: Federal Courts and the Law* (Princeton University Press 1998).

123 Allan James and Aroney Nicholas, 'An Uncommon Court: How the High Court of Australia Has Undermined Australian Federalism' (2008) 30 Sydney Law Review; Allan (n 62).

124 Davis (n 54).

125 Australian Parliament, Joint Select Committee on Constitutional Recognition of Aboriginal and Torres Strait Islander Peoples (n 12) 25.

126 Ibid 24.

127 Ibid.

128 James and Nicholas (n 123).

> idea that, by following this method the judges will avoid imposing their own subjective and idiosyncratic views upon the authoritative text of the constitution. The ironic result to adopt Herbert's terminology has been a most uncommon body of constitutional law, generated by a most uncommon court, using what appear to be the most orthodox techniques of common law reasoning, applied to the text of the constitution.[129]

The prerogative to adopt constitutional literalism as the favoured method of the constitutional text is not unique to Australia. The US Supreme Court, for instance, has, over the years, relied on textual formalism to define the role of American Indians as dependent nations.[130] Scalia, one of the most influential judges of our time, has defended the literal approach in several instances.[131] However, in the case of Australia, statutory textualism has resulted in an increase in the level of anxiety among minorities.[132] 'The High Court has largely applied a strict literal interpretation of civil and political rights, reducing their operation to mere procedural requirements rather than serving as substantive civil or political protections'.[133] The *Kartinyeri v Commonwealth* case engages, for instance, the constitutional legitimacy of a federal statute (the Hindmarsh Island Bridge Act 1997) that suspended the validity of the Heritage Act exclusively for the members of the Kartinyeri tribe.[134] The answer by the majority of the justices was that a federal power to make law includes the prerogative to revoke such a law.[135] However, Justices Gaudron, Gummow and Hayne, in a joint decision, stated that a race power, as it is currently inserted in the constitution, allows

---

[129] Nicholas Aroney and James Allan, 'An Uncommon Court: How the High Court of Australia Has Undermined Australian Federalism' (2008) 30 Sydney Law Review 245, 245; Australian Parliament, Joint Select Committee on Constitutional Recognition of Aboriginal and Torres Strait Islander Peoples (n 12) 25.

[130] Pommersheim (n 38).

[131] Antonin Scalia and Bryan Andrew Garner, *Reading Law: The Interpretation of Legal Texts* (Kindle edition) (West 2012) Contextual Canon; Scalia (n 127) 3–49.

[132] Vito Breda, *The Objectivity of Judicial Decisions: A Comparative Analysis of Nine Jurisdictions* (new edition, Peter Lang 2016).

[133] 'Submission to Joint Select Committee on Constitutional Recognition of Aboriginal and Torres Strait Islander Peoples, Australian Indigenous Leadership Centre' (n 12) 59.

[134] Aboriginal and Torres Strait Islander Heritage Protection Act no. 79.

[135] *Kartinyeri v Commonwealth* (n 58) 12, 47, 57, 174.

parliament to pass reasonable legislation that hinders a racial group.[136] Justice Kirby disagreed.[137] Kirby pointed out that, after the 1967 referendum section 51 (xxvi) prevents parliament from passing legislation that is discriminating of Aboriginal Peoples.[138]

The debate over the soundness of *Kartinyeri v Commonwealth* is only incidental to the issue discussed in this section of the chapter. That is, the unpredictability of the High Court's jurisprudence hinders, albeit indirectly, the process of recognition of identity-based constitutional claims. For instance, in the *Kartinyeri v Commonwealth* case, the High Court had the consequence of suggesting (albeit only by way of a dictum) that the purpose of race power was not altered by the 1967 referendum that intended to eliminate racial dissemination.[139] Hindmarsh Island is a tourist destination relatively close to urban areas of Adelaide. Before the opening of the bridge in 2001, the island was connected to the mainland by a cable ferry. In 1990, the Government of South Australia signed a deed with Binalong Pty Ltd, an estate developer that was already active on the island, that committed the government to financing 50 per cent of the bridge.[140] The deed, however, was drafted in a way that exposed the Government of South Australia, in case of a breach of contract, for the full financial loss of Binalong Pty Ltd. It is unclear whether the government intended to take such a financial liability which wildly exceeded the estimated cost of the entire project.[141] The cost of the bridge was estimated at around $3 million, yet reimbursement for the potential collapse of Binalong Pty Ltd, in case of a breach of contract by the government, could exceed $12 million.[142] Unfortunately, the bridge had to be built in an area that was perceived by the Kartinyeri tribe as part of their cultural heritage and that could have been protected by the Aboriginal and Torres Strait Islander Heritage Protection Act 1984.[143] However, the parliament, by passing the Hindmarsh Island Bridge Act

---

136 My emphasis: *Kartinyeri v Commonwealth* (n 58) 361 para 30.

137 Ibid 153.

138 Ibid 157.

139 Sawer (n 40); Robert Dubler, 'Race and the Constitution' (2002) 76 Australian Law Journal 456; O'Faircheallaigh (n 14).

140 Australian Parliament, 'Bills Digest 50 1996–97 Hindmarsh Island Bridge Bill 1996'.

141 Ibid.

142 '[D]amages payable by the South Australian Government could amount to at least $12.5 million if the bridge is not built and Binalong Pty Ltd successfully sues for breach of contract'. Ibid.

143 Aboriginal and Torres Strait Islander Heritage Protection Act no. 79 Part II.

1997, excluded the Aboriginal cultural sites in the area of the bridge from the safeguard of the Aboriginal and Torres Strait Islander Heritage Protection Act 1984.[144]

This is, again, a tangential issue but, as an example of ad hoc legislation that falls short of Fuller's generality-of-law requirement, it is difficult to find a neater example than the Hindmarsh Island Bridge Act 1997.[145] The Aboriginal and Torres Strait Islander Heritage Protection Act 1984 was enacted under the race power and aims, if some conditions were met, at protecting the cultural assets of Aboriginal Peoples and Torres Strait Islanders from private or public interference. The Hindmarsh Bridge Act 1997 had the opposite purpose, that is, to prevent members of the Kartinyeri tribe from demanding the protection of aspects of their cultural heritage from the negative effects of a private/public joint business venture. If a parliament has the power to enact the act, it also has the power to amend that act.

It was therefore appropriate for the High Court to discuss whether the Hindmarsh Bridge Act 1997 could be included on the heads of power of section 51 (xxvi). The section reads, it is worth remembering, as follows: 'the people of any race, other than the aboriginal race in any State, for whom it is deemed necessary to make special laws'. The High Court was to ask whether the combination of the proposition 'for' and pronoun 'whom' was intended to have a neutral or a positive meaning. The issue is squarely engaged by Gaudron.

> 'Yes' case for the 1967 referendum [...] identified two purposes attending the proposed law, which upon its approval in accordance with s 128 of the Constitution, deleted the words 'other than the aboriginal race in any State' from s 51(xxvi) of the Constitution [...] Given the limited nature of the purposes thus disclosed and given, also, that as a matter of language and syntax, the amendment was apt to achieve those purposes, and only those purposes, it is not possible, in my view, to treat s 51(xxvi) as *limited to laws which benefit Aboriginal Australians* if it is not similarly limited with respect to the people of other races.[146]

---

[144] Pengelley (n 21). The motivation for choosing the name Hindmarsh Island Bridge Act 1997 for a statutory measure that had the only aim of amending the Torres Strait Islander Heritage Protection Act 1984 is also a matter of speculation. The Hindmarsh Island Bridge Act 1997 could be considered, as Brennan and McHugh pointed out, a technical amendment of the Aboriginal and Torres Strait Islander Heritage Protection Act 1984. Brennan and McHugh in *Kartinyeri v Commonwealth* (n 58) para 15.

[145] Lon L Fuller, *The Morality of Law* (Yale University Press 1969) 46.

[146] My emphasis: *Kartinyeri v Commonwealth* (n 58) 361 para 30.

The 1967 constitutional reform that was intended to eliminate the power to legislate in a way that hindered Aboriginal Peoples and Torres Strait Islanders could not, according to Gaudron, be considered as having changed the racist prerogative of the 1900 parliament. The prerogative to discriminate against a group of individuals is, Gaudron continues, trammelled only by the requirement of reasonableness.

Notwithstanding that it is difficult to envisage circumstances in which a law which operated to the disadvantage of the people of a racial minority might validly be enacted under s 51 (xxvi) of the constitution, the test of constitutional validity is not whether it is a beneficial law. Rather, the test is whether the law in question 'is reasonably capable' of being viewed as appropriate and adapted to a real and relevant difference which the parliament might reasonably judge to exist.[147]

As mentioned, Gaudron's stance qualified the High Court position expressed in *Commonwealth v Tasmania*. It did so in a way that might appear unprovable for several reasons.[148] Firstly, Gaudron argues that in *Kartinyeri v Commonwealth* the High Court should consider the discriminatory effects of the Hindmarsh Island Bridge Act 1997 as predicable.[149] Section 51 (xxvi) allocates a legislative power to the commonwealth parliament, and thus parliament has, within the limit of reasonableness, the prerogative to decide how to use it.[150] The concept of reasonableness is not, however, a purely political concept. In common law jurisdictions it is a criterion of statutory interpretation that helps judges in the task of reducing the number of incongruent interpretations.[151] Hart's example of the 'no vehicles in the park' rule is often used to show how judges adopt a series of interpretative methods to exclude textual interpretations that might produce incoherent pragmatic results.[152] MacCormick moves Hart's requirement of rationality a step

---

[147] My emphasis: ibid para 45.

[148] *Commonwealth v Tasmania ('Tasmanian Dam case')* [1983] HCA 21.

[149] Hindmarsh Island Bridge Act 1997.

[150] *Kartinyeri v Commonwealth* (n 58) para 40.

[151] Thomas S Kuhn, *The Structure of Scientific Revolutions: 50th Anniversary Edition* (University of Chicago Press 2012) 23–35; Vito Breda and Lidia Rodak, 'Introduction', in Vito Breda and Lidia Rodak (eds), *Diverse Narratives of Legal Objectivity: An Interdisciplinary Perspective* (Peter Lang 2016) 7; Neil MacCormick, 'Reasonableness and Objectivity' (1998) 74 Notre Dame Law Review 1575.

[152] 'The point must be not merely that a judicial decision to be rational must be made in the light of some conception of what ought to be, but that the aims, the social policies and purposes to which judges should appeal if their decisions are to be rational, are themselves to be considered as part of the law'. HLA Hart,

further when he explains, for instance, that reasonableness is one of the qualifiers of statutory rational interpretations which help in understanding the core meaning of a norm.[153] In particular, reasonableness is, according to MacCormick, a necessary requirement of an objective interpretation.[154]

This assertion appears to move the debate over the 'appropriateness' of a rule to another indeterminate set of references. However, reasonableness is not an indeterminate concept,[155] and more importantly, it is not an exclusive prerogative of parliament to qualify it (as Gaudron appears to suggest in *Kartinyeri v Commonwealth*). The High Court has, for instance, qualified the concept of reasonableness in *Shaddock & Assoc Proprietary, Ltd v Parramatta City Council*.[156] The House of Lords has a well-established line of authority that explains the implications of reasonableness in the areas of statutory interpretation which directly engage the area of racial discrimination.[157] In the case *Mandla v Lee*, for instance, the House of Lords considered the effects of statutory interpretation in a racial discrimination case.[158]

In *Mandla v Lee*, Lord Fraser argued that a legalistic interpretation of section 3(1) of the Race Relations Act 1976 was untenable in cases that such a textual reading produced the effect of discriminating against a group of individuals who were perceived to be part of an ethnic group.[159] Section 3(1) defines the types of groups against whom discriminatory practices would have been considered illegitimate. Racial and ethnic origins could not, for instance, be grounds for direct and indirect discrimination. However, and for historical reasons, English law does

'Positivism and the Separation of Law and Morals' (1958) 71 Harvard Law Review 593, 612. A recent review is provided in Pierre Schlag, 'No Vehicles in the Park' (1999) 23 Seattle University Law Review 381.

[153] MacCormick, 'Reasonableness and Objectivity' (n 151).

[154] Ibid.

[155] Ibid 1537.

[156] *Shaddock & Assoc Proprietary, Ltd v Parramatta City Council* (1981) 150 CLR 225 (High Court) 231.

[157] Vito Breda, 'The Concept of Objectivity in the UK Supreme Court Through a Comparative Looking Glass' in Vito Breda and Lidia Rodak (eds), *Diverse Narratives of Legal Objectivity: An Interdisciplinary Perspective* (Peter Lang 2016); Vito Breda and Mateo Vricella, 'English Pragmatism and Italian Virtue: A Comparative Analysis of the Regime of Illegally Obtained Evidence in Civil Law Proceedings between Italy and England' (2014) 21 Maastricht Journal of European and Comparative Law 428.

[158] *Mandla (Sewa Singh) and Another (Appellants) v Dowell Lee and Other (Respondents) [1983] (HL)* 2 AC 548 (House of Lords).

[159] Ibid 565.

explicitly allow for religious discrimination.[160] In *Mandla v Lee*, Mr Mandla was an orthodox Sikh and his religious beliefs prevented him from taking off his turban and cutting his hair as required by private school regulations. At the appeal stage, Lord Denning interpreted section 3(1) literally and disqualified individuals such as Mr Mandla from the protection of the Race Relations Act 1976.[161] In deciding whether the Sikhs were of ethnic origin, Lord Denning relied on a set of definitions taken from the 1890 edition of the English Oxford Dictionary which distinguished ethnic cultures, ethnic origins and racial groups.[162] The definition, perhaps unsurprisingly given the recent acceptance of racial Darwinism, constructed the concept of ethnicity as a biological concept related to but distinguished from race.[163]

After 1950 and the isolation of DNA, the biological nature of racial taxonomy has been discredited.[164] It was therefore expected that, at the appeal stage of *Mandla v Lee*, Lord Denning would purport that the aim of the Race Relations Act 1976 was to protect only racial groups and communities which were biologically part of an ethnic group. By distinguishing 'biological communities' from 'ethnic groups', cultural minorities such as the Sikhs could be discriminated against in England and Wales. The distinction might also include Jews, and to prevent such a critique, Denning inserted, in obiter, a criterion to distinguish biological Jews from religious Jews (which, by deduction, we should assume could be discriminated against *sic*).[165] The scientific reference in Lord Denning's obiter is in another pre-1940 book titled *We Europeans: A Survey of 'Racial' Problems*.[166] It is one of the judge's expected activities to select the type of scientific references with which to evaluate the

---

160 Race Relations Act 1976 (C74).

161 *Mandla (Sewa Singh) and Another v Dowell Lee and Another [1983]* QB 1 (Court of Appeal).

162 Ibid 7.

163 Michael Banton, *Racial Theories* (Cambridge University Press 1998) 184; Charles Darwin, *The Descent of Man* (Prometheus Books 1997).

164 Banton (n 163) 3; F H C Crick and J D Watson, 'The Complementary Structure of Deoxyribonucleic Acid' (1954) 223 Proceedings of the Royal Society A: Mathematical, Physical and Engineering Sciences 80; Reynolds (n 10) 9.

165 *Mandla (Sewa Singh) and Another v Dowell Lee and Another [1983]* (n 161) 5.

166 Julian Huxley, Alfred Cort Haddon and Sir Alexander Morris Carr-Saunders, *We Europeans: A Survey of 'Racial' Problems* (Harper 1936) 8; Banton (n 163) 97.

plausibility of a claim,[167] and given that the concept of race is often considered a conceptual rabbit hole, so to speak, the choice of one definition of race among a large spectrum of potential significances is likely to lead to different judicial outcomes.[168] An increased level of research, it is reasonable to suggest, would allow for the protection of the Sikhs under the current legislation. Indeed, Lord Denning's reasoning came out wanting in the House of Lords because it did not consider one of the distinctive elements of the common law practice of statutory interpretation that requires, among other aspects, a reflection on the pragmatic effects of a literal interpretation.[169]

However, there are two general elements of the *Mandla v Lee* case that have relevance in the *Kartinyeri v Commonwealth* case. Firstly, a judicial evaluation of legal material is an internal textual analysis which seeks to qualify the core meaning of a text.[170] Secondly, consequentialism, understood as the analysis of the potential effects of a statutory interpretation, is one of the legal practices that judges are expected to adopt in their decisions. It is so because common law is, in comparison with civil law, intended to project its effects on future decisions.[171] In the view expressed in the majority of *Kartinyeri v Commonwealth*, there is little that indicates an analysis of the potential implications of the decision.

It is noteworthy that Justice Gaudron's attempt to justify the reasonableness of the Hindmarsh Island Bridge Act 1997 by considering racial discrimination is, in certain circumstances, an appropriate policy.

> The second matter which flows from the requirement that there be some matter or circumstance upon which the Parliament might reasonably form the judgment that there is some difference pertaining to the people of a particular race which necessitates some special law is that the law must be reasonably capable of being viewed as appropriate and adapted to the difference asserted.[172]

The reasoning is plausible on a general level, yet it is difficult to speculate over an instance, similar to the *Kartinyeri* case, in which a

---

[167] Jules L Coleman and Brian Leiter, 'Determinacy, Objectivity, and Authority' (1993) University of Pennsylvania Law Review 549, 559.

[168] Banton (n 163) 3, 12; Breda and Rodak (n 157); MacCormick, 'Reasonableness and Objectivity' (n 151).

[169] *Mandla (Sewa Singh) and Another (Appellants) v Dowell Lee and Other (Respondents) [1983] (HL)* (n 158) 7.

[170] Coleman and Leiter (n 167).

[171] Breda and Vricella (n 157) 429.

[172] *Kartinyeri v Commonwealth* (n 58) para 41.

liberal democracy might find it reasonable to pass legislation that negatively discriminates against an economically depressed ethnic minority that has been historically persecuted.[173]

This point is well engaged in Kirby's dissenting opinion.[174] Kirby pointed out that the case is about the legitimated extent of the race power in the Australian constitution and not whether the Hindmarsh Island Bridge Act 1997 is a legitimate amendment, as suggested by Brennan and McHugh,[175] of the Aboriginal and Torres Strait Islander Heritage Protection Act 1984. In particular, the dilemma was whether section 51 (xxvi) allowed negative discrimination after the 1967 referendum.[176] A similar issue was, Kirby noted, already engaged by Justice Murphy in *Commonwealth v Tasmania.*[177]

As mentioned earlier, Murphy's rendering of the implications of the 1967 referendum on the interpretation of section 51 (xxvii) is particularly concise.

> A broad reading of this power is that it authorises any law for the benefit, physical and mental, of the people of the race for whom Parliament deems it necessary to pass special laws [...] To hold otherwise would be to make a mockery of the decision of the people to delete from s 51(xxvi) the words 'other than the aboriginal race in any State'.[178]

Justice Brennan, in the *Commonwealth v Tasmania* case, appears to concur with Murphy's interpretation of the amended section 51 (xxvii).[179] Brennan noted, for instance, the implausibility of racial classification in scientific terms. He included a reference to the aforementioned *Mandla v Lee* case.[180] Finally, Brennan concluded that statutory measures which hinder a group of individuals who are perceived as part of a racial minority would not be considered compatible with the Australian constitution.

If the power under section 51 (xxvi) were restricted to a discriminatory conferring of legal rights or a discriminatory imposition of legal obligations on the people of a race, laws for the general protection of historical

---

173 Australian Government – Referendum Council (n 13) 20.

174 *Kartinyeri v Commonwealth* (n 58) paras 103–177.

175 Ibid 353 para 9.

176 Ibid para 126.

177 *Commonwealth v Tasmania ('Tasmanian Dam case')* (n 148).

178 *Kartinyeri v Commonwealth* (n 58) para 126; *Commonwealth v Tasmania ('Tasmanian Dam case')* (n 148) para 70.

179 *Commonwealth v Tasmania ('Tasmanian Dam case')* (n 148) para 77.

180 Ibid 538 para 82.

memorabilia, of religious or spiritual shrines, or cultural practices which are of particular significance to the people of particular races, it would not be valid.[181]

If Brennan's narrative were combined with Murphy's set of sharp remarks, it would have suggested that the only line of interpretation of section 51 (xxvi) that should be considered legitimate is the one to protect minorities. However, in *Kartinyeri v Commonwealth*, the majority of the High Court instead considered the heads of power expressed in section 51 (xxvi) as only limited by a gross violation of common law principles. In short, the Hight Court went in a different direction.[182]

Again, the aim of this section is not to evaluate the decision, rather to point out the large variation, in comparison with other constitutional jurisdictions considered in this book, in the chosen epistemic methods that the High Court decided to adopt. The effect of having an eclectic use of textual material has, in the case of constitutional reforms such as the one that seeks to substantially recognize Aboriginal Peoples' and Torres Strait Islanders' identity claims, a twofold effect. Firstly, given that the High Court is likely to interpret the wording of the new section as a self-standing rule without making any reference to the political and social context, there is a moderate risk that the reference to ethnicity might still be interpreted in a way that allows parliament to discriminate against Aboriginal Peoples and Torres Strait Islanders.[183]

Secondly, there is a legitimate concern that the High Court might interpret, whatever the final result of a successful constitutional reform might be, in a way that unreasonably hinders key economic aspects of Australian development.[184] This point is engaged, albeit indirectly, by the Business Council of Australia's submission to the Joint Select Committee on Constitutional Recognition of Aboriginal and Torres Strait Islander Peoples. The Business Council of Australia represents the interests of mining companies (that contribute to over 30 per cent of Australian

---

[181] Ibid 539 para 84.

[182] Aroney and Allan (n 129).

[183] Marcia Langton, 'Trapped in the Aboriginal Reality Show [The Howard Government Intervention in Northern Territory Aboriginal Communities. Paper in: Re-Imagining Australia. Schultz, Julianne (ed.)]' [2008] Griffith Review 143; Antony Thalia, 'The Northern Territory Intervention: The Ongoing Story of Withheld Indigenous Money' [2008] Ngiya: Talk the Law 2; Langton (n 21); Megan Davis and others, 'International Human Rights Law, Women's Rights and the Intervention' (2009) 7 Indigenous Law Bulletin 11.

[184] The Business Council of Australia, 'Submission to the Joint Select Committee on Constitutional Recognition of Aboriginal and Torres Strait Islander Peoples'; Allan (n 62).

exports)[185] and larger Australian financial institutions (that directly contribute 10 per cent of the national gross domestic product). Both mining companies and the financial sector have a vested interest in limiting the recognition of Aboriginal Peoples' and Torres Strait Islanders' substantive claims over land resources.[186]

To sum up, there are concerns, some of which might be reasonable, regarding how the High Court might handle a successful constitutional recognition of the Aboriginal Peoples' and Torres Strait Islanders' identity-based claims. Indirectly, such concerns slow the pace of the process of recognition.[187]

CONCLUSION

In the near future, Aboriginal Peoples and Torres Strait Islanders are unlikely to obtain constitutional recognition. The Australian constitution has hitherto not recognized the role of Aboriginal Peoples and Torres Strait Islanders and it is, perhaps, unique in granting the possibility to its parliament of passing legislation which discriminates negatively against members of economically depressed racial minorities.[188]

This chapter discussed the role that Aboriginal Peoples and Torres Strait Islanders had and will continue to have in fostering the development of a multinational constitutional system. As for other legal systems considered in this book, identity-based constitutional claims might or might not be recognized for a series of overlapping reasons. In the case of Australia, the political campaign supported by Aboriginal Peoples and Torres Strait Islanders and public institutions is hindered by misinformation. In particular, large parts of the Australian population perceived the allocation of rights to Aboriginal Peoples and Torres Strait Islanders as unfair.[189] These concerns are often void of empirical support, but they are periodically voiced in the media.[190] I also explained that the High Court's preferred method of interpretation of the constitution (which is

---

[185] Peter Downes and others, 'The Effect of the Mining Boom on the Australian Economy' (2014) 8 Reserve Bank of Australia Research Discussion Paper 1, 10.

[186] O'Faircheallaigh (n 14) 16; Downes and others (n 185).

[187] Davis (n 54).

[188] Williams (n 25).

[189] Henderson and Borrello (n 119).

[190] United Nations Committee on the Elimination of Racial Discrimination (n 45).

based on textualism) tends to deliver diverging lines of authority. The result of such instability is to increase the level of anxiety related to the allocation of minority rights and, by proxy, to reduce the speed of constitutional reforms such as the one promoted by Aboriginal Peoples and Torres Strait Islanders.[191]

[191] Gershevitch, Lamoin and Dawes (n 77); Williams (n 25).

Bibliography

INTERNATIONAL TREATIES

King of Great Britain and King of France, 'The Definitive Treaty of Peace and Friendship between His Britannick Majesty, the Most Christian King, and the King of Spain (The Treaty of Paris)'

'Treaty of Peace (Treaty of Paris) 30 Stat. 1754 Treaty Series 343 Signed 12/10/1898, Ratified 11/3/1899'

'Treaty of Peace between the Allied and Associated Powers and Austria; Protocol, Declaration and Special Declaration' [1920] ATS 3

BIBLIOGRAPHY

Abadie A and Gardeazabal J, 'The Economic Costs of Conflict: A Case Study of the Basque Country' (2003) 93 The American Economic Review 113

Ablavsky G, '"With the Indian Tribes": Race, Citizenship, and Original Constitutional Meanings' (Social Science Research Network 2017) SSRN Scholarly Paper ID 3082038 https://papers.ssrn.com/abstract=3082038 (accessed 2 January 2018)

Aboriginal and Torres Strait Islander Heritage Protection Act no. 79 1984

Acierno S, 'The Order of the Spanish Constitutional Court on the Proposal to Convert the Basque Country into a Freely Associated Community: Keeping Hands off Constitutional Politics' (2005) 3 International Journal of Constitutional Law 687

Act of Union 1840 (officially British North America Act 1840) 3 & 4 Victoria, Ch 35

AG (Que) v Quebec Protestant School Boards [1984] C 17821, 2 SCR 66

Agranoff R and Gallarín JAR, 'Toward Federal Democracy in Spain: An Examination of Intergovernmental Relations' (1997) 27 Publius: The Journal of Federalism 1

Ahuna v Dept of Hawaiian Home Lands 640 P2d 1161 (1982)

Akers DL, 'Choctaw' in Richard Schaefer, *Encyclopedia of Race, Ethnicity, and Society* (SAGE 2008)

Alan T, 'Scotland and Wales: The Evolution of Devolution' in Robert Hazell (ed), *Constitutional Futures Revisited: Britain's Constitution to 2020* (Palgrave Macmillan 2008)

Alaska Chapter, Associated General Contractors of America v Pierce 694 F2d 1162 (9th Cir 1982)

Albert R, 'The Structure of Constitutional Amendment Rules' (2014) 49 Wake Forest Law Review 913

Albert R, 'The Theory and Doctrine of Unconstitutional Constitutional Amendment in Canada' (2015) 41 Queen's Law Journal 176

Albertazzi D and McDonnell D, 'The Lega Nord Back in Government' (2010) 33 West European Politics 1318

Alcock A, 'The South Tyrol Autonomy' [2001] A short introduction. University of Ulster http://www.geography.ryerson.ca/wayne/Geo773-F2013/South-Tyrol-Autonomy.pdf (accessed 5 July 2015)

Aldrich JH, 'Rational Choice and Turnout' (1993) 37 American Journal of Political Science 246

Aleinikoff TA, 'Puerto Rico and the Constitution: Conundrums and Prospects' (1994) 11 Constitutional Commentary 15

Aleinikoff TA, 'Securing Tribal Sovereignty: A Theory for Overturning Lone Wolf Symposium – Lone Wolf v. Hitchcock: One Hundred Years Later' (2002) 38 Tulsa Law Review 57

Allan J, 'The Document We Have Sure Ain't Broken, so Why Change It?' (Sydney, 30 January 2014) http://www.theaustralian.com.au/opinion/the-document-we-have-sure-aint-broken-so-why-change-it/story-e6frg6zo-1226813351770 (accessed 18 April 2016)

Allen B and Russo M, *Revisioning Italy: National Identity and Global Culture* (University of Minnesota Press 1997) http://ebookcentral.proquest.com/lib/usq/detail.action?docID=310410 (accessed 18 December 2017)

Allison J, *The English Historical Constitution: Continuity, Change and European Effects* (first edition, Cambridge University Press 2007)

American Samoa Constitution (copy provided by the American Samoa Bar Association) http://www.asbar.org/ (accessed 22 November 2017)

An Act Respecting Constitutional Amendments, SC 1996, c 1

An Act Respecting the Exercise of the Fundamental Rights and Prerogatives of the Québec People and the Québec State, CQLR c E-20.2 2001

An Act to Give Effect to the Requirement for Clarity as Set out in the Opinion of the Supreme Court of Canada in the Quebec Secession Reference, SC 2000, c 26 2000

ANCSA, Pub. L. No. 92-203, 85 Stat. 688 (1971) (codified as amended at 4 3U.S.C. §§ 1601–1629h (2012))

Anderson A, 'Organised Crime, Mafia and Governments' in Sam Peltzman and Gianluca Fiorentini (eds), *The Economics of Organised Crime* (Cambridge University Press 1997)
Anderson B, *Imagined Communities: Reflections on the Origin and Spread of Nationalism* (Verso 1983)
Anderson GW and others, 'Gavin Anderson et al: The Independence Referendum, Legality and the Contested Constitution: Widening the Debate' http://ukconstitutionallaw.org/2012/01/31/gavin-anderson-et-al-the-independence-referendum-legality-and-the-contested-constitution-widening-the-debate/ (accessed 24 November 2012)
Andreu Castellà J, *La Sentencia Del Tribunal Constitucional 31/2010, Sobre El Estatuto de Autonomía de Cataluña y Su Significado Para El Futuro Del Estado Autonómico* (Fundación Ciudadanía y Valores 2010)
Angelo A, *Constitutional Law in New Zealand* (Kluwer Law International 2011)
Angelo T, 'To Be or Not to Be … Integrated, That Is the Problem of Islands' [2002] Revue Juridique Polynésienne 87
Antonini L, *Federalismo all'italiana: Dietro le quinte della grande incompiuta. Quello che ogni cittadino dovrebbe sapere* (Marsilio Editori 2013)
Appiah A, *Cosmopolitanism: Ethics in a World of Strangers* (Allen Lane 2006)
Arel D, 'Political Stability in Multinational Democracies', in James Tully and Alain-G Ganon (ed), *Multinational Democracies* (first edition, Cambridge University Press 2001)
Armstrong v United States 182 US 243 (1901)
Aroney N and Allan J, 'An Uncommon Court: How the High Court of Australia Has Undermined Australian Federalism' (2008) 30 Sydney Law Review 245
Attorney General of Canada v Lavell (C)
Attwood B, *Telling the Truth About Aboriginal History* (Allen & Unwin 2005)
Austin J, *The Province of Jurisprudence Determined* (John Murray 1832)
Australia Act 1986 c 2
Avolio G, 'Institutions of Self-Government' in Jens Woelk, Francesco Palermo and Joseph Marko (eds), *Tolerance Through Law: Self Governance and Group Rights in South Tyrol* (Brill 2007)
Axa General Insurance Ltd, Petitioners, vol 2 (2010)
Ayres S, 'Examining the Role of "Informal Governance"' (Political Studies Association 2016) https://www.bristol.ac.uk/sps/research/projects/completed/2016/examining-the-role-of-informal-governance/ (accessed 8 January 2018)

Baba ML, 'Anthropology and Transnational Migration: A Focus on Policy' (2013) 51 International Migration 1
Babcock HM, 'A Civic-Republican Vision of Domestic Dependent Nations in the Twenty-First Century: Tribal Sovereignty Re-Envisioned, Reinvigorated, and Re-Empowered' (2005) 2005 Utah Law Review 443
Baldwin SE, 'The Constitutional Questions Incident to the Acquisition and Government by the United States of Island Territory' [1899] Harvard Law Review 393
Balzac v Porto Rico 258 US 298 (1922)
Bankes N, 'The Implications of the Tsilhqot'in (William) and Grassy Narrows (Keewatin) Decisions of the Supreme Court of Canada for the Natural Resources Industries' (2015) 33 Journal of Energy & Natural Resources Law 188
Banton M, *Racial Theories* (Cambridge University Press 1998)
Barrena X, '*Estas Son Las 46 Peticiones de Carles Puigdemont a Mariano Rajoy*' (elperiodico, 20 April 2016) http://www.elperiodico.com/es/politica/20160420/las-cuarenta-seis-peticiones-puigdemont-rajoy-moncloa-5070904 (accessed 4 January 2018)
Barreto AA, 'American Identity, Congress, and the Puerto Rico Statehood Debate' (2016) 16 Studies in Ethnicity and Nationalism 100
Barry Maley, 'Abandon Change to Constitution' (2014) The Australian 10
Basic Law for the Federal Republic of Germany in the revised version published in the Federal Law Gazette Part III as last amended by the Act of 11 July 2012 (Federal Law Gazette I p. 1478) 100–101
Basque Government, Propuesta Estatuto político de la Comunidad de Euskadi 2003 [127/000001]
Bauman Z, *In Search of Politics* (Polity 1999)
Bauman Z, 'Identity in the Globalising World' (2001) 9 Social Anthropology 121
Bauman Z, 'Living in the Era of Liquid Modernity' (2001) 22 Cambridge Anthropology 1
Bauman Z, 'Identity: Then, Now, What For?' in M Kempny and A Jawlowska (eds), *Identity in Transformation: Postmodernity, Postcommunism, and Globalization* (Praeger 2002)
Bauman Z, 'Soil, Blood and Identity' (1992) 40 *The Sociological Review* 675
Bean JJ, *Race and Liberty in America* (University Press of Kentucky 2009)
Bel G, *Disdain, Distrust and Dissolution: The Surge of Support for Independence in Catalonia* (Sussex Academic Press 2015)
Benjamin SM, 'Equal Protection and the Special Relationship: The Case of Native Hawaiians' (1996) 106 The Yale Law Journal 537

Bill of Rights [1688] Chapter 2 1 Will and Mar Sess 3 1689
Billig M, *Banal Nationalism* (Sage 1995)
Bochsler D and Hug S, 'How Minorities Fare under Referendums: A Cross-National Study' (2015) 38 Electoral Studies 206
Bogdanor V, *Devolution in the United Kingdom* (Oxford University Press 1999)
Bogdanor V, *Devolution in the United Kingdom* (updated and reissued edition, Oxford University Press 2001)
Bogdanor V, *The British Constitution in the Twentieth Century* (published for the British Academy by Oxford University Press 2003)
Bogdanor V, *The New British Constitution* (Hart 2009)
Bonaventura FD, 'Italy and Lega Nord: Stories of Communities, National (Dis)Integration and Spaces of (Restricted) Citizenship' (2016) 7 Società Mutamento Politica: Rivista Italiana di Sociologia 289
Boronow C, 'Closing the Accountability Gap for Indian Tribes: Balancing the Right To Self-Determination with the Right to a Remedy' (2012) 98 Virginia Law Review 1373
Borrows J, 'Questioning Canada's Title to Land: The Rule of Law, Aboriginal Peoples and Colonialism' in Law Commission of Canada and British Columbia Treaty Commission (Canada) (eds), *Speaking Truth to Power: A Treaty Forum* (Law Commission of Canada; British Columbia Treaty Commission 2001)
Borrows J, *Recovering Canada: The Resurgence of Indigenous Law* (University of Toronto Press 2002)
Borrows J, *Freedom and Indigenous Constitutionalism* (University of Toronto Press, Scholarly Publishing Division 2016)
Bowers P, 'The Sewel Convention' [2005] House of Commons Library Standard http://researchbriefings.files.parliament.uk/documents/SN02084/SN02084.pdf (accessed 26 October 2015)
Boyle K and Hadden T, 'The Peace Process in Northern Ireland' (1995) 71 International Affairs 269
Breda V, 'The Incoherence of the Patriotic State: A Critique of Constitutional Patriotism' (2004) 10 Res Publica 247
Breda V, 'A European Constitution in a Multinational Europe or a Multinational Constitution for Europe?' (2006) 12 European Law Journal 330
Breda V, 'Constitutional Identities in a Liquid Society' in Jiri Priban (ed), *Liquid Society and its Law* (Routledge 2007)
Breda V, 'Constitutional Futures Revisited: Britain's Constitution to 2020 Edited by Robert Hazell [Book Review]' [2011] Public Law 446
Breda V, 'La Devolution de Escocia y El Referéndum de 2014: Cuáles Son Las Repercusiones Potenciales En España?' [2013] Teoria y Realidad Constitucional 69

Breda V, 'An Odd Partnership: Identity-Based Constitutional Claims in Modern Democracy' in Fiona Jenkins, Mark Nolan and Kim Rubenstein (eds), *Allegiance and Identity in a Globalised World* (Cambridge University Press 2014)

Breda V, 'How to Reverse the Italian Brain Drain: A Master Class from Australia' (2014) 52 International Migration 64

Breda V, 'Lingering with Intent: The UK Constitutional Review' in Miodrag A Jovanovic (ed), *Constitutional Review and Democracy* (Eleven International 2015)

Breda V, 'Indigenous Australians and the Constitutional Reform: Learning from a Very British Experience', in Simon Young, Jennifer Nielsen and Jeremy Patrick (eds), *Constitutional Recognition of First Peoples in Australia: Theories and Comparative Perspectives* (Federation Press 2016)

Breda V, 'The Concept of Objectivity in the UK Supreme Court Through a Comparative Looking Glass' in Vito Breda and Lidia Rodak (eds), *Diverse Narratives of Legal Objectivity: An Interdisciplinary Perspective* (Peter Lang 2016)

Breda V, *The Objectivity of Judicial Decisions: A Comparative Analysis of Nine Jurisdictions* (new edition, Peter Lang AG 2016)

Breda V, 'Constitutional Patriotism' in Mortimer Sellers and Stephan Kirste (eds), *Encyclopedia of the Philosophy of Law and Social Philosophy* (Springer Netherlands 2017)

Breda V, 'Constitutional Patriotism: Redux' in Mitja Sardoc (ed), *Handbook of Patriotism* (Springer 2018)

Breda V and Rodak L, 'Introduction' in Vito Breda and Lidia Rodak (eds), *Diverse Narratives of Legal Objectivity: An Interdisciplinary Perspective* (Peter Lang 2016)

Breda V and Vricella M, 'English Pragmatism and Italian Virtue: A Comparative Analysis of the Regime of Illegally Obtained Evidence in Civil Law Proceedings between Italy and England' (2014) 21 Maastricht Journal of European and Comparative Law 428

Brett J, *The Australian Liberals and the Moral Middle Class* (Cambridge University Press 2003)

British North America Act 1867 (c 3)

Broberg G and Roll-Hansen N, *Eugenics and the Welfare State: Norway, Sweden, Denmark, and Finland* (Michigan State University Press 2005) https://muse.jhu.edu/book/40871 (accessed 1 December 2017)

Brown A, McCrone D and Paterson L, *Politics and Society in Scotland* (Macmillan 1996)

Cabrelli D and Siems M, 'Convergence, Legal Origins, and Transplants in Comparative Corporate Law: A Case-Based and Quantitative Analysis' (2015) 63 American Journal of Comparative Law 109

Caciagli M, 'The Long Life of Clientelism in Southern Italy' in Junichi Kawata (ed), *Comparing Political Corruption and Clientelism* (Ashgate 2006)

Calder et al v Attorney-General of British Columbia (AG) [1973] S.C.R. 313

Calvanese E, *Media e immigrazione tra stereotipi e pregiudizi: la rappresentazione dello straniero nel racconto giornalistico* (FrancoAngeli 2011)

Cambridge University Act 1856 c 88

Caron J-F, 'The Exclusive Nature of Quebec's Contemporary Nationalism: The Pitfalls of Civic Nationalism' (2014) 47 International Journal of Canadian Studies 221

Cass DZ, 'Re-Thinking Self-Determination: A Critical Analysis of Current International Law Theories' (1992) 18 Syracuse Journal of International Law & Commerce 21

Cassell L, 'Some Reflections on Hydroelectric Development and the Land Rights of the Innu Who Live in Quebec and Those Who Live in Labrador' (2013) 1 Journal of Human Rights in the Commonwealth 3

Cento Bull A, 'Lega Nord: A Case of Simulative Politics?' (2009) 14 South European Society and Politics 129

Cervi M and Montanelli I, *L' Italia Del Novecento* (Rizzoli 1998)

Charles Hunter McIntosh v John Jeremyn Symonds [1847] NZSC 1, NZPCC 388

Chase OG, 'American "Exceptionalism" and Comparative Procedure' (2002) 50 The American Journal of Comparative Law 277

Cherokee Nation v Georgia 30 US 1 (1831) 30 US 1

Chock JML, 'One Hundred Years of Illegitimacy: International Legal Analysis of the Illegal Overthrow of the Hawaiian Monarchy, Hawai'i's Annexation, and Possible Reparations' (1995) 17 University of Hawai'i Law Review 463

Cities and Local Government Devolution Act 2016 c1

Clarke J and others (eds), *Hanks Australian Constitutional Law: Materials and Commentary* (ninth edition, LexisNexis Butterworths 2013)

Coffman T, *The Island Edge of America: A Political History of Hawai'i* (University of Hawai'i Press 2003)

Coleman JL and Leiter B, 'Determinacy, Objectivity, and Authority' (1993) University of Pennsylvania Law Review 549

Colino C and Pino E, '15. Spain: The Consolidation of Strong Regional Governments and the Limits of Local Decentralization' in John Loughlin, Frank Hendriks and Anders Lidström (eds), *The Oxford Handbook of Local and Regional Democracy in Europe*, vol 1 (first edition, Oxford University Press)

Commission on Scottish Devolution and Calman KC, *Serving Scotland Better: Scotland and the United Kingdom in the 21st Century* (The Commission 2009)

Commonwealth of Australia Constitution Act 1900

Commonwealth v Tasmania ('Tasmanian Dam case') [1983] HCA 21

Constitution Amendment (Recognition of Aboriginal People) Act 2010 (NSW) 2010

Constitution Amendment (Recognition of Aboriginal People) Act 2015 (WA)

Constitution of the Italian Republic 1948

Constitution (Preamble) Amendment Act 2010 (QLD) (3)

Constitutional Act 1791 131 c 31

Constitutional Court (Italy), Decision no. 29 2014

Constitutional Court (Italy), Decision no. 118 2015

Constitutional Court (Spain), Decision no. 31 28/06/2010 172 (Suplemento 11409) BOE 1

Constitutional Court (Spain), Decision no. 40 26/07/1981 193 BOE

Constitutional Court (Spain), Recurso: 1638-2017

Constitutional Law no. 2 26.02.1948

Constitutional Law no. 3 26.02.1948

Constitutional Law no. 4 26.02.1948

Constitutional Law no. 5 26.02.1948

Constitutional Law no. 1 10.11.1971

Constitutional Law no. 1 22.11.1999

Constitutional Law no. 1 31.1963

Constitutional Law no. 3 18.10.2001

Controller and Auditor-General v Sir Ronald Davison (CA 226/95) [1996] NZLR 278 (Court of Appeal)

Cook Islands Constitution Act 1964 no. 69

Corso G and Lopilato V, *Il diritto amministrativo dopo le riforme costituzionali. Parte generale* (Giuffrè Editore 2006)

Costello KA, 'Rice v. Cayetano: Trouble in Paradise for Native Hawaiians Claiming Special Relationship Status Notes' (2000) 79 North Carolina Law Review 812

Coulthard GS, *Red Skin, White Masks: Rejecting the Colonial Politics of Recognition* (University of Minnesota Press 2014)

Crosby RD and King M, *The Musket Wars: A History of Inter-Iwi Conflict 1806–45* (Raupo 1999)

Cross JT and Lomond KM, 'The Civil Rights of the Aboriginal Peoples of the United States and Canada' (1993) 10 Arizona Journal of International & Comparative Law 253

Darwin C, *The Descent of Man* (Prometheus Books 1997)

Daum CW and Ishiwata E, 'From the Myth of Formal Equality to the Politics of Social Justice: Race and the Legal Attack on Native Entitlements' (2010) 44 Law & Society Review 843
Dávila AM, *Sponsored Identities: Cultural Politics in Puerto Rico* (Temple University Press 1997)
Davis M, 'Political Timetables Trump Workable Timetables: Indigenous Constitutional Recognition and the Temptation of Symbolism over Substance' in Simon Young, Jennifer Nielsen and Jeremy Patrick (eds), *Constitutional Recognition of First Peoples in Australia: Theories and Comparative Perspectives* (Federation Press 2016)
Davis M and others, 'International Human Rights Law, Women's Rights and the Intervention' (2009) 7 Indigenous Law Bulletin 11
Dawson M, 'From the Backroom to the Front Line: Making Constitutional History or Encounters with the Constitution: Patriation, Meech Lake, and Charlottetown' (2012) 57 McGill Law Journal/Revue de droit de McGill 955
Decree no. 670 31.08.1972
Dekavalla M, 'Framing Referendum Campaigns: The 2014 Scottish Independence Referendum in the Press' [2016] Media, Culture & Society 0163443715620929
Delgamuukw v British Columbia [1997] C 23799, 3 SCR 1010
DeLima v Bidwell 182 US 1 (1901)
Dellinger W, 'The Legitimacy of Constitutional Change: Rethinking the Amendment Process' (1983) 97 Harvard Law Review 386
Desjardins AB, 'Michael Keating and John McGarry (eds), Minority Nationalism and the Changing International Order' (2002) 8 Nationalism and Ethnic Politics 120
Diamond J, *Guns, Germs and Steel. A Short History of Everybody in the Last 13,000 Years* (Kindle edition) (Vintage 2005)
Dicey AV, *Introduction to the Study of the Law of the Constitution* (Macmillan 1889)
Dicey AV, *The Law of the Constitution*, John Allison (ed) (Oxford University Press 2013)
Di Martino P, Felice E and Vasta M, 'The Curious Case of the Coexistence of Two "Access-Orders": Explaining the Italian Regional Divide' (Department of Economics, University of Siena 2017)
Dionne X and Gagnon A-G, *L'évolution Des Relations Fédérales-Provinciales Au Canada* (Presses de l'Université du Québec 2017)
Dixon R and Ginsburg T (eds), *Comparative Constitutional Law in Asia* (Edward Elgar Publishing 2014)
Dixon R and Holden R, 'Constitutional Amendment Rules' in Tom Ginsburg (ed), *Comparative Constitutional Design* (Cambridge University Press 2012)

Dodson PL and others, 'Recognising Aboriginal and Torres Strait Islander Peoples in the Constitution: Report of the Expert Panel' (Department of Families, Housing, Community Services & Indigenous Affairs 2012)
Dooley v United States 182 US 222 (1901)
Downes v Bidwell 182 US 244 (1901)
Downes P and others, 'The Effect of the Mining Boom on the Australian Economy' (2014) 8 Reserve Bank of Australia Research Discussion Paper 1
Drew KF, *Magna Carta* (Greenwood 2004)
Duany J, *The Puerto Rican Nation on the Move: Identities on the Island & in the United States* (University of North Carolina Press 2002)
Duany J, *Puerto Rico: What Everyone Needs to Know* (Oxford University Press 2017)
Dubler R, 'Race and the Constitution' (2002) 76 Australian Law Journal 456
Dulio DA and Thurber JA, 'America's Two-Party System: Friend or Foe?' (2000) 52 Administrative Law Review 769
Elazar DJ, 'Religious Diversity and Federalism' (2001) International Social Science Journal 3
Electoral Act 1993 N.87 1993
Erb H-P and others, 'Processing Minority and Majority Communications: The Role of Conflict with Prior Attitudes' (2002) 28 Personality and Social Psychology Bulletin 1172
Espadaler Fossas E, *El principio dispositivo en el Estado autonómico* (2008) Revista de Derecho Político 151
Espadaler Fossas E, *Competencia En Materia de Cultura. Comentario a La Sentencia 31/2010* [2010] Revista catalana de dret públic 328
Espadaler Fossas E, *El Estatuto Como Norma y Su Función Constitucional. Comentario a La Sentencia 31/2010* [2010] Revista catalana de dret públic 91
Espadaler Fossas E, *El Control de Constitucionalitat Dels Estatuts d'autonomia* [2011] Revista catalana de dret públic 21
European Communities Act 1972 c 68
Evans G and Trystan D, 'Why Was 1997 Different?' in Bridget Taylor and Katarina Thomson (eds), *Scotland and Wales Nations Again?* (University of Wales Press 1999) http://search.ebscohost.com/login.aspx?direct=true&scope=site&db=nlebk&db=nlabk&AN=27094 (accessed 14 June 2013)
Ewing KD, 'The Human Rights Act and Parliamentary Democracy' (1999) 62 The Modern Law Review 79
Executive TS, 'Choosing Scotland's Future, a National Conversation' (2007)

Faleomavaega EFH, 'Brief of the Honorable Eni F.H. Faleomavaega as Amicus Curiae in Support of Defendants – Civil Action No. 12-1143-RJL' http://www.asbar.org/images/legal_issues/citizenship/tuaua%20v%20%20us%20faleomavaega%20amicus%20brief.pdf (accessed 24 July 2017)

Faure Y-A, 'Jeitinho and Other Related Phenomena in Contemporary Brazil' in Daniel Bach and Mamoudou Gazibo (eds), *Neopatrimonialism in Africa and Beyond* (Routledge 2013)

Felice E, *Perché Il Sud è Rimasto Indietro* (Il Mulino 2013)

Fiorentini G and Peltzman S, *The Economics of Organised Crime* (Cambridge University Press 1997)

Fisher J, 'Whither the Parties' in Robert Hazell (ed), *Constitutional Futures Revisited: Britain's Constitution To 2020* (Palgrave Macmillan 2008)

Fojas C, *Islands of Empire: Pop Culture and U.S. Power* (University of Texas Press 2014)

Font-Guzmán J, 'Confronting a Colonial Legacy: Asserting Puerto Rican Identity by Legally Renouncing US Citizenship' (2013) 25 Centro: Journal of the Center for Puerto Rican Studies

Font-Guzmán J, *Experiencing Puerto Rican Citizenship and Cultural Nationalism* (Springer 2016)

Foreshore and Seabed Act 2004 N. 93 (repealed by the Marine and Coastal Area (Takutai Moana) Act 2011 N. 3 2004

Foster H, 'Getting There' in Law Commission of Canada and British Columbia Treaty Commission (Canada) (eds), *Speaking Truth to Power: A Treaty Forum* (Law Commission of Canada; British Columbia Treaty Commission 2001)

French Constitution 1958

Fukuyama F, *The Origins of Political Order: From Prehuman Times to the French Revolution* (Profile Books 2012)

Fukuyama F, *Political Order and Political Decay: From the Industrial Revolution to the Globalisation of Democracy* (Profile Books 2014)

Fuller L, *The Morality of Law* (Yale University Press 1969)

Gagnon A (ed), *La Baie James* (Editions du Jour 1973)

Gagnon A, 'Québec-Canada's Constitutional Dossier' in *Quebec* (University of Toronto Press 2004) http://www.jstor.org/stable/10.3138/j.ctt2tv5rx.10

Gagnon A, *Political Dynamics in Quebec: Charting Concepts and Imagining Political Avenues* (Cambridge University Press 2017)

Gagnon A and Boucher F, in Alain-G Gagnon and Brian Tanguay (eds), *Canadian Parties in Transition*, (fourth edition, University of Toronto Press, Higher Education Division 2016)

Gagnon A and Dionne X, *Historiographies et Fédéralisme Au Canada* [2009] Revista d'estudis autonòmics i federals 10
Gagnon A and Sauca JM, *Negotiating Diversity Identity, Pluralism and Democracy* (PIE Peter Lang 2014)
Gagnon A and Tanguay B (eds), *Canadian Parties in Transition* (fourth edition, University of Toronto Press, Higher Education Division 2016)
Gagnon A and Tully J (eds), *Multinational Democracies* (Cambridge University Press 2001)
Gash T, Randall J and Sims S, 'Achieving Political Decentralisation' (2014) Institute for Government
Geddis A and Ruru J, 'Places as Persons: Creating a New Framework for Māori-Crown Relations' (speech to biennial Public Law Conference, Melbourne 2018)
Gellner E, *Nations and Nationalism* (Basil Blackwell 1983)
Gellner E, *Nationalism* (Phoenix 1998)
Gershevitch C, Lamoin A and Dawes C, 'Racism in Australia: Is Denial Still Plausible?' (2010) 3 Race/ethnicity: Multidisciplinary Global Contexts 229
Getches DH, 'Beyond Indian Law: The Rehnquist Court's Pursuit of States' Rights, Color-Blind Justice and Mainstream Values' (2001) 86 Minnesota Law Review 267
Gibbins R and Laforest G (eds), *Beyond the Impasse: Towards Reconciliation* (McGill-Queen's University Press 1998)
Ginsborg P, *A History of Contemporary Italy: Society and Politics, 1943–1988* (Palgrave Macmillan 2003)
Ginsborg P, *Italy and Its Discontents 1980–2001: Family, Civil Society, State* (new edition, Penguin 2003)
Ginsburg T and Posner EA, 'Subconstitutionalism' (2010) 62 Stanford Law Review 1583
Giordano B, 'The Contrasting Geographies of "Padania": The Case of the Lega Nord in Northern Italy' (2001) 33 Area 27
Glenn HP, *Legal Traditions of the World: Sustainable Diversity in Law* (Oxford University Press 2010)
Godbout J-F and Smaz M, 'Party Development in the Early Decades of the Australian Parliament: A New Perspective' (2016) 51 Australian Journal of Political Science 478
Goetze v United States 182 US 221 (1901)
Gold TW, *The Lega Nord and Contemporary Politics in Italy* (Palgrave Macmillan 2003)
Goldstein LF, *The U.S. Supreme Court and Racial Minorities: Two Centuries of Judicial Review on Trial* (Edward Elgar Publishing 2017)
Government of Wales Act 1998 c 38
Government of Wales Act 2006 c 32

Graham H, *War and its Shadow: Spain's Civil War in Europe's Long Twentieth Century* (Sussex Academic Press 2012)

Graham LR and Penny HG, 'Performing Indigeneity: Emergent Identity, Self-Determination, and Sovereignty' in Laura R Graham and H Glenn Penny (eds), *Performing Indigeneity: Global Histories and Contemporary Experiences* (University of Nebraska Press 2014)

Graziadei M, 'Legal Transplants and the Frontiers of Legal Knowledge' (2009) 10 Theoretical Inquiries in Law 723

Greer SL and Jarman H, 'What Whitehall?: Definitions, Demographics and the Changing Home Civil Service' (2010) 25 Public Policy and Administration 251

Grigg K and Manderson L, 'Developing the Australian Racism, Acceptance, and Cultural-Ethnocentrism Scale (RACES)' (2015) 32 The Australian Educational and Developmental Psychologist 1

Grigg K and Manderson L, 'The Australian Racism, Acceptance, and Cultural-Ethnocentrism Scale (RACES): Item Response Theory Findings' (2016) 15 International Journal for Equity in Health 49

Gros-Louis et autres v La Société de développement de la Baie James et autres [1974] RP 38

Grote G, 'Gehen Oder Bleiben? – Die Identitätskrise Der Deutschsprachigen Südtiroler in Optanten- Und Dableibergedichten Der Optionszeit' (2004) 37 Modern Austrian Literature 47

Grote G, *The South Tyrol Question, 1866–2010: From National Rage to Regional State* (Peter Lang 2012)

Guerin v The Queen [1984] C 17507, 2 SCR 335

Habermas J, *The Theory of Communicative Action, Volume 1: Reason and the Rationalization of Society* (Beacon Press 1985)

Habermas J, *The Structural Transformation of the Public Sphere: An Inquiry into a Category of Bourgeois Society* (The MIT Press 1991)

Habermas J, 'Popular Sovereignty as Procedure' in William Rehg (ed), *Deliberative Democracy: Essays on Reason and Politics* (MIT 1997)

Habermas J, 'On the Relation Between the Nation, the Rule of Law and Democracy' in Pablo De Greiff and Ciaran Cronin (eds), *The Inclusion of the Other: Studies in Political Theory* (The MIT Press 2000)

Hadden T and Boyle K, 'Northern Ireland: Conflict and Conflict Resolution' in K Rupesinghe (ed), *Ethnic Conflict and Human Right* (United Nations University Press 1988)

Haida Nation v British Columbia (Minister of Forests) [2004] SCC 29419, 3 SCR 511

Haljan D, *Constitutionalising Secession* (Hart Publishing 2014)

Hamlet of Baker Lake v Canada (Indian Affairs and Northern Development) (C)

Hannum H, *Autonomy, Sovereignty, and Self-Determination: The Accommodation of Conflicting Rights* (University of Pennsylvania Press 2011)

Harrop C, 'The Sewel Convention. An Assessment of the Process of Westminster Legislating on Devolved Matters Report Prepared for the Scottish Executive Constitution Unit' http://archive.scottish.parliament.uk/business/committees/procedures/papers-05/prp05-02.pdf (accessed 29 October 2015)

Hart HLA, 'Positivism and the Separation of Law and Morals' (1958) 71 Harvard Law Review 593

Hawaii v Office of Hawaiian Affairs 556 US 163 (2009)

Hawaiian Homes Commission Act (Act of July 9, 1921, c 42, 42 Stat 108) 2011

Haynie KL and Junn J, *New Race Politics in America* (Cambridge University Press 2008)

Hazell R, *Constitutional Futures: A History of the Next Ten Years* (Oxford University Press 1999)

Hazell R, *An Unstable Union: Devolution and the English Question: State of the Union Annual Lecture* (Constitution Unit, School of Public Policy, University College London 2000)

Hazell R, *The English Question* (Manchester University Press 2006)

Hazell R, *Constitutional Futures Revisited: Britain's Constitution to 2020* (Palgrave Macmillan 2008)

Hazell R, 'Constitutional Reform in the United Kingdom: Past, Present and Future' in Caroline Morris, Jonathan Boston and Petra Butler (eds), *Reconstituting the Constitution* (Springer 2011)

Hazell R, *Devolution and the Future of the Unio*n (The Constitution Unit 2015)

Hazell R and Glover M, 'Introduction: Forecasting Constitutional Futures' in Robert Hazell (ed), *Constitutional Futures Revisited: Britain's Constitution to 2020* (Palgrave Macmillan 2008)

Headrick DR, 'The Tools of Imperialism: Technology and the Expansion of European Colonial Empires in the Nineteenth Century' (1979) The Journal of Modern History 231

Henderson A and others, 'England, Englishness and Brexit' (2016) 87 The Political Quarterly 187

Henderson A and Borrello E, 'Abbott Facing Internal Rebellion on Indigenous Recognition Push' (ABC News, 20 August 2015) http://www.abc.net.au/news/2015-08-20/abbott-facing-rebellion-on-indigenous-recognition/6711708 (accessed 19 April 2016)

Henderson JY, 'Dialogical Governance: A Mechanism of Constitutional Governance' (2009) 72 Saskatchewan Law Review 29

Hiebert JL, 'Parliamentary Bills of Rights: An Alternative Model?' (2006) 69 The Modern Law Review 7
Hindmarsh Island Bridge Act 1997
Hirschfield M, 'The Alaska Native Claims Settlement Act: Tribal Sovereignty and the Corporate Form' (1992) 101 The Yale Law Journal 1331
Hirschl R, *Comparative Matters: The Renaissance of Comparative Constitutional Law* (Oxford University Press 2014)
Hobsbawm E, *The Age of Revolution, 1789–1848* (New American Library 1962)
Hobsbawm E, *Nations and Nationalism since 1780: Programme, Myth, Reality* (Cambridge University Press 1992)
Hobsbawm E, *Age Of Empire: 1875–1914* (Hachette 2010)
Hofschneider PB, *A Campaign for Political Rights on the Island of Guam, 1899–1950* (CNMI Division of Historic Preservation 2001)
Hogg PW, 'Formal Amendment of the Constitution of Canada' (1992) 55 Law & Contemporary Problems 253
Hogg PW, 'Canada: From Privy Council to Supreme Court' in Jeffrey Goldsworthy (ed), *Interpreting Constitutions: A Comparative Study* (Oxford University Press 2007)
Hogg PW, *Constitutional Law of Canada* (Carswell 2009)
Hogg PW, 'Canadian Constitutional Law: Presentation to the Annual Conference of International Association of Law Libraries' (2013) 41 International Journal of Legal Information 58
Hong KNS, 'Understanding Native Hawaiian Rights: Mistakes and Consequences of Rice v. Cayetano' (2008) 15 Asian American Law Journal 9
Hooper A, 'Tokelau: A Sort of "Self-Governing" Sort of "Colony"' (2008) 43 The Journal of Pacific History 331
Horey JE, 'The Right of Self-Government in the Commonwealth of the Northern Mariana Islands' (2003) 4 Asian-Pacific Law & Policy Journal 180
Houkamau CA and Sibley CG, 'The Revised Multidimensional Model of Māori Identity and Cultural Engagement (MMM-ICE2)' (2015) 122 Social Indicators Research 279
House of Lords Act 1999 c 34
Hułas M and Fel S (eds), *Intricacies of Patriotism: Towards a Complexity of Patriotic Allegiance* (Peter Lang 2015)
Huntsman J, *The Future of Tokelau: Decolonising Agendas, 1975–2006* (Auckland University Press 2013)
Hutchinson J and Smith AD, 'Introduction' in John Hutchinson and Anthony D Smith (eds), *Nationalism* (Oxford University Press 1994)
Huxley J, Haddon AC and Carr-Saunders SAM, *We Europeans: A Survey of 'Racial' Problems* (Harper 1936)

Huus v New York & Porto Rico Steamship Co 182 US 392 (1901)
Ignatieff M, *Blood & Belonging: Journeys into the New Nationalism* (Vintage 1994)
Ignatieff M, *The Warrior's Honor: Ethnic War and the Modern Conscience* (Vintage 1999)
Immigration Restriction Act 1901
Indian Civil Rights Act of 1968, 82 Stat. 73.
Islam MR and Jahjah M, 'Predictors of Young Australians' Attitudes Toward Aboriginals, Asians And Arabs' (2001) 29 Social Behavior and Personality: An International Journal 569
Jackson VC, 'The (Myth of Un)Amendability of the US Constitution and the Democratic Component of Constitutionalism' (2015) 13 International Journal of Constitutional Law 575
James A and Nicholas A, 'An Uncommon Court: How the High Court of Australia Has Undermined Australian Federalism' (2008) 30 Sydney Law Review
Johnson v M'Intosh [1823] US LEXIS 293 (US Supreme Court)
Johnston K, 'Maori Legal Developments' (2017) New Zealand Law Review 131
Kahkewistahaw First Nation v Taypotat [2015] SCC 35518, 2 SCR 548
Kalolo K, 'Tokelau' (2007) 19 The Contemporary Pacific 256
Kalt JP and Singer JW, 'Myths and Realities of Tribal Sovereignty: The Law and Economics of Indian Self-Rule' (Social Science Research Network 2004) SSRN Scholarly Paper ID 529084 https://papers.ssrn.com/abstract=529084 (accessed 21 April 2017)
Kanatewat et al v James Bay Development Corp et al (1973) 1 SCR 48 (C)
Kant I, *To Perpetual Peace: A Philosophical Sketch* (Ted Humphrey transl, Hackett 2003)
Kao GY and Copulsky JE, 'The Pledge of Allegiance and the Meanings and Limits of Civil Religion' (2007) 75 Journal of the American Academy of Religion 121
Kartinyeri v Commonwealth [1998] HCA 22, 195 CLR 337
Kauanui JK, 'The Politics of Blood and Sovereignty in Rice v. Cayetano' (2002) 25 Political and Legal Anthropology Review 110
Keating M, 'Stateless Nation-Building: Quebec, Catalonia and Scotland in the Changing State System' (1997) 3 Nations and Nationalism 689
Keating M, 'What's Wrong with Asymmetrical Government?' (1998) 8 Regional & Federal Studies 195
Keating M, 'Par Delà La Souveraineté. La Démocratie Plurinationale Dans Un Monde Post-Souverain' in Jocelyn Maclure and Alain-G Gagnon (eds), *Repères en Mutation: Identité et Citoyenneté dans le Québec Contemporain* (Québec Amérique 2001)

Keating M, 'So Many Nations, so Few States: Territory and Nationalism in the Global Era' in James Tully and Alain Gagnon (eds), *Multinational Democracies* (Cambridge University Press 2001)

Keating M, 'Rethinking Sovereignty: Independence-Lite, Devolution-Max and National Accommodation' [2012] Revista d'Estudis Autonomics i Federals 9

Keating M, *Rescaling the European State: The Making of Territory and the Rise of the Meso* (first edition, Oxford University Press 2013)

Keating M and Bray Z, 'Renegotiating Sovereignty: Basque Nationalism and the Rise and Fall of the Ibarretxe Plan' (2006) 5 Ethnopolitics 347

Keating M and Wilson A, 'Regions with Regionalism? The Rescaling of Interest Groups in Six European States' (2014) 53 European Journal of Political Research 840

Kedourie E, *Nationalism* (Hutchinson 1960)

Kellas J, *The Scottish Political System* (Cambridge University Press 1989)

Kelsen H, *Pure Theory of Law* (Lawbook Exchange 2005)

Kincaid J, 'Territorial Neutrality and Cultural Pluralism in American Federalism: Is the United States the Archenemy of Peripheral Nationalism?' (2016) 22 Swiss Political Science Review 565

King George III, 'Royal Proclamation, 1763 (UK), No. 1'

Kirch PV and Rallu J-L, *The Growth and Collapse of Pacific Island Societies: Archaeological and Demographic Perspectives* (University of Hawai'i Press 2007)

Kirkland C and Wood M, 'Legitimacy and Legitimization in Low Turnout Ballots' (2017) 52 Government and Opposition 511

Koch S, *The Presidential Nuclear Initiatives of 1991–1992* (National Defense University Press 2012)

Kontiadēs XI (ed), 'Constitutional Change Engineering' in *Engineering Constitutional Change: A Comparative Perspective on Europe, Canada and the USA* (Routledge 2013)

Kostakopoulou D, 'Thick, Thin and Thinner Patriotisms: Is This All There Is?' (2006) 26 Oxford Journal of Legal Studies 73

Kuhn TS, *The Structure of Scientific Revolutions: 50th Anniversary Edition* (University of Chicago Press 2012)

Kumm M, 'Idea of Thick Constitutional Patriotism and Its Implications for the Role and Structure of European Legal History' (2005) 6 German Law Journal 319

Kwaymullina A, 'Recognition, Referendums and Relationships: Indigenous Worldviews, Constitutional Change, and the "Spirit" of 1967' in Simon Young, Jennifer Nielsen and Jeremy Patrick (eds), *Constitutional Recognition of First Peoples in Australia: Theories and Comparative Perspectives* (Federation Press 2016)

Kymlicka W, *Multicultural Citizenship: A Liberal Theory of Minority Rights* (Clarendon Press 1995)

Kymlicka W, 'Multinational Federalism in Canada; Rethinking the Partnership' in Roger Gibbins and Guy Laforest (eds), *Beyond the Impasse: Towards Reconciliation* (McGill-Queen's University Press 1998)

Laden AS, *Reasonably Radical: Deliberative Liberalism and the Politics of Identity* (Cornell University Press 2001)

Lajoie A, 'What Constitutional Law Doesn't Want to Hear about History' in Law Commission of Canada and British Columbia Treaty Commission (Canada) (eds), *Speaking Truth to Power: A Treaty Forum* (Law Commission of Canada; British Columbia Treaty Commission 2001)

Langdell CC, 'The Status of Our New Territories' (1899) Harvard Law Review 365

Langton M, 'Trapped in the Aboriginal Reality Show [The Howard Government Intervention in Northern Territory Aboriginal Communities. Paper in: Re-Imagining Australia. Schultz, Julianne (ed)]' (2008) Griffith Review 143

Langton M, 'Indigenous Exceptionalism and the Constitutional "Race Power"' (2013) Space, Place and Culture 1

Lantschner E, 'History of the South Tyrol Conflict and Its Settlement' in Jens Woelk, Francesco Palermo and Joseph Marko (eds), *Tolerance Through Law: Self Governance and Group Rights in South Tyrol* (Brill 2007)

Law no. 482 15 December 1999

Lawson G and Seidman G, *The Constitution of Empire* (Yale University Press 2004)

Leclair J, 'Canada's Unfathomable Unwritten Constitutional Principles' (2001) 27 Queen's Law Journal 389

Leclair J, 'Judicial Review in Canadian Constitutional Law: A Brief Overview' (2004) 36 The George Washington International Law Review 543

LeDuc L, 'Referendums and Deliberative Democracy' (2015) 38 Electoral Studies 139

Legislative Decree no. 92 2008

Legislative proposal, pursuant to Section 2 [2] of the Regional Law of the 19th June 2014, no. 15: 'Modalities and Contents for the Recognition for the Increase of Specific Forms of Autonomy for the Veneto Region, pursuant to the third paragraph of Article 116 of the Constitution', 2017

Leibowitz AH, 'American Samoa: Decline of a Culture' (1980) 10 California Western International Law Journal 220

Le Sueur A, Sunkin M and Murkens JE, *Public Law: Text, Cases, and Materials* (third edition, Oxford University Press 2016)

Levy R and Orr G, *The Law of Deliberative Democracy* (Routledge 2016)

Lexier R, 'Two Nations in Canada: The New Democratic Party, the Waffle Movement and Nationalism in Quebec/Deux Nations Au Canada: Le Nouveau Parti Démocrate, Le "Waffle" et Le Nationalisme Au Québec' (2017) 30 British Journal of Canadian Studies 1

Ley 7/2014, de 21 de abril, por la que se modifica la Ley 12/2002, de 23 de mayo, por la que se aprueba el Concierto Económico con la Comunidad Autónoma del País Vasco 2014 97

Ley 12/1981, de 13 de mayo por la que se aprueba el Concierto Economico con la Comunidad Autónoma del Pais Vasco 1981

Ley no. 7 2/2/2017 Ley para la descolonizazion Immediata de Puerto Rico

Ley Orgánica 1/1981, de 6 de abril, de Estatuto de Autonomía para Galicia 1981

Ley Orgánica 1/1995, de 13 de marzo, de Estatuto de Autonomía de Ceuta 1995

Ley Orgánica 1/2007, de 28 de febrero, de reforma del Estatuto de Autonomía de las Illes Balears 2007

Ley Orgánica 1/2011, de 28 de enero, de reforma del Estatuto de Autonomía de la Comunidad Autónoma de Extremadura 2011

Ley Orgánica 2/1995, de 13 de marzo, de Estatuto de Autonomía de Melilla 1995

Ley Orgánica 2/2007, de 19 de marzo, de reforma del Estatuto de Autonomía para Andalucía 2007

Ley Orgánica 3/1979, de 18 de diciembre, de Estatuto de Autonomía para el País Vasco 1979

Ley Orgánica 3/1983, de 25 de febrero, de Estatuto de Autonomía de la Comunidad de Madrid 1983

Ley Orgánica 4/1979, de 18 de diciembre, Estatuto de Autonomía de Cataluña 1979

Ley Orgánica 4/1982, de 9 de junio, de Estatuto de Autonomía para la Región de Murcia 1982

Ley Orgánica 5/1982, de 1 de julio, de Estatuto de Autonomía de la Comunidad Valenciana 1982

Ley Orgánica 5/2007, de 20 de abril, de reforma del Estatuto de Autonomía de Aragón 2007

Ley Orgánica 6/2006, de 19 de julio, de reforma del Estatuto de Autonomía de Cataluña 2006

Ley Orgánica 7/1981, de 30 de diciembre, de Estatuto de Autonomía para Asturias 1982

Ley Orgánica 8/1981, de 30 de diciembre, de Estatuto de Autonomía para Cantabria 1982

Ley Orgánica 9/1982, de 10 de agosto, de Estatuto de Autonomía de Castilla-La Mancha 1982

Ley Orgánica 10/1982, de 10 de agosto, de Estatuto de Autonomía de Canarias 1982

Ley Orgánica 13/1982, de 10 de agosto, de reintegración y amejoramiento del Régimen Foral de Navarra 1982

Ley Orgánica 14/2007, de 30 de noviembre, de reforma del Estatuto de Autonomía de Castilla y León 2007

Lluch J, *Visions of Sovereignty, Nationalism and Accommodation in Multinational Democracies* (University of Pennsylvania Press 2014)

Locke J, *The Second Treatise on Civil Government* (Prometheus Books 1986)

Lone Wolf v Hitchcock 187 US 553 (1903)

Lopez Guerra L, 'Luis Lopez Guerra Former Judge, Tribunal Constitutional (Constitutional Court) Spain' (2005) 3 International Journal of Constitutional Law 567

López LP, 'El Derecho de Autodeterminación En España: Breve Explicación Para Extranjeros Estupefactos y Nacionales Incautos' [2016] Revista d'estudis autonòmics i federals 46

Loughlin M, 'Constituent Power Subverted: From English Constitutional Argument to British Constitutional Practice' in Martin Loughlin and Neil Walker (eds), *The Paradox of Constitutionalism: Constituent Power and Constitutional Form* (Oxford University Press 2007)

Lutz DS, 'Toward a Theory of Constitutional Amendment' (1994) 88 The American Political Science Review 355

Lutz DS, *Colonial Origins of the American Constitution* (Liberty Fund 1977) http://ebookcentral.proquest.com/lib/usq/detail.action?docID=3327341 (accessed 27 November 2017)

Mabo v Queensland (No 2) [1992] HCA 23

MacCormick N, 'Reasonableness and Objectivity' (1998) 74 Notre Dame Law Review 1575

MacCormick N, *Questioning Sovereignty Law, State and Nation in the European Commonwealth* (Oxford University Press 1999)

MacCormick N, 'Is There a Constitutional Path to Scottish Independence?' (2000) 53 Parliamentary Affairs 721

MacKenzie MK, 'Ke Ala Loa – The Long Road: Native Hawaiian Sovereignty and the State of Hawai'i' (2012) 47 Tulsa Law Review 621

Maclure J, *Quebec Identity: The Challenge of Pluralism* (McGill-Queen's University Press 2014)

Maclure J, Gagnon A-G and McGill University (eds), *Repères En Mutation: Identité et Citoyenneté Dans Le Québec Contemporain* (Québec Amérique 2001)

Mandla (Sewa Singh) and Another (Appellants) v Dowell Lee and Others (Respondents) [1983] (HL) 2 AC 548 (House of Lords)

Mandla (Sewa Singh) and Another v Dowell Lee and Another [1983] QB 1 (Court of Appeal England)

Maori Representation Act 1867 (31 Victoriae 1867 N. 47) 1867

Mancini S, 'Secession and Self-Determination' in Michel Rosenfeld and András Sajó (eds), *The Oxford Handbook of Comparative Constitutional Law* (Oxford University Press 2012)

Marrani D, 'Will New Caledonia Be Another Tokelau?' (2006) 31 Alternative Law Journal 102

Marsh I, 'Beyond the Two Party System: New Zealand and Australia? [Address to The Sydney Institute, 11 June 1996]' (1996) 8 Sydney Papers 40

Mascher S and Young S, 'Rights-Based "Recognition": The Canadian Experience' in Simon Young, Jennifer Nielsen and Jeremy Patrick (eds), *Constitutional Recognition of First Peoples in Australia: Theories and Comparative Perspectives* (Federation Press 2016)

Matamonasa-Bennett A, 'Cherokee' in Richard Schaefer, *Encyclopedia of Race, Ethnicity, and Society* (SAGE 2008)

McCrone D, *Understanding Scotland: The Sociology of a Nation* (second edition, Routledge 2001)

McHugh PG, 'Anthropology on Trial: The Hindmarsh Island Bridge Controversy (1993–2001)' in James Nafziger (ed), *Comparative Law and Anthropology* (Edward Elgar Publishing 2017)

Mclean I, 'Report of the Commission on the Consequences of Devolution for the House of Commons (the McKay Commission)' (2013) 84 The Political Quarterly 395

McNeill RS, 'In a Class by Themselves: A Proposal to Incorporate Tribal Courts into the Federal Court System without Compromising Their Unique Status as Domestic Dependent Nations The Washington and Lee Law Alumni Association Student Notes' (2008) 65 Washington and Lee Law Review 283

Mellor D, 'Contemporary Racism in Australia: The Experiences of Aborigines' (2003) 29 Personality and Social Psychology Bulletin 474

Metcalfe P, *A Dangerous Idea: The Alaska Native Brotherhood and the Struggle for Indigenous Rights* (University of Alaska Press 2014)

Migration Act 1958 no. 131

Mill JS, *Considerations on Representative Government* (Prometheus Books 1991)

Miller RJ, 'American Indian Constitutions and Their Influence on the United States Constitution' [2016] https://papers.ssrn.com/sol3/papers.cfm?abstract_id=2739936 (accessed 4 October 2017)

Minder R, Kulish N and Geitner P, 'Spain Accepts Bailout Deal From Europeans for its Banks', *The New York Times* (9 June 2012) https://www.nytimes.com/2012/06/10/business/global/spain-moves-closer-to-bailout-of-banks.html (accessed 5 January 2018)

Monella LM, 'Monitoraggio Autonomia – Lombardia e Veneto, Cosa Succede Dopo Il Voto' (euronews, 23 November 2017) http://it.euronews.com/2017/11/23/monitoraggio-autonomia-lombardia-e-veneto-cosa-succede-dopo-il-referendum (accessed 14 December 2017)

Morano-Foadi S, 'Key Issues and Causes of the Italian Brain Drain' (2006) 19 Innovation: The European Journal of Social Science Research 209

Morata F and Popartan L, 'Spain' in Michael J Baun and Dan Marek (eds), *EU Cohesion Policy after Enlargement* (Palgrave Macmillan 2008)

Morris S, 'Indigenous Constitutional Recognition, Non-Discrimination and Equality before the Law: Why Reform is Necessary' (2011) 7 Indigenous Law Bulletin 7

Morris S, 'Re-Evaluating Mabo: The Case for Native Title Reform to Remove Discrimination and Promote Economic Opportunity' (2012) 5 Land, Rights, Laws: Issues of Native Title 1

Morton v Mancari 417 US 535 (1974)

Moses AD, *Genocide and Settler Society: Frontier Violence and Stolen Indigenous Children in Australian History*, vol 6 (Berghahn 2004)

Mulgan R and Aimer P, *Politics in New Zealand* (Auckland University Press 2013)

Mullen T, 'The Brexit Case and Constitutional Conventions' (2017) 21 Edinburgh Law Review 442

Müller J-W, 'A "Thick" Constitutional Patriotism for the EU? On Morality, Memory and Militancy'in Law and Democracy in the Post-National Union, CIDEL Report (Oslo: Arena 375, 2006)

Müller J-W, *Constitutional Patriotism* (Princeton University Press 2007)

Müller J-W, 'A General Theory of Constitutional Patriotism' (2008) 6 International Journal of Constitutional Law 72

Müller J-W, 'Seven Ways to Misunderstand Constitutional Patriotism' (2009) 25 Notizie di Politeia 20

Müller SC and Meyers GD, 'Mabo – Through the Eyes of the Media (Part II): The Land Fund Legislation' (1995) 2 Deakin Law Review 99

Nairn T, *The Break-Up of Britain: Crisis and Neonationalism* (second expanded, NLB and Verso Editions 1981)

National Bank v County of Yankton 101 US 129 (1879)

Native Title Act 1993 no. 110

Nencioni P, 'L'Accademia Della Crusca e La Lingua Italiana' in Paolo Ramat, Hans-Josef Niederehe and EFK Koerner (eds), *History of Linguistics in Italy* (John Benjamins 1986)

New Zealand Maori Council v Attorney-General (1987) 1 NZLR 641 (Court of Appeal)

Nichols R and Singh J, *Freedom and Democracy in an Imperial Context: Dialogues with James Tully* (Routledge 2014)

Nielsen J, 'Breaking the Silence: The Importance of Constitutional Change' in Simon Young, Jennifer Nielsen and Jeremy Patrick (eds), *Constitutional Recognition of First Peoples in Australia: Theories and Comparative Perspectives* (Federation Press 2016)

Ninet A and Mateu A, 'Spain's Multinational Constitution: A Lost Opportunity?' (2008) 17 Constitutional Forum 19

Northern Ireland Act 1998 c 47

Northern Ireland (St Andrews Agreement) Act 2006 c 53

Norton P, *Parliament in British Politics* (Palgrave Macmillan 2013)

O'Cinneide C, 'The New Human Rights Culture' in Robert Hazell (ed), *Constitutional Futures Revisited: Britain's Constitution to 2020* (Palgrave Macmillan 2008)

Official Languages Act (1969) 1970, R.S.C, c 2

O'Leary B, 'Debating Consociational Politics: Normative and Explanatory Arguments' in Sidney John Roderick Noel (ed), *From Power Sharing to Democracy: Post-Conflict Institutions in Ethnically Divided Societies* (McGill-Queen's University Press 2005)

Oklopcic Z, 'Constitutional (Re) Vision: Sovereign Peoples, New Constituent Powers, and the Formation of Constitutional Orders in the Balkans' (2012) 19 Constellations 81

Oliver D, *Constitutional Reform in the UK* (Oxford University Press 2003)

Oliver, P, 'Canada @ 150' https://ukconstitutionallaw.org/2017/11/02/peter-oliver-canada-150/ (accessed 2 November 2017)

Oliver P, Macklem P and Rosiers ND, *The Oxford Handbook of the Canadian Constitution* (Oxford University Press 2017)

O'Neill M, *The Struggle for the European Constitution: A Past and Future History* (Routledge 2008)

Orange C, *The Treaty of Waitangi* (Bridget Williams 2015)

Order 135/2004 [2004]

O'Sullivan D, 'Needs, Rights and "One Law for All": Contemporary Debates in New Zealand Maori Politics' (2008) 41 Canadian Journal of Political Science/Revue canadienne de science politique 973

O'Sullivan D, 'The Treaty of Waitangi in Contemporary New Zealand Politics' (2008)

Oxford University Act 1854 c 81

Pacific Island Labourers Act 1901 no. 16

Palermo F, 'South Tyrol's Special Status within the Italian Constitution' in Jens Woelk, Francesco Palermo and Joseph Marko (eds), *South Tyrol's Special Status within the Italian Constitution* (Brill 2007)

Palermo F, 'Italy: A Federal Country without Federalism?' in Michael Burgess and G Alan Tarr (eds), *Constitutional Dynamics in Federal Systems: Sub-National Perspectives* (McGill-Queen's University Press 2012)

Palermo F and Wilson A, 'The Dynamics of Decentralization in Italy: Towards a Federal Solution?' [2013] European Diversity & Autonomy Papers http://webfolder.eurac.edu/eurac/publications/edap/2013_edap 04.pdf (accessed 19 June 2015)

Palermo F, Obwexer W and Happacher E (eds), *I 40 Anni Del Secondo Statuto Di Autonomia: L'autonomia Speciale Della Provincia Autonoma Di Bolzano Nel Contesto Dell'integrazione Europea* (Wolters Kluwer Italia; CEDAM 2014)

Pap AL, 'Ethno-Racial Identity (Politics) by Law: "Fraud" and "Choice"' (2017) 45 Nationalities Papers 968

Paringatai K, 'Maori Identity Development Outside of Tribal Environments' (2014) 26 Aotearoa New Zealand Social Work 47

Paterson L, 'Sources of Support for the SNP' in Catherine Bromley and others (eds), *Has Devolution Delivered?* (Edinburgh University Press 2006)

Payne A and Sutton P, 'Towards a Security Policy for Small Island and Enclave Developing States' in Anthony Payne and Paul Sutton (eds), *Size and Survival* (Routledge 2014)

Pearson E, '2014 Essay Winner: "Constitutionally Speaking We Are Still Basically White Australia, However Much We Boast That We Have Changed", Says Former High Court Justice Michael Kirby. Do You Agree? Does the Constitution Need to Be Changed? If so How?' (2014) 8 Indigenous Law Bulletin 31

Pedersen A and others, 'Attitudes toward Aboriginal Australians in City and Country Settings' (2000) 35 Australian Psychologist 109

Pendleton Civil Service Reform Act 1883 c 27

Pengelley N, 'The Hindmarsh Island Bridge Act: Must Laws Based on the Race Power Be for the "Benefit" of Aborigines and Torres Strait Islanders?' (1998) 20 Sydney Law Review 144

Perez MP, 'Pacific Identities beyond US Racial Formations: The Case of Chamorro Ambivalence and Flux' (2002) 8 Social Identities 457

Perez MP, 'Colonialism, Americanization, and Indigenous Identity: A Research Note on Chamorro Identity in Guam' (2005) 25 Sociological Spectrum 571

Perju V, 'Constitutional Transplants, Borrowing, and Migrations' https://papers.ssrn.com/sol3/papers.cfm?abstract_id=1982230 (accessed 26 January 2017)

Peterlini HK, *Südtiroler Bombenjahre: Von Blut und Tränen zum Happy End?* (Raetia 2005)

Pommersheim F, *Braid of Feathers: American Indian Law and Contemporary Tribal Life* (University of California Press 1997)

Pommersheim F, *Broken Landscape: Indians, Indian Tribes, and the Constitution* (Oxford University Press 2009)

Pommersheim F, 'At the Crossroads: A New and Unfortunate Paradigm of Tribal Sovereignty' (2010) 55 South Dakota Law Review 48

Pommersheim F, 'The Crazy Horse Malt Liquor Case: From Tradition to Modernity and Halfway Back' (2012) 57 South Dakota Law Review 42

Price R, 'New Zealand's Interim Treaty Settlement and Arrangements – Building Blocks of Certainty' in Law Commission of Canada and British Columbia Treaty Commission (Canada) (eds), *Speaking Truth to Power: A Treaty Forum* (Law Commission of Canada; British Columbia Treaty Commission 2001)

Price R and Quentin-Baxter A, 'New Zealand Model of Free Association: What Does it Mean for New Zealand' (2008) 39 Victoria University of Wellington Law Review 607

Pub. L. 103-150 – S. J. Res. 19 – 103rd Congress (1993–1994): A joint resolution to acknowledge the 100th anniversary of the January 17, 1893 overthrow of the Kingdom of Hawaii, and to offer an apology to Native Hawaiians on behalf of the United States for the overthrow of the Kingdom of Hawaii 1993

Pub. L. 56-339: An Act to provide a government for the Territory of Hawaii 1900, 599

Pub. L. 64-368: Puerto Rican Federal Relations Act of 1917 (Foraker Act)

Pub. L. 83-517: Revised Organic Act of the Virgin Islands 1954 Pub. L. 83-517

Pub. L. 86-3: An Act to provide for the admission of the State of Hawaii into the Union (Hawaii Admission Act) 1959

Pub. L. 111-118 – S. J. Res. 14 – 111th Congress (2009–2010): A joint resolution to acknowledge a long history of official depredations and ill-conceived policies by the Federal Government regarding Indian tribes and offer an apology to all Native Peoples on behalf of the United States 2009

Pub. L. 114-187: 48 U.S.C. § 2101 et seq Puerto Rico Oversight, Management, and Economic Stability Act or PROMESA 2016

Pub. L. 111-19: To provide for the reconsideration and revision of the proposed constitution of the United States Virgin Islands to correct provisions inconsistent with the Constitution and Federal law.

Quimby F, 'Fortress Guåhån: Chamorro Nationalism, Regional Economic Integration and US Defence Interests Shape Guam's Recent History' (2011) 46 The Journal of Pacific History 357

R (on the Application of Jackson) v Attorney General, vol 1 (UKHL 2005)

R v Pamajewon [1996] C 24596, 2 SCR 821

R v Sparrow [1990] C 20311, 1 SCR 1075

R v Van der Peet [1996] C 23803, 2 SCR 507

Race Relations Act 1976 c 74

Randolph CF, 'Constitutional Aspects of Annexation' (1898) 12 Harvard Law Review 291

Rea D, 'Government Expenditure and Revenue in New Zealand: A Brief Overview' 5 Policy Quarterly 58

Recovery of Medical Costs for Asbestos Diseases (Wales) Bill (Reference By The Counsel General For Wales) [2015] UKSC 3

Reference re Amendment to the Canadian Constitution [1982] C 16904, 2 SCR 791

Reference re Secession of Quebec [1998] 2 SCR 217 [1998] 217

Reference re Senate Reform [2014] SCC 35203, 1 SCR 704

Referendum Act, SC 1992, c 30

Regional Law no. 15 19.06.2014

Regional Law no. 15 19.06.2014

Renan E, *What is a Nation?* (Presses-Pocket 1882)

Reynolds H, *Dispossession: Black Australians and White Invaders* (second edition, Allen & Unwin 1996)

Reynolds H, *An Indelible Stain?: The Question of Genocide in Australia's History* (Penguin 2001)

Rezvani DA, 'The Basis of Puerto Rico's Constitutional Status: Colony, Compact, or "Federacy"?' (2007) 122 Political Science Quarterly 115

Rice v Cayetano 528 US 495 (2000)

Ristroph EB, 'Traditional Cultural Districts: An Opportunity for Alaska Tribes to Protect Subsistence Rights and Traditional Lands' (2014) 31 Alaska Law Review 211

Roberts CL, 'A Desert Grows between Us – The Sovereignty Paradox at the Intersection of Tribal and Federal Courts The Washington and Lee Law Alumni Association Student Notes' (2008) 65 Washington and Lee Law Review 347

Rohrer J and Herr J, *Haoles in Hawai'i* (University of Hawai'i Press 2010)

Roper v Simmons 543 US 551 (2005)

Rose-Ackerman S, 'Citizens and Technocrats: An Essay on Trust, Public Participation, and Government Legitimacy' in Susan Rose-Ackerman, Peter L Lindseth and Emerson Blake (eds), *Comparative Administrative Law* (Edward Elgar Publishing 2010)

Rosenfeld M, *The Identity Of The Constitutional Subject* (Routledge 2010)

Rosenfeld M, 'Constitutional Identity' in Michel Rosenfeld and András Sajó (eds), *The Oxford Handbook of Comparative Constitutional Law* (Oxford University Press 2012)

Ross A, *New Zealand Aspirations in the Pacific in the Nineteenth Century* (Clarendon Press 1964)

Royal Succession Act 2013 N.149

Ruru J and Crosbie A, 'Key to Unlocking Landlocked Maori Land: The Extension of the Maori Land Court's Jurisdiction' (2004) 10 Canterbury Law Review 318

Sajó A and Klein C, 'Constitution-Making; Progress and Substance' in Michel Rosenfeld and András Sajó (eds), *The Oxford Handbook of Comparative Constitutional Law* (Oxford University Press 2012)

Salisbury RF, *A Homeland for the Cree: Regional Development in James Bay, 1971–1981* (McGill-Queen's University Press 1986)

Sanders VA, 'A Tribal Advocate's Critique of Proposed ANCSA Amendments: Perpetuating a Broken Corporate Assimilationist Policy' (2016) 33 Alaska Law Review 303

Santamaria D, 'Orientamenti Della Linguistica Italiana Del Primo Ottocento' in Paolo Ramat, Hans-Josef Niederehe and EFK Koerner (eds), *History of Linguistics in Italy* (John Benjamins 1986)

Santiago J, 'Religion, Secularisation and Nationalism in Quebec and the Basque Country: A Comparative Approach' (2015) 21 Nations and Nationalism 120

Sargiacomo M and others, 'Accounting and the Fight against Corruption in Italian Government Procurement: A Longitudinal Critical Analysis (1992–2014)' (2015) 28 Critical Perspectives on Accounting 89

Sawer G, 'Australian Constitution and the Australian Aborigine', (1966) 2 Federal Law Review 17

Scalia A, *A Matter of Interpretation: Federal Courts and the Law* (Princeton University Press 1998)

Scalia A and Garner BA, *Reading Law: The Interpretation of Legal Texts* (Kindle edition) (West 2012)

Scarano F, *Tra Mussolini e Hitler. Le opzioni dei sudtirolesi nella politica estera fascista: Le opzioni dei sudtirolesi nella politica estera fascista* (FrancoAngeli 2012)

Schachter J and Funk A, 'Sovereignty, Indigeneity, Identities: Perspectives from Hawai'i' (2012) 18 Social Identities 399

Schlag P, 'No Vehicles in the Park' (1999) 23 Seattle University Law Review 381

Schneider J (ed), *Italy's 'Southern Question': Orientalism in One Country* (Berg 3PL 1998)

Schwartz A, 'Patriotism or Integrity? Constitutional Community in Divided Societies' (2011) 31 Oxford Journal of Legal Studies 503

Scotland Act 1998 c 46

Scotland Act 2012 c 11

Scotland Act 2016 c 11

Scott A, 'The Role of Concordats in the New Governance of Britain: Taking Subsidiarity Seriously?' (2001) 5 Edinburgh Law Review 21

Scottish Independence Referendum Act 2013 asp 14

Scottish Independence Referendum (Franchise) Act 2013 asp 13

Seuffert N, *Jurisprudence of National Identity: Kaleidoscopes of Imperialism and Globalisation from Aotearoa New Zealand* (Ashgate 2006)

Shaddock & Assoc Proprietary, Ltd v Parramatta City Council (1981) 150 CLR 225 (High Court)

Sierp A, 'Minority Language Protection in Italy: Linguistic Minorities and the Media' (2008) 4 Journal of Contemporary European Research 303

Singer JW, 'Property and Coercion in Federal Indian Law: The Conflict between Critical and Complacent Pragmatism Symposium on the Renaissance of Pragmatism in American Legal Thought: Comments' (1989) 63 Southern California Law Review 1821

Smith AD, *Theories of Nationalism* (Duckworth 1971)

Smith AD, *The Ethnic Origins of Nations* (Basil Blackwell 1986)

Smith AD, *Ethnicity and Nationalism* (Brill 1992)

Smith AD, 'The Origins of Nations' in John Hutchinson and Anthony D Smith (eds), *Nationalism* (Oxford University Press 1994)

Smith AD, *Nationalism: Theory, Ideology, History* (Polity Press/ Blackwell 2001)

Smith JE, *Quasi-Religions: Humanism, Marxism, and Nationalism* (Macmillan 1994)

Smith R, 'The Bitter Roots of Puerto Rican Citizenship.' in Christina Duffy Burnett and Burke Marshall (eds), *Foreign in a Domestic Sense: Puerto Rico, American Expansion, and the Constitution* (Duke University Press 2001)

Spagnuolo L, 'Italy's Tactical Nuclear Weapons | BASIC – British American Security Information Council' http://www.basicint.org/publications/laura-spagnuolo-research-and-policy-officer/2011/italys-tactical-nuclear-weapons (accessed 8 July 2015)

Spanish Constitution 1978
Stavenhagen R, 'Commission on Human Rights: Report of the Special Rapporteur on the Situation of Human Rights and Fundamental Freedoms of Indigenous People. Addendum: Mission To New Zealand' (Commission on Human Rights – Economic and Social Council, 2006)
St Catharines Milling and Lumber Co v R (C)
Steininger R, *South Tyrol: A Minority Conflict of the Twentieth Century* (Transaction 2003)
Stern KD, 'John Locke and the Declaration of Independence' (1966) 15 The Cleveland State Law Review 186
Stevenson G, *Parallel Paths: The Development of Nationalism in Ireland and Quebec* (McGill-Queen's University Press 2006)
Stewart H, Walker P and Carrell S, 'Theresa May Rejects Nicola Sturgeon's Referendum Demand', *The Guardian* (16 March 2017) http://www.theguardian.com/politics/2017/mar/16/theresa-may-rejects-nicola-sturgeons-scottish-referendum-demand (accessed 9 January 2018)
St Germain J, *Broken Treaties* (University of Nebraska Press 2009)
Stone Sweet A, 'Judicialization and the Construction of Governance' (1999) 32 Comparative Political Studies 147
Te Runanga o Wharekauri Rekohu Inc v Attorney General (1992) 2 NZLR 301 (Court of Appeal)
Teubner G, 'Legal Irritants: Good Faith in British Law or How Unifying Law Ends up in New Divergences' (1998) 61 The Modern Law Review 11
Thalia A, 'The Northern Territory Intervention: The Ongoing Story of Withheld Indigenous Money' (2008) Ngiya: Talk the Law 2
Thayer JB, 'The Origin and Scope of the American Doctrine of Constitutional Law' (1893) 7 Harvard Law Review 129
Thayer JB, 'Our New Possessions' (1899) 12 Harvard Law Review 464
The Australian Constitution 1901
The Constitution Act, 1867, 30 & 31 Vict, Ch 3 (renamed from the British North America Act 1867 by the Constitution Act 1982 section 53 (2))
The Constitution Act 1982
The Constitution Act, 1982, being Schedule B to the Canada Act 1982 (UK), 1982, Ch 11
The New Zealand Constitution Act 1852 Ch 72 1852
The Nineteenth Amendment of The Constitution Act, 1998
The Northern Ireland Act 1998 c 47
The Quebec Act 1774 14 c 83

Thomas MD, Thomas DW and Snow NA, 'Rational Irrationality and the Political Process of Repeal: The Women's Organization for National Prohibition Reform and the 21st Amendment' (2013) 66 Kyklos 130

Tierney S, *Constitutional Law and National Pluralism* (Oxford University Press 2004)

Tierney S, 'Giving with One Hand: Scottish Devolution within a Unitary State' (2007) 5 International Journal of Constitutional Law 4

Tierney S, 'Constitutional Referendums: A Theoretical Enquiry' (2009) 72 The Modern Law Review 360

Tierney S, *Constitutional Referendums: The Theory and Practice of Republican Deliberation* (Oxford University Press 2012)

Tierney S, 'The Referendum on Scottish Independence: A Process as Well as an Event' (2014) 18 Edinburgh Law Review 245

Tierney S, 'Popular Constitutional Amendment: Referendums and Constitutional Change in Canada and the United Kingdom' (2015) 41 Queen's Law Journal 41

Tierney S, 'Reclaiming Politics: Popular Democracy in Britain after the Scottish Referendum' (2015) Political Quarterly 226

Tierney S, 'Towards a Federal United Kingdom? Lessons from America' (2015) Political Insight 16

Tocqueville A de, *Democracy in America* (JP Mayer ed, George Lawrence transl, Harper Perennial Modern Classics edition, Harper Perennial Modern Classics 2006)

Tokelau Act 1948 N. 24 (as at 20 September 2007)

Tonge J, 'Supplying Confidence or Trouble? The Deal Between the Democratic Unionist Party and the Conservative Party' (2017) 88 The Political Quarterly 412

Toniolo G (ed), *The Oxford Handbook of the Italian Economy Since Unification* (Oxford University Press 2013)

Townend A, 'Tokelau's 2006 Referendum on Self-Government' (2007) 5 New Zealand Journal of Public and International Law 127

Trask H-K, *From a Native Daughter: Colonialism and Sovereignty in Hawaii* (revised ed, University of Hawai'i Press 1999)

Treaty of Waitangi Act 1975 N. 114 1975

Treaty of Waitangi (State Enterprises) Act 1988 N. 105

Trench A, 'Scotland and Wales: The Evolution of Devolution' in Robert Hazell (ed), *Constitutional Futures Revisited: Britain's Constitution to 2020* (Palgrave Macmillan 2008)

Trench A, 'Tying the UK Together?' in Robert Hazell (ed), *Constitutional Futures Revisited: Britain's Constitution to 2020* (Palgrave Macmillan 2008)

Trench A, 'Making "Reserved Powers" Work for Wales' https://constitution-unit.com/2015/09/24/making-reserved-powers-work-for-wales/ (accessed 8 January 2018)
Truth and Reconciliation Commission of Canada, *Honouring the Truth, Reconciling for the Future: Summary of the Final Report of the Truth and Reconciliation Commission of Canada* (2015)
Tsilhqot'in Nation v British Columbia [2014] SCC 34986, 2 SCR 257
Tuaua v United States 788 F 3 d (DC Cir 2015)
Tully J, 'Diversity's Gambit Declined' in Curtis Cook (ed), *Constitutional Predicament: Canada after the Referendum of 1992* (McGill-Queen's University Press 1994)
Tully J, *Strange Multiplicity: Constitutionalism in an Age of Diversity* (Cambridge University Press 1995)
Tully J, 'Struggles over Recognition and Distribution' (2000) 7 Constellations 469
Tully J, 'The Challenge of Reimagining Citizenship and Belonging in Multicultural and Multinational Societies' in Catriona McKinnon and Iain Hampsher-Monk (eds), *The Demands of Citizenship* (Continuum 2000)
Tully J, 'Introduction' in James Tully and Alain Gagnon (eds), *Multinational Democracies* (Cambridge University Press 2001)
Tully J, 'Introduction' in Law Commission of Canada and British Columbia Treaty Commission (Canada) (eds), *Speaking Truth to Power: A Treaty Forum* (Law Commission of Canada; British Columbia Treaty Commission 2001)
Tully J, 'The Unfreedom of the Moderns in Comparison to their Ideals of Constitutional Democracy' (2002) 65 Modern Law Review 204
Tully J, 'The Imperialism of Modern Constitutional Democracy' in Martin Loughlin and Neil Walker (eds), *The Paradox of Constitutionalism: Constituent Power and Constitutional Form* (Oxford University Press 2007)
Turano L, 'Spain: Banning Political Parties as a Response to Basque Terrorism' (2003) 1 International Journal of Constitutional Law 730
Turgeon L and Gagnon A-G, 'The Representation of Ethnic and Linguistic Groups in the Federal Civil Service of Belgium and Canada' (2013) 56 Canadian Public Administration 565
Tushnet M, 'Policy Distortion and Democratic Debilitation: Comparative Illumination of the Countermajoritarian Difficulty' (1995) 94 Michigan Law Review 245
Tushnet M, 'The Possibilities of Comparative Constitutional Law' (1999) 108 The Yale Law Journal 1225
Tushnet M, *Advanced Introduction to Comparative Constitutional Law* (Edward Elgar Publishing 2014)

Twomey A, 'The Race Power – Its Replacement and Interpretation' (2012) 40 Federal Law Review 413

Unger JW, *Discursive Construction of the Scots Language: Education, Politics and Everyday Life* (John Benjamins Publishing Company 2013)

Union with Scotland (Amendment) Act 1707 c 40 6 Ann

Universities Tests Act 1871 c 26

Wales Act 2014 c 29

Wales Act 2017 c 4

US v Kagama US 375 (1886)

US v Winans 371 US 375 (1905)

US Supreme Court Order List: 579 June 13, 2016

Wi Parata v Bishop of Wellington [1877] 3 NZ Jur (NS) 72

Van Dyke JM, 'The Political Status of the Native Hawaiian People' (1998) 17 Yale Law & Policy Review 95

Van Dyke JM, *Who Owns the Crown Lands of Hawaii?* (University of Hawai'i Press 2008)

Van Dyke JM, Amore-Siah CD and Berkley-Coats GW, 'Self-Determination for Nonself-Governing Peoples and for Indigenous Peoples: The Cases of Guam and Hawai'i' (1996) 18 University of Hawai'i Law Review 623

Vazquez CG, 'A Business Entity by Any Other Name: Corporation: Community and Kinship' (2016) 33 Alaska Law Review 353

Villazor RC, 'Blood Quantum Land Laws and the Race versus Political Identity Dilemma' (2008) 96 California Law Review 801

Vintró J, 'Legalidad y Consulta Soberanista En Cataluña, Por Joan Vintró' http://idpbarcelona.net/legalidad-y-consulta-soberanista-en-cataluna/ (accessed 4 January 2018)

Viver C, 'Por Favor, No Disparen Contra El Pianista. Mito y Realidad Del (Mal Llamado) Principio Dispositivo' [2008] Revista Española de Derecho Constitucional 339

Viver C, 'Spain's Constitution and Statutes of Autonomy: Explaining the Evolution of Political Decentralization' in Michael Burgess and G Alan Tarr (eds), *Constitutional Dynamics in Federal Systems: Sub-National Perspectives* (McGill-Queen's University Press 2012)

Walker N, 'The Idea of Constitutional Pluralism' (2002) 65 The Modern Law Review 317

Wallace J, 'New Zealand Human Rights Commission' (1989) 58 Nordic Journal of International Law 155

Walters MD, 'Histories of Colonialism, Legality, and Aboriginality' (2007) 57 University of Toronto Law Journal 819

Wardle DL, 'Reason to Ratify: The Influence of John Locke's Religious Beliefs on the Creation and Adoption of the United States Constitution' (2002) 26 Seattle University Law Review 291

Watson A, *Legal Transplants: An Approach to Comparative Law* (new edition, University of Virginia Press 1988)

West D and Chafets Z, 'Is America's Two-Party System Broken?' (2012) 144 New York Times Upfront 22

White TH, 'A Difference of Perspective? Māori Members of Parliament and Te Ao Māori in Parliament' (2016) 68 Political Science 175

Williams v Lee 358 US 217 (1959)

Williams C, 'Recognition of National Justice for Quebec: A Canadian Conundrum' in Steve Fenton and Stephen May (eds), *Ethnonational Identities* (Palgrave Macmillan 2002)

Williams G, 'Removing Racism from Australia's Constitutional DNA' (2012) 37 Alternative Law Journal 151

Williams P and others, 'The Legitimacy of Catalonia's Exercise of its Right to Decide' (2017)

Wilson R and Wilford R, 'Northern Ireland: Polarisation or Normalisation?' in Robert Hazell (ed), *Constitutional Futures Revisited: Britain's Constitution to 2020* (Palgrave Macmillan 2008)

Wisthaler V, 'Identity Politics in the Educational System in South Tyrol: Balancing between Minority Protection and the Need to Manage Diversity' (2013) 13 Studies in Ethnicity and Nationalism 358

Woelk J, 'What it Means to Be Special in Relations with the Central State: Institutions and Procedures' in Jens Woelk, Francesco Palermo and Joseph Marko (eds), *Tolerance Through Law: Self Governance and Group Rights in South Tyrol* (Brill 2007)

Woelk J, Palermo F and Marko J, *Tolerance through Law* (Martinus Nijhoff 2008)

Wolff S, 'The Institutional Structure of Regional Consociations in Brussels, Northern Ireland, and South Tyrol' (2004) 10 Nationalism and Ethnic Politics 387

Worcester v State of Georgia 31 US 515 (1831)

Wyn Jones R and Scully R, *Wales Says Yes: Devolution and the 2011 Welsh Referendum* (University Of Wales Press 2012)

Young S, 'Cultural Timelessness and Colonial Tethers: Australian Native Title in Historical and Comparative Perspective' (2008) 12 Australian Indigenous Law Review 60

Young S, Nielsen J and Patrick J, 'Preface' in Simon Young, Jennifer Nielsen and Jeremy Patrick (eds), *Constitutional Recognition of First Peoples in Australia: Theories and Comparative Perspectives* (Federation Press 2016)

Zinn H, *A People's History of the United States: 1492–Present* (Kindle edition) (HarperCollins 2003)
Zubiri Oria I, *The Economic Agreement between the Basque Country and Spain* (Ad Concordiam 2010) http://www.nber.org/papers/w2588 (accessed 11 December 2015)
Zulaika J, 'Specificities: Tropics of Terror: From Guernica's "Natives" to Global "Terrorists"' (1998) 4 Social Identities 93
Zulaika J, *Basque Violence: Metaphor and Sacrament* (University of Nevada Press 2000)
Zulaika J, *Terrorism: The Self-Fulfilling Prophecy* (University of Chicago Press 2010)

DOCUMENTS AND REPORTS

'Agreement between France, Russia, Great Britain' https://archive.org/stream/agreementbetween00franrich#page/n5/mode/2up (accessed 4 July 2015)
'Articles of Agreement for a Treaty Between Great Britain and Ireland, London, 6/12/1921' http://www.nationalarchives.ie/topics/anglo_irish/dfaexhib2.html (accessed 19 August 2015)
Australian Government, Australian Human Rights Commission, National Anti-Racism Strategy Consultation Report July 2012 (2012) http://www.rwi.lu.se/NHRIDB/Asia/Australia/NationalAnti-racismStrategyConsultationReportJuly2012.pdf (accessed 11 December 2017)
Australian Government, Department of Immigration and Border Protection, 'Fact Sheet – Abolition of the "White Australia" Policy' http://www.border.gov.au/about/corporate/information/fact-sheets/08abolition (accessed 6 December 2017)
Australian Government, Referendum Council, 'Final Report' https://www.referendumcouncil.org.au/final-report (2017)
Australian Indigenous Leadership Centre, 'Submission to Joint Select Committee on Constitutional Recognition of Aboriginal and Torres Strait Islander Peoples' (2014)
Australian Parliament, 'Bills Digest 50 1996–97 Hindmarsh Island Bridge Bill 1996'
Australian Parliament, Human Rights and Equal Opportunity Commission, 'Bringing Them Home: Report of the National Inquiry into the Separation of Aboriginal and Torres Strait Islander Children from Their Families' (Human Rights and Equal Opportunity Commission 1997)
Australian Parliament, Joint Select Committee on Constitutional Recognition of Aboriginal and Torres Strait Islander Peoples, 'Interim Report' (2014)

Australian Parliament, Joint Select Committee on Constitutional Recognition of Aboriginal and Torres Strait Islander Peoples, 'Final Report' (2015)

Australian Parliament, Senate Standing Committe – Legal and Constitutional Affairs, 'Unfinished Business: Indigenous Stolen Wages' (Senate Standing Committee on Legal and Constitutional Affairs 2006)

Banca d 'Italia, 'Economie Regionali L'economia Delle Regioni Italiane Dinamiche Recenti e Aspetti Strutturali' (2017)

Business Council of Australia, 'Submission to the Joint Select Committee on Constitutional Recognition of Aboriginal and Torres Strait Islander Peoples' (2012)

Catalonian Parliament, 'Resolution 5/X of the Parliament of Catalonia, Adopting the Declaration of Sovereignty and Right to Decide of the People of Catalonia' https://www.parlament.cat/document/intrade/7176 (accessed 5 January 2018)

Central Intelligence Agency, 'The World Factbook: Amerian Samoa' https://www.cia.gov/library/publications/the-world-factbook/geos/aq.html (accessed 20 June 2017)

Central Intelligence Agency, 'The World Factbook: Cook Islands' https://www.cia.gov/library/publications/the-world-factbook/geos/print_cw.html (accessed 2 January 2016)

Central Intelligence Agency, 'The World Factbook: Holy See' https://www.cia.gov/library/publications/the-world-factbook/geos/vt.html (accessed 19 December 2017)

Central Intelligence Agency, 'The World Factbook: Niue' https://www.cia.gov/library/publications/the-world-factbook/geos/ne.html (accessed 2 January 2016)

Central Intelligence Agency, 'The World Factbook: San Marino' https://www.cia.gov/library/publications/the-world-factbook/geos/sm.html (accessed 19 December 2017)

Central Intelligence Agency, 'The World Factbook: Australia–Oceania: Guam' https://www.cia.gov/library/publications/the-world-factbook/geos/gq.html (accessed 29 July 2017)

Central Intelligence Agency, 'The World Factbook: Australia–Oceania: Northern Mariana Islands' https://www.cia.gov/library/publications/the-world-factbook/geos/cq.html (accessed 28 July 2017)

Central Intelligence Agency, 'The World Factbook: Tokelau' https://www.cia.gov/library/publications/the-world-factbook/geos/tl.html (accessed 2 January 2016)

Commission HR and others, 'Human Rights in New Zealand Today' [2004] Wellington: Human Rights Commission

Commission on Self-Determination, 'The Draft of Guam Commonwealth Act' (1989)

Committee GBPH of CSA, 'The Sewel Convention: The Westminster Perspective; Fourth Report of Session 2005–06; Report, Together with Formal Minutes, Oral and Written Evidence' (The Stationery Office 2006)

Committee GBPH of CSA, 'The Referendum on Separation for Scotland: Making the Process Legal, Second Report of Session 2012–13, Report, Together with Formal Minutes' (The Stationery Office 2012)

Committee of the Regions, 'EU Communication Policy and Plan D' (2006)

Committees: Indian Affairs – Congress USA, 'S. Rept. 108-310 – To Acknowledge a Long History of Official Depredations and Illconceived Policies by The United States Government Regarding Indian Tribes and Offer an Apology to All Native Peoples on Behalf of The United States' https://www.congress.gov/congressional-report/108th-congress/senate-report/310/1 (accessed 15 June 2017)

Congress USA, 'Proposed Virgin Islands Constitution from the Fifth Constitutional Convention: Oversight Hearing before the Subcommittee on Insular Affairs, Oceans, and Wildlife of the Committee on Natural Resources', US House of Representatives, One Hundred Eleventh Congress, Second Session, Wednesday, 17 March 2010 (Washington 2010)

Congress USA, Congressional Research Service, 'Political Status of Puerto Rico: Options for Congress' (2017)

Constitutional Court (Spain) 'List of 2004 Orders' (Constitutional Court Database) http://www.tribunalconstitucional.es/en/jurisprudencia/Pages/Autos.aspx?sel=2004 (accessed 8 December 2015)

Debates (Hansard) No. 87 – 27 November 2006 (39-1) – House of Commons of Canada

'Deed Concerning the Tokelau International Trust Fund' (2014)

Department of the Interior and Department of Justice, 'From Mauka To Makai: The River of Justice Must Flow Freely Report on the Reconciliation Process between the Federal Government and Native Hawaiians' https://www.doi.gov/sites/doi.gov/files/migrated/ohr/library/upload/Mauka-to-Makai-Report-2.pdf (accessed 14 June 2017)

Devolution Commission, 'Serving Scotland Better: Scotland and the United Kingdom in the 21st Century' (2009)

Direzione Nazional Antimafia, 'Relazione Annuale Sulle Attività Svolte Dal Procuratore Nazionale Antimafia e Dalla Direzione Nazionale Antimafia Nonché Sulle Dinamiche e Strategie Della Criminalità Organizzata Di Tipo Mafioso Nel Periodo 1° Luglio 2013–30 Giugno 2014' http://www.stampoantimafioso.it/wp-content/uploads/2015/05/Relazione%20DNA%202013-2014.pdf (accessed 17 June 2015)

Eurostat, 'Gross Domestic Product (GDP) per Inhabitant in Purchasing Power Standards (PPS) in Relation to the EU-28 Average, by NUTS 2 Regions, 2015 (% of the EU-28 Average, EU-28 = 100)'
Fiji Minister of Foreign Affairs (as per Mr Luke Daunivalu), 'Special Committee on Decolonization Concludes Session with Approval of Draft Resolution on Tokelau, Another Containing Report on Organizational Matters | Meetings Coverage and Press Releases' http://www.un.org/press/en/2011/gacol3227.doc.htm (accessed 9 January 2016)
Government of Australia (Federal), Office of the Minister for Aboriginal and Torres Strait Islander Affairs, 'Rebutting the Myths: Some Facts about Aboriginal and Torres Strait Islander Affairs' (Aust Government Publishing Service 1994)
Government of Australia (Federal), Australian Bureau of Statistics, 'Census: Aboriginal and Torres Strait Islander Population' http://www.abs.gov.au/ausstats/abs@.nsf/MediaRealesesByCatalogue/02D50FAA9987D6B7CA25814800087E03?OpenDocument (accessed 12 December 2017)
Government of Canada, Canadian Parliament Special Committee on Indian Self-Goverment, 'Indian Self-Government of Canada, Report of the Special Committee on Indian Self-Government (The Penner Report)' http://www.metismuseum.ca/resource.php/148890 (accessed 8 October 2017)
Government of Canada, 'Consensus Report on the Constitution: Final Text' (Charlottetown Accord) 1992
Government of Canada, 'Constitutional Accord (Meech Lake Accord)' 1987
Government of Canada, 'First Ministers and National Aboriginal Leaders: Strengthening Relationships and Closing the Gap Document (Kelowna Accord)'
Government of Canada, 'Sustaining Momentum: The Government of Canada's Fourth and Final Report in Response to the Kelowna Accord Implementation Act 2011-12'
Government of Canada, 'Statement of the Government of Canada on Indian Policy (The White Paper, 1969)' (2008) report http://www.aadnc-aandc.gc.ca/eng/1100100010189/1100100010191 (accessed 13 October 2017)
Government of Canada, 'The Government of Canada's Approach to Implementation of the Inherent Right and the Negotiation of Aboriginal Self-Government' (3 November 2008) http://www.aadnc-aandc.gc.ca/eng/1100100031843/1100100031844 (accessed 11 October 2017)
Government of New Zealand, 'Māori Population Estimates: At 30 June 2017 – Tables' http://www.stats.govt.nz/browse_for_stats/population/

estimates_and_projections/MaoriPopulationEstimates_HOTPAt30Jun 17.aspx (accessed 27 November 2017)
Government of New Zealand, 'New Zealand Legislation: List of Amendments Incorporated of the Treaty of Waitangi Act 1975 (Including Claims Settlement)' http://www.legislation.govt.nz/act/public/1975/0114/latest/versions.aspx (accessed 3 February 2016)
Government of New Zealand, 'Report on the Crown's Foreshore and Seabed Policy' (Legislation Direct 2004)
Government of New Zealand, Government of Tokelau, 'Deed Concerning the Tokelau International Trust Fund (Wellington)' (2004)
Government of New Zealand, New Zealand and Waitangi Tribunal, 'Report of the Waitangi Tribunal on the Te Reo Maori Claim (WAI 11)' (Department of Justice 1989)
Government of New Zealand, New Zealand Election Study, '2005 Mass Survey. Most Important Issue? Major Categories' http://www.nzes.org/exec/show/freq_2005a (accessed 3 February 2016)
Government of New Zealand, Royal Commission on Auckland Governance, 'Report of the Commission on the Consequences of Devolution for the House of Commons (McKay Report)' http://webarchive.nationalarchives.gov.uk/20130403030652/http://tmc.independent.gov.uk/wp-content/uploads/2013/03/The-McKay-Commission_Main-Report_25-March-20131.pdf (accessed 21 October 2015)
Government of New Zealand, Royal Commission on the Constitution 1969–1973, 'Volume I, Report (Cmnd 5460)' http://web-archives.univ-pau.fr/english/kilbrandonchap10.pdf (accessed 20 August 2015)
Government of New Zealand, Stats, 'National Population Estimates: At 30 June 2017' http://www.stats.govt.nz/browse_for_stats/population/estimates_and_projections/NationalPopulationEstimates_HOTPAt30Jun 17.aspx (accessed 27 November 2017)
Government of New Zealand, The Crown and Ngatikahu ki Whangaroa, 'Deed of Settlement (Ngatikahu Ki Whangaroa's Claim)' https://www.govt.nz/dmsdocument/6281.pdf (accessed 3 February 2016)
Government of New Zealand, The Waitangi Tribunal, 'Report of the Waitangi Tribunal on Yhe Motunui – Waitara Claim' (1983) http://www.justice.govt.nz/tribunals/waitangi-tribunal/Reports/wai0006/06 title (accessed 28 January 2016)
Government of Quebec, 'Draft Bill on the Sovereignty of Quebec 1995'
Government of Quebec, 'James Bay and Northern Quebec Agreement'
Government of Quebec, 'Québec-Canada: A New Deal. The Québec Government Proposal for a New Partnership Between Equals: Sovereignty-Association – Independence of Québec'
Government of Quebec,'Quebecers Our Way to Be Canadians [2017]'

Government of Scotland, 'A National Conversation – Your Scotland Your Voice' 2012
Government of Scotland, 'Final Appellate Jurisdiction in the Scottish Legal System' (Scottish Government 2010)
Government of Scotland, 'Free Personal and Nursing Care' (30 July 2012) http://www.gov.scot/Topics/Health/Support-Social-Care/Support/Adult-Social-Care/Free-Personal-Nursing-Care (accessed 8 January 2018)
Government of Scotland, 'Key Facts on the Sewel Convention' (1 July 1997)
Government of Scotland, 'List of Contributions, Scotland's Future: A National Conversation', (2012) http://www.scotland.gov.uk/Topics/a-national-conversation/NC-contributions-inds-org (accessed 1 January 2012)
Government of Scotland, 'Your Scotland, Your Referendum'. Time Table to 2014, 2012
Government of Scotland and UK Government, 'Agreement between the United Kingdom Government and the Scottish Government on a Referendum on Independence for Scotland' http://www.scotland.gov.uk/About/Government/concordats/Referendum-on-independence
Government of Spain and Renedo Aguado C, 'Nuevos Estatutos de Autonomía Comparados (Ministero de La Presidencia)' http://www.cepc.gob.es/docs/boletin-de-documentacion-n%C2%BA35/presentacion rev1.pdf?sfvrsn=0 (accessed 4 December 2015)
Government of Tokelau, 'Referendum Commission, Self Determination Package, Voting Procedure' http://www.tokelau.org.nz/About+Us/Government/Self+Determination+Package.html (accessed 12 January 2016)
Hamilton G, 'Our 2014 Election Policies, Maori Affairs (National Party)' https://www.national.org.nz/docs/default-source/PDF/2014/policy/maori-affairs-policy.pdf (accessed 3 February 2016)
Holden H, 'The Commission on Scottish Devolution – The Calman Commission' (2010) 29 Scottish Affairs http://researchbriefings.files.parliament.uk/documents/SN04744/SN04744.pdf (accessed 10 January 2016)
'I·CONnect – A Plea for Dialogue: An Open Letter on Catalonia from Constitutional & International Law Scholars' http://www.iconnectblog.com/2017/10/a-plea-for-dialogue-an-open-letter-on-catalonia-from-constitutional-international-law-scholars/ (accessed 21 October 2017)
ISTAT, 'Trentino Alto Adige (Environment and Energy Data Set)' (13 December 2010) http://www.istat.it (accessed 20 December 2017)
ISTAT, 'L'uso Della Lingua Italiana, Dei Dialetti e Di Altre Lingue in Italia, Statistiche, Rapporto 2012' (2014)

Labour Party Manifesto http://www.labour-party.org.uk/manifestos/1997/1997-labour-manifesto.shtml (accessed 12 March 2014)

Law Commission of Canada and British Columbia Treaty Commission (Canada) (eds), 'Speaking Truth to Power: A Treaty Forum' (Law Commission of Canada; British Columbia Treaty Commission 2001)

Ministero Dell'Interno, 'Archivio Storico Delle Elezioni – Camera Del 13 Aprile 2008' http://elezionistorico.interno.it/index.php?tpel=C&dtel=13/04/2008&tpa=I&tpe=I&lev0=0&levsut0=0&lev1=2&levsut1=1&ne1=2&es0=S&es1=S&ms=S (accessed 1 May 2015)

Ministry of Justice (New Zealand), 'International Covenant on Economic, Social and Cultural Rights' http://www.justice.govt.nz/policy/constitutional-law-and-human-rights/human-rights/international-human-rights-instruments/international-human-rights-instruments-1/international-covenant-on-economic-social-and-cultural-rights (accessed 5 February 2016)

National Party (New Zealand), 'Press Release: Deed of Settlement Signed with Ngatikahu Ki Whangaroa' https://www.national.org.nz/news/news/media-releases/detail/2015/12/20/Deed-of-Settlement-signed-with-Ngatikahu-ki-Whangaroa (accessed 3 February 2016)

National Records of Scotland, 'Scotland's Census 2011 – Interactive Maps | Census Data Explorer.' http://www.scotlandscensus.gov.uk/ods-web/datavis.jsp?theme=Language_September_2013 (accessed 9 January 2018)

NationMaster.com, 'Encyclopedia: Demographics of San Marino' (2004) http://www.nationmaster.com/encyclopedia/Demographics-of-San-Marino (accessed 4 April 1930)

NATO, 'NATO Mini. Comm. Taormina, Italy, 17–18 Nov 1991'

Newspoll, 'Recognition of Aboriginal and Torres Strait Islander Peoples in the Australian Constitution – National Survey'

Pew Research Center, 'The Parties on the Eve of the 2016 Election: Two Coalitions, Moving Further Apart – Party Affiliation among Voters: 1992–2016'

Plaid Cymru, 'Manifesto 2017'

Province of British Columbia, 'Reconciliation & Other Agreements – Province of British Columbia' http://www2.gov.bc.ca/gov/content/environment/natural-resource-stewardship/consulting-with-first-nations/first-nations-negotiations/reconciliation-other-agreements (accessed 13 October 2017)

President of the USA, 'Memorandum for the Heads of Executive Departments and Agencies Regarding Puerto Rico' https://www2.pr.gov/agencias/FederalFunds/Puerto_Rico_Guidance/Documents/Federal%20Regulations/Memorandum%20for%20the%20Heads%20of%

20Executive%20Departments%20and%20Agencies%20regarding%20Puerto%20Rico%20Eligibility.pdf (accessed 7 August 2017)

President of the USA, 'Report by the Task Force on Puerto Rico's Status' http://charma.uprm.edu/~angel/Puerto_Rico/reporte_status.pdf (accessed 3 August 2017)

Regione Autonoma Friuli Venezia Giulia, Comunità Linguistiche Regionali http://www.regione.fvg.it/rafvg/cms/RAFVG/cultura-sport/patrimonio-culturale/comunita-linguistiche/ (accessed 18 December 2017)

Scottish Government, 'Agreement Between the Scottish Government and the United Kingdom Government on the Referendum on Independence for Scotland' (12 October 2012) http://www.scotland.gov.uk/About/Government/concordats/Referendum-on-independence (accessed 27 October 2012)

Scottish National Party, 'Manifesto 2011' http://votesnp.com/campaigns/SNP_Manifesto_2011_lowRes.pdf (accessed 8 January 2018)

Scottish National Party, 'Manifesto (2017)'

Soroa JMR, 'Números y Razones' (eldiario.es) http://www.eldiario.es/norte/vientodelnorte/Numeros-razones_6_724837516.html (accessed 5 January 2018)

Tokelau Government and New Zealand Government, 'Joint Statement of The Principles Of Partnership Between New Zealand and Tokelau' http://www.tokelau.org.nz/About+Us/Government.html (accessed 14 January 2016)

UK Government, 'Report of the Smith Commission for Further Devolution of Powers to the Scottish Parliament' (November 2014)

UK Government and the Government of Ireland, 'The Belfast Agreement: An Agreement Reached at the Multi-Party Talks on Northern Ireland 1998. CM 3883 (the Belfast Agreement)'

UK Parliament, 'Memorandum of Understanding and Supplementary Agreements between the United Kingdom Government, Scottish Ministers and the Cabinet of the National Assembly for Wales (CM 4444)'

UK Parliament, Northcote S and Trevelyan CE, 'The Northcote–Trevelyan Report' (1853)

United Nations, 'Article 14, Analytical Summary of Practice – Resolutions 1497 (XV) and 1661 (XVI) 31/10/1960 346-357'

United Nations, 'The United Nations and Decolonization' http://www.un.org/en/decolonization/specialcommittee.shtml (accessed 9 January 2016)

United Nations, 'The United Nations and Decolonization: Non-Self-Governing Territories (United Nations Secretariat 2015 Working Papers on NSGTs)' http://www.un.org/en/decolonization/nonselfgovterritories.shtml (accessed 5 February 2016)

United Nations, American Samoa (A/AC.109/2017/i), 'The Special Committee on the Situation with Regard to the Implementation of the Declaration on the Granting of Independence to Colonial Countries and Peoples' http://legal.un.org/repertory/art14/english/rep_supp3_vol1-art14_e.pdf (accessed 5 July 2015)

United Nations, 'General Assembly Resolution Defining the Three Options for Self-Determination General Assembly Resolution 1541 (XV)'

United Nations, 'General Assembly Resolution no. 2200A (XXI) International Covenant on Economic, Social and Cultural Rights'

United Nations, 'General Assembly Resolution no. 57/137. Question of Tokelau'

United Nations, Committee on the Elimination of Racial Discrimination, 'Concluding Observations on the Eighteenth to Twentieth Periodic Reports of Australia'

United Nations, General Assembly, 'General Assembly Resolution no. 1514 Declaration on the Granting of Independence to Colonial Countries and Peoples'

United Nations, Secretary-General, 'Secretary-General Gratified by Conduct Of Tokelau's Self-Determination Referendum' http://www.un.org/press/en/2007/sgsm11238.doc.htm (accessed 13 January 2016)

United Nations, Visiting Mission to Tokelau, 1986 (ed), Report of the United Nations Visiting Mission to Tokelau, 1986 (UN 7)

US Census Bureau: Department of Commerce, Economics and Statistics Administration, 'FFF: American Indian and Alaska Native Heritage Month: November 2015' https://www.census.gov/newsroom/facts-for-features/2015/cb15-ff22.html (accessed 14 June 2017)

US Census Bureau: Department of Commerce, Economics and Statistics Administration, 'Native Hawaiian and Other Pacific Islander Alone or in Combination with One or More Other Races (500–599) & (100–299) or (300, A01–Z99) or (400–999)' https://factfinder.census.gov/faces/tableservices/jsf/pages/productview.xhtml?src=bkmk (accessed 16 June 2017)

US Census Bureau: Department of Commerce, Economics and Statistics Administration, 'Question of Guam: Draft Resolution Submitted by the Chair Special Committee on the Situation with Regard to the Implementation of the Declaration on the Granting of Independence to Colonial Countries and Peoples 2017 A /AC.109/2017/L.18' https://www.un.org/press/en/2017/gacol3313.doc.htm (accessed 10 July 2017)

US Census Bureau: Department of Commerce, Economics and Statistics Administration, 'State Population Totals Tables: 2010–2016 – Nation, States, Counties, and Puerto Rico Population' https://www.census.gov/data/tables/2016/demo/popest/state-total.html (accessed 22 July 2017)

US Census Bureau: Department of Commerce, Economics and Statistics Administration, 'U.S. Census Bureau QuickFacts Selected: Puerto Rico' https://www.census.gov/quickfacts/table/PST045216/72 (accessed 20 June 2017)

US Census Bureau: Department of Commerce, Economics and Statistics Administration, 'U.S. Census Bureau Releases 2010 – Census Population Counts for American Samoa' https://www.census.gov/2010census/news/releases/operations/cb11-cn177.html (accessed 22 July 2017)

US Census Bureau: Department of Commerce, Economics and Statistics Administration, 'United States Virgin Islands (A/AC.109/2017/16). The Special Committee on the Situation with Regard to the Implementation of the Declaration on the Granting of Independence to Colonial Countries and Peoples'

Welsh Government, 'Wales in Figures 2010' http://gov.wales/statistics-and-research/wales-figures/?lang=en (accessed 9 January 2018)

NEWS REPORTS

Carrell S, 'Scotland Promised Extra Tax and Legal Powers for Referendum No Vote', *The Guardian* (4 August 2014) http://www.theguardian.com/politics/2014/aug/05/scotland-promised-new-powers-no-vote-referendum (accessed 8 January 2018)

Carrington D, 'UK Cancels Pioneering £1bn Carbon Capture and Storage Competition', *The Guardian* (25 November 2015) http://www.theguardian.com/environment/2015/nov/25/uk-cancels-pioneering-1bn-carbon-capture-and-storage-competition (accessed 10 January 2018)

'Catalonia Asks Spain for 9bn Euros', BBC News (29 January 2013) http://www.bbc.com/news/world-europe-21254010 (accessed 5 January 2018)

Cuddy A, 'Live: Pro-Independence Parties Claim Victory in Catalan Election', euronews (21 December 2017) http://www.euronews.com/2017/12/21/follow-live-catalonia-votes-in-regional-election (accessed 5 January 2018)

'Developments in the Law – The U.S. Territories' (2016) 130 Harvard Law Review 1616

'Firenze, Concorsi Truccati: "E" Il Vile Commercio Dei Posti', Repubblica.it (25 September 2017) http://firenze.repubblica.it/cronaca/2017/09/25/news/firenze_concorsi_truccati_arrestati_sette_docenti_universitari-176440964/ (accessed 20 December 2017)

'Huge Catalan Protest in Barcelona', BBC News (10 July 2010) http://www.bbc.com/news/10588494 (accessed 4 January 2018)

'Italy Knows How to Solve Catalonia's Problem', Bloomberg.com (12 October 2017) https://www.bloomberg.com/view/articles/2017-10-12/italy-knows-how-to-solve-catalonia-s-problem (accessed 16 October 2017)

'Mengele Family Keeps Uneasy Silence', *Tribune Digital – Chicago Tribune* http://articles.chicagotribune.com/1985-06-09/news/8502060229_1_guenzburg-martha-mengele-dr-josef-mengele (accessed 21 December 2017)

Moriarty G, 'Arlene Foster Seeks Return to Direct Rule if Deadlock is Not Broken', *Irish Times* (1 January 2018) https://www.irishtimes.com/news/ireland/irish-news/arlene-foster-seeks-return-to-direct-rule-if-deadlock-is-not-broken-1.3342249 (accessed 7 January 2018)

'Nazisti, in Sud Tirolo Il Rifugio Delle SS in Fuga – La Repubblica.It' (Archivio – la Repubblica.it) http://ricerca.repubblica.it/repubblica/archivio/repubblica/2008/10/28/nazisti-in-sud-tirolo-il-rifugio-delle.html (accessed 20 December 2017)

Roger M, 'Las 23 Demandas de Mas a Rajoy: Financiación, Competencias y Lengua', *El País* (1 August 2014) https://elpais.com/ccaa/2014/08/01/catalunya/1406913058_166638.html (accessed 4 January 2018)

'Scottish Independence Referendum Deal Signed by Cameron and Salmond', *The Guardian* (15 October 2012) https://www.theguardian.com/politics/2012/oct/15/scottish-independence-referendum-cameron-salmond (accessed 8 January 2018)

Scuola R, 'Augusto Fantozzi e i 7 Arrestati: Ecco Chi Sono i Docenti Dello Scandalo Concorsi Truccati', *Corriere della Sera* (25 September 2017) http://www.corriere.it/scuola/universita/cards/corruzione-universita-ecco-chi-sono-docenti-arrestati-dove-insegnano/ex-ministro-fantozzi_principale.shtml (accessed 20 December 2017)

Street L and others, 'Hispanics' http://www.pewresearch.org/data-trend/society-and-demographics/hispanics/ (accessed 8 August 2017)

'Trident Missiles "could Be Relocated to Plymouth from Independent Scotland"', UK News, *The Guardian* https://www.theguardian.com/uk-news/2014/aug/14/trident-missiles-relocate-plymouth-independent-scotland-rusi-report (accessed 10 January 2018)

'U.S. to Start Moving Okinawa-Based Marines to Guam in 2024', *The Japan Times Online* (27 April 2017) http://www.japantimes.co.jp/news/2017/04/27/national/politics-diplomacy/u-s-start-moving-okinawa-based-marines-guam-2024/ (accessed 29 July 2017)

Walsh MW, 'How Puerto Rico is Grappling With a Debt Crisis', *The New York Times* (16 May 2017) https://www.nytimes.com/interactive/2017/business/dealbook/puerto-rico-debt-bankruptcy.html (accessed 4 August 2017)

BLOG REPORTS

Casanas Adam E, 'The Referendum on Catalonian Independence: The Position of the Catalan Authorities' https://ukconstitutionallaw.org/2017/10/03/elisenda-casanas-adam-the-referendum-on-catalonian-independence-the-position-of-the-catalan-authorities/ (accessed 4 January 2018)

Casanas Adam E, 'Too Little, Too Late? The Spanish Government's Proposals to Resolve the Current Conflict with Catalonia | ConstitutionNet' http://www.constitutionnet.org/news/too-little-too-late-spanish-governments-proposals-resolve-current-conflict-catalonia (accessed 4 January 2018)

'Debate: J. H.H. Weiler: Scotland and the EU: A Comment' http://ukconstitutionallaw.org/2014/09/10/debate-j-h-h-weiler-scotland-and-the-eu-a-comment/ (accessed 13 August 2015)

'Debate: Jo Murkens: Scotland and the EU: A Comment' http://ukconstitutionallaw.org/2014/09/10/debate-jo-murkens-scotland-and-the-eu-a-comment/ (accessed 13 August 2015)

'Debate: Sionaidh Douglas-Scott: Why the EU Should Welcome an Independent Scotland' http://ukconstitutionallaw.org/2014/09/10/debate-sionaidh-douglas-scott-why-the-eu-should-welcome-an-independent-scotland/ (accessed 13 August 2015)

Estrada-Cañamares M and Díez Sánchez L, 'National Law Changes in Spain – Constitutional Change through Euro Crisis Law' (2014) http://eurocrisislaw.eui.eu/country/spain/topic/national-law-changes/ (accessed 4 January 2018)

García Oliva J, 'Javier Garcia Oliva: Catalonia in Spain? The Future Ahead' https://ukconstitutionallaw.org/2014/11/10/javier-garcia-oliva-catalonia-in-spain-the-future-ahead/ (accessed 4 January 2018)

García Oliva J, 'Javier Garcia Oliva: The Referendum on Catalonian Independence: The Position of the Spanish Authorities' https://ukconstitutionallaw.org/2017/10/03/javier-garcia-oliva-the-referendum-on-catalonian-independence-the-position-of-the-spanish-authorities/ (accessed 4 January 2018)

Goodall K and others, 'Community Experiences of Sectarianism' http://storre.stir.ac.uk/handle/1893/21622 (accessed 13 July 2015)

Guibernau M, 'Calls for Independence in Catalonia Are Part of an Evolution of Spain's Democracy That the Country's Constitution May Have to Come to Accommodate. | EUROPP' http://blogs.lse.ac.uk/europpblog/2012/10/08/catalonia-independence-spain-constitution/ (accessed 2 November 2012)

I·CONnect, 'Catalonia: Is There a "Right" to Secession?', iconnectblog.com http://www.iconnectblog.com/2017/10/catalonia-is-there-a-right-to-secession/ (accessed 21 October 2017)

Index